The Future of Business Schools

The Future of Business Schools

Purpose, Action, and Impact

Edited by

Rico J. Baldegger
Dean and Professor, School of Management Fribourg (HEG-FR), University of Applied Sciences & Arts Western Switzerland

Ayman El Tarabishy
President & CEO, International Council for Small Business (ICSB), Deputy Chair, Department of Management, School of Business, The George Washington University, USA

David B. Audretsch
Indiana University, USA and the Department of Innovation Management and Entrepreneurship, University of Klagenfurt, Austria

Dafna Kariv
Professor of Entrepreneurship; Head of the dual degree Entrepreneurship-Business Administration, Adelson School of Entrepreneurship, Reichman University (RUNI), Herzliya, Israel

Katia Passerini
Provost and Executive Vice President, Seton Hall University, South Orange, New Jersey, USA

Wee-Liang Tan
Associate Professor of Strategic Management, Lee Kong Chian School of Management, Singapore Management University, Singapore

Edward Elgar
PUBLISHING

Cheltenham, UK • Northampton, MA, USA

Published by
Edward Elgar Publishing Limited
The Lypiatts
15 Lansdown Road
Cheltenham
Glos GL50 2JA
UK

Edward Elgar Publishing, Inc.
William Pratt House
9 Dewey Court
Northampton
Massachusetts 01060
USA

Paperback edition 2024

A catalogue record for this book
is available from the British Library

Library of Congress Control Number: 2022944609

This book is available electronically in the **Elgar**online
Business subject collection
http://dx.doi.org/10.4337/9781800889224

ISBN 978 1 80088 921 7 (cased)
ISBN 978 1 80088 922 4 (eBook)
ISBN 978 1 0353 4056 9 (paperback)

Printed and bound by CPI Group (UK) Ltd, Croydon, CR0 4YY

Contents

Figures

Tables

Contributors

Wolfgang Amann graduated from the University of St. Gallen, Switzerland, with a doctorate in International Strategy. He is also a graduate of key faculty development programmes. He currently serves as Professor of Strategy and Leadership, as well as Academic Director of the degree, open enrolment and custom programs of HEC Paris in Qatar. He has received several research, teaching and impact awards as well as honorary professorships. Most notably, he won five CEMS best course awards.

Rico J. Baldegger is Dean and Professor of Entrepreneurship, Strategy and Innovation at the School of Management Fribourg (HEG-FR), University of Applied Sciences and Arts Western Switzerland. His area of expertise is entrepreneurship and innovation. His academic background includes a Master (Business & Economics) from the University of St. Gallen (1985) and a Ph.D. in SME & Entrepreneurship from the University of Fribourg (1995). His regular activities include teaching and key notes in Europe, the USA, Singapore, and Australia. Professor Baldegger's broad professional experience in entrepreneurship and management includes the fields of leadership, human resources, IT, and branding. He has created several start-ups in Europe and the US and was founder and CEO of a management consultant company. Today, he is on the board of several companies, acting as a Business Angel and supporting the entrepreneurial ecosystem in Switzerland. Rico Baldegger has more than a hundred publications, including several books. His research focuses on the innovation process of entrepreneurs, the internationalization process of start-ups and SMEs, new venture creation, and growth management.

Martine Boutary is Professor of International Business at TBS Education (France). Her research interests are international issues, and more specifically about offshoring process and internationalization of small and medium-sized enterprises (SMEs). She is Advisor for French Foreign Trade, appointed by the French prime minister.

Valeria Budinich is a Systems Entrepreneurship Advisor at the Legatum Center at MIT Sloan, Cambridge, Massachussets, USA. She is an innovator working at the intersection of business and society. As a system changer at Ashoka, she pioneered 'hybrid value chains' and enabled over 50 hybrid business models, impacting the lives of millions of people. She is the co-author, with Olivier Kayser, of *Scaling up Business Solutions to Social Problems* (Palgrave, 2015).

Heather Cairns-Lee is Affiliate Professor of Leadership at IMD in Switzerland, Advisory Board Member of Fribourg School of Management and Visiting Scholar at Surrey Business School. Her award-winning PhD focuses on how leaders make meaning. Her teaching, research and facilitation concern the development of self-awareness and authenticity, leadership and group dynamics, and communication and sensemaking in organizations.

Paul G. Davies, DBA, is Senior Lecturer in Strategic Thinking and Programme Director for the MBA in Swansea University, UK. Areas of research include exploring the collaborative interaction within organic food companies and the strategic supply chain capacity requirements for the renewable energy sector. Both topics draw on aspects of power, motivation and strategy and have generated a number of journal and conference papers as well as informing industry practice.

Alisée de Tonnac is Co-founder and Co-CEO of Seedstars, a Swiss-based investment holding with a mission to impact people's lives in emerging markets through technology and entrepreneurship. She is Advisory Board Member of Fribourg School of Management and a member of the Swiss National Innovation Council. She is highly acclaimed as social entrepreneur Forbes 30 under 30, Innovation Fellow of Wired UK, 50.

Ayman El Tarabishy, PhD, is currently the President and CEO of the International Council for Small Business (ICSB). He is also the Deputy Chairperson, Department of Management, GW School of Business. He is the only Faculty Member in GW who lectures in nationally ranked programs. In 2021, he was voted as the Best Online Faculty at the GW. He played a central role in creating and promoting the United Nations Micro, Small, and Medium-Sized Enterprises (MSMEs) Day.

Rosangela Feola, PhD, is Assistant Professor of Management at the University of Salerno, Italy, and Affiliate Research Fellow at IPAG Business School, Paris, France. She is member of Lisa Lab, a Research Center on Innovative Entrepreneurship and Academic Spin-Off, at the University of Salerno. Her research interests are mainly related to entrepreneurial processes, technology transfer and innovative start-up. She is co-author of several publications on national and international journals including *R&D Management, Journal of Small Business Management, Small Business Economics* and *Journal of Cleaner Production.*

Elisabeth Fröhlich studied at the Ludwig Maximilian University in Munich and at the University of Cologne in Germany. As Professor for Strategic

Procurement Management, she leads the CBS International Business School as president. She is also a board member of several scientific organizations, including PRME (PRME board and chair of the GNC), spokesperson for the Cologne Science Round and Business Ambassador City of Cologne. She researches sustainable supply chain management, sustainable purchasing, strategic supplier management, agility and digitalisation in purchasing.

Inés Gabarret holds a PhD in Management Sciences with a specialization in entrepreneurship from the University of Montpellier, France, and a HDR (authorization to direct research) from the same university. She is a professor and researcher at ESSCA School of Management and at LAREQUOI, Paris-Saclay University, France.

Michael J. Harrison has been Professor for over a decade at Framingham State University, Massachusetts, USA, and is the Chair of the Department of Marketing, where he teaches Marketing and International Business courses. He has over 22 years of business experience working with world-class organizations. He has published in peer-reviewed journals and presented scholarly articles at Oxford University and Cambridge University. He was a nominee for the Oxford Journal Global Top 50 Educators Award and a Teaching Fellow at Harvard University.

Nancy A. Hubbard, DPhil, FRSA, is Dean and Professor of Management at the University of Lynchburg, Virginia, USA, Professor in Management and a Fellow in the Royal Society for the Encouragement of Arts, Manufactures, and Commerce. She has over 20 years of mergers and acquisition, change and strategy consulting experience in addition to teaching at Lynchburg, Goucher College, the University of Oxford, and serving as Visiting Professor at IAE Aix-Marseille University and SKOLKOVO. She holds her doctorate in Management from the University of Oxford.

Louisa Huxtable-Thomas is Associate Professor in the School of Management at Swansea University, UK, and leads on engagement and impact, as well as coordinating Executive Education provision. Combining theories and empirical knowledge gleaned from the fields of business, social science, education and psychology, her research interests relate to how people's behaviors, either as leaders, entrepreneurs or policy makers have an influence on societal and economic welfare.

Mark Darius Juszczak is currently Assistant Professor at the Collins College of Professional Studies at St. John's University in New York City, USA. He is also Expert Advisor in Technology and Human Rights to the Vatican Mission to the United Nations. He holds a doctorate in Education from Teachers College Columbia University, with a specialization in industrial innovation and knowledge management. He has worked in over 40 countries and is the author of numerous academic articles.

Anja Karlshaus studied at the University of Cologne, Santa Clara University, and the European Business School. In 2009, she took over the HRM professorship at CBS International Business School in Cologne, Germany, and became Dean of the Business Administration and Sustainable Management faculty in 2019. Moreover, she was employed at Dresdner Bank, Allianz Group, and Commerzbank from 1999 to 2016 and is currently a member of various working groups such as DIHK, IHK, City of Cologne, State of NWR. She researches sustainability, diversity and agile HR.

Wafa Khlif is Professor of Management Accounting at TBS Education, Spain. Her research interests are on board director efficiency, corporate board roles, duties and composition as well as issues in accounting and audit. Her research has been published in various leading international journals such as *International Small Business Journal, Society and Business Review, Technovation.*

Werner Krings graduated from Henley Business School at the University of Reading, UK, with a doctorate in Marketing. He is Adjunct Professor at Framingham State University, Massachusetts, USA, where he teaches Digital/social media and International Marketing. He teaches Entrepreneurship and Innovation at EM Normandie, Oxford, UK, and Institut Francophone International, Hanoi, Vietnam. He has more than two decades of business development, marketing, sales, and consulting experience with European and US organizations. His research has been published in international books and journals, including *Industrial Marketing Management.*

Mary Kate Naatus is KPMG Dean and Professor of Business at the Frank J. Guarini School of Business at Saint Peter's University, New Jersey, USA, where she was also Department Chair and Founding Director of Ignite Institute for Business Innovation. Prior to that, she was Program Director at NJIT. From 2000 to 2002, she served in the Peace Corps in El Salvador. She has a PhD from Rutgers University, an MBA from New Jersey Institute of Technology and a BA in Journalism from The College of New Jersey.

Roger Palmer is Governor at Sparsholt College, Sparsholt (Winchester), Andover, Director, Orca Associates Ltd and Non Executive Director at Westley Enterprises Ltd. He was Dean of the Business School at Bournemouth University, UK. Formerly, he was Professor of Marketing and Head of the School of Management at Henley Business School, where he teaches and supervises. He gained extensive business experience at board and CEO levels in the chemical, agri-food and pharma sectors. He received his PhD from the Cranfield

School of Management, UK, and has published extensively and taught and consulted internationally. His interests include business marketing, relationship and value management, and marketing strategy and implementation.

Katia Passerini is Provost and Executive Vice President of Seton Hall University, New Jersey, USA. Prior to this, she was Distinguished Chair, Dean of the Collins College of Professional Studies and Professor at St. John's. From 2003 to 2016, she was Professor and Hurlburt Chair of MIS and Dean of the Albert Dorman Honors College (2013–16) at the New Jersey Institute of Technology (NJIT). She holds MBA and PhD degrees in MIS from George Washington University. She has published over 100 peer-reviewed articles.

Kevin Pon is Associate Dean for International Development and Accreditations at ESDES Lyon Business School in France. He obtained his PhD in Management from the University of Buckinghamshire and has published articles on the international strategy of companies and schools. He teaches international marketing and management at ESDES. He has over 25 years experience in teaching and has occupied various positions in other schools. He has set up franchises abroad to deliver French management programs internationally such as in China, Morocco and Tunisia and teaches internationally.

Gaby Probst is Head of Pedagogical Development and member of the Board of Management at the School of Management in Fribourg, Switzerland (HEG)// HES-SO University of Applied Sciences and Arts Western Switzerland, where she teaches business German and coaches all faculty members in their pedagogical process. Her special focus lies in the field of online education with a major interest in active learning, an area in which she provides professional training for faculty and publishes research articles.

Francesca Pucciarelli is Assistant Professor in Marketing, and Turin Campus Academic Director of MBA in International Management at ESCP Business School, Turin, Italy. Her research interests concern higher education evolution, challenges and competitiveness with a special focus on business schools. She is a founding member of the ESCP Business School Big Data Research Center and part of the Creativity Research Center.

Danica Purg is Professor of Leadership, the President of IEDC-Bled School of Management, Slovenia, the President of CEEMAN and the President of the Alliance of Management Development Associations in Rising Economies. She is one of the founding members of PRME and twice led the PRME Steering Committee; in 2013 and in 2020. IEDC was the first PRME Champion in CEE. She is the author of books in the field of innovations in management education, sustainability and art & leadership.

Fernande Raine is CEO and Founder, The History Co:Lab, Boston, Massachusetts, USA. She is an entrepreneur committed to making history fuel for a better future. After gaining a PhD in History at Yale, three years at McKinsey, and 15 years of being an intrapreneur with Ashoka, she launched the History Co:Lab in 2018, following the model outlined in her book chapter. Since then, the Co:Lab has incubated a transatlantic network for inspired teaching and an award-winning youth podcast UnTextbooked.

Francesco Rattalino is Full Professor of Strategy and Management, and Turin Campus Dean at ESCP Business School, Turin, Italy. His published research focuses on strategy execution, sustainability, family business and internationalisation theory, with a focus on how family firms survive over a long period of time and internationalize their business. He is on the steering committee of the NEWLEAD (Innovative Leadership and Change Management in Higher Education) consortium, an Erasmus+-funded initiative aimed at equipping university leaders to successfully steer complex institutional transformation agendas.

Nicole Saliba-Chalhoub, analytical psychotherapist, is a Full Professor at the Holy Spirit University of Kaslik (USEK), in Lebanon, where she has been teaching literary hermeneutics, applied psychoanalysis and aesthetics of postmodernism since 1998. Her articles and books tackle, in particular, the unconscious of literary texts. Her latest book is entitled *From Depressive Discomfort to Artistic Surpassing* (2017).

Christophe Schmitt is a Full Professor at IAE Metz School of Management in France. He holds the Chair Entreprendre and runs its related incubator. He is also Associate Professor at the Louvain School of Management (Belgium) and at the Haute Ecole de Gestion de Fribourg (Switzerland). His articles and books focus on the development of entrepreneurial action's theory. His latest book is entitled *New Perspectives in Entrepreneurship: From the Telegraph Model to the Orchestra's One* (2020).

Marcela Schweitzer, PhD, with more than 25 years of experience in education and cognitive psychology, is a specialist in intellectual development, in the relationship between learning, cognition and emotion. She is Professor of Psychology at the Catholic University of the West and at the University of Angers in France. She is also Manager of the pedagogical support center of ESSCA School of Management, France; Director of MRS coaching, training and consulting; and Member of the Association for Research on Development of Competencies (ARDECO).

Norean R. Sharpe, PhD, is Dean and the Joseph H. and Maria C. Schwartz Chair in Decision Sciences at the Tobin College of Business at St. John's

University, New York, USA. Within the Tobin College resides the Center in Enterprise Risk Management and the Maurice R. Greenberg School of Risk Management, Insurance, and Actuarial Science. An accomplished researcher in the field of analytics, she has served as a consultant worldwide on issues of accreditation and earned her PhD in Systems Engineering from the University of Virginia.

Mark Somers is Professor of Management and Organizational Behavior at the Martin Tuchman School of Management at New Jersey Institute of Technology, USA. He holds an MBA degree in Organizational Psychology from Baruch College and a doctorate in Business with specialization in Organizational Behavior from the Graduate Center of the City University of New York. His research is focused on organizational and occupational socialization, work attitudes and work performance, employee well-being, and applications of machine learning in organizational research.

Agata Stachowicz-Stanusch is Full Professor of Management at Canadian University Dubai, UAE. She is the author of over 80 research papers and has more than 16 books published by leading houses. In 2015, she was the Chair of the ITC. She serves in editorial roles for a number of publications and has been an active member of the UN Global Compact PRME initiative for more than ten years.

Kristian J. Sund is Professor of Strategic Management at Roskilde University in Denmark. His research on business model innovation, uncertainty and management education has appeared in outlets like *MIT Sloan Management Review*, *Journal of Business Research* and *Studies in Higher Education*. He holds a doctorate in Management and Licentiate (MSc) in Economics from the University of Lausanne, and an MA from the Ecole Polytechnique Fédérale de Lausanne (EPFL), where he also completed his post-doc.

Shiv K. Tripathi is Vice-Chancellor at Atmiya University, India. He leads the Humanistic Management Network, India Chapter. He has 24 years of experience in teaching research and education management. He served as Professor and Dean at IIHMR University and CMR University, Jaipur; Executive Director (Management) at Chandigarh University; Vice-Chancellor at Mahatma Gandhi University, Meghalaya; Professor and Head of Business Studies at Mzumbe University in Tanzania; and Dean, Faculty of Management at VBS Purvanchal University.

Francesco Venuti, Ph.D., is Associate Professor of Accounting in the Financial Reporting and Audit Department at ESCP Business School, Turin, Italy. He is Associate Dean for the Executive MBA and also the Director of the Master in International Food & Beverage Management. His teaching experience covers a wide range of different contexts and grades, including executive education and online (MOOC) courses. His major fields of research include financial accounting and reporting (with a focus on insurance companies), nonfinancial disclosure, pedagogy and teaching innovation.

Paul L. Walker, PhD, is the Schiro/Zurich Chair in ERM at St. John's University and the Tobin College of Business, New York, USA. He co-developed one of the first courses on Enterprise Risk Management (ERM) and has trained executives and boards around the world on ERM. He has conducted ERM research at many companies. He also leads the graduate degree programs in ERM and runs the Center for Excellence in ERM at St. John's University.

Diana Wells is President Emerita of Ashoka, serves on Ashoka's Global Leadership Team, and leads Ashoka's Impact & Evidence unit. As a Fulbright and Woodrow Wilson Scholar, her PhD research focused on identity and social movements. She has taught Anthropology at Georgetown University and served as a Trustee of Brown University.

Laura Zizka has been a faculty member of EHL Hospitality Business School// HES-SO University of Applied Sciences and Arts Western Switzerland, Lausanne, Switzerland, since 2002. As Associate Professor, she teaches Academic Writing and Crisis/Strategic Communication to undergraduate and graduate students and supervises both undergraduate and graduate theses. Her teaching philosophy revolves around lifelong learning, application of transferable 'soft' skills, and positive social change. She chairs the Examination Board and is a Peer Pedagogical Coach. She is a member of the Swiss Faculty Development Network (SFDN) and has presented papers in international conferences.

Foreword

Marc Gruber

The advent of business schools can be traced back to the 18th century, with the first institutions specializing in accounting, such as the Aula do Comércio in Lisbon, Portugal, founded in 1759. But it was not until the 19th century when – in the wake of the industrial revolution – a professionalized business administration was required in order to capitalize on the new possibilities offered by mass production and to master the complexities of the 'modern corporation'.

As a response to these growing needs, numerous business schools were founded across Europe and the United States and began teaching subjects such as finance, sales and general management to wider audiences. Over the decades, these institutions added topics such as human resource management, strategy, innovation, corporate social responsibility and many others to their teaching portfolios – thereby reflecting our growing knowledge of managerial activities, firms and their stakeholders, and a growing need to further professionalize the management of organizations in increasingly challenging, international competitive settings.

Time and again, business schools have proven that they can adapt their offerings to the evolving needs of individuals and businesses, as well as the societies in which they operate as educational and research institutions. Yet, as many argue, the challenges business schools are facing today are more fundamental than ever before. For instance, the Grand Challenges that our societies are facing require business schools to become leaders in redefining the purpose of business organizations to encompass wider definitions of value creation and to become more meaningful platforms for diverse internal and external audiences. The manifold technological disruptions enable powerful new forms of content delivery (e.g., digital channels augmented by machine learning), give rise to alternative, competing business school concepts (e.g., virtual schools; social networks offering degrees), require the development of new content and degrees (e.g., in computational sciences), and demand new solutions at the interface between human beings, digitalization and smart machines.

In light of these and other key challenges, we need to explore and evaluate multiple ways in which we can reinvent business schools and turn them into indispensable providers and partners for the years and decades to come. In bringing together manifold ideas, observations and recommendations, the present book plays an instrumental role in achieving this important ambition and vision. Business schools strive to educate the leaders of the future – and if they do their job in a forward-looking manner that is sensitive to major developments and disruptive shifts, they can leverage their prominent positions as trusted educational institutions to become leading agents of change towards a better future – for the individual, for businesses, for communities, for societies, and for our planet.

Full Professor at Ecole Polytechnique Fédérale de Lausanne (EPFL),
Switzerland
Editor-in-Chief of Academy of Management Journal (AMJ)

Foreword

Louis Jacques Filion

How relevant are business school programs in today's world? This question has begun to generate a lot of attention from public and private sector agencies alike. Yet, in all the reports that have been published, one observation stands out: the courses offered by many business schools should be better adapted to the requirements of organizations and societies. For example, in the United States, the Ford Foundation has long insisted on this need for change.

Others, including the Carnegie Foundation, have noted that business school programs tend to focus too much on theory and not enough on practice. In other words, business schools, like the universities to which they are attached, tend to produce students with heads full of theories rather than well-developed minds adjusted to the context of today's workplace.

Therefore, I was especially thrilled to read a book that tackles this topic precisely. Its six editors, all known for their leading-edge work, were courageous enough to address what is a thorny subject by inviting business school professors, researchers, and leaders to share their opinions and suggestions. The widely different views expressed by authors from various contexts and countries provide a great deal of food for thought.

One aspect that emerges clearly from the book is the importance of innovation and sustainability as two of the most significant dimensions of the modern world. In many cases, the authors refer implicitly or explicitly to the 17 United Nations Sustainable Development Goals (SDGs) promoted vigorously since 2016. However, radical changes are needed to support the growing interest of younger generations in creating a more ecologically responsible and sustainable society.

The many examples of innovations in business schools described by the book's authors provide some exciting reference points and suggest paths that will help change the way we view university-level management education. As a result, the entrepreneurs, executives, leaders, and managers of the future will need to think differently about addressing the challenges they will face in an evolving world.

The pace of change in that world is accelerating exponentially, and business schools must adjust if they are to prepare tomorrow's leaders for the roles they will play. Every chapter in this book adds to the long list of topics that must be considered as we move forward toward renewal. In addition, the book presents a wealth of ideas for business school stakeholders on topics ranging from course content, program structures, and research topics to teaching materials and a host of other aspects.

This is a book that is both thought-provoking and inspiring. It is impossible to read it without concluding that we must change how we look at education in business schools. Thanks to the editors and authors for their ground-breaking ideas. They have opened the door to new, avant-garde approaches that should encourage us to think differently about how tomorrow's business leaders should be trained.

Emeritus Professor
HEC Montréal

Introduction to *The Future of Business Schools*

Rico J. Baldegger

INTRODUCTION: HELPING CREATE A SUSTAINABLE WORLD – THE ROLE OF BUSINESS SCHOOLS IN A NEW AND DYNAMIC WORLD

Business schools' overall purpose, relevance, and impact as societal actors are under attack. Even the question of what is their purpose in the future? How can business schools reinvent themselves to remain relevant to society? These questions are at the center of the ongoing debate about business schools in the 21st century. These thoughts echo some influential works on the role of business schools, such as 'The future of business schools,' published in 2005 by Gabriel Hawawini from INSEAD, France, followed by Chia and Holt's article in 2008 and Dyllick's article in 2015, including the recent article from 2020 of Krishnamurthy that discussed the various reciprocal relationships of business schools with their stakeholders. The underlining premise of these publications across time remains focused on securing the relevance, sustainability, and an accepted purpose and destiny of business schools.

This debate addresses the relevance and content of business school curricula and to what extent their research and training orientations can be made more purposeful to society. This book contributes to this debate by providing a rich plethora of ideas, experiences, and studies that address the renewal process of business schools. Thus, various stakeholders of business schools contribute to the discussion on the future of business schools by addressing an array of expectations and challenges. Our book reflects the changes in the perceived value that business schools bring through the lenses of different stakeholders. In addition, it resonates with the richness in the perceived roles that business schools embody in their ecosystems, especially in times of change, for example, COVID-19, the Russia-Ukraine war, the turbulent swings in the stock markets, the rising global unemployment, among others, in which business schools were expected to generate and lead innovative, relevant, and possible responses that the new conditions created. Entrepreneurs, professionals, and scholars from different schools of thought and research interests, including those focusing on ecological, ethical, and social impacts, have contributed to this book. Their contributions represent the book's three parts that address critical areas of current challenges: complexity, sustainability, and destiny. We will discuss each part next.

COMPLEXITY

How can we know where we are headed in the future is unpredictably complex? Consequently, how and what do we teach our students to be equipped with the skills and mindsets that would enable them to manage complexity? And how do we engage the ecosystems and business school stakeholders to facilitate and promote the creation of relevant, helping learning premises for our students? Environments embody continual uncertainty and complexity. Business schools are expected to tackle this complexity by building skills, abilities, mindsets, and resilience that future managers (i.e., current students) can use, redeploy, and modify under various conditions.

To determine possible futures, building on a deeper understanding of the evolving environment increasingly turning into the long-envisioned VUCA world – volatile, uncertain, complex, and ambiguous – is crucial. There is a contrast between these environmental characteristics and established, current business school approaches. For instance, to what extent is the current focus in research and teaching on individual actors and their agency still relevant when environmental shifts are increasingly collective and systemic? And can the typically linear, deductive approaches still provide valid predictions and insights in such complex, interdependent dynamics? In this book, suggestions are made to the contrary: environmental complexity does not require even more specialized, but rather more holistic responses by business schools, mainly as multiple specializations and disciplines 'explain' complexities, consequently providing close-grained answers to manage complexity, which may preclude the development of integrative, innovative responses to dynamic changes. For instance, such holistic responses are needed at the disciplinary level. This creates institutional challenges: How can cross-disciplinarity, multidisciplinarity, or interdisciplinarity be achieved in a discipline-based specialization in the research and teaching system? Holistic responses are also needed at the geographical and cultural level, which again require institutional renewal: How can local, regional, and international perspectives be integrated? What does this imply for traditional on-off student exchanges? Can international experiences be integrated more seamlessly throughout the studies in a hybrid mode between in-person interaction and virtual participation? How can new technologies simplify the complexities, for example, virtual classes, digitalized learning systems, or online programs, and how do we guarantee that students and faculty of diverse areas have equal access to such technologies? These technologies embody agile solutions for various challenges, from student exchange programs (virtually) to creating international teams for a project, formulating global research projects, to the 'New Normal' in which classes can be virtual or hybrid. These are just some examples provided in this book for exploring answers to the challenge of complexity. The COVID-19 crisis has created a sudden, unique level of complexity and thereby an extraordinary impetus for change from which many insights can and should be drawn. Such sudden, unforeseen complex changes represent a form of uncertainty that is unprecedented to higher education institutions and thus not only require rethinking research and teaching approaches and introducing and professionalizing risk management approaches for higher education. Overall, the challenge of environmental complexity clarifies that business schools cannot remain reactive actors who adapt to changes – they would always be too late, with too few technological changes, and thus constantly remain misfits. Instead, business schools need the ability to develop and act upon what authors call 'practical wisdom.' Overall, the future of business schools thus may lie in becoming proactive co-creators of their environments and, at times, assuming the leadership role of a disruptive innovator to develop novel creative solutions for advancing academic, corporate, and societal interests in the 21st century and beyond (Bagley et al., 2020). Due to the environment's complexity, the best way to predict the future of business schools may be to create it.

SUSTAINABILITY

How can we achieve sustainability in a complex, unpredictable world? The second part of the book addresses this debate. However, the core of the discussion seems to focus on current and future contributions of management sciences to address sustainable development and the 17 United Nations (UN) Sustainable Development Goals (SDGs) accepted by the world community since 2016. Business schools need to be involved in this global debate and solve the challenge of defining and implementing corporate responsibility from within and in direct and indirect impacts on nature and society.

Sustainability has turned into the umbrella term that encompasses all the dimensions that contribute to sustainable business operations, for example, social, environmental, and economic performance, known and established as the triple-bottom-line of people, planet, and profit (Painter-Morland & Ten Bos, 2011, p. 288). The central question for business schools is to study and propose how corporate actors can combine and reconcile binding interactions among the economy, society, and the environment into the 21st century and beyond. Some solutions have to be innovative and even disruptive.

One crucial challenge for business schools is their future research and education capacities to address and inspire corporate responsibility, impact entrepreneurship, and sustainable leadership (Markman et al., 2019). This means how a sound and balanced combination of human, financial, technical, and social capital can deliver responsible strategies to manage multinational enterprises (MNEs), large firms, and small and medium-sized enterprises (SMEs) and lead, both conceptually and in practice, to new business models and new products and services with high value for a better society.

Another challenge is exploring how firms can drive impact-oriented deliverables for sustainable development and achieve most SDGs. In other words, it means how corporations can contribute socio-economic and technical solutions for good, for nature and the people, at the grassroots level and regional, international, and global levels. This also means how firms can do well and do good.

Such orientations also include a revisited participation in sustainable development for and within business schools based on reviewing appropriate combinations of practice to science and science to practice, applied research, and training at all degree and continued education levels. In addition, more than 800 business schools have signed up to the UN Global Compact's Principles for Responsible Management Education, which were drawn up in 2007 and require them to submit progress reports.

DESTINY

The third part of the book presents recent trends and views on the pertinence and use of Management Education. We have passed a long way from Herbert Simon's (1967) view on the purpose of business schools: 'The purpose of a business school is to train managers for the practice of management as a profession and to develop new knowledge that may be relevant to improving the operation of business' (p. 5). Research has proved that today's students pinpoint the purpose of business schools in delivering a broader education that captures human, environmental, and economic perspectives to be used as valuable resources in their consequence success as managers. Stakeholders see the purpose of business schools as the means to shape the students' knowledge, skills, mindsets, and overall profile, to harmonize the stakeholders' envisioned future society. These perspectives may be refuted, thus setting a substantial challenge in front of business schools in determining the direction by promising their purposes as perceived by the students and stakeholders; hence a salient impetus to explore this aspect through our book. The chapters explain the various perspectives between academia and industry and the essential role of critical thinking, resilience, and empathy for future leaders. This part covers ideas to reshape and reframe a responsible and sustainable pedagogy. The broader societal changes, including the seemingly overnight shift to remote working and education at all levels, have profoundly changed how we live, learn, and work. Business schools were able to take a leading role in addressing these shifting needs, expectations, and cultural and societal norms, by continuing to embrace new collaborative tools and models of interaction and curriculum delivery that allow more profound levels of global engagement, industry connectedness, and transparency in the post-COVID-19 educational landscape.

DETAILED OVERVIEW OF THE BOOK

As indicated, the book has three distinct parts. Part I of the book gives an overview of sensemaking in business schools and the challenge of navigating complexity and preparing for uncertainty. Wolfgang Amann, Agata Stachowicz-Stanusch, and Shiv K. Tripathi focus on the dynamics of business environments that are now frequently described as VUCA – volatile, uncertain, complex, and ambiguous. They consider the COVID-19 pandemic outbreak in 2020 as a case in point. Therefore, strategies, business models, tactics, and plans were challenged for the year. In this situation, executives worldwide did not suffer from insufficient general knowledge about strategizing, business modeling, or planning. This research project posits that practical wisdom is what practitioners need to survive and thrive. The chapter provides insights based on exploratory research and presents a state-of-the-art framework for fostering such practical understanding. The process foresees a three-act process and six concrete steps to take practical wisdom to the next level. The insights gained contribute to a better return on education (ROE). It also prepares the learner more aptly for this VUCA world. This chapter focuses on the tremendous potential of emphasizing practical wisdom more than ever before. As a result, program graduates will receive a higher return on their investment (ROI) and education (ROE). Schools should aspire to add more value, discuss relevantly, and evolve into better contributors.

Mary Kate Naatus, Katia Passerini, Kevin Pon, and Mark Somers focus on business schools post COVID-19, and the significant impact on internationalization of business education, especially in Europe, where physical mobility across countries has been particularly affected. They discuss three aspects of a post-pandemic environment: the pandemic as an impetus for change; implications for education; and implications for academic administration, especially in administering international programs.

The authors argue that the pandemic has also been the catalyst to lay down new internationalization rules and bring unique hidden benefits to other areas of the business school's perimeter. The cosmic shifts the pandemic brought about in our collective thinking have disrupted long-held practices and approaches to global education and have reduced some resistance to interdisciplinarity.

Institutions can maintain that heightened infusion of creativity when planning internationalization strategies and processes through a more inclusive lens. In other administrative areas, continued gains can be made in the post-pandemic environment. By shifting away from traditional notions of student exchange as one of the few internationalization opportunities and providing more incentives and facilitated processes for engaging a much broader spectrum of global virtual interactions between students and faculty, far more students are likely to benefit, and we can establish deeper global connections among institutions.

Nicole Saliba-Chalhoud and Christophe Schmitt explore the crucial issue of the academic model of global studies, presenting them as a new challenge for higher education, especially when business schools must train students to become systemic citizens to gain in complexity as much as for a better societal impact. They underline the effect of global studies in the education framework, with international studies still somewhat absent. The origins of global studies are presented, their philosophy is highlighted, and some of their implementations are indicated in different universities worldwide. They highlight the ties between cross-disciplinary, multidisciplinary, and interdisciplinary education, ensuring bonds with the territories by linking the local, regional, and international perspectives.

Martine Boutary and Wafa Khlif start by asking: Breaking out of the paradox loop: a metamorphosis for Business Schools? They highlight the paradoxical situation in which business schools are evolving, based mainly on observations of French schools. Responsible for educating individuals in business management, these business schools are confronted, on the one hand, with the demands of their stakeholders – students and companies, in particular – for performance, growth, and short-term efficiency and, on the other hand, with a demanding society that is facing a fragile environment and limited resources.

They posit that this can turn useless if business school leaders do nothing to tackle the three following fundamental paradoxes. The first one is about deified individuals, endowed with 'an exclusive property right' that grants them the 'power to act,' yet fragile, as they are so disconnected from their context/reality – even their planet. The second is the paradox of using what tend to be linear models and deductive approaches to analyze and represent certainty in a world that is unstable and uncertain. The third paradox is a complex world, sliced up as needed by simplistic, quantified economic models. Caring, questioning, and transversality could be the three pillars to embrace these paradoxes and carry new business schools into a renewed society. We propose some avenues for reflection and actions in this context.

Werner Krings, Michael J. Harrison, and Roger Palmer contribute to the debate on designing future viable business schools to assume the leadership role of a disruptive innovator and develop creative solutions for advancing academic, corporate, and societal interests in the 21st century and beyond. In summer 2021, they conducted 40 semi-structured interviews with first-rate entrepreneurs, professors, and students of North America, Western/Eastern Europe, and the Asia-Pacific, focusing on urgent topics. The outcome provides a comprehensive overview, examining the issues from various angles, providing guidelines on proper action steps to impact entrepreneurship as an added value, and aligning business education by partnering with enterprises forging sustainability while advancing teaching and learning approaches. In addition, the authors highlight the importance of Social Capital to form forward-looking synergies with business-related disciplines, for example, Science, Technology, Engineering, and Mathematics (STEM).

The last chapter of Part I by Norean R. Sharpe, Nancy A. Hubbard, and Paul L. Walker provides a review of recent and practical research in the discipline of Enterprise Risk Management (ERM) as it applies to higher education; here, we find recommendations for including ERM in operational business processes and sharing insights into building a curriculum in ERM at business schools. This book has many applications and cases that could be incorporated into a business curriculum. For example, one chapter discusses disruption and innovation in detail and how ERM practices can be applied to make creation more successful, including using strategic disruption workshops, developing a series of new business models, and techniques that help map out and analyze the business model. Higher educational institutions would be wise to implement ERM practices and apply them to themselves. It would also seem wise to promote intellectual scholarship and curriculum in this area to prepare students better to be more successful future leaders.

Elisabeth Fröhlich, Anja Karlshaus, and Danica Purg open Part II with the story of two business schools that embraced responsible management education (RME) at a very early stage in their history. The chapter illustrates why it is urgently necessary to rethink economic strategies and train sustainable leaders. The authors explain why RME is becoming the central task of every business school. Only responsible leaders can initiate the necessary changes to successfully implement resilient business strategies in today's complex and volatile environment. In this context, it becomes apparent that traditional teaching formats are reaching their limits.

The chapter gives insights on 'Sustainable Leadership' principles and the 'Artful Leadership' approach. In the search for management and leadership development that prepares for coping with the complexities of the 21st century, new elements have been added to the educational concept and methods. The hypothesis is that the same characteristics can define new leadership as art:

inspiration, imagination, intuition, authenticity, and skills. The aim is to offer a tool that enables managers and business leaders to reflect on their leadership mindset and style. However, it can be stated in conclusion that the need for appropriate holistic teaching approaches is more urgent than ever – not just since the COVID-19 crisis, which has strongly reinforced our conviction in sustainability and vividly highlighted the interconnected and interdependent nature of the world's social, ecological, and economic systems.

In the second chapter of Part II, Ayman El Tarabishy and Rosangela Feola analyze how Humane Entrepreneurship could create the conditions to harness the potential of the millennial generation, therefore increasing the innovation and competitiveness of their companies and the wellness of society more broadly. They outline that millennials are considered the unluckiest generation in the world, but at the same time, studies show that they are one of the most talented and creative generations. So, the critical question becomes understanding how firms can activate the potential of millennials to produce positive effects for both individuals and organizations. The emerging model of Humane Entrepreneurship could potentially represent the missing link between firms and millennials. The Humane Entrepreneurship model maintains that firms need to integrate the traditional orientation toward business and profit (Entrepreneurial Orientation) with two additional elements: the attention toward Humane Resources involved in the firm (Humane Orientation) and attention to the environment and society (Sustainable Orientation).

Valeria Budinich, Fernande Raine, and Diana Wells explain Ashoka's research with 120 world-leading system changers, suggesting a powerful playbook for business leaders seeking to enable their teams to create and capture value in today's economy in new ways. Their study examines how more business leaders across industries and geographies can become system changers who reimagine and reshape industries for all. Over two years, Ashoka consulted 120 leading system changers through its global network of social entrepreneurs. This research tapped into 40 years of Ashoka's expertise in identifying system changers as 'Ashoka Fellows' and integrating them into a global, supportive community.

The authors explain how Ashoka Fellows are selected through a rigorous process that assesses the impact potential of the new system change idea and the creativity and entrepreneurial skills of the system changer. Most of these Fellows lead citizen sector organizations with national or international impact. As of 2022, Ashoka has elected more than 4,000 Fellows in 90 countries through a selection process that uses consistent criteria. Across the levers of leadership (how they lead themselves, others, and systems), the authors have identified five capability dimensions that system changers manifest: building purpose through empathy, embracing continuous change, having the courage to be different, being biased to action, and collaborating for impact.

Heather Cairns-Lee and Alisée de Tonnac conclude Part II of the book by drawing on the 17th Sustainable Development Goal – partnerships. The chapter suggests that business schools need to recast themselves as partners in learning to multiply their contribution to an equitable, inclusive, and innovative society. Business schools have increased over the last 60 years to become a dominant education model and a revenue stream for many universities. However, they have been criticized for focusing on business, prioritizing their etymological origins of commerce and trade at the expense of a broader remit to nurture an inclusive and sustainable society. Again, language is crucial, as it shapes the narratives that signal what is valued. They suggest that recasting business schools as learning partnerships increases their relevance to identifying and developing the skills and mindsets needed by a fast-changing society. These include an entrepreneurial education that supports the development of creative responses to the changing needs and emerging challenges faced by individuals, organizations, and society.

Part III delivers views on the pertinence and the use of management education which reflect recent trends. In the first chapter, Inés Gabaret and Marcela Schweitzer question the competencies needed for the managerial roles of the future and propose resilience and empathy as fundamental capacities to allow managers to deal with uncertain and complex environments. Empathy and resilience, and more broadly, emotional intelligence, can be learned and, therefore, taught. This chapter aims to propose an insightful approach to understanding emotions and insights on how to help the managers of the future develop their and others' abilities. Emotions are essential determinants of behavior and achievement at work and influence companies' social climate and productivity. The content they propose goes beyond simple interventions on soft skills development, as it is common to see. Instead, the proposal invites students to study, understand, and conceptualize in action. With a systemic and reflective approach, the learner is at the center of the knowledge-building process to analyze emotional skills, emotions, behaviors, and implications for individuals and organizations.

Paul G. Davies and Louisa Huxtable-Thomas outline key insights into business schools' role, acting as valuable interlocutors and interpreters between academia and industry and providing helpful employees for today's complex work environments. The example of the MBA course development illustrates how these challenges create a relevant and stimulating learning environment that can equip graduates for varied careers in an increasingly complex and changeable environment.

On the one hand, they explore how a clear philosophy to the course provides a more substantial base to build the critical thinking skills essential to creating more informed decision-makers. On the other hand, a more practical consideration is that innovation is encouraged – even demanded – to maintain a competitive position. Still, long-established systems that are not always comfortable with change are in place. We recognize many examples of innovative course design practices within business schools but raise this point to articulate that a course does not exist in isolation. Understanding the course systems is imperative to avoid unrealistic expectations and, more fatally, impractical learning experiences for students. The authors argue that understanding the balance of these two elements can enable an innovative practice that furthers the potential of business schools to foster critical thinkers who will shape the broader organizational practice into the future.

Gaby Probst and Laura Zizka critically review how business schools have faced challenges over the past few decades, such as choosing and using technology, attracting students to a competitive world, and meeting the real-world demands of the industries they train their students in.

Careers and career paths have become more fluid and less predictable. New jobs have been characterized as 'de-specialized,' where flexibility and adaptation to change have become the new normal. Business schools have attempted to adapt by providing innovative programs based on competencies and applied knowledge. Nonetheless, no challenge has been as brutal and all-encompassing as the brusque shift to online education due to the COVID-19 pandemic. Any discrepancies or inequalities in teaching and learning were accentuated in the then-introduced emergency remote environment. Nevertheless, the pandemic has also offered opportunities to reshape, reframe, and reconsider business school practices, especially when developing a responsible and sustainable pedagogy.

Mark Darius Juszczak outlines a new type of degree program – a computational MBA program – that will meet the challenges of companies operating in theaters of unusual complexity and uncertainty from a process and methods perspective. The increasing complexity in computational systems embedded within traditional finance and business organizations and the broad democratization of computational tools are serving the needs of computational social science.

Drawing on the strength of similar programs, a distinct computational MBA degree appears imminent. It will be fundamentally different in its research and methodology, drawing on tools in computational social science to generate new methods of strategic analysis. Graduates of a computational MBA degree will be pulled toward those businesses that operate with high degrees of uncertainty. They will have competencies that traditional MBA graduates do not have and do not require. Instead, they will be sought out by companies and employers that operate under unique environments of technological risk, social uncertainty, and other forms of complexity that do not bear equally on all markets.

Francesca Pucciarelli, Francesco Rattalino, and Francesco Venuti continue with a chapter focused on the ongoing digital transformation of higher education. Hybrid models differ from the existing blended model. Remote and face-to-face teaching is made available simultaneously and at a scale enabling each student to choose the mode of each educational activity. Implementation paths and implications of the hybrid education model are at the center of the debate on the future of business schools. The chapter analyzes the latest scholarly literature on the opportunities and challenges of the hybrid education model. The ESCP Business School's transition to hybrid education impacts teaching, research, and campus practices. The chapter concludes by highlighting that the digital transformation cannot divorce itself from the future of business schools, and the hybrid education model could (and should) expedite more sustainable practices in management education.

The last chapter of Part III, written by Kristian J. Sund, extends the book's scope on gender and ability at entry. The author starts by asking: Looking to the future: will male students underperform in the business school? Although women remain under-represented at top management and board levels around the world, the tables are said to have turned within the context of education. An increasingly accepted stylized fact in both lower and higher education is those female students demonstrate higher academic achievement than males. This has led to a 'boy discourse' surrounding the consequences of such outperformance. Yet, recent evidence seems to question this discourse. The author presents the results of an empirical study of the sex effect at a sizeable London-based business school. The data include measures of sex, ability at entry, age at entry, and final degree classification. Ability at entry is a statistically significant predictor of subsequent undergraduate academic performance. However, contrary to the prediction of the boy discourse, no evidence of a sex effect could be confirmed.

REFERENCES

Bagley, C.E., Sulkowski, A.J., Nelson, J.S., Waddock, S., & Shrivastava, P. (2020). A path to developing more insightful business school graduates: A systems-based, experimental approach to integrating law, strategy, and sustainability. *Academy of Management Learning and Education*, 19(4), 541–68. https://doi.org/10.5465/amle.2018.0036

Chia, R., & Holt, R. (2008). The nature of knowledge in business schools. *Academy of Management Learning and Education*, 7(4), 471–86.

Dyllick, T. (2015). Responsible management education for a sustainable world: The challenges for business schools. *Journal of Management Development*, 34(1), 16–33.

Hawawini, G. (2005). The future of business schools. *Journal of Management Development*, 24(1), 770–83.

Krishnamurthy, S. (2020). The future of business education: A commentary in the shadow of the Covid-19 pandemic. *Journal of Business Research*, 117, 1–5.

Markman, G.D., Waldron, T.L., Gianiodis, P.T., & Espina, M.I. (2019). E pluribus unum: Impact entrepreneurship as a solution to grand challenges. *Academy of Management Perspectives*, 33(4), 371–82. https://doi.org/10.5465/amp.2019.0130

Painter-Morland, M., & Ten Bos, R. (eds) (2011). *Business Ethics and Continental Philosophy*. Cambridge: Cambridge University Press.

Simon, H.A. (1967). The business school a problem in organizational design. *Journal of Management Studies*, 4(1), 1–16.

PART I

Sensemaking in business schools: navigating
complexity and preparing for uncertainty

1. Building the business schools of the future with a strong focus on practical wisdom for a VUCA world

Wolfgang Amann, Agata Stachowicz-Stanusch and Shiv K. Tripathi

1.1 INTRODUCTION: WHAT IS ONE OF THE CORE PROBLEMS?

The COVID-19 pandemic challenged many business schools and their business models. Many were not ready to substantially increase their online offer, compensate for drastically reduced executive education income and lower numbers of incoming international students, and the overall uncertainty about the length of the lockdown. What professors have been teaching in classrooms about volatile, uncertain, complex, and ambiguous environments – or VUCA – challenged institutions and their leadership teams probably like never before (cf. Betof et al., 2014). Nevertheless, even before COVID-19, it dawned on many industry experts that business as usual could not be an option. Business schools have been under fire. Management education guru Mintzberg (2004) questioned the relevance of what was conveyed, clarifying that institutions may well produce MBAs but not managers. Spender and Locke (2011) ask if business schools had been hijacked by the elites. Swanson and Frederick (2011) criticize that institutions turned into silent partners in crime as ethics education was not effective. Amann et al. (2011) saw business schools under fire as they risked over-commercialization, shied away from applying the lessons they teach in the classroom to themselves, and were too slow to adapt. Hernandez et al. (2021) detail that even before the COVID-19 pandemic causing at times warlike conditions, 50 percent of leaders failed. How did business schools help before and during the crisis? How did they enable smooth transitions in the post-COVID period?

Walk the talk, being a role model, conveying ethics, and balancing the commercial as well as academic goals inarguably represent challenges. However, this chapter argues that the core logic of what ideal outcomes of education in a business school means is changing. Executives from around the world currently drown in too much knowledge. Never before did they have access to more books, articles, studies, seminars, or consultancies. Expert frameworks, such as Kotter's (2012) infamous eight steps for managing change or Kim and Mauborgne's (2014) blue ocean strategy framework with numerous caselettes, are easily accessible. The available body of knowledge continues to grow, with as many as four new leadership books being published per day, rapidly adding to the 57,000 volumes available on Amazon (Iarocci, 2015). Executives would have a hard time even watching and learning from the 3,000+ TED talks on sound leadership and management accessible to them (Zao-Sander, 2007).

One would expect flourishing organizations, innovative strategies, and successful product launches in blue ocean markets left and right. Reality is more daunting than that. For example, Cândido and Santos (2015) review critically that 50–90 percent of strategic initiatives fail even if they take place in one's industry with which the leaders of an organization are highly familiar with. Joshi et al. (2020) add to this reality check that M&A figures remain disappointing – with a success rate below 30 percent. Attempts to diversify often disappoint and lead to spin-offs later. Schwetzler and Reimund (2003) show that valuations of conglomerates are significantly lower, referring to inabilities to realize synergies fully. Forth et al. (2020) and Shooter (2021) reveal in their two independent studies that 70 percent of digital transformations fail as well – one of today's most critical challenges, aggravated and accelerated by COVID-19. Shooter (2021) elaborates that only 16 percent yield a lasting and noteworthy impact. Are graduates equipped with the right mindsets, skills, and tools to embrace these challenges? Do business schools provide the quantity and quality of solutions for business and society in light of these statistics and the increasingly turbulent VUCA world?

This chapter takes a clear stance and questions if current practices and learning outcomes suffice. When it comes to creating the future of business schools, it calls for a 'leadershift' (Maxwell, 2019) – a significant reorientation by institutional leaders – toward a stronger focus on practical wisdom, that is, phronesis.

CAPS (2017) substantiates this need of changing the focus as merely 37 percent of executive education clients notice any real impact of an executive education intervention once participants return to their workplaces; 34 percent only see customer satisfaction improving; a mere 32 percent record profit margins getting impacted. These figures do not support the claim that business schools add all the value they could. Before delving deeper in Section 1.3 into what this means and how it can be done, the following section first aims to clarify that there is not just one type of business schools, and therefore, there is no one-size-fits-all solution. The suggested solution of emphasizing practical wisdom applies to various types of institutions to varying degrees.

1.2   NO ONE SIZE FITS ALL: WHAT DO WE MEAN BY 'BUSINESS SCHOOL'?

Writing about business schools must first acknowledge that institutions are diverse (Lorange, 2002). D'Alessio and Avolio (2011) clarify that 'there is no single model or size for business schools' (p. 21). Even in the US with the highest number of well-developed schools, numerous variations persist, according to Engwall (2007). Table 1.1 outlines key categorization attempts. Are there four, five, six, or seven main gestalt types? Various others disagree both on the number as well as the criteria to distinguish them. D'Alessio and Avolio (2011) emphasize the organizational context in which a business school is embedded. Ivory et al. (2006) draw a two-by-two matrix with the first dimension asking if a school prioritizes organizational impact versus scholarly impact. The second dimension investigates if a school views teaching versus research as a strength to be prioritized. The resulting four types view a 'professional school' pursuing organizational impact and emphasizing teaching, a 'knowledge economy' viewing schools as research-intense institutions focused on organizational impact, a 'social science' place directing efforts toward scholarly impact via research, and finally, a 'liberal arts' being a teaching-intensive institution focused on scholarly impact. In turn, the authors argue that a lack of clarity too frequently confuses all stakeholders. Too few institutions can honestly claim to be all four effectively.

Iniguez de Onzono (2011) offers a competing typology, once more on two dimensions. He positions schools along the first continuum of either a very limited or broad range of programs and simultaneously on the second continuum of a more limited or more pronounced international reputation. Lorange (2002) as the former leader of the Norwegian school of business and International Institute for Management Development (IMD) differentiates various types of institutions based on how they embrace competition, yet with different foci than Iniguez de Onzono (2011). Lorange (2002) sets institutions apart based on whether they are adaptive, proactive, entrepreneurial, rationally managed, or dynamic.

It soon becomes clear that no one size fits all. Schools have their idiosyncrasies. Their aspirations, priorities, scope, resources, as well as opportunities, and barriers to moving into the future diverge. This chapter's main topic of practical wisdom plays a different role across types of schools:

- Any institution emphasizing scholarly impact primarily – be it a teaching-focused liberal arts or a social science-oriented place – is likely to emphasize practical wisdom less. However, the question remains how to stay relevant for course practitioners who have to survive and thrive in

Table 1.1   *Types of business schools*

Authors	Number and types
D'Alessio and Avolio (2011)	Six types: Model 1: Operates as part of a university Model 2: Operates on the same campus Model 3: Belongs to university and relies on distinct brand Model 4: Operates financially independently while still belonging to a university Model 5: Operates as a stand-alone, financially independent entity Model 6: Operates independently and works toward a university
Ivory et al. (2006)	Four types: 1. Professional school – pursuing organizational impact and emphasizing teaching 2. Knowledge economy – research-intense institutions focused on organizational impact 3. Social science – directing efforts toward scholarly impact via research 4. Liberal arts – teaching-intensive institutions focused on scholarly impact
Iniguez de Onzono (2011)	Seven types: 1. Boutiques 2. Executive education centers 3. Local providers 4. International postgraduate schools 5. Global integrated schools 6. Regional champions 7. Bigger public universities
Lorange (2002)	Five types: 1. Adaptive 2. Proactive 3. Entrepreneurial 4. Rationally governed and managed 5. Dynamic

Source: Amann (2021).

a VUCA world. A minimum degree of practical wisdom will always have to be fostered and ensured.

- In contrast, a professional school prioritizing teaching and organizational impact will more strongly foster practical wisdom in the classroom. Faculty members would include more practitioners, case studies, problem-based learning, and possibly even field trips to remain as close to reality as possible.
- Equally, a knowledge economy will pursue practical wisdom, yet with a slightly different route. Practical wisdom receives more space in the applied research to be carried out, producing resources in the form of books or articles of higher relevance to organizations.

1.3   PRACTICAL WISDOM DEFINED: WHAT DOES IT REFER TO?

In the literature on phronesis and phronesizing, four essential parts emerge as relevant and as portrayed in Figure 1.1. Literature addresses the questions of 'who' qualifies as phronimons, that is, a learner and acquirer of practical wisdom. Past research equally scrutinizes the context in which phronesizing takes place in terms of 'where.' In addition, past attempts explored the process as well as outcomes of phronesizing. All of the past definitions tend to view phronesis as a virtue worth acquiring, mostly in a lengthy and even life-long journey. How phronesizing is done remains hidden in a black box.

In contrast, our understanding of phronesizing moves beyond it being a desirable virtue. It is key to survival, be it at an organizational or an individual leader's level. The questions shift toward how to optimize the process of acquiring, leveraging, and renewing it – ideally at an ever-faster pace as the VUCA world by definition is turbulent and solutions short-lived. Understood in its version 2.0 as the meta-capability to strategically deal with complexity

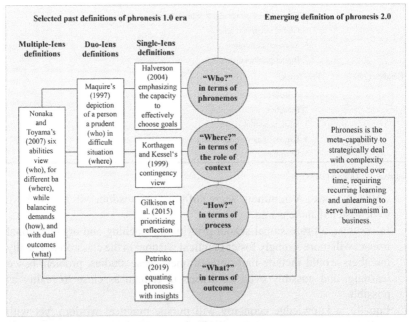

Source: Based on Amann (2021).

Figure 1.1   *Past and emerging definition of phronesis*

encountered during a specific episode and across episodes over time, requiring learning and unlearning to serve humanism in business, we call for positioning it as a central learning outcome for business schools. It perpetuates the ethical component, the perception of it being something learned and not born with, and clarifies what value created in business schools can mean.

We deem practical wisdom essential for graduates and their organizations. Jordan et al. (2020) outline that a leader has to navigate seven tensions. Leaders have to find the right balance between:

- Being an expert versus a learner of new things.
- Being the constant versus the adaptor.
- Being the visionary versus the tactician.
- Being the teller versus the listener.
- Being the power holder versus the power sharer.
- Being the intuitionist versus the analyst.
- Being the perfectionist versus the pragmatic accelerator.

When, how, and for how long and in what intensity a leader positions himself or herself along these seven dimensions requires sound judgment. Practical wisdom can help navigate. The likelihood exists, though, that any solution on how to position oneself will only be temporary. Versatility over time based on practical wisdom will be essential. Yet, how to build it? The subsequent section will shed light on our research methodology before Section 1.5 continues with the emerging solution based on our proposed framework.

1.4 RESEARCH METHODOLOGY: HOW DID WE ARRIVE AT OUR INSIGHTS?

The study producing the results for this chapter builds on a constructivist grounded theory approach. As little was known – not about the millennia-old concept of phronesis but the process of honing it, especially in a leadership development context – a constructivist approach and exploratory analysis was promising (cf. Amann, 2021 for a full and critical review of the methodology). The study zoomed in on a top-ranked business school and its EMBA graduates. Graduates represent an insightful target group for in-depth interviews, offering substantial 'information power' (Aldiabat & Le Navanec, 2018), as they had experienced the entire learning journey as well as how learning is applied in the real world after graduation. An EMBA program of 18 months also ensures sufficient time to grow practical wisdom in contrast to a shorter executive education intervention. Overall, 32 interviewees shared their experiences before saturation was deemed to kick in, causing an interview cut-off point. An established grounded theorizing process modeled after Charmaz (2006, 2012) led to the framework presented in the next section.

1.5   A STATE-OF-THE-ART FRAMEWORK FOR PHRONESIZING: WHAT DO WE NEED TO ENSURE WHEN SECURING THE FUTURE OF BUSINESS SCHOOLS?

Practical wisdom does not only emerge from a single source of acting and learning. Kristjánsson (2021) foresees many possible interventions, and our own research visualized in Figure 1.2 outlines essential steps in the context of a business school's set of classes. It relies on the idea of a duologue as an established form of interaction in theatre. The two actors are the faculty members with direct exposure to course participants and the actual learner. A duologue prescribes only two key actors as being of importance, and this is what the exploratory interviews reveal. Taking the idea of a duologue as a form of a dialogue between two groups, our model foresees three acts as outlined in the following. All of the individual core tasks can be summarized with the 6Cs:

- Act 1 – calibration: The faculty calibrates what they offer and do in the classroom to the actual audience. An undergraduate course participant ought to receive a different treatment, content, and learning journey from the seasoned executive. EMBA candidates require a C-level view more than a pre-experienced candidate. Updating course contents and andragogy is a must.
- Act 2 – cannonading: Faculty members launch their divers and numerous learning stimuli, intentionally working toward overstimulating to increase the mental bandwidth of learners and ensure there are elements of the learning journey delivered in line with the preferred learning styles represented in the classroom. According to the meshing hypothesis, learners absorb more and sustain their motivation to learn more if their preferences are met.
- Act 3 – careening: The professors ensure their learning journeys are truly transformational and not merely inspirational. They effectively deploy means to change behaviors via feedback and feedforward techniques, catalyzing behavioral change beyond mere knowledge increases.

As visualized in Figure 1.2, the learners contribute their distinct part in each of the three acts. They play an active role. Only if they fulfill their tasks would phronesizing take place based on the interviews carried out:

- Act 1 – cultivating learning motivation: The learners endeavor to focus on intrinsic learning motivation. Pursuing a 'degree on the wall,' chasing higher pay, pursuing promotion, etc., represent extrinsic factors. Instead, they focus on personal growth and upgrading their skills to reach the next level in their development. They aspire to become a better version of themselves as part of an ambitious learning community.

- Act 2 – cherry-picking: The modern learner understands one's speed and versatility to learn may well be the only sustainable competitive advantage. He or she knows how to learn better and selects the most urgent fields to grow in. Therefore, each learner should be encouraged to identify a unique learning journey.
- Act 3 – cutting ties: The learner must withstand the temptation to see the responsibility for one's learning with the faculty or program director. Instead, one has to own the learning journey, be fully aware of the responsibility to drive learning and plan the right rhythm, speed, and intensity of further growth. The right dose of exploration of new areas must be matched with the once more personal dose of exploitation of existing knowledge

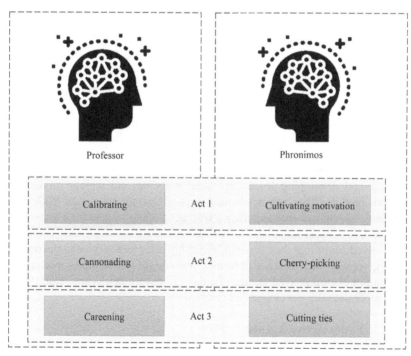

Source: Amann (2021).

Figure 1.2   *The 6C-duolog theory of phronesizing*

and skillsets. Personal development plans, actively seeking feedback and feedforward, and regularly measuring with the help of psychometric tests can foster progress.

1.6   RECOMMENDATIONS: WHAT SHALL WE DO NOW?

The chapter continues in this section with our top three recommendations for the future of business schools. They first addresses the school's leadership team as the helm of any organization must provide the most conducive context for a winning performance. Our recommendations continue for individual directors and faculty members, and we close by reiterating that no one size fits all. Situational factors and local contexts matter.

1.6.1   A Fish Rots from Its Head Down

Business schools must rely on soundly educated leaders themselves. Not only do they require situational factors and specific adaptations of how school leaders function, they also need to evolve their organizations over time. Be it technological change, e.g., triggered by artificial intelligence (AI) (cf. Stachowicz-Stanusch et al., 2021), internationalization, the right degree of commercialization, or the ways their institutions cope with crises, e.g., due to COVID-19, agility and versatility represent not only topics to be taught in the classroom, but school leaders need to walk the talk themselves. Thus, it is essential to build a well-developed leadership pipeline. Merely promoting professors based on their research or teaching accomplishments but without actual experience to manage complex and larger systems is too risky. Any professionally managed school should build a multi-stage leadership pipeline, spotting and developing leadership talent early beyond merely relying on external recruits. The (non-academic) corporate sector runs such leadership pipelines, having gathered experience with developing leaders for a long time. This is, in our observation, hardly the case in business schools. Many deans we interviewed admit that they serve in leadership roles as a service to the organization, yet with their hearts still beating for thought leadership in research or teaching in classrooms. More must be done to ensure that school leaders are more professionally developed and selected.

1.6.2   Foster Active Agents

Beyond this call for better leaders at the helm of business schools, we equally issue a call to all other organizational members in business schools. Sociology differentiates between agency and structure (Kabele, 2010). The school is the structure, and staff members operate in it. They perceive varying degrees of discretion and may well await their structure to provide them with instructions. Alternatively, they can see what kind of discretion they have to drive their own development and innovations. Never before have international opportunities to collaborate and learn from and with each other been as abundantly available as now. Numerous webinars and faculty exchange platforms exist so that even in more resource-poor organizations, eager faculty members can liaise with experts globally, upgrade their skillsets, design, and deliver more unique, impactful, and practical wisdom-oriented learning journeys. Faculty members can do so nowadays without working at elite institutions. However, it all starts with adopting full responsibility for one's quality in the delivery and being even more of an active agent than before to embrace opportunities. The speed of exploring innovations, adopting them, and refining them over time should accelerate. Expectations rise for graduates, and so they do for faculty members and their institutions. A key litmus test for business schools is whether they genuinely ready their graduates and their organizations for the VUCA world and all of its adversity. Our recommendation is to be realistic and pragmatic. Not all faculty members will be able or willing to jump on this bandwagon toward more wisdom orientation. There should be no discrimination against those who are unable or unwilling. With whom to build more practical wisdom, though, should be a consideration when hiring or training talent. The tenure system does not naturally foster system-wide change anyway and often seems to cement the status quo. Incentives could come from policy innovations regarding research funds or lower teaching 'loads' for promising faculty members excelling at wisdom creation. Also, the entire organization does not have to be focused on practical wisdom exclusively. Undergraduate education can still focus to a large extent on building the foundation. Over time, the experts on practical wisdom should grow numberwise in order to add more value. Another stakeholder group requires separate attention – alums. The idea is not to communicate any possible devaluing of their accomplishments during their studies or of their degree overall. This would foster more inertia. The communication should be along the lines of 'good can always be done better,' portraying the institution as a thought leader and innovator, which may well increase the value of a degree and could also render the influx of new alums to alum associations more interesting. Equally, boards of trustees should see this refocusing on practical wisdom as added value, not as criticism of their past work. As outlined above, the fish rot starts from its head down. Therefore, the crucial dialogue skills so essential to include and communicate across diverse stakeholder groups must be in place to ensure sufficient progress and not getting stuck in the say-do gap.

1.6.3   Horses for Courses

We have clarified above that institutions differ. The priorities, success recipes, onboarded faculty experts, and resource allocation may well diverge. Routes to practical wisdom and the role it plays vary from business school to business school. Nonetheless, we see room for improvement across the main gestalts of institutions. Too much focus remains on traditional approaches to learning and measuring learning outcomes. The reorientation toward practical wisdom requires system-wide changes. A post-module satisfaction survey with the same survey items and smiley sheets to be filled out by participants will not do justice to much-needed innovations. Faculty development requires resources in terms of time and attention. Traditional program directors and deans may have fallen in love with their dated solutions. Innovative business schools readying themselves for the future will need different solutions, experts, and professional change management to transition to the subsequent trajectory. In addition, institutions should become more open to experimenting with structural innovations. Structure follows strategy is a famous insight when creating peak performance organizations. Why not create units in charge of creating more awareness for practical wisdom? They could have the mandate to identify key priorities and projects to pilot initiatives. Stakeholder dialogues with various types of organizations could identify low hanging fruits and most pressing topics to explore first. There could be a unit focus on non-governmental organizations (NGOs) and what practical wisdom insights they need. There could be a parallel unit for the government sector, small enterprises, mid-size companies, and the larger recruiters. Next to types of organizations, these units could be themes based, such as sustainability, inflation, pandemics, etc. The idea is not to replace other centers but to focus on catalyzing wisdom creation and dissemination beyond knowledge. Different horses for different courses and this should reflect in structures as well! Instead of modelling competitors, idiosyncratic strategies should see schools diverge, creating richer and a more diverse landscape of institutions.

1.7   CONCLUSIONS: WHAT DID WE PROMISE TO EXPLAIN?

In this chapter, we aspired to contribute to the debate on building the business school of the future. We acknowledged that several industry gurus, such as Mintzberg (2004), amongst many others, became very critical of several developments. In contrast, we adopted not a standpoint of criticism but a constructive contribution to how progress can be made. As the world is likely to become even more VUCA in the future, with shorter and shorter times to recover between crises and changes, turning graduates into even better learners represents a helpful way forward. However, the field of learning both from a process as well as an outcome perspective is enormous. Many sciences contribute to a better understanding of patterns and dynamics at work. This chapter focuses on the tremendous potential of emphasizing practical wisdom more so than ever before. Program graduates will receive a higher return on their investment (ROI) and their education (ROE). Schools should aspire to add more value, discuss how they are relevant, and evolve into even better contributors. We were carefully acknowledging that institutions diverge and not all prioritize organizational impact via teaching. Yet, if teaching takes place, it can add more value. This is the call to action of this chapter.

REFERENCES

Aldiabat, K. and Le Navenec, C. (2018) 'Philosophical roots of classic grounded theory: Its foundations in symbolic interactionism', *Qualitative Report*, 16(4), pp. 1063–80.

Amann, W. (2021) *How to Build Practical Wisdom in Executive Education*. New Delhi: Walnut.

Amann, W., Pirson, M., Spitzeck, H., Dierksmeier, C., and Von Kimakowitz, E. (eds) (2011) *Business Schools under Fire – Humanistic Management Education as the Way Forward*. London: Palgrave Macmillan.

Betof, E., Owens, L., and Todd, S. (2014) 'The key to success in a VUCA world: Leaders as teachers is the winning strategy that great companies have used to manage volatility, uncertainty, complexity, and ambiguity (VUCA) confronting their leaders', *T+D*, 68(7), pp. 38–44.

Cândido, C. and Santos, S. (2015) *Strategy Implementation: What Is the Failure Rate?* Cambridge: Cambridge University Press.

CAPS (2017) *The impact of executive education. A review of current practice and trends*. https://charteredabs.org/wp-content/uploads/2017/12/Impact-of-Executive-Education-Chartered-ABS.pdf. Accessed on August 18, 2022.

Charmaz, K. (2006) *Constructing Grounded Theory: A Practical Guide through Qualitative Analysis*. Thousand Oaks, CA: Sage.

Charmaz, K. (2012) 'Qualitative interviewing and grounded theory analysis'. In F. Gubrium, A. Holstein, A. Marvasti, and K. McKinney (eds), *The SAGE Handbook of Interview Research: The Complexity of the Craft* (pp. 675–94). Thousand Oaks, CA: Sage.

D'Alessio, F. and Avolio, B. (2011) 'Business schools and resources constraints: A task for deans or magicians?', *Research in Higher Education Journal*, 13, pp. 1–37.

Engwall, L. (2007) 'The anatomy of management education', *Scandinavian Journal of Management*, 23(1), pp. 4–35.

Forth, P., Reichert, T., de Laubier, R., and Chakraborty, S. (2020) *Flipping the odds of digital transformation success*. https://www.bcg.com/publications/2020/increasing-odds-of-success-in-digital-transformation. Accessed on August 18, 2022.

Halverson, R. (2004) 'Accessing, documenting and communicating the phronesis of school leadership practice', *American Journal of Education*, 111(1), pp. 90–122.

Hernandez, M., Khattab, J., and Hoopes, Chr. (2021) 'Why good leaders fail', *MIT Sloan Management Review*. https://sloanreview.mit.edu/article/why-good-leaders

-fail/?use_credit=251ea36cd4aeed340c0ac860d09f05b8. Accessed on August 18, 2022.

Iarocci, J. (2015) *Why are there so many leadership books? Here are 5 reasons.* https://serveleadnow.com/why–are–there–so–many–leadership–books/. Accessed on August 18, 2022.

Iniguez de Onzono, S. (2011) *The Learning Curve.* London: Palgrave Macmillan.

Ivory, C., Misekll, P., Shipton, H., White A., and Moeslein, K. (2006) *The future of UK business schools.* AIM research. http://wi1.uni-erlangen.de/files/busschool.pdf. Accessed on August 18, 2022.

Jordan, J., Wade, M. and Teracino, E. (2020) 'Every leader needs to navigate these 7 tensions', *Harvard Business Review.* https://hbr-org.cdn.ampproject.org/c/s/hbr.org/amp/2020/02/every-leader-needs-to-navigate-these-7-tensions. Accessed on August 18, 2022.

Joshi, M., Sanchez, C., and Mudde, P. (2020) 'Improving the MandA success rate: Identity may be the key', *Journal of Business Strategy*, 41(1), pp. 50–7.

Kabele, J. (2010) 'The agency/structure dilemma: A coordination solution', *Journal for the Theory of Social Behaviour*, 40(3), 314–38.

Kim, W. and Mauborgne, R. (2014) 'Blue ocean leadership: Are your employees fully engaged in moving your company forward? Here's how to release their untapped talent and energy', *Harvard Business Review*, 5, pp. 60–72.

Korthagen, F. and Kessels, J. (1999) 'Linking theory and practice: Changing the pedagogy of teacher education', *Educational Researcher*, 28(4), pp. 4–17.

Kotter, J. (2012) *Leading Change.* Cambridge MA: Harvard Business Press.

Kristjánsson, K. (2021) 'Twenty-two testable hypotheses about phronesis: Outlining an educational research programme', *British Educational Research Journal.* https://bera-journals.onlinelibrary.wiley.com/doi/full/10.1002/berj.3727. Accessed on August 18, 2022.

Lorange, P. (2002) *New Vision for Management Education: Leadership Challenges.* Oxford: Pergamon.

Maguire, S. (1997) 'Business ethics: A compromise between politics and virtue', *Journal of Business Ethics*, 16, pp. 1411–18.

Maxwell, J. (2019) *Leadershift: The 11 Essential Changes Every Leader Must Embrace.* New York: HarperCollins.

Mintzberg, H. (2004) *Managers Not MBAs: A Hard Look at the Soft Practice of Managing and Management Development.* Hoboken, NJ: Prentice Hall.

Nonaka, I. and Toyama, R. (2007). 'Strategic management as distributed practical wisdom (phronesis)', *Industrial & Corporate Change*, 16(3), pp. 371–94.

Petrinko, E. (2019) 'Teachers' perspective on wise education', *Journal of Teacher Education for Sustainability*, 21(1), pp. 67–75.

Schwetzler, B. and Reimund, C. (2003) Conglomerate discount and cash distortion: New evidence from Germany. https://papers.ssrn.com/sol3/pape rs.cfm?abstract_id=392321. Accessed on August 18, 2022.

Shooter, K. (2021) *Unlocking success in digital transformations.* https://www.technologymagazine.com/data-and-data-analytics/mckinsey-unlocking-success-digital-transformations. Accessed on August 18, 2022.

Spender, J.-C. and Locke, R.R. (2011) *Confronting Managerialism: How the Business Elite and Their Schools Threw Our Lives out of Balance.* London: Zed Books.

Stachowicz-Stanusch, A., Amann, W., and Tripath, S. (2021) *Principles of Responsible Management Education (PRME) in the Age of Artificial Intelligence (AI) – Opportunities, Threats, and the Way Forward.* Charlotte, NC: IAP.

Swanson, D. and Frederick, W. (2011) 'Are business schools silent partners in corporate crime?', *Journal of Corporate Citizenship*, 9(1), pp. 24–7.

Zao-Sander, M. (2007) 'A 2×2 matrix to help you prioritize the skills to learn right now', *Harvard Business Review*. https://hbr.org/2017/09/a-2x2-matrix-to-help-you-prioritize-the-skills-to-learn-right-now. Accessed on August 18, 2022.

2. Post-COVID-19 future of hybrid education: internationalization, inclusion, opportunities

Mary Kate Naatus, Katia Passerini, Kevin Pon and Mark Somers

2.1 INTRODUCTION: THE GLOBAL EVOLUTION OF BUSINESS SCHOOLS AND THE PANDEMIC AS A FACTOR OF CHANGE

Today, as in the past, business schools prepare students for entry into an ever-changing job market and ultimately into a profession. Business schools, therefore, have an obligation to stay updated on trends in a highly dynamic world that is gradually getting smaller due to the pervasive technological advances, especially in digital communication. This global access to technology and digital communication further pushes business schools' need to internationalize to give students the best possible advantage to successfully enter the increasingly borderless and diverse job market. The 'imperative' of internationalization has been described among the most impactful substantive development in the history of American education (Groennings, 1987; Pon, 2007).

At the same time, there are still many unanswered questions about the internationalization of higher education concerning its meaning, implementation, and strategic aspects of development, and there is room for continued research to be carried out. This evolution is not limited to just one region of the world – nor to the larger, more prestigious educational institutions that may have more financial and human means to internationalize – but also to smaller schools. The problem for these schools is that they lack, or at the very least, have fewer resources to internationalize. Nevertheless, they must do so to continue attracting students to their institutions and preparing them for future careers in a globalized world, where many peers are already bilingual, if not trilingual.

2.1.1 Business Schools' Traditional Limitations in 'Global Thinking': Reductionism and Empiricism

Management education has been subject to ongoing criticism during the past decade. Concerns have been raised that business schools have developed curricula that have little application to management practice, have relied on analytics as a substitute for addressing societal problems, and have remained insular while the world undergoes disruptive changes and finally becomes more diverse and pluralistic, at all levels including the C-suites. Critics have described management education as in a constant state of crisis and have wondered why remedies to well-documented problems have emerged slowly, if at all (Bandera et al., 2020).

The coronavirus pandemic presented a much more urgent crisis that required immediate attention. Thus, it forced business schools and their leaders to adapt more quickly and imaginatively than they were accustomed to. In order to better understand both the challenges and opportunities that COVID-19 presented, it is helpful to examine the sources of resistance that led to the ongoing concerns about the value and efficacy of management education. Those sources are best viewed as a mindset grounded in two fundamental and mostly unexamined philosophies: reductionism and empiricism. Each is pernicious in its own way, but when combined, they create a mindset rooted in rigidity and determinism. That is, a mindset with an emphasis on affirming what is known to be true rather than an openness to examining the assumptions and consequences associated with that mindset.

Reductionism is based on the general notion that the whole can be better understood by breaking it into its component pieces (Sarkar, 1992). Reductionist thinking, therefore, seeks to deconstruct a larger entity to make it simpler and easier to understand. Once deconstructed, the epistemology behind reductionism involves finding levels of association among component pieces, which presumably offer a more parsimonious and accurate representation of a broader entity (Verschuren, 2001). Empiricism complements reductionism because it is based on observation and objective measurement to build models to better understand phenomena of interest (Bunge, 1967). Empiricism eschews intuition, creativity, and exploration and emphasizes logic, reason, and objective analysis.

The coronavirus pandemic challenged both empiricism and reductionism. With respect to empiricism, the pandemic produced uncertainty and confusion to the point where empirical analysis was greatly limited. Even treatment protocols were improvised as physicians took risks and hoped for the best. The pandemic also made it clear that reductionism was of minimal value in developing effective responses. This was a global problem on a massive scale that could not be broken into component pieces to devise optimized solutions. Such an approach was not only folly, but it was also deadly.

2.1.2   COVID-19 as an Enabler for Global Thinking

With the abrupt questioning of their fundamental methods grounded in reductionism and empiricism, business schools were left without their two most treasured tools, facing an environment that was rapidly changing, highly unpredictable, and posing potentially existential threats. Further, at the height of the pandemic, there was no consensus about a return to normalcy as empirically derived predictive models generated a wide range of possible outcomes, most of which proved inaccurate. As daunting as this environment was, it was sufficiently disruptive to unfreeze business schools to the point where they began to see their missions, curricula, and value in new ways; that is, holistically, globally, and inclusively. It is at this point where we can begin to discuss the opportunities and possibilities for business schools in a slowly emerging post-pandemic environment. It is our belief that these possibilities would not have been fully considered and would not be realized without this extraordinary event (i.e., pandemic) due to the entrenched business school mindset. It is in this spirit that we explore these renewed possibilities.

Perhaps the most compelling aspect of the coronavirus pandemic was how quickly the problem morphed from a local to a regional and then to a global problem that required coordinated global solutions. The ineffectiveness of closed borders and closed minds pointed to the importance of new ways of thinking and new forms of action. In a sense, the pandemic served as a laboratory and a lesson for business schools to change their mindsets. In particular, internationalization can be redefined as a philosophy that can reposition business schools to better meet stakeholder and societal expectations rather than as a strategy that increases influence and revenue.

2.1.3   Internationalization and Knowledge Sharing 2.0

This rethinking of internationalization is useful in gaining new insights into management pedagogy and the role of business schools in society. With regard to the former, 'international' business schools typically opened satellite campuses in other (usually distant) locations and/or actively recruited students from other parts of the world. However, there was usually very little contact between students and faculty at the home and satellite campuses. The pandemic forced business schools to teach virtually, and the rapid adoption of conferencing technologies highlighted the value of connecting students across sites so that classrooms became global. These newfound connections set the stage for alliances and partnerships to evolve into networks that span multiple institutions and regions. With respect to the latter, although pressure has been increasing for business schools to demonstrate their value to society (Tufano, 2020), those efforts are decidedly local in nature. However, the societal problems where business schools can play a role in addressing are not local (e.g., wealth inequality, climate change, sustainability) in nature. Thus, to meet stakeholder expectations, business schools must have an international perspective, and to do so requires partnerships and alliances that are global in scope. The pandemic taught us about the importance of knowledge and information sharing and highlighted the critical value of deep, globally distributed knowledge clusters. That model is well suited to meeting the societal challenges that business schools are expected to address. In so doing, problem definition becomes better framed, resources are leveraged, valued is added through cooperation, and the focused, empirical, market-driven solutions that have been proposed in the past and that have not fared well (Rapaccioli, Franch and Christie, 2021) are replaced with ideas and initiatives that are more relevant to issues at hand.

2.2 IMPLICATIONS FOR ACADEMIA: INTERNATIONALIZATION, TEACHING, LEARNING, AND RESEARCH POST-PANDEMIC

Due to the pandemic restrictions, student mobility was greatly reduced for the academic year 2020–21 and will continue to be restricted until all national borders are fully open. With the appearance of successive waves of the pandemic returning, mobility (particularly in Europe where mobility is highly embedded in existing programs) had to be achieved with a number of innovative ideas developed and implemented rapidly. This is particularly true of the French business schools' model of internationalization where compulsory mobility is an integral part of the curriculum and students out of a five-year program leading to a master's degree may have to spend up to two semesters abroad prior to and as a condition of completing their degree (Naatus et al., 2015). Two initiatives that have emerged in order to satisfy the international aspect of such academic programs include Collaborative Online International Learning and virtual international mobility of faculty and students.

2.2.1 Collaborative Online International Learning

Collaborative Online International Learning (COIL) initiatives have been enhancing global student engagement since 2004. COIL provides a platform and framework for connecting students across the globe, using online tools and video conferencing. The purpose of COIL partnerships is to enhance intercultural interaction and understanding through meaningful online engagement, providing a powerful and cost-effective global experience (Marcillo-Gómez and Desilus, 2016). In Fall of 2020, we piloted an online global collaboration in international marketing classes in New Jersey, USA, and Lyon, France. Students from the Catholic University of Lyon and Saint Peter's University worked in international teams to develop marketing plans for a simulated opening of a new Walt Disney Theme Park location. In this case, the elimination of in-person study abroad due to COVID-19 prompted faculty to develop this partner initiative completely online. With the mass adoption of Zoom and other virtual meeting tools, there was a small learning curve, and cross-cultural learning outcomes were very positive. With so many students and faculty now familiar with Zoom and comfortable communicating in the distributed and hybrid classroom environment, programs like COIL are likely to accelerate learning outcomes associated with cross-cultural communication, international business, and aligned topics. A similar initiative has now extended to multiple partners in the USA, including Seton Hall University which is working with students' teams across multiple continents.

2.2.2   Organizing Faculty for Virtual Mobility

Due to pandemic-related barriers for traditional travel for both scholarly research and teaching, the obvious alternative was to use technology and digital learning to bring internationalization into the classroom. From an anecdotal poll of faculty in our network, there has been a significant increase in virtual collaboration with students, faculty, and industry experts from the local, regional, national, and global communities, with the added flexibility of Zoom discussions, which were far less common prior to the pandemic. Many academic conferences and scholarly networks converted to a virtual format throughout the pandemic, and while many academics are eager for more in-person interaction and live co-located conferences again, some form virtual engagement for research and scholarship is here to stay. With more constraints on academic budgets facing many of our higher education institutions, including a virtual option for participation in conferences and other professional events can ultimately be beneficial and more inclusive.

In addition, there are endless opportunities to bring in international faculty from partner universities to enhance internationalization at home using virtual communication tools, which in some ways may replace mobility with global partner universities or at the very least will continue to supplement live, in-person global immersion academic experiences. Rather than waiting to meet, pre-during-post interactions can now easily take place among faculty and students.

2.2.3 New Comparative Research Opportunities

In addition, the acceleration of the use of digital and technological tools in global teaching has also opened opportunities for new comparative research on the integrated international learning, both from the standpoint of learning outcomes but also around understanding management frameworks that emerge in different continents, with different foundations (Naatus et al., 2015). In a few words, the students can adopt a global lens also in the material studied, not just the classroom projects. The reference literature and textbooks can easily expand, and new textbook can be written leveraging the comparative experiences.

2.3 IMPLICATIONS FOR ACADEMIC ADMINISTRATION: THE DIGITALIZATION OF ANY PROCESS

As many have already demonstrated, institutions of higher education have adapted to internationalization in other ways but perhaps the one area that has been impacted, which is often neglected in the research, is how the pandemic brought about hidden benefits in the way our schools are run on an administrative level. Many long overdue improvements in efficiency have resulted for many organizations and higher education institutions during the pandemic due to necessity in the remote and hybrid work experience.

Prior to March of 2020 when many higher education institutions lagged well behind other industries in terms of digitally driven business models, many administrators and students were bogged down in paperwork requiring multiple signatures to enact even the most mundane transaction (Gallagher and Palmer, 2020). It may have taken a global pandemic to prompt many colleges and universities to digitize processes, from academic transactions and approvals to billing and human resources functions. This pandemic-induced technological transformation comes at a time when the value proposition of a college degree is being questioned and an emphasis on student satisfaction and a customer-oriented approach is increasing. Providing seamless student services from the time of admission to graduation is expected, and similar expectations permeate hiring, finance and budgeting and other areas of administration. Other common technologies adopted at an accelerated rate during the past year and a half include more digital credentialing, digital tutoring options for students and a shift to digital promotional materials and communications.

Many types of activities, from student orientations and recruitment events to alumni and donor engagement events had to move to a fully remote format, and in some instances have yielded extremely positive results. This broad-level digitization in higher education should have taken place several decades earlier, but many institutions of higher learning lagged behind. The pandemic forced a quick move to remote education and remote work, shaking academic institutions out of their comfort zone and instigating many long overdue changes in this area. The gains in efficiency, learner/student experience, transparency and accountability and productivity are evident, and it is likely that these gains not only will remain but will continue to accelerate into the future.

2.3.1   Academic Administration and Enhanced International Development of Business Schools

When it comes to administrative approaches directly linked to internationalization that have been impacted by the pandemic, there have been cosmic shifts in the landscape during the pandemic. We know that virtual collaboration across borders and regions is here to stay, but this cannot replicate the deep level of internationalization that many higher education institutions seek and that many have become dependent on. A significant portion of colleges and universities emphasize global engagement and internationalization on the list of key strategic goals. However, the way this is operationalized and the resources in place to support internationalization seem to vary widely across institutions. For some institutions, international student enrollment is a primary focus area of internationalization, and with more than five million students a year applying for international admission globally, is a potentially lucrative approach (Healey, 2016, 2018). According to an article by the Century Foundation, international students studying in the USA contribute over $44 billion annually to the US economy and make up about 5 percent of total student enrollment (Hall, Curtis and Wofford, 2020). The financial implications of a potential drastic reduction in international student enrollment are significant, and at some institutions heavily dependent on international tuition revenue, at a crisis level. Many institutions have global campus locations overseas, or International Branch Campuses (IBCs) which present unique opportunities for international enrollment expansion and a deep level of global involvement, but also present challenges such as oversight, staffing, cultural adaptation, transparency, and financial and reputational risk (Healey, 2016, 2018). It is too early to assess the specific impact of COVID-19 at the more than 200 IBCs on a global scale. Along the continuum of international involvement are global fellowships and research partnerships, virtual exchanges and internship programs for students and internationalization of the curriculum. These types of experiences can be replicated or even enhanced in the post-COVID-19 world by infusing virtual mobility strategies defined above such as COIL, reducing the cost, in terms of both time and money, for meaningful international involvement for a much broader group of students and faculty.

To support these now disrupted higher education institutions plan for the future, while acknowledging the challenges and opportunities of internationalization in the post-COVID-19 environment, we summarize several recommendations for maintaining and expanding global experiences.

2.3.2 Developing a Deeper Internationalization Strategy with Existing Partners

Rethinking the new possibilities of global partners is a great starting point. Existing MOUs (Memoranda of Understanding) may outline student and faculty exchanges with some wording around other types of collaboration, but the specifics of the agreements can become more multifaceted. Beyond sending and receiving faculty and students both physically and virtually, other possibilities include developing dual degree programs offered simultaneously, developing international consortia to examine critical areas of research with global implications, and facilitating meaningful experiential learning, service, and volunteer opportunities with a global component. Taking an inventory of existing global partners and identifying high priority institutions with existing synergies offers a chance to escalate impact and pathways with current partners. Institutions can reconsider whether they want to cultivate a larger number of partner universities or deepen their engagement with a smaller group of partners. University networks, such as the International Association of Jesuit Universities, and many other international academic networks, such as the International Federation of Catholic Universities, can provide powerful forums for developing and growing partner relationships.

Another avenue to consider is augmenting existing partner relationships through an interdisciplinary lens. Bringing more cohesion with existing partners can be accomplished in a multidisciplinary fashion. For example, one school's or department's partner within a university can become another department's partner, and partners can leverage each other to establish additional connections by sharing collaborative efforts organized around strategic initiatives.

2.3.3 Rethinking of International Programs

The rethinking of international engagement to consider a variety of models beyond physical exchange and travel may lead to greater access to a broader range of students from diverse socio-economic backgrounds. For example, a general reduction in costs for globally immersive virtual experiences, environmental benefits with fewer people traveling and other impacts can open new sustainable and more equitable opportunities. Financial resources can then be used for dual purposes, lower traveling costs may generate funding to spend on international teaching and learning stipends, with online classes taught by international staff from other countries (Hudzik, 2020). Reimagining international programs as a menu or continuum of activities with many milestones to onboard and involve more individuals can help broaden outcomes and expose a larger percentage of the university community to international experiences.

2.3.4   Maintaining and Nurturing Virtual Connections

Beyond the specific focus on internationalization, many of the gains and lessons learned from a powerful shift of mindset and enhanced adoption of digitalization of functions and processes has led to its use on a national level to create greater links between higher education institutions and its varied stakeholders. From connecting virtually with alumni and corporate partners for guest lectures, consulting engagement with student teams and professional training to creating innovative virtual and hybrid experiential programs with mentors and corporate partners, where geography is less of a barrier, the opportunities are truly immense. Many schools and faculty members have found that in the new digital environment, barriers have been reduced for engaging busy professionals, both locally or globally into our academic settings, classrooms, and programs. By reducing costs and time with virtual discussions, conversations, lectures, and collaboration, only one's imagination can set the boundaries. It may have taken the globally disruptive pandemic to illuminate what should have been obvious, but also represents an example of the tendency to do things in the same way, using the same approaches until forced to reconsider and change.

The challenge is to create unique, personalized, and satisfying experiences or components of these virtual experiences and events, so that students can feel like they are part of a community, creating social connections and being able to express themselves fully. Zoom fatigue is real and needs to be balanced with other types of engagement. Staff meetings, board meetings, faculty meetings and a host of other gatherings that may have been purely in person in the past may become purely virtual or hybrid going forward, maintaining efficiencies generated throughout the remote pandemic environment. Creating working groups and breakout discussions and interspersing direct interaction when available can help maximize team and group formation and productivity.

2.4   INTERNATIONAL COLLABORATIONS TO FOSTER A NEW GLOBAL MINDSET

The pandemic is expected to morph into a manageable endemic virus and people are expected to learn how to live with this new virus (Vaishnav, Dalal

Table 2.1   *Summary of new internationalization opportunities*

Opportunities for Academia	Opportunities for Academic Administration
Collaborative Online International Learning (COIL)	Enhanced business process digitalization
Organizing Faculty for Virtual Mobility	Developing a more comprehensive or deep internationalization strategy with existing partners
New Comparative Research Opportunities	Rethinking of international programs
	Maintaining and nurturing virtual connections

and Javed, 2020). This gradual decrease in a state of crisis should provide business schools with the stability to begin to plan for the future. In so doing, challenges will shift from operational to financial and behavioral as business schools begin to adjust to more normal environments. In this regard, internationalization poses new challenges that span differences in mindset, culture, and expectations because the nature of cooperation post-pandemic is qualitatively different. That is, the focus is not on expansion and exploring new opportunities for growth, but rather in melding educational models and methods to devise new ways of designing and delivering curricula.

One challenge is integrating American and European approaches to management education. American business schools emphasize quantitative models, short-term results, profitability, and innovation while their European counterparts place greater emphasis on societal impacts, employee rights, experiential learning, and long-term planning. Merging these mindsets can broaden the focus of business schools to consider a broader array of stakeholders and broader set of outcome measures so that an international ethos can be used as a model for preparing the next generation of managers for corporations that are international rather than multinational. The internationalization of support services and business school operations, in turn, can serve as an incubator or sandbox that can provide insights for corporations as they are increasingly faced with similar challenges. As such, internationalization is not a strategy, but rather a logic or a way of being, and it presents a large number of opportunities that we summarize in Table 2.1.

However, for these opportunities to be fully realized, it is necessary to come to terms with the nature of relationships among business schools that are forged. Revenue models have typically taken precedence so that if financial returns were not apparent within a given period of time, partnerships were not justifiable especially when American partners were involved. Post-pandemic internationalization of business schools raises the possibility of long-term relationships in which exchange of ideas, experiences, and knowledge takes precedence over exchange of revenue. Although such relationships might take some time to generate positive cash flow, longer-term thinking suggests that value added goes beyond short-term financial returns. In this regard, enduring relationships can generate long-term value added while economic partnerships might be fleeting, assuming that we can rethink the current structure that is limited and misaligned with international cost elements.

In order to capture the value of internationalization of business education, a compelling vision is needed. To be responsive to a wide range of stakeholders seems to require networks of relationships that are both deep and dynamic. Business school leaders have the opportunity to develop visions for those networks that define a clear, compelling future for their notions of internationalization. Doing so redefines the current model of business schools as standalone entities with a given value that is all too often defined by external agencies such as ranking services to assess the degree to which a given business school has built an ecosystem and a network to provide an international experience. Visioning is about defining the nature of that experience.

Finally, it is important to ensure that students are presented with a compelling value proposition that addresses their needs and aspirations. A digitally connected, international experience presents business schools with the opportunity to reshape curricula to both meet student expectations and the challenges of an increasingly interdependent world. Satisfaction with courses and instructors can be replaced with satisfaction with preparation, learning experiences and contact with students from other parts of the world. Student satisfaction, thus, is redefined from an episodic event to an ongoing process that captures one's connectedness to others.

2.5   CONCLUSIONS

The pandemic has certainly brought about a disruption in our way of thinking within business schools and higher education in general, but it has also been the catalyst to lay down new rules in internationalization and bring new hidden benefits in other areas of the perimeter of the business school. The cosmic shifts brought about in our collective way of thinking due to the pandemic have disrupted long-held practices and approaches to global education and have reduced some resistance to interdisciplinarity. The forceful and sudden disruption of empiricism and reductionism, long valued by business schools, may have had the unforeseen consequence of unfreezing business schools, allowing leaders and faculty to view their missions and curricula through a new, more holistic, and global lens. That is, through a lens that is more inclusive. The same forces have allowed intuition, creativity, and exploration to play a more active role in planning and decision-making in the midst of the emergency situation spurred by the pandemic. If institutions can maintain that heightened infusion of creativity when approaching planning for internationalization strategies and processes, and in other areas of administration, in the post-pandemic environment, there are continued gains that can be made. While this chapter has focused principally on internationalization as it relates to the pandemic-driven disruption, there are other major areas of business disruption than higher education. From IT acceleration and advances in connectivity and automation to improvements in global supply chain and increased global competition, universities must continue to adapt strategy, faculty research, course delivery and content and modes of communicating and working to take advantage of opportunities and become more agile and flexible with the evolving environment.

The broader societal changes, including the seemingly overnight shift to remote working and remote education at all levels, have profoundly changed the way we live, learn, and work. Business schools have the opportunity to take a leading role in addressing these shifting needs, expectations, and cultural and societal norms, by continuing to embrace new collaborative tools and models of interaction and curriculum delivery that allow deeper levels of global engagement, industry connectedness, and transparency in the post-COVID-19 educational landscape. By shifting away from traditional notions of student exchange as one of the few internationalization opportunities and providing more incentives and facilitated processes for engaging a much broader spectrum of global virtual interactions between students and faculty, it is likely that far more students can benefit, and we can establish deeper global connections among institutions. These types of benefits should be identified and leveraged, and not just tossed aside when and if we are 'back to normal,' and the more traditional programs of student exchange and immersive travel courses can once again run normally. As in many areas of life, work, and education, the disruptions and ensuing adaptations of the COVID-19 pandemic can provide valuable lessons and models moving forward, and the suggestions presented in this review are only one example of how important it is to take these changes to the next level of opportunity generation.

REFERENCES

Bandera, C., Somers, M., Naatus, M.K. and Passerini, K. (2020) 'Disruptions as opportunities for new thinking: Applying the studio model to business education', *Knowledge Management Research & Practice*, 18(1), pp. 81–92. doi:10.1080/14778238.2019.1621225.

Bunge, M. (1967) 'The turn of the tide', in *Quantum Theory and Reality*. Berlin and Heidelberg: Springer, pp. 1–6.

Gallagher, S. and Palmer, J. (2020) 'The pandemic pushed universities online: The change was long overdue', *Harvard Business Review*, September 29. Available at: https://hbr.org/2020/09/the-pandemic-pushed-universities-online-the-change-was-long-overdue (accessed July 28, 2022).

Groennings, S.O. (1987) *The Impact of Economic Globalization on Higher Education*. New England Board of Higher Education.

Hall, S., Curtis, R. and Wofford, C. (2020) 'What states can do to protect students from predatory for-profit colleges: A 2020 toolkit for state policy makers.', *Century Foundation*. Available at: https://production-tcf.imgix.net/app/uploads/2020/05/24175433/5.22_toolkit_for-profit-colleges_withoutembargo1.pdf (accessed July 28, 2022).

Healey, N.M. (2016) 'The challenges of leading an international branch campus: The "lived experience" of in-country senior managers', *Journal of Studies in International Education*, 20(1), pp. 61–78.

Healey, N.M. (2018) 'The challenges of managing transnational education partnerships: The views of "home-based" managers vs "in-country" managers', *International Journal of Educational Management*, 32(2), 241–56.

Hudzik, J.K. (2020) 'Post-COVID higher education internationalization', *Trends & Insights*, p. 7.

Marcillo-Gómez, M. and Desilus, B. (2016) 'Collaborative online international learning experience in practice: Opportunities and challenges', *Journal of Technology Management & Innovation*, 11(1), pp. 30–35.

Naatus, M.K., Passerini, K., Pon, K. and Somers, M. (2015) 'Do we know what they know? Comparing US and French undergraduate students' knowledge of core business concepts', *Journal of Management Development*, 34(8), pp. 922–40.

Pon, K. (2007) 'An evaluation of the internationalisation process in schools of management in France: The experience of four schools of management'. Available at: https://uobrep.openrepository.com/handle/10547/299499 (accessed October 10, 2021).

Rapaccioli, D., Franch, J. and Christie, J. (2021) *A Hunger for a Better World | AACSB*. Available at: https://www.aacsb.edu/insights/2021/august/hunger-for-a-better-world (accessed October 10, 2021).

Sarkar, S. (1992) 'Models of reduction and categories of reductionism', *Synthese*, 91(3), pp. 167–94.

Tufano, P. (2020) 'A bolder vision for business schools', *Harvard Business Review*, 11.

Vaishnav, M., Dalal, P.K. and Javed, A. (2020) 'When will the pandemic end?', *Indian Journal of Psychiatry*, 62(Suppl. 3), pp. S330–S334. doi:10.4103/psychiatry.IndianJPsychiatry_1030_20.

Verschuren, P.J. (2001) 'Holism versus reductionism in modern social science research', *Quality and Quantity*, 35(4), pp. 389–405.

3. Expanding and renewing teaching and learning: towards Global Studies

Nicole Saliba-Chalhoub and Christophe Schmitt

This chapter allows us to present a concept that is still little tackled in the French-speaking world: Global Studies. While they are strongly present in the Anglo-Saxon world, it would be interesting to examine them in a different framework, the French-speaking one (we mean by the adjective "French-speaking" the type of academic system), namely a framework in which Global Studies are still rather absent. By "Global Studies," we mean academic programs with a focus on globality, global facts, but also facts in their entirety, in their socio-geopolitical dimension and historical depth. Global Studies establish ties between the cross-disciplinary, the multidisciplinary and the interdisciplinary, ensuring bonds with the territories by linking the local, the regional and the international, as well as cultural refocusing and decentering.

Therefore, it is first necessary to understand their origins and their underlying philosophy; this is the purpose of the first section. In the second section, we will present a global study experience carried out in the field of entrepreneurship within a French business school. In conclusion, we will revisit the contribution of Global Studies, more particularly in the context of entrepreneurship at the university.

3.1 ORIGINS AND TOPICALITY OF GLOBAL STUDIES

It is not possible to identify one single source for the idea of introducing what we could later call in the context of the Higher Education sector: "Global Studies." The very concept of "global" is polysemous and complex. Although it is relatively new, it already has a whole history and different stages of development that correspond to different meanings (Ravano, 2021).

However, we could choose to refer to the original Canadian model which, aiming to explain to the essentially French-speaking world the peculiarities of politics in Canada and Quebec, had encountered serious difficulties in conveying its message and was forced to opt for a global approach to politics in order to make it understandable. It was back in 1976 when Professor André Bernard, following long years of painstaking work and resource modeling, published his book entitled *La politique au Canada et au Québec* (Politics in Canada and Quebec), using systemic insight as a research and analysis tool, the only one likely to convey the message to the reader according to the author, a specialist in political sciences. The book in question was received as the bible of the history of politics in Canada and Quebec. In fact, this history was introduced and analyzed in the light of a well-developed set of interactional components that have specifically generated such politics and not another, some of which may seem at first glance surprising to say the least: the climate, environment, geographical location, morphology of the territory, demographic curve, structures of the populations, family, religion, school, media, working conditions, syndicates, associations, organization of political parties, elections, pressure groups, participation, etc. The list is very long and cannot be exhaustive. Nevertheless, while seeking to introduce the politics of his country to the French-speaking populations, more particularly to the French,[1] the researcher felt compelled to seize the globality of the context in order to successfully convey the tiniest characteristics in a way that is quite acceptable to uninformed readers. By adding the component of complexity, and more particularly by linking the global to the local, he thus avoided seeing his project, completely hampered at the beginning, fall apart and come to a halt.

From another perspective, we could go back to the 1980s, particularly to the USA with the emergence of minimalism, an art movement that we consider nowadays, and with hindsight, as the ancestor of Global Studies. For the followers of this movement, it consisted in getting rid of unnecessary details while endeavoring to refine each art in such a way as to make it interact with other arts, thereby generating the desired multidisciplinarity. Hence, unexpected encounters emerged at the time between artistic disciplines hitherto completely unrelated to each other, namely, painting and choreography, sculpture and music, photography and theatrical performance, etc. For a long time, these encounters were perceived as academic and artistic "collaboration." Minimalism has progressively achieved a genuine blend, moving from multidisciplinarity to interdisciplinarity, in other words, from cohabitation to complexity, by accessing, according to the American academic jargon, what has since been referred to as the comprehensive approach, that is, the global approach.

Whether at the level of Bachelor of Arts or Bachelor of Sciences, the course offerings have soon witnessed the emergence of a 30 percent of courses common to all disciplines, known as General Education Requirements (GER), aiming to provide students with a foundation of cross-curricular and global knowledge and skills. To this was added later the possibility of combining one's major, both in the undergraduate (BA/BS) and graduate studies (MA/MS), with a related program known as minor, not necessarily associated with the chosen major. We can clearly notice at this point the efforts needed to bridge the different disciplines and, beyond that, the various academic units that offer them.

In Europe, the emergence of a comprehensive or global approach's ambition has unfolded in a different way than in the Anglo-Saxon world, described above. Indeed, the steppingstones of Global Studies were the disciplines of history, geography and international relations, the initial challenge being to analyze the global world in its historical depth and geographical features, as well as its socio-political dimensions. It also consisted in successfully bringing together teams of researchers working on topics where various disciplines of human and social sciences could intersect. Finally, the aim was to contextualize the work within multidisciplinary and transdisciplinary perspectives, both theoretical and analytical, rather than within the framework of professionalization of the said curricula.

As for East Asia, we could evoke the case of Japan. For instance, Doshisha University established in April 2010 the Graduate School of Global Studies, whose challenges were exposed by stating the following: "The contemporary world is facing rivalries among ethnic communities, international conflicts, peacebuilding, economic inequalities, gender relations; in other words, problems which go beyond borders and regions. In order to respond to this complexity stemming from globalization, we need intelligence to build the structures that would allow the coexistence of human beings. It is in this context that the Graduate School of Global Studies was founded in April 2010."[2] There are three curricula offered by the said School:

- Global Studies;
- Cross-regional Studies;
- Regional Studies.

These curricula are structured in a way that makes it possible for students enrolled in one of them to take and validate courses from the other two simultaneously (50%; 25%; 25%). Also, to be admitted to the doctoral program, they could strive for the major of Global Studies.

Nowadays, formal courses in Global Studies are offered in the USA. Contrary to what one might think, these courses are not focused on the study of globalization, which constitutes a ground for analysis in many academic fields: economics, sociology, environment, public health, etc. Global Studies, for their part, which are not therefore a study of globalization, supported by systemic philosophy, integrate a wide variety of disciplines, knowledge and know-how, by linking the local to the global. This is why we could rather talk about "glocal" studies, considering the micro as the foundation of the macro and, sometimes, inversely, ranging from the national to the transnational, from multidisciplinary to interdisciplinary, from cultural to transcultural, from history to contemporaneity and, more particularly, from problems to be defined to targeted solutions to be sought. Students specializing in these fields even prefer describing their studies as Critical Globalization Studies, implying that the challenge of their education is not to accumulate knowledge but to understand their world and the world as a whole, to act within the world and for the world.

These Global Studies have been conducted based on a systemic approach, as we say above. They aim at a better understanding of the world and, even more, a better flow of knowledge. Because if the latter is stored, unshared, frozen, it would be useless and would end up fading away, even though the *raison d'être* of higher education and research lies in the transmission and retransmission of knowledge ...

Given that, in today's world, our dominant development models of the last 30 years are no longer suitable and are even leading us into a dead end, it could be very interesting and appropriate, nowadays, to consider the establishment of educational paths, in all countries and universities, dedicated to Global Studies, in order to better understand a world that is increasingly globalized and paradoxically less and less shared, especially in terms of values, cultures, development projects, responsibility and sustainability.

In fact, how to understand a world where, despite the trade liberalization, delocalization of some activities, massive development of telecommunications, fluidification of financial movements, internationalization of mindsets, breakdown of borders, etc., we are witnessing the rise of increasingly proven difficulties from cultural exchanges and openness to diversity, to civilizational and individual peculiarities, as well as the emergence of anti-globalization and alter-globalization movements, to mention just a few..

In this respect, it seems necessary, even urgent, to reconsider our approaches to today's world, particularly based on our academic and scientific position as researchers to move towards more dialogical and more global attitudes without necessarily being encompassing (in the sense of unifying and standardizing).

It goes without saying that some curricula among the ones French-speaking universities offer adopt a "glocal" approach in their implementation. They could therefore serve as an example and support for what it would be worth establishing and, even more, institutionalizing. In this same vein, we propose, in the remainder of the chapter, to shed light on an example of Global Studies within a French business school and, more particularly, around entrepreneurship training.

3.2   AN EXAMPLE OF GLOBAL STUDIES: ENTREPRENEURISHIP AT IAE METZ SCHOOL OF MANAGEMENT

IAE Metz is a French public business school, part of the national network of IAEs in France. The development of entrepreneurship is first and foremost a regional aspiration to respond collectively to the challenge of promoting the development of an entrepreneurial culture through experience (Hagg & Kurczewska, 2021; Pepin, 2017[3]). In Global Studies' perspective, it is not only about questioning a dominant thought, essentially centered on enterprises' creation; but above all it is about addressing the different dimensions of a socio-economic theme in order to gain a better understanding of them. This objective has been identified as a missing link in relation to what could exist in the Lorraine region in terms of entrepreneurship. An impetus has been generated around this proposal to integrate public and private partners, from a "glocal" approach's perspective.

Developing entrepreneurship within IAE Metz has promptly raised a fundamental question: what pedagogy should be implemented? Literature on this point, for over 20 years, shows that entrepreneurship cannot be taught in the same way as other disciplines (Champy-Remoussenard & Starck, 2018; Schieb-Bienfait, 2000; Toutain et al., 2020). The choice we made is in line with the pedagogies we have seen at work, whether in Canada at HEC Montréal and at the University of Quebec in Trois-Rivières, in Switzerland at the School of Management of Fribourg (HEG-FR), in Morocco at Universiapolis of Agadir, in Mauritius at the Institut de la Francophonie pour l'Entrepreneuriat affiliated to the AUF, or in Belgium at the Louvain School of Management in Louvain-la-Neuve. Beyond pedagogy by project or by action, it is about putting the students in an entrepreneurial situation, so that they can have a first experience of immersion in the entrepreneurial field (Berglund, 2007; Schmitt, 2017). The idea is to get rid of simple educational simulations. Moreover, the objective is to get students to "undertake themselves" and, consequently, to experience, in whole or in part, what entrepreneurs go through when developing their projects. To this end, we have introduced original and global approach courses linked to the culture of IAE Metz and the university's student life services. The objective is to help students to consider the different facets of the same object, in this case the object of entrepreneurship. For instance, through sports and physical expression, students get the chance to explore concepts such as risk, relationship to others, uncertainty, etc., which are all skills that will be encountered in entrepreneurship.

3.2.1   A Common Thread: Undertake Oneself in Order to Live an Entrepreneurial Experience

Developing an entrepreneurial culture does not mean exclusively instilling the desire or the will to "start a business." It is more about being interested in the gaseous state of entrepreneurship, too often forgotten in favor of the state of crystallization. Based on this observation, our aim is to allow students to have the opportunity to live, in different forms, an entrepreneurial experience (Hagg & Kurczewska, 2021). We firmly subscribe to a phenomenological perspective (Berglund, 2007; Sarasvathy & Berglund, 2010; Schmitt, 2020), that is, based on the analysis of the lived experience of the students, we offer focused courses, no longer simply an opportunity, with importance given to the development of planning, but also on the entrepreneur and his context, in other words on an understanding of oneself and others, that is, the entrepreneurial act.

Usually supported by observation, traditional teaching methods in entrepreneurship, implemented within IAE Metz School of Management, do not seem to be suitable for a student audience. Indeed, the latter are not very credible with all the stakeholders of the entrepreneurial project; they give little results in terms of student-led projects. This lack of credibility can be explained at different levels:

- The entrepreneur: having little or no experience, the student often suffers from a lack of confidence in himself and in his project, especially when he is called upon to present it (Pepin, 2017).
- The business opportunity: often limited to a conceptual level, the business opportunity has not been confronted with the reality on the ground to test its robustness and its appropriation (Tremblay & Carrier, 2006). By remaining in observation, the demonstration of the interest of the business opportunity remains weak.
- The stakeholders in the context: this corresponds to the way these stakeholders view the project. In comparison to the projects they can see go by, those of the students seem to suffer from a lack of maturity which can be explained by their poor experience in the field in which they wish to embark (Hagg & Kurczewska, 2021).

To meet these needs, IAE Metz has sought to set up approaches that are part of an experiential logic (Berglund, 2007; Hagg & Kurczewska, 2021; Schmitt, 2015, 2017, 2020). These approaches, in many respects, are original. In particular, they promote the adoption of reflective postures based on confrontation with stakeholders (Champy-Remoussenard & Starck, 2018). Taking as a springboard an entrepreneurial experience based on an idea of their choice and which is the symbol of their relationship to the world, the students were approached by the entrepreneurial process from different aspects. In this logic, the students were, for example, offered training courses where they were led by using paint to express the added value of their project, of their personal view of the world. Another example is the use of sport to simulate entrepreneurial situations: boxing to understand the relationship with others or the impact of their action; climbing to understand self-confidence, letting go or even risk. Alongside these courses, students had more traditional lessons. However, each training must enrich their thinking about their entrepreneurial project. Therefore, entrepreneurial project, as a form of experience, becomes the pretext for a global approach.

Another dimension has also been worked on through these different actions: the collective. Indeed, the entrepreneur is not a socially isolated actor. On the contrary, he or she is in constant contact with the stakeholders of their entrepreneurial project. These actions also make it possible to break the isolation in which the entrepreneur could find himself when developing his project and promotes the global approach to it.

3.2.2   Business Units: The Entrepreneurship System at IAE Metz

To meet these needs for experience, we have developed at IAE Metz a course called Business Unit. The purpose is to set up various resources and means to carry out a project and give it the opportunity to achieve growth in the market. In other words, we lead students to build a business opportunity starting from a defined idea. Students who benefit from this system are generally those who, instead of doing an internship in an enterprise, prefer to work on their own entrepreneurial project. For this reason, they receive a payment equivalent to what they could receive if they were interns in a certain enterprise, not to forget the possibility of benefiting from additional start-up funds depending on the progress of their project. Through the novelty of this system, the aim was to create ahead of time a student-entrepreneur status at IAE Metz.

In fact, the students find themselves in a fairly new position: they become stakeholders in their own project. As Filion recalls (1999, p. 40), "one of the great differences between the entrepreneur and the other stakeholders who work in organization is that the entrepreneur defines the object that will determine his own future." It is far from easy. Regarding behavior, we can identify the problems and hesitations towards endorsing this dimension. Often too involved in the logic of doing, students discover with the Business Unit system another logic: the logic of conception. In line with Simon's work *The Sciences of the Artificial* (1996), the aim is to (re)introduce this often-forgotten dimension within the educational mechanisms.

3.2.3   An Action-oriented Philosophy: The Entrepreneurial Act

If we look at the various experiments carried out internationally (Berglund, 2007; Hagg & Kurczewska, 2021; Kyrö & Carrier, 2005; Pepin, 2017; Schmitt, 2005, 2008), those which can be considered successful are clearly the ones where the logic of the business plan is called into question. In recent years, a recurring question about entrepreneurship has been raised: should we burn the business plan (Cohen, 2008; Nlemvo & Witmeur, 2010)? This question mainly concerns the logic of observation underlying the business plan. In fact, it would be enough to observe one's environment to understand it and develop an action plan that would be feasible to implement subsequently. Clearly inspired by the planning period, this logic is currently raising concerns and even more so for students who are project leaders and who have little or no experience nor funds. The business plan places the project leader within an act that should be qualified as rational and conventional (Joas, 1996).

Alongside this logic, we find another one more rooted in pragmatism: the entrepreneurial act. The IAE Metz experience is totally in line with this logic. Our starting point consists in arguing that if entrepreneurship is a cultural problem, it would be appropriate to bring another culture and therefore another way of approaching it, another way of teaching it, another way of acting, etc. It is in this perspective that the Business Unit course has, from the very beginning, moved away from the sacrosanct business plan. The objective is twofold: to develop a scenario based on the students' ideas and to lead them to confront their scenario with action, facts and the stakeholders in the field. It is in action that students can find answers to their questions, and it is always action that brings up questions that could not have been raised otherwise. By working on a scenario and confronting it with reality, students give meaning and coherence to their project, making it also possible to assess the robustness of the scenario. In the end, the students manage to find partners to develop their initial idea and to mobilize the necessary resources and means in order to take their project forward. The entrepreneurial act reverses the relationship with the action that could be found in the business plan (Schmitt, 2017). It is no longer a question of observing and then acting, but rather of being able to do both at the same time. Students who take the Business Unit course are required to make a field demonstration on the interest of their project. This constitutes an integral part of the environment in which they will operate. The experience carried out by each student becomes the starting point for their construction of meaning and the actions they will subsequently undertake. A non-negligible point of this logic is the development of salutogenic aspects (Torrès, 2014) such as self-esteem, consistency of the project with one's life plan, and taking control of one's own destiny.

3.2.4 Business Units: An Innovative Course through Experience

The fact that experience plays an essential role in entrepreneurial development has led to the development of an innovative course, off the beaten path. The three points mentioned above have guided the development of the Business Unit course offered to the IAE Metz students:

- Me: self-awareness;
- My project: development of the business opportunity;
- My ecosystem: familiarity with one's context.

Self-knowledge mainly refers to entrepreneurial skills and competences (Aouni & Surlemont, 2007; Loué et al., 2008). As we are following a logic of action, certain entrepreneurial dimensions should be brought to life to the project leaders. For this purpose, it was necessary to work on reproducing entrepreneurial situations through other fields, where students are put in situations where entrepreneurial skills and competences are mobilized. The situations we offer to the students are highly varied and relate more generally to sports and culture. In terms of sports, students are encouraged to practice climbing, badminton and French boxing. In terms of culture, students are motivated to do painting, music, theater and body language activities. In these various situations, students get the opportunity to fine-tune and consolidate their skills or competencies such as leadership, confidence, relationship to others, project expression, success, failure and sharing of experience.

Familiarity with the context refers to the need to identify the stakeholders of the ecosystem and how this latter works. Once again, it is not a question of merely contemplating and describing this ecosystem. This way of doing things is very reassuring for students and leaves them in their comfort zone, since it does not generally require strong interaction with the stakeholders of the ecosystem. In the Business Unit approach, the most important thing is to submit the scenario chosen by students for their project to the stakeholders of their ecosystem. They are therefore asked to interpret their scenarios to these stakeholders, since it is the scenario that guides fieldwork and information seeking. Students are clearly faced with inferences, that is, actions that establish links between the components of the scenario and an ecosystem leading to the demonstration of acceptance, rejection or probability of this same scenario. The method adopted by experts is perhaps favored over survey methods. As Hatem et al. (1993) and Maleki (2009) point out, the assumptions made by a group of experts are generally more reliable than those made by groups of individuals surveyed randomly. For the students, this involves organizing the consultation of experts, synchronously or asynchronously, on a specific subject.

The development of the business opportunity is the third pillar of the Business Units course. First, the main objective is to build the scenario of the students' project in order to rationalize the initial idea. Second, it requires the concretization of the scenario into a product, service or demonstration of the initial idea. The student then strives to embody their project beyond words. This embodiment can go as far as selling the product or service to validate the interest of this scenario. The development of the business opportunity not only gives students confidence but also inspires confidence among the stakeholders of the ecosystem. For instance, it is easier to go and meet a funder, accompanied with already accomplished elements, such as turnover, partnership with a supplier, etc., than only with a business plan that remains too often in the stage of observation.

It is worth noting that the aforementioned three points are intrinsically linked and should not be understood in terms of precedence.

As we may have noticed after reading this chapter, not only do Global Studies represent a new academic field, but even more than that, another way of understanding university teaching and learning by students as the agents of their own educational journey, citizens of a globalization that they are invited to understand and within which they will have to act and succeed, by considering several stakeholders that are not always harmoniously linked. As we could see through the example of entrepreneurship training at the IAE Metz Business School, the use of Global Studies makes it possible to innovate pedagogically and better integrate students into their training. More precisely, this allows us to place students in the very center of training and pedagogical reflections. Since the establishment of Global Studies at IAE Metz, it has been the component of the university with the largest number of students-entrepreneurs.

In all cases, we should endeavor to convince students that knowledge in today's world, the very one that could be the passport to cross all borders and to deeply and empathetically understand the magnitude of our world and its countless peculiarities, is the one that develops by favoring multidisciplinarity, interdisciplinarity, cross-disciplinarity, ties with the territory and the dialogical grasp of cultural rootedness and decentering, that one grows through the unavoidable encounter of concepts, situations and contexts, a genuine Borromean knot for approaching and undertaking life in its complexity.

NOTES

1. There are four essential characteristics that distinguish Canada's politics from that of France, or even more contrast them: the federal organization of power, constitutional monarchy, parliamentarism and division of the political parties.
2. http://global-studies.doshisha.ac.jp/fr/ (accessed March 1, 2021).
3. In this part of the chapter, the literature review is mainly focused on the topic of entrepreneurial experience.

REFERENCES

Aouni, Z., Surlemont, B. (2007), Le processus d'acquisition des compétences entre-preneuriales: une approche cognitive, *5e Congrès international de l'Académie de l'entrepreneuriat*, Sherbrooke, October 4–5.

Berglund, H. (2007), Researching entrepreneurship as lived experience, in Neergaard, H. and Ulhøi, J. (eds), *Handbook of Qualitative Research Methods in Entrepreneurship*. Cheltenham, UK and Northampton, MA, USA: Edward Elgar, pp. 75–93.

Bernard, A. (1976), *La politique au Canada et au Québec*. Montréal: Presses de l'Uni-versité du Québec.

Champy-Remoussenard, P., Starck, S. (2018). *Apprendre à entreprendre: Politiques et pratiques éducatives*. Louvain-la-Neuve: De Boeck Supérieur.

Cohen, R. (2008), Faut-il brûler les plans d'affaires? *L'Expansion Management Review*, 1(128), 22–30.

Filion, L.J. (1999), *Tintin, Minville, l'entrepreneur et la potion magique*. Québec: FIDES.

Hagg, G., Kurczewska, A. (2021), Toward a learning philosophy based on experience in entrepreneurship education, *Entrepreneurship Education and Pedagogy*, 4(1), 4–29.

Hatem, F., Cazes, B., Roubelat, F. (1993), *La prospective. Pratiques et méthodes*. Paris: Gestion Economica.

Joas, H. (1996), *The Creativity of Action*. Chicago, IL: Chicago University Press.

Juergensmeyer, M. (2013), What is Global Studies? *Globalizations*, 10(6), 765–9. doi: 10.1080/14747731.2013.845956

Kyrö, P., Carrier, C. (2005), *The Dynamics of Learning Entrepreneurship in a Cross-cultural University Context*. Tampere, FL: University of Tampere.

Loué, C., Laviolette, E., Bonnafos-Boucher, M. (2008), L'entrepreneur à l'épreuve de ses compétences: Eléments de construction d'un référentiel en situation d'incuba-tion. *Revue de l'Entrepreneuriat*, 7u(1), 63–83.

Maleki, K. (2009), *Méthodes quantitatives de consultation d'experts*. Editions Publibook.

Nlemvo, F., Witmeur, O. (2010). Faut-il vraiment brûler les plans d'affaires? *L'expansion entrepreneuriat*, 6, 46–50.

Pepin, M. (2017). S'entreprendre pour apprendre à l'école primaire: un défi péda-gogique. *Entreprendre & Innover*, 33, 18–28. https://doi.org/10.3917/entin.033 .0018

Ravano, L. (2021), La notion de *global South* et l'histoire de la pensée politique, *Inventions du Sud*, 16, 1–20.

Sarasvathy, S.D., Berglund, H. (2010), On the relevance of decision making in entrepreneurial decision making, in Lohrke, F. and Landstrom H. (eds), *Historical Foundations of Entrepreneurship Research*. Cheltenham, UK and Northampton, MA, USA: Edward Elgar, pp. 163–84.

Schieb-Bienfait, N. (2000), Etat des réflexions actualles sur l'enseignement de l'en-trepreneuriat en France, in T. Verstraete (ed.), *Histoire de l'entrepreneuriat*. Caen: EMS Management & Société, pp. 133–48.

Schmitt, C. (2005), *Université et entrepreneuriat: une relation en quête de sens*. Paris: L'Harmattan.

Schmitt, C. (2008), *Regards sur l'évolution des pratiques entrepreneuriales*. Québec: Presses de l'Université du Québec.

Schmitt, C. (2015), *L'agir entrepreneurial*. Montréal: Presses de l'Université du Québec.

Schmitt, C. (2017), *La fabrique de l'entrepreneuriat*. Paris: Dunod.

Schmitt, C. (2020), *Nouvelles perspectives en entrepreneuriat, du modèle du télégraphe au modèle de l'orchestre*. Paris: Vuibert.

Simon, H.A. (1996), *The Sciences of the Artificial*. Cambridge, MA: MIT Press.

Torrès, O. (2014), Vers une salutogénèse entrepreneuriale, in Torrès O. (ed.), *La santé du dirigeant, de la souffrance patronale à l'entrepreneuriat salutaire*. Brussels: De Boeck, pp. 211–12.

Toutain, O., Fayolle, A., Barès, F. (2020). La transformation numérique dans l'éducation et l'accompagnement à l'entrepreneuriat. *Entreprendre & Innover*, 47, 5–9. https://doi.org/10.3917/entin.047.0005

Tremblay, M., Carrier, C. (2006), Développement de la recherche sur l'identification collective d'opportunités: assises et perspectives. *Revue de l'entrepreneuriat*, 5(2), 69–88.

4. A new call for Business Schools: breaking out of the paradox loop

Martine Boutary and Wafa Khlif

4.1 INTRODUCTION

Since their creation, French Business Schools have responded to industry's need for a pragmatically trained workforce, which they have achieved by taking a liberal economic approach and using teaching methods based on cases preferably from Harvard Business School. Beyond these pedagogical methods, Business Schools (hereafter b-schools) are anchored in a "modern" Cartesian school of thought; progress resides in man's capacity to understand Nature, to shape it, and ultimately become its "masters and possessors" in a form of divine providence. From this perspective, the primary objective of the education system is high efficiency in the business world. The development of effective and efficient tools in all areas of management thus appears to have been prioritized over the teaching of problematization skills. The business model seems clear: the teaching is designed to be efficient, straightforward, depoliticized, standardized and globalized for "universal" performance. There is a predominance of technical, instrumental and decontextualized approaches, while debate is not an objective, and neutrality is encouraged.

Management courses have certainly evolved, in particular thanks to the fairly early introduction of research. Their (learning) objectives have shifted from the conservative transmission of knowledge by economic actors themselves to the creation and transmission of more disembodied and "scientific" knowledge that is mainly focused on a quest for increasingly stronger performance and, sometimes infinite, growth. However, in a context where culture and civilizations are in transition, where the world's political, economic and technological data is being disrupted, notably with the emergence of Big Data, and of connected objects and transhumanist thinking, certain limitations are emerging. Several economic actors are already warning that b-schools' teaching is too analytical, too narrow, too specialized (Thomas et al. 2013) and sometimes too simplistic with perilous knowledge shortcuts. The actors, individuals and organizations have to cope with the primacy of short-term efficiency, in response to demands for rapid growth and shareholder returns in an extremely competitive world in which competition is somewhat more linked to external references than to internal wills.

Thus far it has been management tools, instrumentally represented companies, pragmatism as a value, and demand for predictability that have guided teaching activity. B-schools seem to favor the perpetuation of the dominant economic model whereby unlimited profit from resource optimization is not questioned. As a result, the emergence of organic, comprehensive behaviors and tools embedded in the planet and, more generally, in respect for living beings is marginalized. To put it more explicitly, profit is still at the forefront, and although consideration of current societal and environmental issues is gaining importance, for several central actors it is still a lesser issue than the demand for financial returns.

Worldwide, b-schools are currently struggling (Friedland and Jain 2020) and are responding by introducing more responsible, sensitive and environmental considerations. We posit that this will be of very little use if b-schools' leaders do nothing to tackle the three fundamental paradoxes that we wish to highlight in this chapter. The first paradox is that of deified individuals endowed with "an exclusive property right" that grants them the "power to act" on an inert world (Latour 2021) and yet they become fragile as they are so disconnected from their context/reality – even their planet. The second is the paradox of using what tend to be linear models and deductive approaches to analyze and represent certainty in a world that is inherently unstable and uncertain. The third paradox is that of a complex world that is sliced up as needed by simplistic, quantified economic models that go so far as to (under)estimate social actors and the living in general, in order to overcome the impossible task of describing them individually (Boudon 1985). We postulate that these three paradoxes are strongly intertwined and thus cannot be reconsidered separately due to the risk of falling back on market considerations rather than on a qualitative and structural metamorphosis for b-schools.

We need to break out of this loop. In the first section, we aim to clarify each of these paradoxes and to examine their causality and impact. In the second section, we provide certain reconsiderations of the roles of individuals and groups, in which we accept uncertainty in management and offer complex reflections to reconcile science and the subjective experience of reality. We call for a return to the reality of the living, making a priority of multiple theorizations rather than ideological, universal theories that are disconnected from any cultural or political roots, and which impose a uniform way of existence.

4.2   THE INTERTWINED PARADOXES OF B-SCHOOLS

Rankings and proximity to companies have procured the superiority of the b-schools system. As a result, the students strive to join high fees schools with one major motivation on graduation: a secure job and all the status that goes with it. The link between diploma and job is made possible by two interrelated assets: (1) the network of alumni who are likely to help members of the same organization/tribe to find employment, and (2) compulsory internships in different companies that make them quickly operational and thus profitable for their employers. These companies are looking for candidates that are already operational and less focused on theoretical developments than university graduates tend to be. Both students and companies were and still are promised practical and experiential learning, based on numerous "cases" and a certain amount of situational simulation to promote the understanding and reproduction of given scenarios. There is no doubt that this process works and allows many corporate executives and managers to advance their professional careers rapidly and for companies to grow and globalize, but at the price of the negative externalities that the prevailing world is experiencing.

Indeed, theories based on partial analysis and the use of specific/exclusive hypotheses and mainly deductive models have made managers blind to the global consequences of their decisions. Supiot (2015) labeled this "reality denial," whereby managers (higher ups or traders, for example) live inside a closed, idealized bubble with no possibility for connection to Nature. The compartmentalization of thinking can lead to the general disempowerment of organizations, which give priority only to the efficiency of each link in the design, production and marketing chains of certain goods and services. Each of these links has a specific functional responsibility, focused on the optimization of certain choices, most often with a financial priority. Although recent discourse on sustainability suggests the introduction of new indicators, these inevitably end up being conditioned nevertheless by economic/financial performance.

In such a scenario, the rewarding of individuals for their partial, short-term successes raises questions both about themselves (the meaning of their work) and about society as a whole (societal responsibility). What individuals should do and what they want to do no longer appear to be coherent. Some scholars have witnessed this tension between their personal lives and postures and professional demands for the reproduction of existing models. Albeit mildly (and highly mediatized), new actors and paradigms are coming into play to readjust managerial practices/models. The notions of sustainable development, the common good, the economy of the living and regeneration are coming to the fore without calling into question the (economic) system itself and its (theoretical) embeddedness.

4.2.1 I Am, Because I Am

We need to look back at numerous political, sociological, psychological and economic constructs to understand how management sciences have examined the "creation" of this 21st-century individual, who is individualistic to the point of egoism and focused on their eco-ego rather than their position as a (human) being who is part of the planet. The critics have not held back:

> Without business schools, accountants, lawyers, Excel spreadsheets, without the continuous work of states to divide tasks between the public and the private, without the continuous training through the invention of new algorithms, without the formatting of property rights, no one would have invented an individual with a radical enough egoism, continuous enough to owe nothing to him/herself and to consider all the others as strangers and all forms of life as resourcesz. (Latour 2021, p. 80)

Ideological choices coupled with the power of management tools can lead to simplified evidence and individual performance choices, in response to poignant but decontextualized questions. Within this dominant ideology, students are trained to become efficient operators/agents who are capable of making technical decisions when faced by apparently complicated problems. Case study questions are expected to lead to operationally effective solutions, which ignore the externalities, complex interrelations and human/social considerations and do not question the essential principle of shareholder interests.[1]

Within the framework of neoliberal non-polemical thinking, these choices may be acceptable, but can we continue to rely solely on the *homos economicus* model of thought, dissociating general interest from private interest? Would it not be better to discuss the reasons and stakes of these choices, not just in terms of overall economic efficiency but also of socio-political responsibility, in order to at least act with a clean conscience?

Decontextualized learning nurtures the emergence of the specialized knowledge worker. Puzzling situations viewed with a silo mentality (accounting approach, marketing approach, etc.) often are solved regardless of the political or human context. For example, a machine's profitability will be assessed considering its production capacity, production time, resource requirements, etc. But consideration is rarely given to the recycling, adverse labor conditions or polluting trans-border transportation that this may generate, among other things. The market study always highlights the potential market returns but rarely the relevance of the overall development of the market, for the same reasons.

While some authors (i.e., Merleau Ponti 1976) state that "it is from the world that we perceive things," students are asked to think dispassionately and deductively in order to make objective decisions and avoid emotions. The individual who studies and makes decisions that way focuses their attention on the task at hand, rather than being sidetracked by other issues. At a distance from other people and places, they deploy a form of survival by tightening their personal universe around themselves and those close to them, in order to avoid a more collective consideration that might challenge them.

Trained thus, the individual feels capable of absolute objectivity. This capacity for action is also reinforced by powerful tools, whereby the instrumentalized individual, who is hyper-connected to abstract situations and individuals (Giddens 2000) that have no context, confirms their selfishness (Elias 1991). These situations are not neutral for organizations which, seeking growth and performance, find themselves in a bind: individualization reduces the capacity for collective intelligence, and consequently creativity and innovation. On the other hand, these "empowered" individuals are drawn into a logic of infinite betterment, which often ends up flattening their values, through assimilation but also through burnout and frustration.

4.2.2 Uncertainty within Closed Systems?

Uncertainty is problematic because it cannot be modeled and is therefore difficult to grasp and teach in an environment that is constantly seeking practical and riskless solutions. It is thus linearized and controlled for economic optimization and in pedagogical settings. In his typology, Lavoie (1985) defines uncertainty as a situation where the set of possible choices is not necessarily known, the possible outcomes are not exhaustively known, and nor are the values of these outcomes. Thus, orthodox economic theory considers the neoclassical agent in a situation of uncertainty with regard to awareness of the range of possible futures, as well as the probability of each of them occurring (Dallery et al. 2010).

To that end, Economics has built on Physics' general equilibrium to draw rigorous market dynamics. Unfortunately, there is a problem with this perilous analogy that has been known since the 1970s: there is no single equilibrium, but several. Linearity implies reasoning in closed systems where the same causes always produce the same effects. This determinism facilitates the lives of modelers and teachers alike. The closure of systems analyzing the mechanisms of life and organizations (which are a network of organic and inorganic elements) can typically lead to their disappearance (e.g., knowledge stored in databases) (Stiegler 2015).

Despite decades of economic and social crisis and turmoil, the reference to the machine still persists in the managerial world. "It is not doubt, it is certainty that drives one mad"[2] and this is exactly what has happened to the widely taught and used models of optimization; in search of certainty, they have gone mad because they are disconnected from uncertain and plural realities. According to Stiegler and Montévil (2019), a critique of contemporary political economy, that is, of modern-day capitalism, requires a conceptual reconsideration of the economy. Here, we are not simply dealing with the living, but with organized inorganic matter. According to these authors, the key is to reconsider knowledge, which has largely been diluted into information that is "partly calculable and intrinsically entropic" (p. 6).

Moreover, quantification systems often support the illusion of certainty. Quantification is at the heart of how humans attempt to make Nature manageable/governable. The highly popular quotation attributed to Drucker both in academia and in the managerial world, "what gets measured gets managed," reflects this desire to bring under control (measure) the management of the uncertain component of companies: the human(s). In this sense, certainty invites us to place human beings and their activity within measurable criteria, in order to frame behaviors rationally, because the figures "tell the truth" and do not distort reality (Supiot 2015). Within this certainty, students learn and understand management through multiple metric tools in order to reinforce objectivity and reduce, accordingly, the rhetorical or emotional risk. But we often forget that calculation hinders the political body (Stiegler 2015).

With the promise of certainty, quantification makes it possible to see and shape human targets in decided structures. By bringing desired features into light, it also serves to hide areas that are off-limits to social debate. Finally, the quantification of Nature means that specific policies and interventions in our ecosystems can be made from often remote and outsourced "computing centers," with vast and often unforeseen implications for those who are quantified and counted, and also with a perverse effect on the counters themselves (Mehrpouya 2021).

4.2.3   Complexity through Simplistic Layers?

The whole is complex, and this can prevent action. In order to understand and control this whole, models, methods and management tools have been developed that involve simplification, assumptions and presuppositions (de Geuser and Fiol 2004). Even if justified, simplifications leave things open to any operation on the parts and, at the same time, feed the rhetoric of complexity. Learning by simplification helps future managers to grasp a situation quickly by removing elements of complexity. In actual fact, the problem only gets worse when learners forget that they are routinizing simplification in order to understand. In that regard, they lose their capacity to view any given problem from broad or multiple perspectives.

Even though it inherently reduces reality, simplification aims to save time and money by cutting costs and making the environment more predictable. Simplification tends to separate humans from the reality they are supposed to be creating through their decisions. Morin (1977) explains that it expresses the disjunction between separate and closed entities. He adds that "knowledge is blind when it is reduced to its sole quantitative dimension and when the economy and business are considered in a compartmentalized way. However, compartmentalizations that are impermeable to each other have become the norm. The dominant logic is utilitarian and short-term" (Morin 2019, p. 27).

Reference to globalization is a powerful example of this widespread use of simplification. It gives substance to a unity manufactured by an inescapable (top-down) standardization and centralization. Both become central drivers for one possible expression of efficiency. Simplification does not make the elements of reality simpler; it risks disempowering and dehumanizing humans in their action on the world (Besnier 2012). The context of the Covid-19 pandemic revealed the limits of this type of analysis: the identified risks did not consider a possible global blockage of inter-continental transport, which did prove to be the case and had an impact on all global production chains. Analysis that is centered on production costs cannot incorporate such a scenario.

Another manifestation of this simplification is the supposed split between body and mind. A simplifying perspective views individuals mainly in terms of their mind (rationality) or intellect. The emotional dimension of individuals is barely noticed, let alone given priority. Simplification also disregards intuition, paradoxically at a time when studies on entrepreneurship are emphasizing its importance in start-ups. Fairly recently, and to compensate for the effects of actors becoming more distant from their humanity, soft skills have disproportionably reappeared on management courses: it is a question of reappropriating the knowledge of being and daring to relate. In what is usually accepted to be a competitive world, emotions are then treated as instruments and offered to students to reinforce their efficiency and performance, but no paradigm shift has occurred. In that regard, Linhart (2015) underlines the risks of an "over-humanization" of professional relations.

As long as the world remains partitioned, sliced up, with some components of the living world excluded, and actions remain decontextualized, actors will lose sense of their actions, and some will try to skip such systems. This is already happening to students who, on graduation, and even when loaded with management tools whose value they recognize, opt for different organizational modalities and work patterns. B-schools' world of certainties and rationality, even if limited, suffers from being isolated from sensitivity. We postulate, following the work by Libois (2018), "that being available to welcome, listen to, observe, and be touched by the other and his/her differences, in contrast to a practice stuck to pre-established objectives and procedures, is part of what makes a profession." We still need to return to this point and will discuss it in the second part of this chapter.

4.3   THE METAMORPHOSIS OF B-SCHOOLS: FROM PROMOTION TO GUIDANCE

> We are all capable of questioning the obvious, of questioning our comfort zones and of stepping back from what they represent. Camus ... argues for a fundamentally human posture of permanent "rebellion", at the heart of the irreducible incompleteness of everything. To adopt such a posture of humility, listening and trying, rather than pride, certainty and efficiency, would be to live again what temperance and moderation were for the Greeks. We can suppose if not hope that, even through its horror, the coronavirus crisis will teach us such a posture again. (Bibard 2020)

We need to move on from merely transmitting knowledge and/or orchestrating classroom activity. There are growing crises on the economic, social, health and climate levels. For decades now, several reports have been highlighting the inequalities in the world and global warming (e.g., IPCC 2021, 2022; World Inequality Report 2022). It seems we need to rethink the choices made by b-schools, not only in terms of strategic positioning but as actors in a changing society: what do these schools educate for and what educational and societal contributions do they make?

Having observed the paradoxes raised above, we now suggest a few avenues for progress: a reconsideration of the *raison d'être* of b-schools, a reinterpretation of the key knowledge to be discussed (setting new frameworks) and an appropriation of the world-environment. The overall idea of these proposals would be to shift, individually as well as collectively and institutionally, from the role of reproducing the managerial elites to the role of guiding the populace towards managerial skills, thus focusing more on creating the circumstances for thinking and co-elaborating contexts rather than reinforcing and optimizing the existing paths.

4.3.1   Instinct to Have, or Reason to Be?

Following the PACTE law in France, many companies are beginning to disclose their *raison d'être*, and b-schools are no exception. However, the *raison d'être* exercise can quickly end at the disclosure level. Friedland and Jain (2020) posit that b-schools are facing a "crisis of purpose" and explain the reasons and consequences of this phenomenon. They mainly link it to the definition of professional success, which is closely linked to capacities for financial accumulation. Although several b-schools are beginning to adhere significantly to the United Nation's Principles of Responsible Management Education (PRME) by integrating ethics, corporate social responsibility (CSR) and sustainability into their core activities (Burchell et al. 2015), this is not so much a redefinition of their activities as it is a (sometimes instrumental) add-on that only legitimizes their very existence (Caplan 2018). It goes without saying that this will require a major reconsideration of thinking, objectives and modes of action, supported by a collective effort that is accepted by all stakeholders.

Having such a *raison d'être* implies a key question: what am I serving as an institution and who am I serving in society? Should we not, as Schlegelmilch (2020) suggests, broaden the scope of action and reflection to educate responsible students who are aware of their roles as (future) managers within society as a whole (Raworth 2018; Schlegelmilch 2020)? This question calls for major consideration of the *raison d'être* within the complexity of the economic mechanisms of societies.

One of the keys would be to start focusing on education before worrying about any kind of business, to let different schools of thought, pedagogies and commitments flourish and express themselves, each feeding the other without opposing and embracing complexity. The western last two-century development has transformed into a dominant progress model where rationality and science are at the center of value consideration. While b-schools focus on problem-solving, Morin (1977) shows that knowledge of complexity requires a new approach and a reform of thinking. Santos et al. (2007) call for "opening up the canon of knowledge" and for the "recognition of the plurality of heterogeneous knowledges (one of them being modern science) and on the sustained and dynamic interconnections between them without compromising their autonomy" (Santos 2007, p. 27). For example, they heavily underline the absence of "South thinking" within western curricula.

It seems relevant to broaden the vision and ambitions of b-schools, so they can foster new, and less classical and normative orientations. The latter would aim to generate and regenerate managerial practices that respect the living world, bridging the gap between awareness and action among b-schools' internal and external actors (Pelluchon 2020), and producing a scheme for the collective and inclusive inhabitation of our planet. From this perspective, there is a need to define common goods (Cornu et al. 2021) as something to be protected for humanity itself to the detriment of individual or corporate interests that maximize profits, and sometimes only in the short term. This approach would help circumvent dual conceptions, such as opposing good and evil, or right and wrong (Libois 2018). The paradoxes are still present, and they must be taken into account rather than eliminated.

The Socratic warning that "an unquestioned life is not worth living" is a good starting point for this fundamental change. It challenges individuals on the coherence between their personal values and their actions. This examination often involves elements of unlearning and creative imagination. There is an urgent need for b-schools to reflect on their intentions, assumptions and moral underpinnings, and also to consider learning as a process of "becoming" – in the Deleuzian sense – more truly responsible. According to Deleuze and Guattari (1987), "becoming" is not a linear development process that requires a prescribed pattern to be followed, but rather a continuous adaptation to what is happening, within which new ideas, practices, norms and values are generated.

It goes without saying that the *raison d'être* is a complex political exercise, as the choices made by b-schools are not independent from an elitist ecosystem. However, and even without challenging the privileges of a certain social class (Pasquali 2021), intentions, and moral foundations, would be the basis and condition for all managerial and educational choices and decisions. This *raison d'être* can generate organic interaction between the different interdependent units of the b-schools (academic, admission, research, financial, promotion, etc.) as it will drive the whole towards a coherent and tangible horizon: back to a better-known ecosystem within which interactions are generated while including benevolence in each intention and action.

4.3.2   The Multiple Voices of Questionable Knowledge

While b-schools focus on (anticipated) problem-solving, there is a need, as presented in the previous section, to develop a comprehensive (technical and behavioral) understanding of the problem within its context. As early as 1977, Edgar Morin denounced the blindness of knowledge by pointing out, among other things, paradigmatic blindness. He invites us as educators to teach relevant knowledge, which considers "glocalized" contexts and their multidimensionality, as well as distrusting reductionist reasoning that often clashes with or constructs false rationalities. He advocates that all teaching cannot be detached from the human question (*homo complexus*) and its earthly identity.

A classical way of dealing with problems is to identify solutions. As a result, the correct solution leads to the acquisition of defined, determined and static knowledge, which is then stored in databases (or textbooks). Paradoxically, the problem can remain unknown, however satisfied the actor is with the operational efficiency of the presented solution. The threat of externalities surfaces here because the solution is only partial and therefore does not answer the complete problem. Learning what the problem is "as such" (Birck 2009, cf. Deleuze), elaborating upon it, is more oriented towards the learning and genesis of a produced rather than received "truth." Deleuze thus defines a "transformed pedagogy" as opening the door to a promise of science:

> To understand the problem as such is to untie it from the complexity it constitutes with the solution that resolves it. Now, what we are most generally given in the concrete experience of school teaching are solved problems, knowledge, or at least

problems awaiting their solutions, with a view to the acquisition of knowledge. (Birck 2009)

B-schools' pedagogy could evolve towards this type of reflection, integrating knowledge as an active capacity, both individually and collectively.

Acting within the framework of environmental change also requires decompartmentalizing knowledge and making science autonomous from capitalism (Stiegler 2015). Capitalism, or neoliberalism, has led us to believe in a kind of organization that is spontaneously oriented towards competition, specialization, offensiveness and individualism (Servigne and Chapelle 2019) and which is no longer sustainable. Senard and Notat (2018), in their report on the preparation of the French PACTE law (2018), state: "We will have to create a different model, which is neither a classic Anglo-Saxon capitalism nor a state capitalism"; "We need to change the paradigm" (Morin 2014). The emphasis on individual well-being, on the development of "talents" intended to bring an individual to the top of his or her abilities and personal success, contributes to this social failure, to the development of inequalities through intensified competition, and to the collapse, at times, of these same individuals who, torn between action and consciousness (Pelluchon 2020), are struck by burnout or other personal or societal malaise.

It is therefore important to start considering knowledge, whatever it may be, always as a way to collectively define what helps to slow down or reduce entropy in this or that field of human existence. As Stiegler (2015) argues, *savoir-faire* (procedure) is articulated as "making sure that what I do does not collapse and lead to chaos," *savoir-vivre* (being) as "knowing how to enrich and individuate the social organization in which I live without destroying it," and finally, *savoir* (concept): "as knowing how to inherit its past only by disrupting it, and disrupt it only by reactivating it." He called for a reconnection with what makes us human: the ability to escape "entropy" by inventing new forms of existence.

4.3.3 De-mechanizing Life

Described by Mendel (1998) in his book depicting action as an adventure, uncertainty in any activity/action is inherent and carries a kind of know-how that has to be identified. Human professions are highly representative of this need to know how to act within uncertainty, which is a source of emotional tension. Paradoxically, the developed organizational models lead to the "management" of distortions and contradictions and compel managers to avoid ambiguities that are sources of mutual incomprehension. The temptation to standardize is high and can lead to individual and collective passivity. As we type these sentences on our keyboard, the machine itself assists us by anticipating our words, diminishing at the same time our ability to visualize our thoughts, meaning we never get to memorize the correct spelling. Technical assistance becomes a key to servitude and uniformity, which may even lead to the disappearance of all individuality.

Colonization by the mechanization of existence goes beyond economic enslavement; it penetrates the spiritual through the time-honored saying that "time is money." This phrase desacralizes life and hijacks the relationship with morality by cloistering it in instrumentalized ethical consensus. It also professionalizes boredom by opening the door to pleasure without effort: acquiring a language in less than a month, becoming an expert in less than a year, an aviator in less than six months, growing a tomato in less than three weeks, etc. As long as you can afford it, anything can be done more quickly. These examples remind us that professional boredom provides greater comfort and laziness, and can put us in a state of intellectual, spiritual and sometimes physical pre-death.

The separation of facts and values has paradoxically undermined thinking and has also disconnected scholars from social practices, especially local ones. Massi et al. (2018) confirm that stability/certainty would be unhelpful for learning. Training for uncertainty means first of all learning to spot the moments when thinking closes down, when it descends into dogmatism, into addiction to certainties. This may start by turning away from the linearity of models and repositioning the living (and not humankind) at the center of the values to be "transmitted." There have been several attempts by 21st century economists to think about uncertainty and depart from the failed models of neoclassical theory. They are essentially based on two key concepts: regeneration and contribution (Stiegler 2020) and calling for in-depth questioning of the institutional conditions that favored the separation of economy and society through the emergence of a self-regulating market (Polanyi 1944 [1983]).

We have also understood the extent to which thinking about independent calculative individuals can lead to forgetting or denying the need for collective organization and/or the defense of common goods. Mutual aid offers a natural solution, by learning from others (Servigne and Chapelle 2019). It is a form of action that could reinvent competition, reintegrate the holistic approach to life, and thus create the conditions for sustainable collective life. Thus, externalities are no longer "managed" by denial, they are taken into consideration and reduced (or even eliminated) if they are negative. The resource economy (without including humans) is designed not to increase individual profit, but to increase collective well-being, which remains to be defined. It is harder and takes more time to define, but it is definitively related to the essence of democracy.

An individual who feels and is the group echoes a strong concept of emptiness.

> Emptiness (Sanskrit: śūnyatā) implies that although phenomena are perceptible to the human mind, they do not intrinsically exist. This is not the same as saying that they do not exist at all, but rather that they exist only in a relative manner. In other words, a key principle of emptiness is that apart from a categorical label, something constituting the self of a given entity, including humans, can never be located in time or space. This contrasts with the prevailing Western psychological view whereby the self is typically deemed to be an independent, definitive and autonomous entity. (Van Gordon et al. 2021, p. 1845)

The self is totally intertwined with the other selves, including not only individuals, but all living beings.

4.4 CONCLUSION

In this chapter, we have tried to highlight the paradoxical situation in which b-schools are evolving, mainly based on observations of French Schools. Responsible for educating individuals in business management, they are confronted, on the one hand, with the demands of their stakeholders – students and companies in particular – for performance, growth and short-term efficiency and, on the other hand, with a demanding society that is facing a fragile environment and finiteness of resources (Latour 2021). Nevertheless, b-schools are still being built on decisions and teaching methods that are designed to reproduce, and improve upon, existing models, which may even be innovative but are still heavily oriented towards increasing inequalities, consumption and profit. Institutionally, they have developed international positions and partnerships that have opened up their potential for recruitment and placement of students, but they have also rendered abstract the notions of localized groups and student promotion (Giddens 2000). In terms of teaching, they have mostly opted for methods that direct thinking towards the search for (correct) solutions to anticipated and delimited problems, often outside a complex context (Morin 2014) in order for (specialized) students to be able to solve problems within one of the managerial disciplines.

However, this search for certainty and systematic risk assessment no longer corresponds to the uncertainties and complexities of the milieu within which actions occur. In this world of interconnectivities, division and disciplinary hierarchy pose limits. In a digitalized world, truth and neutrality of tools are dangerous lures. In a world of injustices, the business ethics approach is a heresy. In a world of meaning, mastery of rationality is a hindrance. In a complex world, value for money in a futurized present is a threat. Finally, in a world where capitalism is becoming a religion, it is dogmatic to continue to teach doctrine and close the door to possible debate. Students, or at least some of them, are demanding a different meaning to their studies or are turning away from existing systems, while companies, satisfied with the operational level of their young recruits, are sometimes offended by their lack of involvement or commitment.

We reflected on possible ways of reconsidering the essence of a b-school. Will it continue to play the role of facilitator and connector of defined stakeholders in a known and stable socio-economic space? We propose a revision of this essence towards a more organic model, where a b-school takes on its full responsibility as a guide in a complex world in perpetual crisis, because we do not teach what we know, but only teach what we are. We suggest a return to the origins of the term *guidonis* from the Frankish *witan* ("to show the way"), which in turn stems from the Indo-European root *weid- ("to know").

In concrete terms, we have chosen to give priority to reflection on the *raison d'être* of these institutions, to avoid "only" modifying schools' practices without questioning their substance and fundamental choices: who is our vis-à-vis? What are the components of our ecosystem? What is our societal contribution? Only then can we ask questions about the How: what paradigms should be taught (liberalism, collectivism, culturalism, colonialism, globalism, complexity, diversity, versatility, local and international), what pedagogical methodologies should be promoted (in and out of the classroom, refocus on work areas, distance ourselves from the "data," link (in the sense of Morin's complexity) teaching within research), what factors should be shared (the vision, the work, the profit), who to integrate and how (all categories of workers, stakeholders of a wider ecosystem) and how to regenerate what are already highly depleted resources and the Living in its diversity (Giraud and Sarr 2021) and at the same time unity (Oughourlian 2020). Dubet (2021) refers to the need to "redefine what is and what makes for solidarity," and "to develop a moral of modesty and seriousness."

Caring, questioning and transversality could be the three pillars that can embrace the aforesaid paradoxes and carry forward a new b-school in a renewed society. We are aware that this might sound naive in a world of inequalities, resource scarcity and political instability, but the social crisis that is everywhere around us is crying out for disruptive rules.

"Business as usual" is tempting because it is quicker and easier, but right now it would be suicidal not to change the paradigm, and to simply stick to the same objectives and the same performance indicators (Fleming 2019). Growth can be re-examined in terms of what underpins it: the nature of what is built is as important as the amount of what is spent. New indicators need to be defined (Giraud and Sarr 2021) to move towards Schools that can add possibility to reality, with a desire to share knowledge, true, but also emotions and different futures. Futures that make technology a docile assistant and not a despot. Futures that idealize beings that are full of compassion and that look with despair upon beings that are full of money. Futures where borders are stiffened against the politics of the private good and the common good finds its stolen meaning again. Futures where the word of an employee is worth more than a speech about value creation. Finally, futures that deny a modernity that tends to separate being from living.

We propose that b-schools should adopt a new guiding role, and for the teaching promoted and provided in them to foster thought as experimentation. As the self does not exist by itself (Oughourlian 2020), b-schools should lead the way towards the building of communities with a single obligation: respect. Within communities, humankind takes its place in the reality of a unified Nature.

NOTES

1. See Oxfam report, 2020: https://www.oxfam.org/fr/communiques-presse/les -benefices-des-entreprises-explosent-les-plus-riches-empochent-des-milliards (accessed July 27, 2022).
2. F. Nietzsche, 1992, *Ecco Homo*, Penguin Classic.

REFERENCES

Besnier, JM 2012, *L'homme simplifié*, Collection Sciences Humaines, Paris: Ed. Fayard

Bibard, L 2020, 'Penser l'après: En quoi Camus est-il indispensable pour nous aider à sortir de la crise?' *The Conversation*, April 17.

Birck, JB 2009, '"Créer des problèmes": Éléments pour une pédagogie des problèmes à partir de G. Deleuze'. https://doi.org/10.4000/ree.4131

Boudon, R 1985, *L'Inégalité des chances*, Paris, Armand Colin 3e édition, Hachette, collection Pluriel.

Burchell J, Kennedy S and Murray A 2015, 'Responsible management education in UK business schools: Critically examining the role of the United Nations Principles for Responsible Management Education as a driver for change'. *Management Learning*, vol. 46, no. 4, pp. 479–97.

Caplan, B 2018, *The Case Against Education: Why the Education System Is a Waste of Time and Money*, Princeton, NJ: Princeton University Press.

Cornu, M, Orsi, F and Rochfeld, J (eds) 2021, *Dictionnaire des biens communs*, Paris: Ed. PUF.

Dallery, T, Eloire, F and Melmies, J 2010, 'L'incertitude au cœur des marchés concrets: Confrontation entre théorie post-keynésienne et sociologie économique structurale', *Innovations*, vol. 31, no.1, pp. 131–56.

de Geuser, F and Fiol, M 2004, 'Le contrôle de gestion entre une dérangeante complexité et une indispensable simplification', *Normes et Mondialisation*, May, France. CD-ROM. halshs- 00593092.

Deleuze, G and Guattari, F 1987, *A Thousand Plateaus: Capitalism and Schizophrenia*, translation and Foreword by Brian Massumi, London: Continuum.

Dubet, F 2021, 'The return of society', *European Journal of Social Theory*, vol. 24, no. 1, pp. 3–21. doi:10.1177/1368431020950541

Elias, N 1991, *La société des individus*, Paris: Fayart.

Fleming, P 2019, 'Dark academia: Despair in the neoliberal business school', *Journal of Management Studies*, vol. 57, no. 6, pp. 1305–11. https://doi.org/10.1111/joms.12521

Friedland, J and Jain, T 2020, 'Reframing the purpose of business education: Crowding-in a culture of moral self-awareness', *Journal of Management Inquiry*, vol. 31, no. 1, pp. 15–29. https://doi.org/10.1177/1056492620940793

Giddens, A 2000, *Les conséquences de la modernité*, Paris: Ed. L'Harmattan.

Giraud, G and Sarr, F 2021, *L'économie à venir*, Paris: Ed. Les liens qui libèrent.

IPCC 2021, https://www.ipcc.ch/report/ar6/wg1/ (accessed July 27, 2022).

IPCC 2022, 'Impacts, adaptation and vulnerability'. https://www.ipcc.ch/report/sixth-assessment-report-working-group-ii/ (accessed July 27, 2022).

Latour, B 2021, *Où suis-je? Leçons du confinement à l'usage des terrestres*, Paris: La Découverte.

Lavoie, M 1985, 'La distinction entre l'incertitude keynésienne et le risque néoclassique', *Économie Appliquée*, vol. 38, no. 2, pp. 493–518.

Libois, J 2018, 'Complexité de l'agir: Une présence qui engage les émotions', *Sociétés et jeunesses en difficulté*, no. 20 (online). http://journals.openedition.org/sejed/8767 (accessed January 12, 2022).

Linhart, D 2015, *La comédie humaine du travail: De la déshumanisation taylorienne à la sur-humanisation managériale*, Paris: Erès, collection 'Sociologie clinique'.

Massi, B, Donahue, CH and Lee, D 2018, 'Volatility facilitates value updating in the prefrontal cortex', *Neuron*, vol. 99, pp. 598–608.

Mehrpouya, A 2021, 'Critical call', *Re-count*. https://www.recountphotoaward.org/

Mendel, G 1998, *L'acte est une aventure: Du sujet métaphysique au sujet de l'actepouvoir*. Paris: La Découverte.

Merleau Ponti, M 1976, (1ère parution 1945), *Phénoménologie de la perception*, Gallimard, Paris: Ed. Tel no. 4.

Morin, E 1977, *La méthode*, Paris: Collection Points, Série Essais.

Morin, E 2014, *Introduction à la pensée complexe*, Paris: Seuil.

Morin, E 2019, *Pour changer de civilisation*, Paris: Essai, Mikros.

Oughourlian, JM 2020, *L'Altérité, de qui souffrez-vous?* Paris: Desclée de Brouwer.

Pasquali, P 2021, *Héritocratie: Les élites, les grandes écoles et les mésaventures du mérite (1870–2020)*, Paris: La Découverte.

Pelluchon, C 2020, *Réparons le monde: Humains, animaux, nature*, Paris: Rivages, coll. "Petite Bibliothèque".

Polanyi, K 1944, *La Grande Transformation: Aux origines politiques et économiques de notre temps*, Gallimard, Paris (reprinted 1983).

Raworth, K 2018, *La théorie du donut*, Paris: Plon.

Santos, BS 2007, 'Beyond abyssal thinking: From global lines to ecologies of knowledges', *Review*, vol. 30, no. 1, pp. 45–89.

Santos, BS, Nunes, JA and Meneses, MP 2007, 'Opening up the canon of knowledge and recognition of difference', in BS Santos (ed.), *Another Knowledge is Possible*, London: Verso, pp. 19–63.

Schlegelmilch, BB 2020, 'Why business schools need radical 1innovations: Drivers and development trajectories', *Journal of Marketing Education*, vol. 42, no. 2, pp. 1–15.

Senard, JD and Notat, N 2018, Rapport *'L'entreprise, objet d'intérêt collectif'*, pour la préparation de la loi française PACTE.

Servigne, P and Chapelle, G 2019, *L'entraide, l'autre loi de la jungle*, Paris: Les liens qui libèrent.

Stiegler, B 2015, 'Sortir de l'anthropocène'. *Multitudes*, vol. 60, pp. 137–46. https://doi.org/10.3917/mult.060.0137

Stiegler, B (ed.) 2020. *Bifurquer: Il n'y a pas d'alternative*, Paris: les Liens qui Libèrent.

Stiegler, B and Montévil, M 2019, 'Entretien sur l'entropie, le vivant et la technique: Deuxième partie', *Links Series* 2. http://links-series.com/n-1-2-virtuel-et-biologie/

Supiot, A 2015, *La gouvernance par les nombres*, Paris: Fayard.

Thomas, H, Lonage, P and Sheth, J 2013, *The Business School in the Twenty-first Century: Emergent Challenges and New Business in Models*. Cambridge: Cambridge University Press.

Van Gordon, W, Sapthiang, S, Barrows, P and Shonin, E 2021, 'Understanding and practicing emptiness', *Mindfulness*, vol. 12, pp. 1845–8. https://doi.org/10.1007/s12671-020-01586-1

World Inequality Report 2022, https://wir2022.wid.world/ (accessed July 27, 2022).

5. Designing disruptive-innovative business schools

Werner Krings, Michael J. Harrison and Roger Palmer

5.1 INTRODUCTION

In a volatile, uncertain, complex, and ambiguous (VUCA) environment (Rodriguez & Rodriguez 2015), business schools and universities are increasingly forced to rethink how to target and serve students, anticipate future knowledge trends, and create value for businesses (Accenture 2021).

Today's environment poses numerous challenges. First, the increasing number of smaller private business schools with various accreditations and rankings dramatically changes the educational infrastructure (Bothwell 2018). Second, the technological and societal changes require reviewing conventional research and teaching methods consistent with the expected learning experiences and outcomes of Generation Y and Z students (Baumöl & Bockshecker 2017). Third, the call for abbreviated study and training periods suggests streamlining the content to balance practitioners' requirements and academic quality standards (Krings 2021). Fourth, decreasing enrollment rates (Astin & Oseguera 2004), especially males (Vedder & Colegrove 2021), and increasing collaboration, alliances, and mergers (Williams 2017) among academic institutions create disruptive-innovative learning models (Schlegelmilch 2020). Fifth, changing values, for example, the focus on online certificates from top-tier business schools and national developments, for example, Brexit, might jeopardize the comparability and recognition of academic degrees (Bennett 2021). Ultimately, global challenges, for example, Covid-19 (Rich 2020), the climate crisis (Collins 2021), present opportunities and threats for international economies that influence academic learning and research and require a (re)positioning of business schools and universities (Rana et al. 2020).

To remain relevant and viable (Arvanitakis & Hornsby 2016), scholars suggest that business schools and universities must develop strategies and show that their curricula include the latest technology, create a unique student/

customer experience, and equip and shape tomorrow's entrepreneurs and leaders (Sharp 2019). In addition, it is essential to impart knowledge and theory which fulfills academic rigor but is relevant to executives and their particular industry (Savović 2020). Nevertheless, drastic changes in both off-campus and online learning environments due to the ongoing Covid-19 pandemic challenge enrollment rates, the justification of fees, and pressures on funding (Newman et al. 2010; Rana et al. 2020).

Therefore, business schools and universities must review and adjust their strategies and policies and become more entrepreneurial to remain attractive to students and ensure profitability (Duderstadt 2001; Savović 2020). For example, top-tier universities targeting high-achieving students should consider that online learning experiences cannot entirely replace face-to-face (F2F) relationship-building. This impedes the accumulation of Social Capital (Karl 2001), critical for choosing a particular Higher Education institution (HEI) (*Economist* 2017).

Likewise, executive education should develop thought and practice leaders capable of innovating more sustainable goods and services (Accenture 2021).

This study contributes to transforming traditional business schools into disruptive-innovative (Christensen 2013) organizations by identifying essential themes aligned with the perspectives of (start-up) entrepreneurs and students from different regions (Krings, 2021; Sebhatu et al. 2021). This results in a profound change in viewpoints and a shift in paradigms from academic-centricity to a real-world focus.

5.2   LITERATURE REVIEW

5.2.1   Higher Education on a global scale

The current global Higher Education Industry situation can be summarized as follows.

Higher Education (HE) has steadily grown over the last decades. The Quacquarelli Symonds (QS) World University Ranking 2021 lists 1,000 leading universities in 80 different locations, with 47 new entrants assessing over 5,500 universities worldwide.

Traditionally, essential criteria for students and job recruiters include the value proposition (salary after graduation), cost of the program (fees), admission tests (GMAT), accreditation, and (inter)national ranking. The accreditation, perceived as a seal of approval, motivates business schools to enhance their program quality continuously and provides students guidance in choosing a particular institution (Bryant 2013).

For example, the 'triple crown' accreditation of the Association to Advance Collegiate Schools of Business (AACSB), the Association of MBAs (AMBA), and the European Foundation for Management Development (EFMD) Quality Improvement System (EQUIS) indicates the 102 top echelon business schools for Master of Business Administration (MBA) programs globally (FIGMAT 2021).

As depicted in Figure 5.1, the most prestigious universities are located in the European, North American, and Latin American regions.

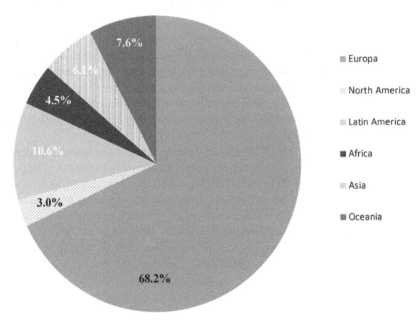

Source: MBAToday (2020).

Figure 5.1   Triple-accredited business schools

The accrediting bodies usually consider the quality of the academic program, faculty, and students (Newman et al. 2010). However, it is noteworthy that for the elite universities (e.g., Harvard, Stanford, and Wharton) that are AACSB accredited, the accreditation plays a subordinate role, that is, as a differentiator because of their global brand and reputation. More importantly, it is relevant whether the business school prepares for a career, for example, in consulting (Harvard) or entrepreneurship (Wharton). Lastly, belonging to the alumni of these organizations establishes career-critical networks (*Economist* 2017).

5.2.2 Higher Education on a National and Regional Scale

Regional or national accreditations, for example, the Foundation for International Business Administration Accreditation (FIBAA) or the International Accreditation Council for Business Education (IACBE), fulfill a similar purpose. However, instead of pursuing top accredited programs that guarantee international program excellence, accomplished practitioners, due to different workplace values (Hui et al. 2020), tend to opt into regionally accredited MBA programs of private universities such as Fachhochschule für Ökonomie und Management (FOM), Framingham State University (FSU). These programs promise to complete quicker at less expense while offering high employability.

5.2.3 Democratization and Diversification of Study Programs

Executive education has experienced increasing competition caused by private educational vendors and disruptors such as social networking and platform sites including LinkedIn and Udemy. These offer various online certifications with relaxed or no admission requirements and more reasonable rates. Moreover, the continuous change of context and content of education (Arvanitakis & Hornsby 2016) might downgrade the quality of education (Brown 2013) for the mass market. Subsequently, traditional business schools are forced to adjust by generating measurable business value to their stakeholders while maintaining a certain educational standard (Dover et al. 2018).

In the UK, for instance, Henley Business School, a globally leading prestigious institution, recognized the opportunity to boost its declining executive MBA enrollment rates by offering government-funded internships for executives and launching a Higher Education pathway program in collaboration with the British Army (Godley 2021).

In the US, for instance, Harvard University offers online certificates for various industries and leadership knowledge that support practitioners acquiring state-of-the-art knowledge at reasonable fees with the side benefit of enhancing their perceived credibility through a certificate from an Ivy League university on social media. Similarly, online and state universities offer reduced admission fees for US veterans and service members (Mantz 2017).

5.2.4 The Diverging Interest of Academics, Students, and Entrepreneurs

Numerous studies have been undertaken on reinventing business schools to ensure institutional success within this landscape of higher education (Newman et al. 2010). Nevertheless, these studies often prioritize the interests of academics, especially when responding to inevitable changes. The focus is on adjusting to increased competition between institutions. In addition, declining enrollment and funding pressures have driven business schools and universities to focus on blended teaching-delivery options and curriculum changes, that is, their primary interests (Rana et al. 2020).

Corporate organizations anticipated digitalization to simplify processes and overcome siloed functions to enhance customer experiences (Krings et al. 2021). By contrast, HEIs tend to maintain their organizational structure characterized by siloed functions and established processes.

Cultural clashes due to departmentalized interests of faculties and researchers are a block to becoming stakeholder-centric (Arvanitakis & Hornsby 2016). In particular, stakeholder-centricity addresses contemporary demands of students, alumni, and businesses to deal effectively with disruptions in the VUCA world, such as multiple career changes, recognizing innovative opportunities, or networking to fund start-ups (Sharp 2019).

In addition, HEIs frequently neglect the proactive leadership role expected from research universities, particularly business schools, through a disconnect of researchers from the real world. As a result, political leaders are helpless and look to the higher education and business sector to anticipate innovative solutions mastering geopolitical challenges such as the crisis-ridden world economy, climate change, and the pandemic (Collins 2021). Similarly, corporate and start-up businesses increasingly require students to become advocates and improve society beyond being a source of knowledge (Arvanitakis & Hornsby 2016).

5.2.5   The Identified Gaps and Contributions

Few scholars noticed the importance of HEIs to step up their efforts to their true mission, that is, meeting these challenges (Brennan & Teichler 2008) and aligning higher education institutional goals and objectives with their stakeholders (Krings 2021).

There is abundant literature on how HEIs might handle the tension between prevalent challenges of today's environment and the disguised opportunities on their own (Accenture 2021; Arvanitakis & Hornsby 2016). On the one hand, scholars derive current HE themes from the interests and viewpoints of academics (Rana et al. 2020). On the other, they develop themes by aligning the orientation of business schools/universities primarily to the resource requirements of these HE organizations (Bridges 2000). However, a primary institution-centric approach calls for high competitiveness among HEIs and excessive demands for funding resources (Newman et al. 2010).

Notable is that no recent studies have looked at and considered the perspectives of entrepreneurs, professors, and students as stakeholders of business schools. In addition, most studies are qualitative and centered around HEIs in a country-specific setting (Newman et al. 2010; Rana et al. 2020) instead of targeting a broader cross-section of regions or societies.

This book chapter contributes by balancing the stakeholder perspectives; an additional contribution consists of expanding the scope from national to global themes (Brennan & Teichler 2008).

In addition, the study lays new ground by addressing different gaps in the literature as follows.

First, shifting the strong orientation of business schools/universities from a rather self-centered interest to meet existential challenges such as competing for funding and determining the quality of education towards global opportunities offered by new technologies like digitalization; the changing demographics and diversity of students; and participating in geo-economical and political interests (Beynaghi et al. 2016; Duderstadt 2001).

Second, merging different perspectives in one study (e.g., academics and practitioners) allows one to arrive at a more balanced viewpoint and overcome biases and interests (Bridges 2000; Rana et al. 2020). Third, casting the net wider by considering academia and practice in various regions supports identifying unanticipated stances (Sharp 2019; Teichler 2003). Fourth, by considering mixed (qualitative-quantitative) methodologies to provide additional evidence.

Consequently, this chapter contributes to the discussion about how business schools/universities can align their priorities with stakeholders' interests to boost (inter)national economic growth (Peters 2007), enhance the collaboration with their academic peers (Savović 2020), and participate in anticipating and tackling global problems (Sebhatu et al. 2021). In particular, by developing a future-oriented education, business schools are expected to be the catalyst to generate innovative solutions and achieve sustainable goals in such areas as climate change and geopolitical dilemmas following the pandemic (Clawson & Page 2010; Collins 2021).

5.3   RESEARCH FRAMEWORK

5.3.1   Research Purpose

This chapter enabled the authors to 'link work across disciplines [business administration, IT, science, technology, engineering, and mathematics, STEM], provide multi-level insights [academics and practitioners], and broaden the scope of [their design] thinking' (Gilson & Goldberg 2015, p. 128).

In addition, following Rich (2020, p. 144), the authors sought a deeper understanding of the disruptive-innovative business school/university (DIBS), that is, as an 'agile university' (Bider & Jalali 2016) to adjust swiftly to technological changes (Duderstadt 2012) and sustainability (Sebhatu et al. 2021) and to proactively anticipate and master instead of passively responding to future unexpected events like the Covid-19 pandemic (Rana et al. 2020).

For this reason, the study was conducted in several regions (Asia-Pacific, Europe, and North America). The targets were 40 thought leaders among practitioners and academics complemented by students. The recruiting criteria were: high-achievers in their particular discipline, business, or peer group. In addition, the sample included students that launched promising start-ups either during their studies or shortly after graduation. This approach seemed critical to integrate different experiences and viewpoints to prevalent themes identified in the literature.

The overall objective is to align the often siloed perspectives of academics and practitioners, faculty, and student bodies (Krings 2021) by creating a stakeholder-oriented culture with excellent learning experiences (Argyris 2010) while collaborating on innovations and sustainability with trailblazer businesses (Accenture 2021).

This approach ensures attracting the ideal students for (under/post)graduate programs, securing enrollment rates, and stimulating the faculty's collaboration with peer HEIs and local and international companies (Mat et al. 2018). Furthermore, by accelerating and enhancing their business process development, for example, marketing processes focusing on superb Stakeholder Experiences (SX), future business schools will achieve recurring revenues and ensure the co-creation of innovative curricula (Krings et al. 2021). Besides enhancing branding and reputation, it is vital to reorientate HEIs aligned with industry, faculty, students, and societal expectations and values (Newman et al. 2010).

Moreover, the pilot study considered the understanding, emotions, and experiences of the three groups to develop a road map on how future business schools/universities remain thought leaders in tackling current challenges, such as health care in Covid-19 and global warming by stimulating innovations (e.g., vaccines and sustainable products) (Beynaghi et al. 2016) to revive the lockdown-shaken international economies (Collins 2021). This pathway suggests more holistic curricula that combine business administration with STEM content focusing on entrepreneurship (Krings 2021; Sebhatu et al. 2021).

5.3.2   Research Contributions

This chapter contributes in several ways as outlined below.

First, by supporting HEIs to transition from a traditional business school/university-centricity towards a disruptive-innovative centricity. This paradigm shift is accomplished by interacting in close alignment and partnership with societal stakeholders. In particular, a DIBS recenters its interests. It creates valuable experiences for its stakeholders (students, businesses, and society in the broadest sense), ensuring its position (Arvanitakis & Hornsby 2016).

Second, such a transformation warrants collaboration with other institutions, creating solutions to global challenges by detecting opportunities early on that trigger innovations and effectively contributing to (inter)national governmental leadership (Collins 2021).

Third, DIBS become forerunners by aligning their stakeholders' interests and corresponding interactions, as highlighted in the conceptual framework in Figure 5.2.

Fourth, this study differs from most country-specific studies by extending the scale from a general national or regional perspective to a multinational or global perspective.

Fifth, by choosing a mix-method approach, this chapter supplements the insights of the literature review by semi-structured interviews with 40 leaders. Finally, this research is very topical by pulse-checking and contrasting the viewpoints of academics (faculty and staff), students, and (start-up) entrepreneurs and avoiding a siloed approach of a study with one particular group exclusively (Krings 2021).

DIBS are expected to provide guidance and leadership development in the post-pandemic world. According to the global risk report, most (84 percent) political, business, and society decision-makers take a pessimistic view of the future (World Economic Forum 2022). Consequently, by expanding the study-relevant themes, that is, constituents are identified and developed that support DIBS to redefine themselves and break new ground compared to their traditional peers that are incapable or unwilling to adapt in a fast-changing world (Duderstadt 2012).

5.3.3   Conceptual Framework and Research Questions

The conceptual model (MacInnis 2011) was created based on the insights from the literature review and the overarching research question: *What are essential constituents for the transformation to a disruptive-innovative business school?*
    With its underlying sub-questions:

RQ1. What are the current and emerging constituents for disruptive-innovative business schools?

RQ2. What suggestions are there to adjust the academic approach, services, alumni support in disruptive-innovative business schools?

The framework answers the research questions and aims at recalibrating, transforming, and strengthening the role of DIBS/universities by providing relevant guidance and leadership to its stakeholders, for example, students, faculty, alumni, businesses (Newman et al. 2010), and society at large (World Economic Forum 2022).

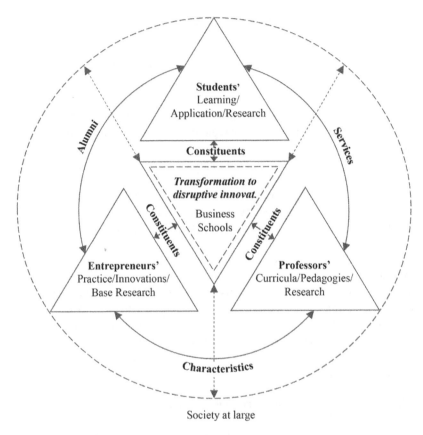

Figure 5.2   Conceptual framework of disruptive-innovative business schools

The conceptual model is the starting point to identify the core themes of creating DIBS. Then, the model is empirically underpinned by the findings of semi-structured interviews with 40 leading entrepreneurs, professors, and students in North America, Europe, and the Asia-Pacific. Thereby, the straight (dotted) lines indicate the (in)direct interactions (transformation), and impact DIBS can make on their stakeholders and society.

5.4 RESEARCH METHODOLOGY

Studies about the current challenges of business schools/universities are conducted primarily qualitatively (Arvanitakis & Hornsby 2016; Bridges 2000; Rana et al. 2020).

5.4.1 Semi-structured Interviews

The data for this research project was gathered during summer 2021. Hence, semi-structured interviews seemed feasible: open-ended questions allowed the participants to express opinions and emotions and probe for action steps concerning a post-pandemic envisioned educational infrastructure. Twelve quantitative statements at a time addressed the questions, 'what *characteristics* should a DIBS have?' 'what *services* should it provide?' and 'how should it support its *alumni*?' (Newman et al. 2010; Rich 2020). Each statement battery applied 7-point Likert scales that were own-developed based on the insights from the literature review to reflect the participants' evaluations (Finstad 2010).

In addition, open questions like 'what were the expectations in a DIBS to distinguish itself from the mass of its peers?', 'what would make it an ideal investment opportunity?' and 'what were the drivers to make the DIBS worthwhile to develop, recommend, or consider for further education?' helped gain richer theme insights. In contrast, some questions probed for past experiences creating barriers to transforming to a DIBS.

Thematic Analysis (TA), an 'inductive method for identifying, analyzing, and reporting patterns within the data' (Braun & Clarke 2006, p. 79), was applied to determine the themes of interest. An independent reviewer supported organizing, categorizing, analyzing, and visualizing the qualitative data of the open-ended questions with Nvivo 12 to ensure intercoder reliability (Kurasaki 2000). Finally, SPSS v28 was applied to evaluate the quantitative part of the primary data.

5.4.2 Participants in the Study

Among the participants were senior decision-makers and faculty of well-established business schools and universities in several regions, gifted students, and successful corporate entrepreneurs and start-ups in the early funding stage. Initially, a minimum of ten interviews per partial sample seemed necessary to ensure theme saturation in thematic analysis (Guest et al. 2012) and accommodate meaningful statistical analyses (Isaac & Michael 1995).

Furthermore, including various perspectives allowed triangulation (Remenyi et al. 2002). The authors conducted 40 interviews with 13 corporate or entrepreneurial leaders, 14 academics with *designations*, that is, Dean, Director, (visiting) Assistant/Associate Professor, and tenured Professor.

The participants were recruited from the primary author's worldwide 17,800 first-degree LinkedIn connections and 300 business/student contacts. The first two groups included experience levels of less than five, five to ten, and more than ten years. In addition, the third group included 13 undergraduate and (post)graduate honor students. Though the study schedule for summer 2021 seemed questionable because of vacation time, a combination of individual email requests and regular status updates on LinkedIn yielded a response rate of .77 (40 of 52) targeted participants.

5.5   DISCUSSION OF THE FINDINGS

The research sparked the interest of the targets, clearly evidenced in the following responses:

- 'Anyway, if *I* can be of assistance to these efforts in a future business school, please let me know. *I* am passionate about this and have always wanted to fix for the generations who come after me,' Funded start-up entrepreneur, Boston, US.
- 'Thanks for sharing this exciting project,' Associate Professor, Reading, UK.
- 'Very comprehensive interview touching on various areas,' Executive MBA student, Tokyo, Japan.

Table 5.1 gives an overview of the socio-demographic background of the participants.

The profile shows a male dominance of 70 percent vs. 30 percent females with an average age of 43.5 years. In addition, four out of five participants belong to either Generation X (42.5 percent) or Y (40.0 percent).

The sample demonstrates diversity from a regional viewpoint, with participants from North America (42.5 percent) followed closely by Western Europe, including the UK (20.0 percent), Germany, Austria, Switzerland (DACH) region (15.0 percent), and Eastern Europe (12.5 percent). The Asia-Pacific region counted for the remaining 10.0 percent.

More than half of the entrepreneurs were start-ups (54.0 percent), followed by small and medium-sized businesses (31.0 percent). Junior and tenured faculty represented 36.0 percent, with a minority of associate professors (28.0 percent). Most students pursued Master of Science or Executive MBA degrees

Table 5.1   *Profile of the participants*

Characteristics of Sample	%	Region	%
Total Sample size (N_{TOT} = 40)	100.0	North America (US, Canada)	42.5
		Western Europe (incl. UK)	20.0
Participants (Subsamples)	%	Germany (D), Austria (A) and	
Entrepreneurs (N_{ENTP} = 13)	32.5	Switzerland (CH) (DACH)	15.0
Professors (N_{PROF} = 14)	35.0	Eastern Europe	12.5
Students (N_{STUD} = 13)	32.5	Asia-Pacific (China, Japan)	10.0
Gender	%	Business Size	%
Male	70.0	Start-ups	54.0
Female	30.0	Small and medium	31.0
		Large	15.0
Generation	%	Faculty Position	%
1946–64 (Baby Boomers)	12.5	Visiting, Assistant Professor	36.0
1965–80 (Generation X)	42.5	Associate Professor	28.0
1981–96 (Generation Y, Millennials)	40.0	Full tenured Professor, President	36.0
1997–2012 (Generation Z)	5.0		
Average Age	Mean	Academic Degree	%
Entrepreneurs	47.7	Undergraduate (BBA, BSc)	31.0
Professors	46.0	Graduate (MBA, MSc)	38.0
Students	36.5	Postgraduate (DBA, Ed.D., PhD.)	31.0

(38.0 percent), while undergraduate and doctoral students were represented in perfect balance (31.0 percent).

5.5.1   Prevalent Themes

First, the discussion addresses the open-ended questions to respond to *RQ1* and *RQ2*. Second, the authors present the following findings on the statement batteries on 'what are the *characteristics* a DIBS should have?' 'what *services* should it provide?' and 'how should it support its *alumni*?' to answer *RQ2*.

Initially, the authors identified 33 themes, with the 11 most prominent ones summarized in Table 5.2. These themes reflect essential aspects and the participants' genuine interest in 'what constituted the DIBS/university?'

Table 5.2   *Eleven constituents of DIBS*

Eleven Constituents of the Future Business School/University	
5. An excellent disruptive-innovative business school is about	aligning the network between students, faculty, and entrepreneurs. Developing human intuition, emphasizing platforms and technology that emulates actual business experience to equip students to be influential players from the get-go. Presents content simple, clear, and understandable, i.e., child-like perspective.
2. A mix of academia and practice	Flexible education, not just brick and mortar. Combination of real-world/business and theoretical education. Career-oriented specialized business education, including professional licenses as optional courses.
3. Funding	The timely supply of funds overcomes a significant barrier for research, studies, and start-ups.
4. Social capital	The strongest currency in the world is the network. It helps to allocate capital in one's network most effectively and work towards shared goals.
5. International collaboration	Transverse skills, e.g., cross-cultural communication and presentation skills, are essential to connect and collaborate, academic exchange, think tank, new technology, and one-on-one mentorship for entrepreneurial ventures.
6. Business school-related problems and challenges	Outdated curricula with a disconnect between academia and real business due to a risk-averse faculty often lacking corporate or entrepreneurial experience while teaching business practice. In addition, students are perceived as 'cash machines,' and the relationship and communication often end at graduation.
7. Internship	Internships, externships, and co-ops should apply and test the academic knowledge in the real world.
8. Suggestions	A shift from testing knowledge and memory to interpreting dynamic data and information. Enrich business curriculum with math, computer science, and information technology courses.
9. School program issues	Lack of addressing the significant challenges that contemporary societies and economies face and adhering to outdated curricula, e.g., the pure profit orientation of businesses. Instead, topics on discovering customers and profits with social and environmental impact should be included.

Eleven Constituents of the Future Business School/University	
10. New generation's challenges	Prepare students for the imminent digitalization and technological revolution with relevant, up-to-date learning content and generate student talent to seize the best entrepreneurial and employment opportunities ahead of time.
11. School and Sustainability	Business schools should become the breeding ground for great business ideas and support their students to realize these. Faculty should build strong connections to enhance collaboration and bear responsibilities in business and society. Finally, higher education should develop leaders with strong ethics who shape their businesses beyond profits.

Therefore, these 11 themes or constituents are central to the discussion about what drives the transformation towards the DIBS?

The concept of 'Social Capital' among the identified themes is not mentioned explicitly in the HE literature though it is implicitly mentioned in various themes such as 'collaboration' and 'alumni.'

A starting point for 'Social Capital' is the resource of social networks, for instance, social ties, mutual trust, and shared values (Lin 2008). Other examples are sharing learning strategies during undergraduate and (post)graduate studies among students, collaborating on research projects among faculties, forming alliances between HEIs, or programs to benefit society (Williams 2017). Finally, social capital is instrumental in leveraging alumni contacts for career progression or funding purposes (*Economist* 2017; Newman et al. 2010).

The boundaries between the themes can be fluid. For instance, theme 6 (problems and challenges) and theme 8 (suggestions) are similar regarding the transition to digital technologies and interdisciplinary curricula, for example, business administration and STEM. Furthermore, the participants expressed that these 11 constituents are essential in designing DIBS that remain viable (Arvanitakis & Hornsby 2016).

5.5.2 Outcome from the Three Statement Batteries

Figures 5.3 to 5.5 show the mean values of the series of 12 statements for each of the three subsamples. Again, the findings indicate significant differences/gaps in the perspectives of entrepreneurs, professors, and students besides some similarities.

For example, while most academics insisted on a high-quality, research-oriented education relying foremost on lecture method (Rana et al. 2020), students and entrepreneurs expressed the need for an application-oriented education characterized by conceptual and design thinking provided by 'pracademic' professors. Contrary to full-tenured research faculty, 'pracademic' professors often have similar academic expertise backed by industry and leadership experiences. They combine lectures with real business case studies and experiential storytelling (Remenyi et al. 2002; Savović 2020).

The identified gaps illustrate entry points or service opportunities that business schools can leverage for their benefit in the transformation process to disruptive-innovative HEIs (Arvanitakis & Hornsby 2016).

5.5.3   Characteristics of Disruptive-Innovative Business Schools

Figure 5.3 shows the main characteristics of DIBS supported by Iniguez (2021).

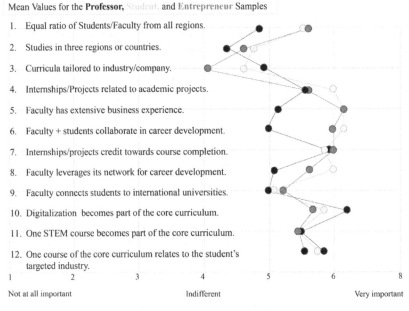

Figure 5.3   *Polarity profile: characteristics of DIBS*

Most participants considered studies in various regions or countries necessary (Statement 2). There are different opinions concerning the industry focus of the curricula (Statements 3 and 12). While professors and students like to tailor the curricula more to a particular industry, entrepreneurs are neutral in this respect.

The answers to the open questions revealed that academics were divided about whether the higher education quality should be compromised for practitioner or social objectives. However, most faculty raised concerns about the inflationary quality of academic education that is student-centered and adjusted to corporate demands.

One professor of an elite European university raised the point that business schools should retain their high educational standards and not compromise. However, business schools are increasingly required to emphasize application- and design-oriented curricula and forms of learning to avoid becoming redundant (Arvanitakis & Hornsby 2016).

Entrepreneurs and professors are unanimous about internships related to academic projects (Statement 4), contrasting with students' perspectives. However, students did feel that faculty should have extensive business experience and collaborate with students in career development (Statements 5 and 6). A DIBS can close these gaps by recruiting a part of their full-time faculty based on academic and professional experiences (Bridges 2000) and developing a sponsorship program where faculty leverage their social capital (Karl 2001) to support their students proactively in career development.

In contrast, professors become trendsetters by viewing digitalization and industry-related courses (Statement 10) as more critical than entrepreneurs, probably because digitalization is still in its infancy. At the same time, all stakeholders agree that STEM has to become part of the core curriculum (Sebhatu et al. 2021).

5.5.4 Services of Disruptive-Innovative Business Schools

Figure 5.4 depicts how the services future business schools should provide are perceived in the three subsamples.

The mean values of the 12 statements suggest incorporating personal development, reflection, and mentorship programs geared to raise the next generations of entrepreneurs or researchers.

Moreover, DIBS should consider mindset coaching to develop students into global citizens and changemakers in their world of work (Bridges 2000; Iniguez 2021). Likewise, case studies relating to real-world issues (Remenyi et al. 2002), including the latest technologies and lecturing methods, enable more adaptable and flexible curricula and learning environments in line with Rana et al. (2020).

5.5.5 Alumni Support of Disruptive-Innovative Business Schools

Alumni networks rankings are essential for business schools (*Economist* 2017). Figure 5.5 illustrates this importance, notably by supporting alumni beyond the widespread homecoming events.

DIBS should redesign their alumni support for career development, job placement, coaching, and mentoring. Especially, 'resilience coaching' is

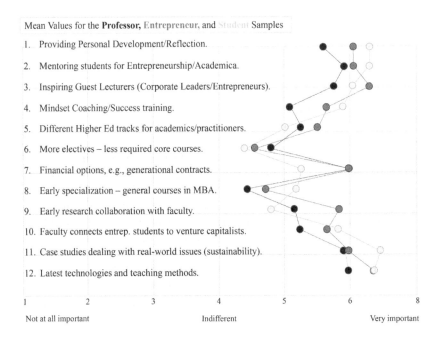

Mean Values for the **Professor,** Entrepreneur, and Student Samples

1. Providing Personal Development/Reflection.
2. Mentoring students for Entrepreneurship/Academica.
3. Inspiring Guest Lecturers (Corporate Leaders/Entrepreneurs).
4. Mindset Coaching/Success training.
5. Different Higher Ed tracks for academics/practitioners.
6. More electives – less required core courses.
7. Financial options, e.g., generational contracts.
8. Early specialization – general courses in MBA.
9. Early research collaboration with faculty.
10. Faculty connects entrep. students to venture capitalists.
11. Case studies dealing with real-world issues (sustainability).
12. Latest technologies and teaching methods.

| 1 | 2 | 3 | 4 | 5 | 6 | 8 |

Not at all important   Indifferent   Very important

Figure 5.4   Polarity profile: services of DIBS

critical to developing 'citizen scholars' to evolve and anticipate innovations, whether in a corporate or entrepreneurial setting (Arvanitakis & Hornsby 2016, p. 16). This has a twofold benefit for both business schools and alumni. On the one hand, students get practical support and do not feel abandoned when they graduate. Nevertheless, on the other hand, they can be earmarked as prospective clients of future services. This alignment of interests creates long-term, mutually beneficial relationships (Krings 2021). For example, providing valuable alumni support before marketing additional professional certificates (Statements 1 and 8) is meaningful in a gig economy typified by multiple career changes. Likewise, entrepreneurs view funding support as essential (Statement 9).

In contrast, faculty and students perceive state-of-the-art business knowledge and design thinking as a critical benefit for society (Statement 12) (Arvanitakis & Hornsby 2016). Moreover, students and entrepreneurs appreciate memberships of business networks/think tanks (Statement 5).

Overall, these findings provide various transformation opportunities to DIBS. In contrast, they also identify conflicts with higher education institutional centricity and associated lack of awareness. If business schools respond

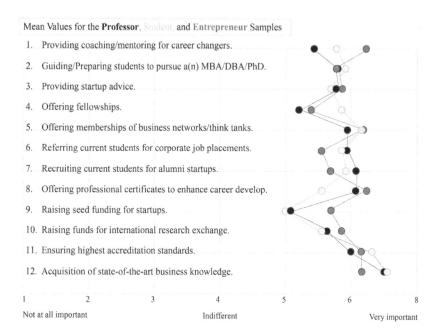

Mean Values for the **Professor**, Student, and Entrepreneur Samples

1. Providing coaching/mentoring for career changers.
2. Guiding/Preparing students to pursue a(n) MBA/DBA/PhD.
3. Providing startup advice.
4. Offering fellowships.
5. Offering memberships of business networks/think tanks.
6. Referring current students for corporate job placements.
7. Recruiting current students for alumni startups.
8. Offering professional certificates to enhance career develop.
9. Raising seed funding for startups.
10. Raising funds for international research exchange.
11. Ensuring highest accreditation standards.
12. Acquisition of state-of-the-art business knowledge.

1　　　　2　　　　3　　　　4　　　　5　　　　6　　　　8

Not at all important　　　　　Indifferent　　　　　Very important

Figure 5.5　　Polarity profile: alumni support of DIBS

to current changes 'as before,' they are sooner or later endangered to become irrelevant (Argyris, 2010).

Consequently, the transformation process to a DIBS can be improved by detecting trends, that is, the gaps where stakeholders are underserved. Then, acting to close these gaps, for instance, by offering the alumni support previously mentioned.

Referring and recruiting current students for corporate or start-up jobs (Statements 6 and 7) in line with Wu et al. (2010) will develop a competitive alumni network and ultimately pay back dividends in charitable giving/ endowments. Though the number of alumni members might be used to brand a business school's reputation, the accurate indicator consists of the quality of alumni support business schools provide (*Economist* 2017).

5.6　　CONCLUSION

DIBS and universities must reflect on their inner structure and transaction processes to better serve their stakeholders' overarching interests. This endeavor includes reviewing and redesigning obsolete processes and isolated curricula to remain relevant and secure funding (Newman et al. 2010). Moreover, it requires creating a 'future-proof' learning and research experience. Faculty must develop their existing and new students into global 'citizen scholars' to create these experiences. Thus, the focus is on 'scholarship and active and engaged citizens' (Arvanitakis & Hornsby 2016, pp. 11–12). Finally, they must connect to practitioners and society by aligning with the millennials' values and being flexible to societal changes. In particular, curricula development should focus on accelerated application and monetization beyond traditional salary orientation. Interdisciplinary content should include STEM, data sciences, and digitalization (Iniguez 2021). In addition, DIBS should lay the groundwork for skills like co-creation, innovations, and entrepreneurship accompanied by holistic leadership development (Vargo & Lusch 2010).

For example, character-building, including emotional intelligence, resilience has to be considered to a greater extent to achieve societal objectives, such as ethics and sustainability (Wu et al. 2010).

Accelerated and flexible curricula and the abbreviation of the overall length of study are achievable by combining academic courses with internships and portfolio building (undergraduate studies) or fast-track management programs and mentorships (graduate studies).

This 'pracademic approach' fosters a higher level of applied learning forms and builds the motivation to start a business during or shortly after graduation. Business schools/universities can rethink their current financial funding situation by initiating 'generation contracts' with students or improving endowments by proactively supporting alumni. In return, alumni commit to coach or mentor current students or give back with parts of their future salaries (My Guide 2021). Existing or new curricula can be revised or co-created with alumni who belong to high-achievers in academia and practice. Faculty can be developed by considering either alumni or outsiders from alliance partners. Overall, it is about creating excellent stakeholder experiences (Krings 2021).

5.6.1   Contributions

This study addressed several gaps in the literature.

First, in contrast to numerous studies focusing primarily on academia, this chapter lays a novel foundation by gathering expert knowledge and opinions from leading (start-up) entrepreneurs, students, and faculty and staff of universities and merging it into one study.

Second, this research widened the scope from general national studies to a multinational project by recruiting participants from several regions.

Third, by applying mixed methodologies, 11 current and merging themes were identified as DIBS constituents impacting the interactions illustrated in the conceptual framework (see Figure 5.2). These constituents addressed our research questions *RQ1* and *RQ2* and were generally supported by a recent study at IE University (Iniguez 2021).

Finally, this research provides practical transformation guidelines based on the 11 constituents identified in the literature, refined and validated by 40 interviews.

Business schools are empowered to:

* undergo a paradigm shift from an institutional-centric to a stakeholder-centric orientation highlighted in the conceptual framework
* become a trendsetter for relevant services by aligning institutional and stakeholder interests illustrated in Figures 5.3 to 5.5
* create excellent stakeholder experiences (SX) by offering meaningful services and support.

5.6.2 Implications

This chapter identified and explored the significant themes that enable DIBS/ universities to alter their course beyond the pandemic in the VUCA world. In addition, the authors identified constituents that enable both globally and regionally leading HEIs to adjust their future approach to the demands of practitioners, students, and faculty, thereby transforming into DIBS. Significant themes include a stronger emphasis on applied learning methods, and social capital to form a virtual and face-to-face network to assume leadership in a dynamic economy and fast-changing society.

The views of successful practitioners, academics, and students in different regions and institutions were aligned to deepen the understanding of tackling the transformation. The focus was to differentiate HEIs to create unique student/faculty/entrepreneur experiences (Newman et al. 2010), becoming preferred partners for collaboration, alliances, or mergers (Williams 2017).

In addition, future quality criteria might be extended to the number of successful start-ups, corporate careers, and societal contributions, for example, meeting specific sustainability objectives by international or global highly ranked business schools (Beynaghi et al. 2016).

5.6.3 Limitations and Future Research

Though the authors reached out to leading experts in their network located in major regions, the time scope did not allow them to gather wider data sets. Consequently, the informative value cannot be generalized to Africa, the Middle East, and Latin America.

Future studies might consider participants in the regions not covered by this research and include technologies, for example, digital platform solutions

(Wirtz et al. 2019), spin-offs of established HEIs, Artificial Intelligence (AI) solutions, to optimize the interconnection between DIBS and their stakeholders. Moreover, the identified 11 constituents should be researched more in-depth. Further research might also optimize processes and overcome siloed functions to accelerate the transition from institutional to stakeholder orientation.

ACKNOWLEDGEMENTS

The authors thank the participants in the semi-structured interviews and the reviewers for their constructive, insightful, and helpful comments that contributed to completing this book chapter.

Special thanks are due to Dr. Tórheðin Jónsveinsson Jensen for supporting the qualitative data analysis with NVivo 12 and Thematic Analysis.

REFERENCES

Accenture 2021, 'Business futures 2021: Signals of change,' accessed August 2021 at https://www.accenture.com/us-en/insights/consulting/business-change.

Argyris, C 2010, *Organizational traps: Leadership, culture, organizational design*, Oxford, Oxford University Press.

Arvanitakis, J and Hornsby, D 2016, 'Are universities redundant?' in J Arvanitakis and DJ Hornsby (eds), *Universities, the citizen scholar and the future of higher education*, New York, Palgrave Macmillan, pp. 7–20.

Astin, AW and Oseguera, L 2004, 'The declining "equity" of American higher education,' *Review of Higher Education*, vol. 27, no. 3, pp. 321–41.

Baumöl, U and Bockshecker, A 2017, 'Evolutionary change of higher education driven by digitalization,' in *Proceedings of the 16th International Conference on Information Technology Based Higher Education and Training (ITHET)*, pp. 1–5.

Bennet, M 2021, 'What Brexit means for Master Degrees, PhDs, and other students,' The FindAPhD Blog, January, accessed April 2021 at https://www.findaphd.com/advice/blog/1863/what-brexit-means-for-masters-degrees-phds-and-other-students.

Beynaghi, A, Trencher, G, Moztarzadeh, F, Mozafari, M, Maknoon, R and Leal Filho W 2016, 'Future sustainability scenarios for universities: Moving beyond the United Nations decade of education for sustainable development,' *Journal of Cleaner Production*, vol. 112, pp. 3646–78.

Bider, I and Jalali, A 2016, 'Agile business process development: Why, how and when – applying Nonaka's theory of knowledge transformation to business process development,' *Information Systems and e-Business Management*, vol. 14, no. 4, pp. 693–731.

Bothwell, E 2018, 'Global boom in private enrollments,' *Times Higher Education*, accessed April 2021 at https://www.insidehighered.com/news/2018/03/08/survey-finds-global-boom-private-higher-education-enrollments.

Braun, V and Clarke, V 2006, 'Using thematic analysis in psychology,' *Qualitative Research in Psychology*, vol. 3, no. 2, pp. 77–101.

Brennan, J and Teichler, U 2008, 'The future of higher education and higher education research,' *Higher Education*, vol. 56, no. 3, pp. 259–64.

Bridges, D 2000, 'Back to the future: The higher education curriculum in the 21st century,' *Cambridge Journal of Education*, vol. 30, no. 1, pp. 37–55.

Brown, S 2013, 'Large-scale innovation and change in UK higher education,' *Research in Learning Technology*, vol. 21, pp. 1–14.

Bryant, M 2013, 'International accreditations as drivers of business school quality improvement,' *Journal of Teaching in International Business*, vol. 24, no. 3–4, pp. 155–67.

Christensen, CM 2013, *The innovator's dilemma: When new technologies cause great firms to fail*, Boston, MA, Harvard Business Review Press.

Clawson, D and Page, M 2010, *The future of higher education*, New York, Routledge.

Collins, C 2021, 'Leadership gems, Ep.3, Dr. Maria Ohisalo, Henley Business School,' accessed September 2021 at https://www.youtube.com/watch?v=lM1EFv7LBsI.

Dover, PA, Manwani, S and Munn D 2018, 'Creating learning solutions for executive education programs,' *International Journal of Management Education*, vol. 16, no. 1, pp. 80–91.

Duderstadt, JJ 2001, 'Preparing for the revolution: The future of the university in the digital age,' in *Proceedings of the Glion III Conference*, pp. 1–16.

Duderstadt, JJ 2012, 'The future of the university: A perspective from the Oort cloud,' *Social Research: An International Quarterly*, vol. 79, no. 3, pp. 579–600.

Economist 2017, 'Alumni networks: Who you know, not what you know? The 15 highest-ranked alumni networks at business schools,' accessed September 2021 at https://www.economist.com/ whichmba/mba-rankings/alumni-network.

European Quality Improvement System (EQUIS) 2021, accessed April 2021 at https://www.efmdglobal.org/accreditations/business-schools/equis/.

F1GMAT 2021, 'Top 100 accredited business schools, only AACSB accreditation for top US business schools,' accessed April 2021 at https://www.f1gmat.com/top-mba-accreditation.

Finstad, K 2010, 'Response interpolation and scale sensitivity: Evidence against 5-point scales,' *Journal of Usability Studies*, vol. 5, no. 3, pp. 104–10.

Godley, A 2021, 'Embracing true internationalisation in business school education,' February 1, Henley Business School, University of Reading, accessed January 2022 at https://www.henley.ac.uk/news/2021/embracing-true-internationalisation-in-business-school-education#.

Gilson, LL and Goldberg, CB 2015, 'Editors' comment: So, what is a conceptual paper?' *Group and Organization Management*, vol. 40, no. 2, pp. 127–30.

Guest, G, MacQueen, KM and Namey, EE 2012, 'Introduction to Applied Thematic Analysis,' *Applied Thematic Analysis*, vol. 3, no. 20, pp. 1–21.

Hui, LQW, Nazir, S, Mengyu Z, Asadullah MA and Khadim, S 2020, 'Organizational identification perceptions and millennials creativity: Testing the mediating role of work engagement and the moderating role work values,' *European Journal of Innovation Management*, vol. 24, no. 5, pp. 1653–78.

Iniguez, S 2021, 'Higher education in 2022: Challenges and trends,' December 18, LinkedIn, accessed January 2022 at https://www.linkedin.com/pulse/higher-education-2022-challenges-trends-santiago-iniguez/.

Isaac, S and Michael, WB 1995, *Handbook in research and evaluation*, 3rd edn, San Diego, CA, Educational and Industrial Testing Services (EDITS).

Karl, KA 2001, *Achieving success through social capital: Tapping the hidden resources in your personal and business networks*, San Francisco, CA, Jossey-Bass.

Krings, W 2021, 'Pedagogical approach: Contribution to developing an innovative business administration program,' Webinar, EM Normandie, March 17, pp. 1–12.

Krings W, Palmer R and Inversini A 2021, 'Industrial marketing management digital media optimization for B2B marketing,' *Industrial Marketing Management*, vol. 93, pp. 174–86.

Kurasaki, KS 2000, 'Intercoder reliability for validating conclusions drawn from open-ended interview data,' *Field Methods*, vol. 12, no. 3, pp. 179–94.

Lin, N 2008, 'A network theory of social capital,' *Handbook of Social Capital*, vol. 50, no. 1, pp. 50–69.

MacInnis, DJ 2011, 'A framework for conceptual contributions in marketing, ' *Journal of Marketing*, vol. 75, no. 4, pp. 136–54.

Mantz, E 2017, 'UNH offers application fee waiver to US Veterans and service members,' *UNH Today*, p. 4995, accessed September 2021 at https://scholars.unh.edu/news/4995.

Mat, N, Noor, N and Mohemad, R 2018, 'Development of collaboration model by integrating information and communication technology (ICT) tools in Higher Education Institutions (HEI),' *International Journal of Information and Education Technology*, vol. 8, no. 11, pp. 798–803.

MBAToday (2020) 'List of triple-accredited business schools (AACSB, EQUIS, AMBA),' accessed July 2021 at https://www.mba.today/guide/triple-accreditation-business-schools.

My Guide 2021, 'Check your entrance qualification and contact universities,' accessed April 2021 at https://www.myguide.de/en/degree-programmes/strategy-organisation/?hec-id=w60785.

Newman, F, Couturier, L and Scurry, J 2010, *The future of higher education: Rhetoric, reality, and the risks of the market*, Hoboken, NJ: John Wiley & Sons.

Peters, M 2007, *Knowledge economy, development and the future of higher education*, Rotterdam, Sense Publishers.

Rana, S, Anand, A, Prashar, S and Haque, MM 2020, 'A perspective on the positioning of Indian business schools post COVID-19 pandemic,' *International Journal of Emerging Markets*, doi: 10.1108/IJOEM-04-2020-0415.

Remenyi, D, Money, A, Price, D and Bannister, F 2002, 'The creation of knowledge through case study research,' *Irish Journal of Management*, vol. 23, no. 2, pp. 1–17.

Rich, M 2020, 'Disruption and the university of the future,' in D Remenyi, KA Grant, and S Singh (eds), *The University of the future: Responding to Covid-19*, Reading, UK, ACIL.

Rodriguez, A and Rodriguez, Y 2015, 'Metaphors for today's leadership: VUCA world, millennial and "Cloud Leaders",' *Journal of Management Development*, vol. 34, no. 7, pp. 854–66.

Savović, S 2020, 'University mergers: New strategies for higher education institutions,' in *Handbook of research on enhancing innovation in Higher Education Institutions*, Hershey, PA: IGI Global, pp. 239–60.

Schlegelmilch, BB 2020, 'Why business schools need radical innovations: Drivers and development trajectories,' *Journal of Marketing Education*, vol. 42, no. 2, pp. 93–107.

Sebhatu, SP, Enquist, B and Edvardsson, B (eds) 2021, *Business transformation for a sustainable future*, Oxon, UK, Routledge.

Sharp, P 2019, 'Knowledge and skills for postgraduate business students of the future,' in D Remenyi, KA Grant and S Singh (eds), *The university of the future: Responding to Covid-19*, Reading, UK, ACIL, pp. 151–64.

Teichler, U 2003, 'The future of higher education and the future of higher education research,' *Tertiary Education & Management*, vol. 9, no. 3, pp.171–85.

QS Top University Ranking 2021, 'Discover the world's top universities. Explore the QS World University Rankings® 2021,' accessed April 2021 at https://www.topuniversities.com/university-rankings/world-university-rankings/2021.

Vargo, SL and Lusch, RF 2010, 'From repeat patronage to value co-creation in service ecosystems: A transcending conceptualization of relationship,' *Journal of Business Market Management*, vol. 4, no. 4, pp. 169–79.

Vedder, R and Colegrove, B 2021, 'Why men are disappearing on campus,' *The Wall Street Journal*, Opinion/Commentary, accessed September 2021 at https://www.wsj.com/articles/gender-inequity-inequality-education-college-university-feminism-family-structure-1163279837.

Williams, J 2017, 'Collaboration, alliance, and merger among higher education institutions,' in *OECD Education Working Paper*, no. 160, Paris, OECD.

Wirtz, J, So, KKF, Mody, MA, Liu, SQ and Chun, HH 2019, 'Platforms in the peer-to-peer sharing economy,' *Journal of Service Management*, vol. 30, no. 4, pp. 452–83.

World Economic Forum 2022, 'The global risks report 2022 17th edition. Executive summary and global risks perception survey 2021–2022 results,' accessed January 2022 at https://www.weforum.org/reports/global-risks-report-2022.

Wu, YCJ, Huang, S, Kuo, L and Wu, WH 2010, 'Management education for sustainability: A web-based content analysis,' *Academy of Management Learning & Education*, vol. 9, no. 3, pp. 520–31.

6. The case for enterprise risk management in business education

Norean R. Sharpe, Nancy A. Hubbard and Paul L. Walker

6.1   INTRODUCTION

As a result of the recent pandemic, critical changes that have been in the background for decades are now at the forefront of educational leadership. Business education is at an inflection point and we are faced with uncertainty, volatility, and risk on multiple levels: How do schools prepare for the future competitive nature of the industry with declining demand and increased centralization at the top-tier programs? How can we use what we have learned from the practice of risk management to educate our students and faculty to increase the relevance of our business curriculum for society? The concepts of enterprise risk management can be used to help business schools identify and manage these questions and challenges.

In nearly all industries – especially in publicly traded companies – an in-depth knowledge and practice of enterprise risk management (ERM) is expected by stakeholders, although implementation of ERM strategies varies across corporations. Even in the US government, each federal agency must adopt an ERM approach (Irving and Walker 2021). Thus, we stipulate that the time has come for higher education, and particularly business schools, to embrace the concepts of ERM. While some universities have hired Chief Risk Officers (CROs), not all universities have done so, and how they are used and integrated into the operation of schools and colleges is inconsistent.

The advantage of ERM is not just in developing strategies to manage risks, it is also in identifying and growing opportunities. To understand current practices and tools for ERM and how these are evolving, the American Productivity & Quality Center (https://www.apqc.org/) recently conducted a global study with Dr. Paul Walker, Director of the Center for Excellence in ERM at St. John's University. The study included a survey with 229 respondents at organizations of all sizes from a diverse range of industries and regions.

The results of the survey indicate that higher education is not alone in lagging behind in the area of ERM; while 37 percent of survey participants said they had defined ERM processes in place, only 25 percent said their ERM process was fully optimized, and approximately 25 percent reported that their ERM program was less than three years old, with a majority reportedly practicing ERM for less than five years (Collins, Vlachos, and Walker 2021). Additionally, less than half of the organizations surveyed employed an executive-level or C-Suite CRO. What the organizations did agree on was the scope of the risks: Strategic, Operational, Financial, Cyber, External, Reputational, and Regulatory. These same risks exist in higher education. This chapter provides a review of recent developments in the discipline of ERM as it applies to higher education and recommendations for both using and teaching ERM at business schools.

6.2   GROWTH OF ENTERPRISE RISK MANAGEMENT

Enterprise risk management is primarily designed to help create, protect, and enhance organizational value and that seems more necessary each year with a world that is volatile and uncertain. Risk management has a history of being linked with the insurance and finance industries but has evolved over the past 50 years to become an instrumental part of strategic leadership for nearly all organizations – both for-profit and not-for-profit.

Professional recognition of the field began when the Insurance Institute of America, founded in 1960, developed a unique series of examinations in 1966 for practitioners to earn the title of Associate in Risk Management (ARM). Growth of the field in the 1970s and 1980s continued to escalate; in 1971, the International Association for the Study of Insurance Economics, commonly known as the Geneva Association, was created and five years later, the American Society of Insurance Management changed its name to the Risk and Insurance Management Society (RIMS), demonstrating the increased focus on the study of risk. In 1986, the Institute for Risk Management was founded in London, eventually leading to qualifying exams to earn Fellow of the Institute of Risk Management. More recently, the International Organization for Standardization (ISO), originally founded to regulate standards for nearly all aspects of manufacturing, began work on guidelines for the practice of risk management in 2005 and published these guidelines in 2009, with revisions issued in 2018 and 2019. These latter publications provide details of strategic integration and assessment techniques used to manage risk. The Committee of Sponsoring Organizations (COSO) updated their published framework for ERM in 2017, and many global organizations reference this framework in their annual reports. Alongside the progress of these professional organizations, there were many academic publications that moved the needle on the application of risk in the disciplines of finance, economics, and data science. For a thorough history of risk management as it relates to all industries, see Kloman and Fraser (2021).

While some researchers see today's primary risks as climate and social, others have documented serious global financial and economic risks. Current business models cannot be effective if they don't foresee and consider risks on a regular basis. Even before COVID-19, many organizational leaders and executives realized that they needed to rethink their approaches to strategic planning. Simultaneously, Wall Street investors were pressuring companies to disrupt themselves or be disrupted. One survey of risk executives in 2018 showed that 88 percent believed risks were growing (Walker 2018), while another 2019 survey (Walker 2019) showed that only 38 percent were confident they had *identified all* of their significant risks.

There is also a growing body of empirical literature examining the value of ERM practices. One paper showed a positive relationship between ERM and firm value (Hoyt and Liebenberg 2011). Another empirical paper explored why ERM adds value and found that part of the answer is that ERM leads to better decision making (Gates, Nicolas, and Walker 2012). Finally, there is also some research on ERM and higher education. One white paper documented a link between negative risk events and reduced applications to the institution with the negative events (Luca, Rooney, and Smith 2016).

In the last several years, the practice and adoption of ERM has been growing around the world. In the public company arena, stock exchanges, such as the NYSE, have already written rules requiring risk management by leadership and board committees. Furthermore, in addition to requiring risk factor disclosure, the Securities Exchange Commission (SEC) has raised the bar for ERM and board risk oversight by making board risk oversight a necessary annual disclosure. Other countries around the world have also begun to mandate versions of ERM including Germany, South Africa, the UK, Singapore, and many others. Some countries have organizations disclose their ERM process and framework, how they are managing their top risks, and even make a declaration that there is no risk that threatens the existent of the organization. Others disclose the role of the board, how they look for emerging risks, and their early warning risk indicators.

How ERM is practiced and where it is focused has also evolved. Early ERM adopters focused on building a process but as organizations get more advanced and as they feel the pressure of increased risk and uncertainty, the efforts tend to become more strategic, focusing on disruption, legacy business models, exogenous risks, risk triggers, culture, and the role of the board. The biggest risk is usually strategic, but this can be more difficult to identify, understand, and manage. The likelihood of disruption is so high that some corporations are beginning to map out new ideas, not based on revenue alone, but also on whether or not they transform the organization. The graph in Figure 6.1 can be used to help organizations think about balancing revenue generation with transformation. Data points can be put in the graph and used to plot new strategies, programs, and initiatives.

Growth and Transformation

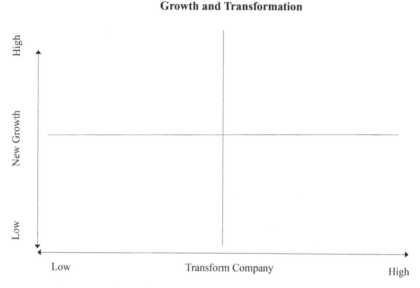

Figure 6.1   Understanding the transformational risk around new ideas

In certain industries, such as banking and insurance, the regulators have added additional ERM requirements. Furthermore, the Department of Justice has included "risk assessment" as part of a properly designed program. Reflecting the seriousness of how regulators view ERM, in 2020 Citicorp received a fine in excess of $400 million for, among other things, "unsound practices with respect to the Bank's enterprise-wide risk management" and "failure to establish an effective risk governance framework" (Benoit 2020). Outside of publicly traded companies, ERM has also spread into areas like the Joint Chief of Staff Manual and into other federal areas. In fact, the Office of Management and Budget circulars now mandate ERM for all federal agencies.

All corporations are experiencing growing external pressure to manage risks. For example, major financial institutions have put considerable pressure on organizations in the area of Environmental, Social, and Governance (ESG)-related risks. Furthermore, a stockholder proposal by Alphabet (Google) investors requested the company conduct a risk assessment of content management. Examples of firms that ignored risks and suffered setbacks include Wells Fargo and Deutsche Bank. As a consequence, there are a growing number of court cases alleging poor risk management and poor risk oversight by leaders and boards. The stakes for organizations are high.

Research on current ERM practices noted that many were building support for their ERM program, where the most common approaches included senior risk communications, formal ERM training, risk reviews with risk owners, risk summits, and embedding ERM champions into the lines of the business (Collins, Vlachos, and Walker 2021). The organizations surveyed identified a variety of methods to analyze risk including brainstorming, formal risk assessments, scenario analysis, probabilistic modeling, and decision trees. Many of the organizations also utilized risk registers, risk scorecards, and risk maps.

The recent pandemic has changed ERM practices for many organizations. Significant efforts have been made in the past year to identify unknown risks, assess risks, and test risk plans. When asked about the benefits of their ERM efforts, the organizations answered that both improved decision making and also risk avoidance were the chief benefits. Better risk awareness was also frequently cited. A full 76 percent stated their ERM program was effective and 82 percent stated their ERM program was driving value (APQC 2021). Of course much work is yet to be done as evidenced by another 58 percent, which stated that a major risk occurred (besides COVID-19) that they had not previously identified. Some of the common expected benefits of a well-designed ERM framework include better decisions, improved performance, improved earnings, fewer surprises, increased resilience, and enhanced long-term success. There is also a growing body of academic empirical research documenting the value of ERM practices.

6.3   NEED FOR ENTERPRISE RISK MANAGEMENT IN HIGHER EDUCATION

All of the increased risk and uncertainty and the increasing set of rules have put considerable pressure on organizations to step up their ERM efforts, including universities. One large university's Board of Regents mandates ERM in its policy manual. A recent study showed that the number of university reputational risk events is growing and that such reputational risks are quite large (Abraham and Walker 2017). Surprisingly, over half stated they might not be able to survive a major reputational risk event. That study also highlighted that one of the top risks going forward is the business model of higher education, specifically, "the viability of sustaining the business model of high tuition, high tuition discount, and diminishing state support weighs heavily on the minds of the leadership of colleges and universities." All of this was with the knowledge of an impending risk – the large demographic shift and subsequent enrollment drop predicted in the US in 2025. And then COVID-19 happened, which accelerated enrollment challenges for smaller institutions and subsequent mergers and acquisitions. The impact of COVID-19 was especially troublesome because of the combination of weak operating models, unsustainable financial models, unembraced digital disruption and change, and university slowness in pivoting to a new reality.

Partly because of the extreme dependency on tuition, the faculty labor market, and volatile student demand, universities are unique organizations. Thus, the standard systems for accountability used by corporations are not easily applied to universities (Birnbaum 1988). However, over the past few decades, institutions of higher education have had to evolve out of necessity to care about compliance and focus on reducing risks to legal claims by both students and employees. Universities have had no choice but to evolve and realize that they are indeed large enterprises, albeit not-for-profit ones (Lundquist 2021). Now, perhaps more than ever, university leaders and those in oversight roles should embrace ERM strategies to manage risk. Educational leadership has been described as having six categories: formal, collegial, political, subjective, ambiguous, and cultural (Bush 2011). Understanding the culture, politics, and vision of a university is critical in implementing appropriate ERM models to effectively reduce risks. This means building a culture of preparing for risk, considering the strategic context environment, understanding assumptions in the strategy, setting objectives, ensuring the strategy matches the environment, and executing on the vision.

The largest risk for universities is nearly always about where and how to compete for students, faculty, and partnerships. Academic leaders and those in oversight roles must understand the value proposition and how current and future students, alumni, and other stakeholders view that value. They must build a competitive business model that delivers on the value promised, not one that is constantly leveraged and leads to constant inefficiencies and big misses on the value. ERM also means identifying the risks, assessing the risks, building responses to manage these risks, and viewing risks from an integrated portfolio approach (or holistic approach). Figure 6.2 shows output from an ERM Summit of business school Deans' attempt at identifying the risk during COVID-19. Tools and approaches like this are one of many new risk tools to help organizations begin the journey in managing risk.

At all universities, new strategies and initiatives should include a risk identification and assessment dimension. Risks in new ventures could consider the ability of the unit to compete in that area, the strategic growth of the area, the competitive advantage they have in that area, etc. New ventures could also identity the top risk drivers of success and build in early warning indicators. Applying ERM requires universities to consider the many dimensions of stra-

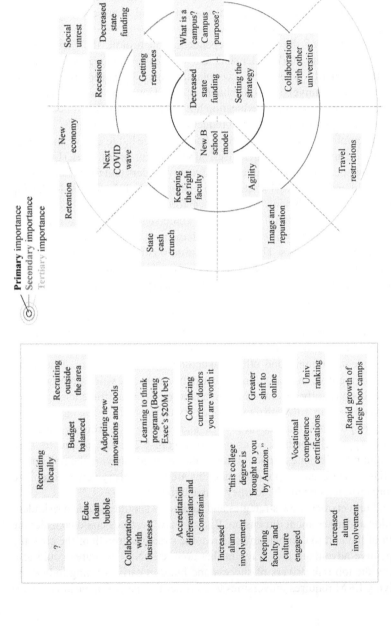

Figure 6.2   Set of risks facing business schools and higher education

tegic risk. Given the change in demographics, discount rates, recruitment regulations, faculty demands, student preferences, and modes of learning, strategic planning is critical to align the organization's vision, goals, and strategies. Finally, there is the risk associated with not executing and implementing the chosen strategy. Any plan will not succeed without the proper financial model, value proposition, risk identification, metrics, and assigned senior leaders.

Large organizations have begun to develop the practice of strategic risk analysis and academia should adopt some of these approaches and tools. Universities should use strategic disruption and black-swan type workshops to help them determine if they have the right strategy, how the world is changing, and what their strategy might be missing. Other approaches include (Walker 2021):

- Emerging risk analysis;
- Operational results analysis;
- Strategic bow-tie analysis;
- Deep risk dive;
- Scenario analysis;
- Game theory;
- Opportunity workshops; and
- Assumptions risk analysis.

Not having an understanding of the changing economy, current challenges, and future risks can be a recipe for failure.

6.4   ROLE OF BOARDS IN RISK MANAGEMENT

When assessing how competently an entity is managed in terms of risk, one often refers to its ultimate decision-making body, the board of directors, or in the case of higher education, the board of trustees. When referring to the US higher education system, this kind of assessment is complicated and variable. There are two-year and four-year colleges and private and public institutions. Publics can be divided further into land grant, top-tier public research universities, military service colleges, and less selective public institutions. Private higher education is even more diverse with highly selective elite institutions, purely undergraduate colleges, others that award graduate degrees, those with religious affiliations, those with discipline affiliations (i.e., liberal arts and engineering/technical colleges), those with enormous endowments, and yet others that are tuition dependent for survival. Considering this heterogeneity, it is not surprising that there is little definitive research in higher education governance in the US. The research that has been conducted is either anecdotal, case study based, or limited to a specific subset, such as land grant universities or those from a certain geography.

Further ambiguity surrounds measuring "success" in higher education – including its governance, effectiveness, and performance especially in terms of risk assessment. Whereas financial performance is objectively determined in for-profit organizations, measurable outcomes for higher education is more nebulous. Enrollment, student success and satisfaction, fundraising, research, and teaching are all used to measure a board of trustee's success despite the board not having a direct and meaningful influence over most of these. One could question which of these constitute the true success of an institution? If one struggles to describe success, how does one measure failure especially in terms of risk assessment?

One generally accepted role of the board of trustees is to oversee the effectiveness of senior management in delivering the agreed organizational objectives – a concept called agency theory. This reduces institutional risk by ensuring senior leadership is competent at their abilities, while the board of trustees' role is to hold them accountable. Having a majority of external board members enhances corporate governance in this capacity, thereby reducing organizational risk. A major flaw in this concept occurs in higher education, however, as the roles and allegiances of board members blur. Very few, if any, higher education board members are truly external. They tend to have some relationship with the institution as donors, alumni, or administrators – in essence, they are all inside board members. Since one rarely hears of the dismissal of senior leadership in higher education due to "poor performance" based on any of these measures, agency theory does not seem applicable in higher education.

Historically, higher education institutions were not supposed to be relevant for society. In fact, they were designed to be detached and rise above the fray, thereby giving more objective commentary on society and its values. This distance was seen as an advantage to ensure their longevity and the academic freedom of faculty. In essence, they served as a buffer between societal pressures and the smooth running of the institution with an almost benevolent and paternalistic perspective. As suggested by Ingram (1997, p. 2), the board of trustees is for all intent, the institution's "legal owner and final authority. It holds the institution's financial, physical, and human assets and operations in trust for future generations. It decides who should benefit from those assets, how, why, and when."

Regardless, some boards of trustees have been criticized for being both overbearing in their meddling and micromanaging, threatening shared governance while alternatively others have been seen to be too lax in their running of institutions, simply rubber stamping the administration's actions. Infighting and bringing partisan politics into the educational sphere adds an additional complexity to public institution boards especially in the current political climate. The gloomy conclusion is that "effective governance by a board is a relatively rare and unnatural act" (Chait, Holland, and Taylor 1996, p. 1). These limitations notwithstanding, conclusions can be drawn from existing research and suggestions made on what constitutes robust governance, thereby enhancing the institution's risk profile.

Public institution boards tend to be homophilous in nature; in land grant universities (which are almost exclusively public), 55 percent of board of trustees members come from industry while another 20 percent are politicians or lawyers (Woodward 2009). Little consideration in these cases is given to the skill set of the appointee and its relevance for the institution at hand. Logically it would follow that board governance suffers because of this and creates greater risk for the institution. Public board selection has come increasingly under scrutiny with decreasing autonomy as the institutions' complexities overlaid with political agendas have dramatically complicated their management. Appointments have become more political in nature in some cases with board seats being given as political favors. One positive byproduct of this is to increase the number of external board members, thereby reducing risk. However, this is countered by increasing budgetary challenges, reactions to shrinking student populations, and public institutional mergers and closures.

European higher education is almost entirely public in nature and can provide some guidance in a more diverse perspective of management. Research from the Netherlands and Portugal highlight the complexities of stakeholder management systems in higher education. In both cases, the respective governments mandated university systems to be modified to bring them in line with the wider stakeholder approach seen in both countries' private and public industries. This includes the extensive use of works councils and advisory groups to assist the boards by ensuring the complexities of major stakeholders' perspectives are communicated. In both countries, institutions were encouraged to create advisory boards of key stakeholder groups. Further, more diverse board memberships were employed representing those groups. Thus, faculty, students, staff including union representation, alumni, administrators as well as local government officials were represented at a board level. This stakeholder approach appears to ensure that the complex network inherent to higher education is considered in establishing long-term objectives and strategy.

A wide variety of initiatives have been suggested to increase performance of public university boards of trustees, and thereby reduce risk. First, and in line with European structures, boards of trustees should develop mechanisms for "trying to balance layers of stakeholder interests with board wisdom" (Kezar 2006, p. 998). If direct representation on the board is not feasible, advisory councils composed of students, faculty, and staff can support this initiative.

This mitigates the inevitable isolation and power distance experienced by boards and thereby reduces risk. Breaking down partisan positions is also seen as key for successful public board management including the breakdown of uncivil behavior. Key to this is a strong agenda with a strategic focus. Extensive financial, strategic, and risk assessment training ensures board members are comfortable with steering the direction of the institution. This is especially relevant when using increasingly diverse groups on a board of trustees. Finally, a clear set of guidelines of expected behavior in difficult or ambiguous situations, as well as enforcement from a strong leader is key to ensure productive behavior.

Private education is no less complicated than public, despite the lack of political appointments. Private institutions are seen to suffer from homophilous board representation due to trustees being replaced with trustees who resemble themselves. Often these trustees are white, male, older alumni donors who have had success in industry; these trustees are sometimes jokingly referred to as "male, pale and stale." While efforts have been made to include a wider net of stakeholder input including women and minorities, representation of these groups is lagging behind at a board level. Not only does this create a less diverse board of trustees, it fails to represent the majority of students in the US higher education system.

The performance of diverse vis-à-vis homophilous boards is surprisingly mixed. On the positive side, homophilous boards are more cohesive, have greater interpersonal communication, exert greater influence on fellow members, and create greater conformity. Yet, this cohesion has been found to decrease effectiveness in governance and raise questions of board legitimacy, especially if the board does not represent the students and faculty of today. Further, some members may feel indebted to their peers for including them and be less likely to voice dissent. All of this can lead to "groupthink" and stifle creativity and innovation as "homophily continues to produce and reinforce dense networks of similar actors" (Perrault 2015, p. 154). In terms of risk management, a board seeped in groupthink is likely to ignore impending challenges to address them innovatively.

Boards can create diversity through a variety of means – including stakeholders of differing gender, race/ethnicity, age, socioeconomic background, and education. The majority of research has found that increases in board diversity engenders a more creative and innovative board presumably due to the variety of perspectives and life experiences held by the membership. They are more engaged in increased vetting of ideas and actions of other board members. More conflict creates more debate especially when examining new or innovative ideas. Diverse groups hold different perspectives that generate different questions; research has found this is particularly true in gender-based differences (Joo 2003). Intangible benefits of heterogeneous board membership include having visible role models for students, greater legitimacy on the entity by being more representative of the student body, and greater trust of decisions taken. These findings, while generally accepted, are not by any means conclusive; however, it is seen that the good created by heterogeneous board governance outweighs the good created by that of homophilous boards. This in turn, enhances board performance and reduces risk of poor decision making due to groupthink.

Many of the actions taken to enhance the performance of public boards of trustees also applies to private institutions. While the political overlay is less apparent, private institutions hold a complex array of stakeholders that should feel they have a voice in the institution's strategy and future. Student, faculty, and staff representation on the board of trustees goes far in ensuring those perspectives are heard. They are effective only with adequate training to ensure those stakeholders can participate fully in situational assessment and decision making. If that is not possible, advisory councils or boards, much like the European stakeholder model, encourage input. Finally, a clear set of expectations of those involved, the development of agreed ethical guidelines, and strong internal leadership to ensure behavioral compliance all facilitate a more diverse decision-making body and, therefore, a more robust consideration of outcomes.

The *2020 Survey of Board Professionals*, a follow-up to a study conducted in 2015, by the Association of Governing Boards of Universities and Colleges (AGB) and United Educators, investigated the reporting relationships, compensation, and years of experience for governing boards. The survey included 228 board professionals from public (34 percent), private/ independent (48 percent), and for-profit (8.5 percent) institutions (9.5 percent were from institutional-related foundations). Study results indicate that board professionals today are being asked to do even more than in the past five years as universities face greater challenges. Some of their findings include (AGB 2021):

- 65 percent were recruited to their position from within the institution;
- 85 percent had other responsibilities within the institution; and
- 55 percent reported an increase in the level of responsibility for the role of board members.

The respondents were most interested in learning more about benchmarking, dashboards, board orientation, managing the board, and board recruitment, retention, and development. Many of those who replied noted that the recent pandemic impacted their workload and increased their board responsibilities. Among the increased responsibilities were greater input on shared governance and guidance on governance matters. Other areas of increase were an increase in scrutiny by the campus community, media, and the public, as well as an increase in demands to report to state and federal organizations on compliance issues.

Given the enhanced need for governing boards to be involved in compliance and risk management matters, we hope that more universities will hire CROs and that more universities will provide enhanced risk management training for all board members. Board risk oversight is especially important and is considered part of the major ERM frameworks that are used by organizations. As noted previously, board risk oversight is also a required SEC disclosure for public companies.

6.5   IMPORTANCE OF TEACHING RISK MANAGEMENT

Increased risk and uncertainty have implications for the academic curriculum at business schools. Deans and other academic leaders can lead by collaborating with faculty to incorporate this type of risk acumen into their curriculum and by working with other academic units at their university. Schools should update their curricular content and materials to incorporate risk management. It is critical to review, revise, and revitalize what is taught at our business schools on a regular basis in both undergraduate and graduate programs to stay current to educate future business leaders of our global workforce.

To assist business schools in preparing for the hybrid campus of the future, managing changes in student demand, and increasing the societal value and impact of a business education, we argue that all schools should both teach the discipline of ERM to their students and hire an ERM executive. The ERM faculty and/or administrator would be responsible for:

- Identifying risks on a periodic basis;
- Managing risks centrally and proactively;
- Using ERM and analytical tools, such as scenario analysis and simulation models;
- Updating the models based on external and internal changes;
- Understanding the costs/benefits of decisions and actions; and
- Communicating the management of risks to the Dean and other leaders.

Many ERM strategies can be applied to understanding recruitment and enrollment models; redistributing financial and physical resources; closing shrinking degree programs and launching new programs; closing satellite campuses; preparing students for an ever-changing workforce; redefining the student experience; and adjusting to a hybrid campus.

At St. John's University, the Tobin College of Business has offered a bachelors and masters degree Risk Management and Insurance since 2001 and a masters degree in Enterprise Risk Management since 2010. These degrees include courses that cover building ERM, identifying risk (i.e., reputational, medical, environmental, and financial), assessing risk, changing the culture, building risk oversight, incorporating uncertainty into decisions, building models with value propositions, and analyzing strategic risk. If the world is rapidly changing, then talent agility must also be taught. We all should be teaching our students to think critically, creatively, and entrepreneurially to embrace risk and change. Business school graduates should be educated to join a workforce that will fully expect them to understand risks and enterprise risk management.

The International Insurance Society (IIS) has identified Global Centers of Insurance Excellence (GCIE) using clearly stated criteria. The university must offer a program or track in insurance, be an AACSB or EQUIS accredited school, and have a curriculum that teaches four distinct areas of risk management and insurance. The program must have at least ten graduates a year over the last four years, provide strong employment results following graduation, and connect to industry partners using an advisory board, campus speakers, career center, internships, or other avenues. For detailed criteria, see www .internationalinsurance.org. Their identified Global Centers of Insurance Excellence are listed in Table 6.1.

Table 6.1   *Global Centers of Insurance Excellence listed alphabetically (2021)*

Appalachian State University	University of Alabama
Ball State University	University of Barcelona
California State University – Fullerton	University of Calgary
City University of London – Cass Business School	Universite Catholique De Louvain
	University of Central Arkansas
Drake University	University of Colorado – Denver
Florida State University	University of Georgia – Terry College of Business
Georgia State University	University of Hamburg
Illinois State University – College of Business	University of Iowa
Ku Leuven	Universite de Lausanne
Lingnan University	University of Mississippi
Munich Risk and Insurance Center	University of North Texas
Peking University	University of South Carolina – Darla Moore School of Business
St. John's University – Tobin College of Business	University of St. Gallen
Sungkyunkwan University	University of Wisconsin – Madison
Temple University – Fox School of Business	University of the Witwatersrand
Tsinghua SEM	Virginia Commonwealth University – School of Business

Given the increase in volatility and risk in higher education, it is clear that universities and business schools have a responsibility to not only provide expertise in risk management to their senior leadership, but to also educate their students in managing, assessing, and modeling risk.

BIBLIOGRAPHY

Abraham, J. and Walker, P. 2017. 'ERM and reputational risk: More talk than action,' https://www.stjohns.edu/sites/default/files/uploads/ERM%20and%20Reputational%20Risk%20White%20Paper.pdf

APQC. 2021. *Evolving Practices in Enterprise Risk Management.*

Association of Governing Boards of Universities and Colleges and United Educators. 2021. *The AGB 2020 Survey of Board Professionals.* Washington, DC: AGB.

Bear, S., Rahman, N., and Post, C. 2010. 'The impact of board diversity and gender composition on corporate social responsibility and firm reputation', *Journal of Business Ethics*, vol. 97, pp. 207–21.

Benoit, D. 2020. 'Regulators fine Citigroup $400 million over "serious ongoing deficiencies,"' *Wall Street Journal*, October 7.

Birnbaum, R. 1988. *How Colleges Work: The Cybernetics of Academic Organization and Leadership.* San Francisco, CA: Jossey-Bass.

Bush, T. 2011. *Theories of Educational Leadership and Management*, 4th edn. London: Sage.

Chait, R., Holland, T., and Taylor, B. 1996. *The Effective Board of Trustees: Improving the Performance of Governing Boards.* New York: American Council on Education and Macmillan.

Collins, R., Vlachos, N., and Walker, P. 2021. 'Enterprise risk management: How to make it a priority', May 25, cfo.com/risk-management/2021/05/enterprise-risk-management-how-to-make-it-a-priority/

Gates, S., Nicolas, J-L., and Walker, P. 2012. 'Enterprise risk management: A process for enhanced management and improved performance,' *Management Accounting Quarterly*, Spring, vol. 13, no. 3, pp. 28–38.

Hoyt, R. and Liebenberg, A. 2011. 'The value of enterprise risk management,' *Journal of Risk and Insurance*, vol. 788, no. 4, pp. 795–822.

Hubbard, N. and Purcell, J. 2001. 'Managing employee expectations during acquisitions', *Human Resource Management Journal*, vol. 11, no. 2, pp. 17–33.

Ingram, R.T. 1997. *Trustee Responsibilities: A Guide for Governing Boards of Public institutions.* Washington, DC: Association of Governing Boards of Universities and Colleges.

Irving, J. and Walker, P. 2021. 'Applying enterprise risk management principles to the U.S. government,' *The CPA Journal*, April/May.

Joo, T. 2003. 'A trip through the maze of "corporate democracy": Shareholder voice and management composition', *St. John's Law Review*, vol. 77, pp. 735–67.

Kang, H., Cheng, M., and Gray, S. 2007. 'Corporate governance and board composition: Diversity and independence of Australian boards', *Corporate Governance: An International Review*, vol. 15, no. 2, pp. 194–207.

Kezar, A. 2006. 'Rethinking public higher education governing boards performance: Results of a national study of governing boards in the United States', *Journal of Higher Education*, vol. 77, no. 6, pp. 968–1008.

Kloman, H. and Fraser, J. 2021. 'A brief history of risk management,' in *Enterprise Risk Management: Today's Leading Research and Best Practices for Tomorrow's Executives*, 2nd edn, edited by J. Fraser, R. Quailm, and B.J. Simkins. Hoboken, NJ: John Wiley & Sons, pp. 23–36.

Luca, M., Rooney, P., and Smith, J. 2016. 'The impact of campus scandals on college applications.' Working paper 16-137. Harvard Business School.

Lundquist, A. 2021. 'Lessons from the Academy: ERM implementation in the university setting,' in *Enterprise Risk Management: Today's Leading Research and Best Practices for Tomorrow's Executives*, 2nd edn, edited by J. Fraser, R. Quailm, and B.J. Simkins. Hoboken, NJ: John Wiley & Sons, pp. 807–40.

Maassen, P. 2000. 'The changing roles of stakeholders in Dutch university governance,' *European Journal of Education*, vol. 35, no. 4, pp. 449–64.

Magalhães, A. and Amaral, A. 2000. 'Portuguese higher education and the imaginary friend: The stakeholders' role in institutional governance,' *European Journal of Education*, vol. 35, no. 4, pp. 439–48.

Perrault, E. 2015. 'Why does board gender diversity matter and how do we get there? The role of shareholder activism in deinstitutionalizing old boys' networks,' *Journal of Business Ethics*, vol. 128, no. 1, pp. 149–65.

Walker, P. 2018. 'The ERM Journey.' Center for Excellence in ERM White Paper Series.

Walker, P. 2019. 'Digital disruption and transformation risks.' Center for Excellence in ERM White Paper Series.

Walker, P. 2021. 'Incorporating risk acumen and enterprise risk management into innovation approaches,' in *Enterprise Risk Management: Today's Leading Research and Best Practices for Tomorrow's Executives*, 2nd edn, edited by J. Fraser, R. Quailm, and B.J. Simkins. Hoboken, NJ: John Wiley & Sons.

Woodward, A. 2009. 'Land-grant university governance: An analysis of board composition and corporate interlocks,' *Agriculture and Human Values*, vol. 26, pp. 121–31.

PART II

Possible future of business schools within the context of the sustainable development challenge

7. Shaping the new normal: business schools as an enabler for promoting a sustainable world – the example of CBS International Business School, Germany and IEDC Bled School of Management, Slovenia

Elisabeth Fröhlich, Anja Karlshaus and Danica Purg

7.1 INTRODUCTION

The current pandemic has clearly shown that economic behaviour must change. Responsible leaders accept the fact that our affluent society and extensive consumption have contributed to this human catastrophe. Only a shift away from traditional business models can lead to a solution to solve several environmental and social problems. Adam Smith's (2018) 'invisible hand' theory offers some interesting insights into tackling this required change, in that it stands for the best possible distribution of resources and thus for the highest achievable level of prosperity in a society. What has been largely overlooked in the practical implementation of the concept is the fact that it is based on the theory of 'moral sentiments'. Thus, it only works in an economic environment characterised by 'sympathy' and 'empathy'. Since this 'moral context' is not present in either our economy or society, governments are expected to intervene to prevent market malfunctions. Consequently, businesses must take on the task of shaping a clear vision of the future world in which we all wish to live. Business schools, in this context, have been given the responsibility to educate the responsible leaders required to do so.

In this respect, CBS International Business School and IEDC-Bled School of Management are highly committed to the six PRME principles (Principles of Responsible Management Education) – purpose, value, method, research, partnership and dialogue (Fröhlich 2022) – representing a United

Nations-supported initiative founded in 2007. As a platform to raise the profile of sustainability in schools around the world, PRME equips today's business students with the understanding and ability to deliver change tomorrow (PRME 2021b). In this chapter, the two principles 'method' and 'research' are addressed referring to introducing research-based innovative educational formats (MBA Artful Leadership and the SDG Teaching Map), to create a 'dialogue' between practice and academia.

However, our current economic model is still focused on efficiency and needs to be changed. Following this line of thought, managers have attempted, for example, to decrease the use of finite resources, to minimise negative ecological effects (EPEA 2021). However, this mires economic behaviour in the 'old days', prevents innovation and will never lead to creative and new ways of replacing harmful materials or stopping human rights violations throughout global supply chains. Effectiveness in the context of sustainable business, on the other hand, focuses on the positive impacts of business on the environment and society, in line with Fullerton's (2015) 'holistic worldview'. Companies evolve into value-adding businesses through problem-solving and are enabled through innovation to create qualitative improvements that benefit our society and the environment. Responsible managers should no longer find answers to the question as to whether they are 'doing things right' (efficiency), but whether they are 'doing the right things' (effectiveness). Effective management can only work 'responsibly' in today's world: 'to not be responsible is not to be effective as a leader' (Waldman & Galvin 2008, p. 327). The described shift leads to an innovative, sustainable business model and is in line with Hallinger and Suriyankietkaews's (2018) view that responsible leaders need to focus on long-term outcomes based on regenerative business models, rather than continuing to pay homage to short-term profits.

In this chapter, learning methods that can help to address the world's current sustainability challenges will be discussed, innovative pedagogical-didactical approaches introduced, and two best practice examples highlighted. The authors intend to inspire in terms of how business schools may contribute directly to the achievement of the Sustainable Development Goals (SDGs) via an 'SDG Teaching Map' training approach, as well as indirectly via an 'Artful Leadership' education programme. The two best practices featured herein offer international insights from CBS International Business School (Germany) and IEDC-Bled School of management (Slovenia). Both universities have many years of experience in the field of responsible management education, as well as a personal, deep and authentic connection to the topic of sustainability.

7.2   RESPONSIBLE MANAGEMENT EDUCATION

In this section, the definitional foundations of the central Sustainable Leadership concept are elaborated, and a compact overview of innovative teaching formats for responsible management education is presented.

7.2.1   Clarification of Terms: 'Sustainable Leadership'

The implementation of a sustainable management strategy requires leaders who live and breathe sustainable values and promote sustainable practices (Metcalf & Benn 2013). In this context, the differentiation between and discussion on the suitability of existing, established and related leadership concepts – such as transformational, charismatic, authentic, participative, servant, shared, artful or ethical leadership – has given rise to the call for a separate leadership model, namely 'Sustainable Leadership' (Shriberg & MacDonald 2013), as current leadership concepts do not fully represent the relevant features and characteristics of sustainable leaders.

Twenty years ago, Andy Hargreaves and Dean Fink founded and defined Sustainable Leadership by setting out a framework of seven principles (Hargreaves & Fink 2003):

1.   Sustainable leadership creates and preserves sustainable learning.
2.   Sustainable leadership secures success over time.
3.   Sustainable leadership sustains the leadership of others.
4.   Sustainable leadership addresses issues of social justice.
5.   Sustainable leadership develops rather than depletes human and material resources.
6.   Sustainable leadership develops environmental diversity and capacity.
7.   Sustainable leadership undertakes activist engagement with the environment.

Although research on the subject is still in its infancy (Burawat 2019), it has already been determined through discussions on the role and responsibility of leaders that they need to solve current societal, environmental and economic challenges such as climate change, pandemics, economic scandals, (societal) inequalities, etc. (Pless & Maak 2011). Sustainable leaders thus promote sustainability values at the individual, organisational and societal levels (Iqbal et al. 2020; Peterlin et al. 2015).

Definitions of 'Responsible Leadership' accordingly encompass issues of 'responsibility', including accountability, appropriate moral decision-making and trust. In other words, the definition of Responsible Leadership is based on a conceptualisation of 'responsible' that is adapted to the leadership context

(Pless & Maak 2011). However, this is not just about semantic variations in the term 'responsibility' – Sustainable Leadership is to be understood as a relational and an ethical construct that describes the responsibility of leaders 'towards others'. As Responsible Leadership focuses on the concerns of others, a definitional specification of who the 'others' are, and what it means to address their concerns, seems necessary (Maak & Pless 2006a).

Sustainable Leadership is sometimes defined primarily (only) in terms of the 'leader-employee relationship' and is characterised in this context by practices such as valuing and developing employees, as well as creating employee-friendly work environments and relationships that consider individual life stages and needs (Avery & Bergsteiner 2011). Other recent definitions, however, focus more broadly on improving the quality of life for all stakeholders (McCann & Holt 2010), that is, not only employees, but also customers, suppliers, shareholders, society, etc. The concept of leadership thus changes from a one-dimensional 'manager-employee' level to a multi-dimensional 'manager-stakeholder' approach (Maak & Pless 2006b), although the goal of improving well-being by respecting social values does not change (Peterlin et al., 2015). According to this view, sustainable leaders strive to focus more on long-term results and sustainable changes rather than on short-term wins (Hallinger & Suriyankietkaew 2018).

Thus, Sustainable Leadership attributes include a sustainable mindset, multi-level systems thinking, stakeholder inclusion, disruptive innovation and long-term activation (United Nations Global Compact 2020). Managers need to understand that businesses cannot be developed separately from the social and environmental contexts in which they operate, and that a holistic view is accordingly essential. They need to identify at what point strategic changes can be made and what needs to be abandoned to generate sustainable success (Davies 2007). They also need to think and act beyond their own organisational system and include and involve stakeholders from inside and outside of their businesses. This increasing complexity also requires sustainable managers to actively drive innovations and find novel solutions to meet these new leadership challenges.

7.2.2   Innovative Teaching Formats for Responsible Management Education

Prof. Dr. Anja Karlshaus – What has formed and inspired me?

Born and raised in rural northern Germany, I had the privilege of a carefree childhood. While my father was a manager in a medium-sized company, my mother worked as a kindergarten teacher. Common to both of them – and a central value of our upbringing – was (and still is) their love for people. My parents had about 25 children in short-term care, held various honorary posts, and even after their retirement, they are still involved in their community.

During my school years at a private former missionary school, where we as students were encouraged to take responsibility for ourselves and others through voluntary projects both within and beyond the curriculum. The positive view of humanity and its associated self-conception was thereby reinforced in a much more global context. This deep-rooted focus on people has certainly shaped and guided my career and research choices and inspired me to pass on corresponding ideas in study and training programmes. As a mother of four children, I am particularly concerned with making the business world a little bit more humane and sustainable, which all starts with the transmission of a respective mindset to those who have – or will have – decision-making power. Being now a professor of human resources management and dean of sustainable management, I am intensively engaged with the question of how sustainability can be conveyed in the best possible way, and therefore enjoy experimenting with new and innovative teaching formats. As a scientist, human being, and mother, I am aware that imparting knowledge requires not only technical and didactic skills – but also authenticity and example. This applies to individuals as well as to business schools.

Sustainability education requires more than cognitive understanding (see Prof. Dr. Anja Karlshaus – What has formed and inspired me?). It needs, according to Shrivastava (2010, p. 443), alternative teaching methods and pedagogical approaches that incorporate physical and emotional engagement and connect head, heart and hand: 'Behavior change requires, among other factors, emotional engagement and passionate commitment. Education for sustainability needs to seriously contend with this basic human fact. Cognitive understanding alone is not sufficient; managers and students need holistic, physical and emotional engagement with sustainability issues.' However, such pedagogical approaches are still rare in management education, although the need to integrate such topics into business school practice has long existed (Starik et al. 2010). For the most part, curricula and teaching methods in business schools focus on teaching topics that directly influence the knowledge and skills needed in a business context. Artistic, creative or teaching methods already directly relating to application possibilities in the course of the study programme are almost non-existent (Molderez & Ceulemans 2019).

Following the seven principles of Sustainable Leadership set out by Hargreaves and Fink (2003), and the demand for a multi-dimensional 'manager-stakeholder' approach (Maak & Pless 2006b), several consequences for training approaches appear. Sustainability education, for example, is about conveying a mindset, where the depth of learning and achieving real success are more desirable outcomes than the superficial testing of performance.

Furthermore, it is about conveying a mindset that promotes discussions about purposes, creative ideas and initiatives – rather than about self-presentation skills or ego references of future managers. And finally, any sustainability education involves training a mindset that embraces diversity and includes a wide variety of perspectives. Such 'normalisation' helps contextualise the issues and signal their importance (Dunfee & Robertson 1988). Integrating sustainability, responsibility and ethics into sustainability education is both important and timely (Rasche & Gilbert 2017). Ideally, such a training concept requires cross-functional learning, network opportunities inside and outside of the university and inspiration from disciplines other than just business. Awareness of the interconnectedness of systems, the increasing complexity in our world and the not one-dimensional or easy-to-solve problems of our time must be addressed. Thus, Shrivastava (2010, p. 443) demands clearly that learning about sustainability requires 'a holistic learning experience'. Furthermore, it is important to note that sustainability education and training can only take place via authentic formats and within authentic environments, in which case the 'hidden curricula' and values practiced at the university must also be strongly considered in this subject area. The hidden curricula and mindsets of lecturers need to match the formal curriculum in responsible management education (Høgdal et al. 2019; Rasche & Gilbert 2017).

Experts agree that competencies such as 'systemic thinking' are of great importance in understanding current societal challenges and being able to shape a more sustainable world. However, as one of the most important sustainability competencies, 'systemic thinking' is also the most difficult skill for students to acquire (Mingers 2015) since traditional teaching formats and methods have reached their limits in this respect.

Alternative teaching methods such as project-based learning, voluntary engagement and service learning, multi-perspective and interdisciplinary thinking approaches and work experience learning are very effective in acquiring relevant sustainability skills (Molderez & Fonseca 2018; Scarff Seatter & Ceulemans 2017). Furthermore, several publications and initial empirical research can be found on innovative approaches to the current status quo of management education on contemporary social and environmental challenges (Clack & Ellison 2018; Rimanoczy et al. 2017), as well as on non-conventional learning methods regarding SDG training (Filho 2021). Moreover, theoretical books and papers that address experimental learning concepts for responsible management education or critical thinking approaches towards a sustainable development education have been published (Hope et al. 2020; Moosmayer et al. 2020; Storey 2020). Furthermore, in addition to these application and experiential learning concepts, the incorporation of digital or blended learning approaches into sustainability education is also being increasingly discussed and implemented (Montiel et al. 2019) – triggered particularly by the circumstances surrounding the pandemic. Non-traditional ways of teaching, such as using creative and artistic concepts, are in contrast rarely found in research and management education (Molderez & Ceulemans 2019; Shrivastava 2010).

7.3   APPLICATION OF INNOVATIVE TEACHING FORMATS TO ADDRESS SUSTAINABILITY CHALLENGES

Due to the numerous political efforts, it can be assumed that the legal sustainability requirements will become more stringent in the future. First and foremost, the 2030 Agenda is a global sustainability strategy that was adopted without restriction by the international community at a United Nations summit in 2015. The 2030 Agenda applies to all countries of the world and contains 17 so-called 'Sustainable Development Goals' to solve the most urgent social, ecological and economic challenges to establish a sustainable and just world (Müller & Siakala 2020). More attention is being paid to politically sensitive issues such as human rights, civil society, democracy, transparency, the role of the media, cyber security, political and economic ethics, etc.

The sustainable challenges in this chapter are defined by the still existing problems in achieving the SDGs. Companies are struggling with numerous shortcomings in attaining the SDGs. However, time should not be wasted in discussing the supposedly insurmountable challenges, but rather consider what will happen if the defined targets of the 2030 Agenda are not met. SDG 15 (see SDG Teaching Map) is used as an example to explain the sustainable challenges that arise if the defined sub-targets are not achieved by 2030. Failing to protect biodiversity would lead to species extinction. Deforestation and erosion would affect the lives of millions of people, as they would lose essential services of well-being and soil productivity. Biodiversity conservation is essential for climate regulation to avoid further worsening of extreme weather situations (Filho et al. 2020).

As all these challenges have an impact on the educational formats, this chapter presents two completely different approaches on how to anchor responsible management education in business schools. The CBS International Business School's approach is to consistently implement the SDGs in its teaching and study programs, an example of which is the SDG Teaching Map. The IEDC-Bled School of Management, on the other hand, enriches its Master programmes by including the innovative element Artful Leadership, referring to the personal leadership journey of its president. Responsible leaders are enabled to reflect on their leadership style in terms of necessary ecological and social changes, thus helping them to adapt to new requirements.

7.3.1   Arts in Management Education at IEDC-Bled School of Management

Prof. Dr. Danica Purg – What has formed and inspired me?

I am a child of the post-war period, born in Yugoslavia, in what is now the Republic of Slovenia. I became as innately aware of the importance of, and differences between, ugliness and beauty. It was my good fortune to have been born into a family that fought against the 'the ugly', i.e., the sources of World War II. Family members devoted their lives to meaningfully creating a more beautiful world for all of us, our communities, and societies. It started with my father, who was active as a blacksmith and a workers' representative in the company, building the family home and still having time to perform in theatrical performances in the broader village. My mother crafted the most delicious cakes for weddings and sewed dresses for the village children. They understood the meaning of these actions, in that they made the lives of others better. We were steeped in the works of our local artists. Almost daily we sang enchanting Slovenian melodies, sketched local settings, and recited the poetry of our land, from the national poet France Prešeren (1800–1849) to the young activist and expressionist Srečko Kosovel (1904–1926). I believe that this inspirational environment and the experience of the highly motivated educators in the schools I attended gave me the courage to establish IEDC and to practise management education differently than 'traditional' – particularly Western – models. That difference involved bringing the arts – whether paintings, plays or musical performances – to our participants, in order to offer the possibility to be inspired by beauty and thereby dwell in meaning (Purg & Sutherland 2017).

7.3.1.1 IEDC-Bled School of Management and its vision

From its inception, IEDC has incorporated cultural, artistic and aesthetic elements in its degrees and other programmes. In a certain sense, this can be considered a disruptive approach to management and leadership development. Why does this happen just at IEDC? One explanation is that IEDC has been a disruptive innovation in and of itself. Founded in the former Yugoslavia, it was a management school in a socio-political environment where one was prohibited from using the term 'management'. Back then, even in official documents, such language was considered technocratic, a way of manipulating people, something in direct opposition to the 'self-management' philosophy and of daily practice. Management was considered a threat to the power of workers (Purg & Walravens 2015). Another – and perhaps even stronger – explanation lies in the history, curiosity and drive of the founder of the school (see Prof. Danica Purg – What has formed and inspired me?). When Prof. Dr.

Danica Purg began the journey to found a new management school 35 years ago (Slovenia has existed for 30 years, IEDC for 35), she sensed the importance of providing participants with artistic experiences as a way to foreground meaning, cultivating beauty as a way of judging the meaning of managerial practice. She wanted to develop pedagogical practices in which, through arts, participants would be confronted with both beauty and ugliness, so they would consciously know how they felt (Purg & Sutherland 2017).

This view on management education has also been increasingly supported by the belief that education dominated by functional knowledge alone cannot prepare contemporary managers and business leaders for the challenges they face in an increasingly complex world. This belief exists every day at IEDC. Described as 'a creative environment for creative leadership', its faculty boasts professionals not only from finance, accounting and marketing, but also from the arts, social sciences and humanities. Its architecture is designed to inspire, and the large collection of original art that adorns its campus deepens participants' thinking and reflection (Purg & Walravens 2015).

This vision has been shared by many scholars in the last decennia. Woodward and Funk (2010) state that in a complex and sometimes chaotic environment, traditional forms of leadership and management development do not offer the tools or the mindset to cope with them; in fact, they can form obstacles, as they do not cultivate holistic, socially responsible views on the world. The challenge is therefore to reimagine these complex realities and to re-envision how to approach them. Edgar Schein (2013) advises consultants to trust their own 'artistic impulse' in deciding what kind of intervention can be made in a human system since there are always more data than one can absorb. Moreover, there will be always surprises, and there will never be enough predictability to determine a 'correct' course of action (Sutherland 2011).

7.3.1.2 Leadership redefined: Artful Leadership
The notion behind Artful Leadership developed in the middle of the 1990s (Tschirhart 1996). It can be considered one of the last results of searching and analysing the phenomena of leadership, the leadership mindset and leadership style, as well as a response to what kind of leadership is demanded today and in the coming decennia. Michael Jones (2006) states in his book *Artful Leadership: Awakening the Commons of Imagination* that leaders will need to develop a capacity for experiencing and understanding a new and more subtle intelligence, a way of knowing that is not a separate function but rather the source of an imaginative response to the world. As a kind of sense organ, this intelligence reaches out and makes tentative contact with wholeness, that is, things of another order than we can see directly, making visible what is hidden to begin to draw into awareness, which cannot yet be heard or seen. Artful Leadership is about imagination, creativity, using one's senses and driving on

Table 7.1   *Art and Leadership at IEDC*

Examples of some specific courses	Learning goals	Comments from learners
Personal development and Art and Leadership through active learning/ painting (provider: a professional artist/ PhD in leadership culture)	Enhancing team-building and interpersonal skills To foster creative thinking and innovative decision-making	It helped me to see how we show up in different contexts and how it impacts our process. Really insightful. Very interesting way of teaching about our identity, creativity, motivation, everything presented through art. I have finally realised things that go wrong in my team. I felt, but I didn't really understand.
Arts and Leadership course using films (provider: a film director/expert in leadership studies)	To be aware of different leadership styles and to reflect on their own style Challenging our own assumptions about life, management and leadership Focusing on the ethical and moral issues of management and leadership	Thank you for showing us the brutal truth of the world and more of who we really are. We could see ourselves in the mirror. It made me more critical. Excellent lecture about seeing life and business through different perspectives. It may be the most useful knowledge in my future career.

Source: Purg and Walravens (2015).

intuition. It also goes beyond easy, pragmatic, short-term and short-sighted solutions by opting to search in any circumstance for the 'most beautiful' way to respond to challenges. It is about leadership that is characterised by transparency, open and trustful relations with stakeholders, social responsibility and sustainability. The Arts and Leadership programme at IEDC aims at developing Artful Leadership amongst managers and business leaders.

7.3.1.3   Arts and Leadership in practice

Arts and Leadership start with certain premises. IEDC's buildings, for instance, are works of art. The open spaces, large terraces, broad windows, and the use of glass make the interior an invigorating space where the beauty of Bled's natural environment also folds into the classroom. Walking into the school, if you did not know where you were, you might think it is an art gallery. IEDC has now stood in Bled for more than 20 years and boasts a permanent collection of more than 200 paintings and sculptures (Mljac & Stepancic 2013).

Even more important than creating a beautiful, inspiring environment has been the integration of Arts in the educational programmes at IEDC. Art generates emotions in the spectator, which are necessary to promote a change towards sustainability. Moreover, it forces us to reflect critically and challenges our comfort zone. Art can also help us to understand better the inter-connections between and interdependencies of social and ecological systems. This gift of artists to make people think critically should also find its way into management education. Pushing boundaries is essential to changing future managers' attitudes towards an innovative topic like sustainability (Ceulemans 2021). Table 7.1 shows examples of selected Artful Leadership courses, their learning goals and comments from learners. The examples show how the programme helps to reflect on leaders' identity, to discover the importance of creativity and motivation, to understand the impact of context and a holistic view, to realise the purpose of leadership and the moral and ethical implications of decisions.

Besides specific courses, educators in functional topics also use metaphors of Art in their lectures, not only because of the vision of the school, but also as a way of becoming aware of the impact of using Art to understand the materials on offer.

7.3.2   The SDG Teaching Map at CBS International Business School

Prof. Dr. Elisabeth Fröhlich – What has formed and inspired me?

Born in the south of Austria, nature and freedom have always played a big role in my life. In addition to its numerous sports weeks, the Austrian school system also includes a visit to Vienna under the title 'The Austrian provinces get to know their capital city.' During one such week, we visited the United Nations Headquarters in Vienna, and I had the great honour of listening to a speech by Kurt Waldheim, the former UN Secretary General. I was so fascinated by this speech that my desire to work for the UN never completely vanished. After my studies in business administration, both doctorate and post-doctorate, I discovered my passion for the functional area of procurement and global supply chains – the part of any company that will have to make a significant contribution to solving our environmental and social challenges. Danica Purg, one of the co-authors of this chapter, appointed me to the Interim Management Board of the UN Global Compact Initiative PRME (Principles for Responsible Management Education) and thus brought me much closer to my childhood dream. During this time, I was able to get to know Mette Morsing, the current PRME Secretariat. She appointed me to the newly founded PRME board. Since then, I have also had the great honour of chairing the Nomination and Governance Committee and actively shaping the work in PRME. This path was made possible by my position as president of the CBS International Business School. For over 10 years, we have believed in the power of a business school to shape a sustainable future for all of us. Together with our students and col-

leagues, we work tirelessly to make responsible management education a little better every day.

7.3.2.1 CBS International Business School and its vision

CBS International Business School (CBS), formerly Cologne Business School, is a state-recognised university of applied sciences with its headquarters in Cologne and various branches throughout Germany. CBS was founded in 1993 and offers degree programmes in all areas: Bachelor, Master, MBA and joint PhD programmes. In recent years, the school has made a name for itself in the field of responsible management education (CBS 2021a). As a PRME signatory, the university is strongly committed to this movement for responsible management education. The president of the CBS is a member of the PRME Board, chairman of the PRME Governance and Nomination Committee and chairman of the PRME DACH Chapter (PRME 2021a). Inspired by her commitment and her interest in the work of the United Nations since her youth, CBS was one of the first business schools to introduce a so-called 'integrated sustainability' curriculum (Kolb et al. 2017, see Prof. Dr. Elisabeth Fröhlich – What has formed and inspired me?). The university offers its students international, future-oriented study programmes with a strong focus on practical business experience. In addition, personal skills are promoted to prepare them for the demands of international companies that need responsible leaders to meet the environmental and social challenges of our time. In response to this evolution of the university, and as part of its rebranding process, CBS has chosen a new slogan, 'Creating Tomorrow', which has led to a new vision as a next step: 'We want to empower, inspire and encourage people to live the lives they want and to actively and responsibly shape change in the world as part of the community' (CBS 2021b). To realise this CBS vision, the economy must be rethought.

7.3.2.2 The SDG Teaching Map: an attempt to meet the ecological and social challenges in management education

As explained above, responsible leaders must create a future business model that supports the sustainable development of both the environment and society. To achieve this challenging objective, the 'Sustainable Development Goals (SDG) Teaching Map' (Fröhlich & Kul 2020) was developed at CBS to fulfil the most important fields of action defined by the United Nations, the so-called 17 SDGs.

> The 2030 Agenda for Sustainable Development, adopted by all United Nations Member States in 2015, provides a shared blueprint for peace and prosperity for people and the planet, now and into the future. At its heart are the 17 Sustainable Development Goals (SDGs), which are an urgent call for action by all countries

– developed and developing – in a global partnership. They recognise that ending poverty and other deprivations must go hand-in-hand with strategies that improve health and education, reduce inequality and spur economic growth – all while tackling climate change and working to preserve our oceans and forests. (United Nations 2021)

To specify Sustainable Leadership in the context of the SDGs, the SDG Teaching Map was implemented, building on the preliminary work of Kolb, Fröhlich and Schmidpeter (2017). The SDG Teaching Map is based on the sustainability performance model, which discusses the relevant dimensions that enable managers to implement requisite sustainable strategies and measures. In the next step, the curricula of all English-taught programmes at CBS were analysed. Based on this evaluation, it was possible to determine which sub-targets of the 17 SDGs were covered by corresponding teaching content and in which courses this content could be found (Fröhlich & Kul 2020). This made it possible to first define the gap with each individual SDG. Some SDGs, such as 8, 10 or 12, are almost completely addressed, while others, such as SDGs 3, 5 or 11, are not yet covered in the CBS curriculum (Fröhlich et al. 2021). In a final step, three specific questions were asked as part of a focus group design: (a) What contents of the 17 sub-targets of the SDGs that have not been covered so far could be incorporated into the curriculum of a business school? (b) How could this content be integrated (e.g., by creating a new lecture or integrating it into existing lectures)? (c) What contents of the sub-targets of the 17 SDGs cannot be represented by a business school (Fröhlich & Kul 2020)?

In the further course of this section, a concrete example will be used to show how a previously identified gap was closed by using an innovative teaching method, illustrated by the example of the '21-Day Challenge' (Fröhlich et al. 2021). This innovative teaching format was developed within the Erasmus+ project ISSUE (2021) and will be briefly discussed in the following paragraph.

7.3.2.3 Innovative teaching formats to tackle responsible management education: the 21-Day Challenge

The 21-Day Challenge is based on collaborative online learning. Different tasks ('challenges') must be completed related to the 17 SDGs. After solving each challenge, the participants receive points, which they can then share in their learning community. Each SDG is represented by three components. First, a short video introduces the respective topic (SDGs 1–17) and provides the necessary knowledge to solve the problems associated with each goal. The second part contains the tasks that need to be worked on. Through discussion and the joint exchange of experiences, the students receive the necessary feedback to solve the challenge. Besides pure task completion, the student also receives points for offering solutions and interactions such as comments, postings or uploads on the provided platform. This is essential to promote exchange and discussion among each other, to raise understanding and awareness of ecological and social challenges relevant to responsible leaders. The 21-Day Challenge offers several possibilities for integration into university teaching. It could be part of a regular lecture using a 'learning diary' in which the participants reflect on what they have learned. Campus challenges with rewards could also be initiated, whereby not only students, but also university staff can participate. A concept draft helps lecturers and students navigate through the game (Fröhlich et al. 2021).

As mentioned before, so far, no lecture has addressed any of the sub-targets of SDG 15, which covers the protection, restoration and promotion of the sustainable use of terrestrial ecosystems: '60% of the world's ecosystem services have been degraded over the past 50 years ... Estimates indicate that 2–5 trillion USD ecosystem services are lost each year from deforestation alone' (SDG Compass 2021). Key business topics such as deforestation and forest degradation, mountain ecosystems and natural habit degradation – to name but a few – are not part of a business school's curriculum – which is where the 21-Day Challenge comes into play, as SDG 15 is indeed included in the field of environmental engineering. In a very informative and concise video entitled 'Save Ecosystems and Biodiversity', business students are introduced to the devastating effects of not halting the destruction of our ecosystems. It also highlights the role of business in addressing some of the most pressing challenges. The idea behind this innovative teaching method is illustrated by two concrete challenges. The first task, 'banish pesticides', asks students to find out how to avoid the use of pesticides in a small individual urban gardening project. Through the consistent search for helpful information, it becomes clear that one's own purchasing behaviour can also encourage companies to rethink. The same applies to the task 'recycled is good'. Students are asked to buy only recyclable products or products made from recycled materials. Here, too, the students are made aware of the challenges companies face, as products made from recycled materials are often perceived as inferior in the market. All of these insights have been taken from this recently invented teaching format as part of the ISSUE project, which will be made available for other universities soon.

While playing this game, students acquire a basic knowledge of all SDGs and understand the fundamental link to economics. The next step to be taken at CBS is to offer an elective course that deals with the in-depth knowledge of environmental science and addresses possible impacts, to help make more sustainable decisions in companies. Thus, questions (a) and (b) raised earlier can be answered. By working on each of the identified gaps in the SDG Teaching Map, CBS will find out in the long run which gaps cannot be closed. And this is where collaborations gain importance. CBS will try to offer lectures from technical universities or hire colleagues who are experts in the field of environmental engineering. In summary, the SDG Teaching Map not only offers the potential to identify these 'content gaps', but it also supports the integration of courses from other disciplines and the use of innovative teaching formats.

7.4 CONCLUSION

In summary, this chapter explains why the future of a business school can only be a sustainable one. Responsible management education is becoming the central task of every business school, because only responsible leaders can initiate the necessary changes to successfully implement resilient business strategies in today's complex and volatile environment.

In this context, it is obvious that traditional teaching formats are reaching their limits. Thus, insights are provided herein in terms of how to educate responsible leaders for a sustainable future by using the two examples of IEDC-Bled School of Management and CBS International Business School, two leading universities in the field of educating responsible leaders.

Coming back to the previously discussed seven principles of Sustainable Leadership (Hargreaves & Fink 2003), the Artful Leadership approach provided by IEDC covers the first three principles. In the search for management and leadership development, which prepares for coping with the complexities of the 21st century, new elements have been added to the educational concept and its methods. The hypothesis is that new leadership can be defined by the same characteristics as Art: inspiration, imagination, intuition, authenticity and skills. The aim is therefore to offer a tool that enables managers and business leaders to reflect deeper on their leadership mindset and style. Furthermore, IEDC is convinced that Arts can still contribute much more to this initiative. This 'inspiring' approach encourages other leaders to follow this vision and ensures success over time, thereby creating and maintaining sustainable learning.

The SDG Teaching Map, on the other hand, offers a broader approach to responsible management education. The innovative 21-Day Challenge teaching method opens up a range of concrete actions that can be considered within a sustainable management framework. Thus, the CBS example helps address principles 4 to 7 of Hargreaves and Fink's (2003) 'Sustainable Leadership' concept. Issues of social justice, the development of human and material resources and ecological diversity and capacity are tackled in the 21-Day Challenge, and concrete measures are devised in a playful way while their feasibility is interrogated. Finally, sustainable leaders are educated to commit themselves to active engagement in the environment.

The authors are aware that the presented sustainability training formats also have their limitations and weaknesses. The quality of sustainability education cannot be determined by a vision, content or curriculum alone – it also depends on the mindset, enthusiasm and didactic competence of the instructors. Thus, teachers need to be involved in the development of training measures and must be comprehensively trained themselves. The opportunities to experiment with content and practical implementation are just as important for the learners as early networking possibilities among the student peer-group and with stakeholders outside the university. In addition, it is important to note that no training measure can ever be final; all training interventions must be evaluated on an ongoing basis. In this regard, tools and impact measures for controlling the effectiveness of the specific sustainability teaching concepts could be optimised. The authors are currently working primarily with quantitative and qualitative student evaluations, which are collected directly at the end of the training session. Long-term behavioural changes, however, cannot be recorded in this way.

Nevertheless, it can be stated in conclusion that the need for appropriate holistic teaching approaches is more urgent than ever – and not just since the Covid-19 crisis, which has strongly reinforced our conviction in sustainability and vividly highlighted the interconnected and interdependent nature of the world's social, ecological and economic systems (Mousa 2021). Both universities are more than willing to travel down this route.

REFERENCES

Avery, GC and Bergsteiner, H 2011, 'Sustainable leadership practices for enhancing business resilience and performance', *Strategy & Leadership*, vol. 39, no. 3, pp, 5–15, DOI:10.1108/10878571111128766.

Burawat, P 2019, 'The relationships among transformational leadership, sustainable leadership, lean manufacturing and sustainability performance in Thai SMEs manufacturing industry', *International Journal of Quality & Reliability Management*, vol. 36, no. 6, pp. 1014–36, DOI:10.1108/IJQRM-09-2017-0178.

CBS 2021a, 'About CBS International Business School', viewed 29 October 2021, https://www.cbs.de/en/about-us/.

CBS 2021b, Neue Hochschulmarke: 'CBS International Business School erfolgreich gestartet', viewed 29 October 2021, https://www.cbs.de/blog/cbs-international -business-school-erfolgreich-gestartet.

Ceulemans, K 2021, 'Using art to foster sustainability thinking in management education', viewed 13 November 2021, https://www.tbsearch.fr/en/using-art-to-foster -sustainability-thinking-in-management-education/.

Clack, L and Ellison, R 2018, 'Innovative approaches to management education', *Journal of Management Policies and Practices*, vol. 6, no. 1, pp. 6–9, DOI:10 .15640/jmpp.v6n1a2.

Davies, B 2007, 'Developing sustainable leadership', *Management in Education*, vol. 21, no. 3, pp. 4–9, DOI:10.1177/0892020607079984.

Dunfee, TW and Robertson, DC 1988, 'Integrating ethics into the business school curriculum', *Journal of Business Ethics*, vol. 7, pp. 847–59.

EPEA 2021, 'Cradle to cradle', viewed 29 October 2021, https://epea.com/ueber-uns/cradle-to-cradle.

Filho, WL 2021, 'Non-conventional learning on sustainable development: Achieving the SDGs', *Environmental Sciences Europe*, vol. 33, no. 97, n.p., DOI: 10.1186/s12302-021-00525-8.

Filho, WL, Wolf, F, Lange Salvia, A, Beynaghi, A, Shulla, K, Kovaleva, M and Vasconcelos, CRP 2020, 'Heading towards an unsustainable world: Some of the implications of not achieving the SDGs', *Discover Sustainability*, n.p., DOI: https://doi.org/10.1007/s43621-020-00002-x.

Fröhlich, E 2022, 'PRME Chapter DACH (Germany, Austria, Switzerland) – striving for positive change – continuous support of the PRME principles', *Responsible Management Education* (ed. PRME), pp. 120–35.

Fröhlich, E and Kul, B 2020, 'The necessity of sustainability in management education', *CSR/Sustainability in Management Education*, JFBS Annals no. 9, Chikura Publishing, Tokyo, pp. 20–32.

Fröhlich, E, Schmitz, M and Damme, S 2021, 'The "Sustainable Development Goals (SDG) Teaching Map" and other innovative teaching formats', in W Filoh, U Azeiteiro, L Brandli, A Lange Salvia and R Pretorius (eds), *Universities, Sustainability and Society: Supporting the Implementation of the Sustainable Development Goals*, Springer Verlag, Cham, pp. 483–500.

Fullerton, J 2015, 'Regenerative capitalism', viewed 29 October 2021, http://www.CapitalInstitute.org/Regenerative-Capitalism.

Hallinger, P and Suriyankietkaew, S 2018, 'Science mapping of the knowledge base on sustainable leadership, 1990–2018', *Sustainability*, vol. 12, no. 10, Article 4846, DOI:10.3390/su10124846.

Hargreaves, A and Fink, D 2003, 'The Seven Principles of Sustainable Leadership', *Educational Leadership*, December.

Høgdal, C, Rasche, A, Schoeneborn, D and Scotti, L 2019, 'Exploring the hidden curriculum in responsible management education', *Academy of Management Proceedings*, DOI: 10.5465/AMBPP.2019.127.

Hope, A, Croney, P and Myers, J 2020, 'Experiential learning for responsible management education', in DC Moosmayer, O Laasch, C Parkes and KG Brown (eds), *The SAGE Handbook of Responsible Management Learning and Education*, Sage, London, pp. 265–79.

Iqbal, Q, Ahmad, NH, Nasim, A and Khan, SAR 2020, 'A moderated-mediation analysis of psychological empowerment: Sustainable leadership and sustainable performance', *Journal of Cleaner Production*, vol. 262, DOI:10.1016/j.jclepro.2020.121429.

ISSUE 2021, 'Developing education tools based on principles and goals of sustainable development', viewed 29 October 2021, http://www.issue-project.eu.

Jones, M 2006, *Artful Leadership: Awakening the Commons of the Imagination*, Trafford Publishing, Bloomington, IN.

Kolb, M, Fröhlich, L and Schmidpeter, R 2017, 'Implementing sustainability as a new normal: Responsible management education – from a private business school's perspective', *International Journal of Management Education*, vol. 15, pp. 280–292, DOI:10.1016/j.ijme.2017.03.009.

Maak, T and Pless, NM 2006a, Responsible leadership in a stakeholder society – a relational perspective', *Journal of Business Ethics*, vol. 66, pp. 99–115, DOI:10.1007/s10551-006-9047-z.

Maak, T and Pless, NM 2006b, *Responsible Leadership*, Routledge, London/New York.

McCann, JT and Holt, RA 2010, 'Servant and sustainable leadership: An analysis in the manufacturing environment', *International Journal of Management Practice*, vol. 4, no. 2, pp. 134–48, DOI:10.1504/IJMP.2010.033691.

Metcalf, L and Benn, S 2013, 'Leadership for sustainability: An evolution of leadership ability', *Journal of Business Ethics*, vol. 112, no. 3, pp. 369–84, DOI:10.1007/s10551-012-1278-6.

Mingers, J 2015, 'Helping business schools engage with real problems: The contribution of critical realism and systems thinking', *European Journal of Operational Research*, vol. 242, no. 1, pp. 316–31, DOI:10.1016/j.ejor.2014.10.058.

Mljac, M and Stepancic, L 2013, '"A collection of three grace", IEDC – a creative environment for creative leadership', IEDC-Bled School of Management, Kranj, Slovenia, pp. 23–31.

Molderez, I and Ceulemans, K 2019, 'The power of art to foster systems thinking, one of the key competencies of education for sustainable development', *Journal of Cleaner Production*, vol. 186, pp. 758–70, DOI:10.1016/j.jclepro.2018.03.120.

Molderez, I and Fonseca, E 2018, 'The efficacy of real-world experiences and service learning for fostering competences for sustainable development in higher education', *Journal of Cleaner Production*, vol. 172, pp. 4397–410, DOI:10.1016/j.jclepro.2017.04.062.

Montiel, I, Delgado-Ceballos, J, Ortiz-de-Mandojana, N and Antolin-Lopez, R 2019, 'Innovation through developing a total enterprise computer simulation: Teaching responsible decision making', *Journal of Business Ethics*, vol. 161, pp. 243–51, DOI: 10.1177%2F1052562920987591.

Moosmayer, DC, Laasch, O, Parkes, C and Brown, KG 2020, *The SAGE Handbook of Responsible Management Learning and Education*, Sage, London.

Mousa, M 2021, 'Responsible management education (RME) post COVID-19: What must change in public business schools?', *Journal of Management Development*, vol. 40, no. 2, pp. 105–20, DOI: 10.1108/JMD-10-2020-0316.

Müller, M and Siakala, S 2020, *Nachhaltiges Lieferkettenmanagement* [Sustainable Supply Chain Management], De Gruyter, Berlin.

Peterlin, J, Pearse, NJ and Dimovski, V 2015, 'Strategic decision making for organizational sustainability: The implications of servant leadership and sustainable leadership approaches', *Economic & Business Review*, vol. 17, no. 3, pp. 273–90, DOI:10.15458/85451.4.

Pless, NM and Maak, T 2011, 'Responsible Leadership: Pathways to the future', in NM Pless and T Maak (eds), *Responsible Leadership*, Springer, Dordrecht, DOI:10.1007/978-94-007-3995-6_2.

PRME 2021a, 'PRME Board Committees & Sub-Committees', viewed 29 October 2021, https://www.unprme.org/prme-board.

PRME 2021b, 'What is PRME?', viewed 13 November 2021, https://www.unprme.org/about.

Purg, D and Sutherland, I 2017, 'Why art in management education? Questioning meaning', *Academy of Management Review*, vol. 42, no. 2, pp. 382–96, DOI: 10.5465/amr.2016.0047.

Purg, D and Walravens, A 2015, 'Arts and Leadership: Vision and practice at the IEDC-Bled School of Management', *Journal of Leadership Studies*, vol. 9, no. 1, pp. 42–7, DOI: 10.1002/jls.21355.

Rasche, A and Gilbert, DU 2017, 'Decoupling responsible management education – why business schools may not walk their talk', *Academy of Management Proceedings*, DOI:10.5465/ambpp.2014.13321.

Rimanoczy, I, Heaton, DP, Baskin, R, Hart, S, LeClair, D, Muff, K, Negri, A and North, J 2017, 'Purpose in action: Paradigm shift in management education for a better world', *Academy of Management Proceedings*, no. 1, n.p., DOI:0.5465/ambpp.2016.17664symposium.

Scarff Seatter, C and Ceulemans, K 2017, 'Teaching sustainability in higher education: Pedagogical styles that make a difference', *Canadian Journal of Higher Education*, vol. 47, no. 2, pp. 47–70, DOI:10.47678/cjhe.v47i2.186284.

Schein, E 2013, 'The role of art and the artist', *Organizational Aesthetics*, vol. 2, no. 1.

SDG Compass 2021, 'The guide for business action on the SDGs', viewed 29 October 2021, http://www.sdg.compass.org.

Shriberg, M and MacDonald, L 2013, 'Sustainability leadership programs: Emerging goals, methods & best practices', *Journal of Sustainability Education*, vol. 5, no. 1, pp. 1–21.

Shrivastava, P 2010, 'Pedagogy of passion for sustainability', *Academy of Management Learning and Education*, vol. 9, no. 3, pp. 44355.

Smith, A 2018, *The Theory of Moral Sentiments*, Digireads, Stilwell.

Starik, M, Rands, G, Marcus, AA and Clark, TS 2010, 'From the guest editors: In search of sustainability in management education', *Academy of Management Learning & Education*, vol. 9, pp. 377–83, DOI:10.5465/AMLE.2010.53791821.

Storey, M 2020, 'Critical responsible management education for sustainable development', in DC Moosmayer, O Laasch, C Parkes and KG Brown (eds), *The SAGE Handbook of Responsible Management Learning and Education*, Sage, London, pp. 110–25.

Sutherland, I 2011, 'Business as unusual: Arts-based learning and practise', The Vision and the Voices of IEDC-Bled School of Management, pp. 190–7.

Tschirhart, M 1996, *Artful Leadership: Managing Stakeholder Problems in Nonprofit Arts Organizations*, Indiana University Press, Bloomington, IN.

United Nations 2021, 'THE 17 GOALS', viewed 29 October 2021, https://sdgs.un.org/goals.

United Nations Global Compact 2020, 'Leadership for the Decade of Action', viewed 29 October 2021, https://www.unglobalcompact.org/library/5745.

Waldman, DA and Galvin, BM 2008, 'Alternative perspectives of responsible leadership', *Organizational Dynamics*, vol. 37, pp. 327–41, DOI:10.1016/j.orgdyn.2008.07.001.

Woodward, J and Funk, C 2010, 'Developing the artist-leader', *Leadership*, vol. 6, no. 3, pp. 295–309, DOI:10.1177/1742715010368768.

8. Healing a hurt generation with humane entrepreneurship and creativity

Ayman El Tarabishy and Rosangela Feola

8.1 INTRODUCTION

Millennials – also known as generation Y – are the newest members of the global workforce, and they have become the largest workforce generation worldwide (Fry 2015). This generational cohort encompasses those born between 1980 and 2000 (Howe & Strauss 2007). In addition, millennials distinguish themselves from earlier generations in several aspects, including their relationship with technology, educational background, and attitudes toward careers and organizations (The Council of Economic Advisers 2015).

However, this generation represents the unluckiest generation in the world (Van Dam 2020). Unlike preceding generations, millennials – whose namesake comes from growing up in the pre-millennium period – grew up during an era of rapid change, characterized by growing economic inequality, ballooning debt, and ever-insecure job prospects (Kurz et al. 2018).

Further, because of the financial crisis during the Great Recession of 2008 and the COVID-19 pandemic crisis in 2020, the average millennial has experienced slower economic growth than any previous generation. As shown by a recent analysis (Rinz 2019), millennials are most severely damaged by these current crises. They will likely bear economic scars from these events throughout their lives regarding lower earnings, less wealth, and delayed personal milestones. In addition, the unique context in which this generation has grown up has shaped their outlook on the world and way of interacting with others. These factors are the source of some of the challenges millennials face in establishing their relationships with firms and the workplace.

Despite their generational setbacks, many studies show that millennials are the most talented, energized, and creative because of their proactive personalities (Hui et al. 2021) and open-mindedness (Gong et al. 2018; Mackey & Sisodia 2012). Howe and Straus (2007) demonstrated that millennials are self-confident and optimistic, team-oriented, focused on achievement and doing their best, and driven to achieve higher continually. Similar research found that this generation is prouder and more assertive than other genera-tions (Twenge & Campbell 2001) and maintains a higher locus of control (Trzesniewski & Donnellan 2010). These common characteristics indicate the generation's potential to assume innovative behaviors and promote innovation (Corgnet et al. 2016; Howe & Strauss 2007).

Furthermore, millennials are known for rejecting individualistic needs in favor of more community-based needs (Hanks et al. 2008). Howe and Strauss (2000) argue that one of the main goals of the millennial generation is to improve and protect the environment for the benefit of future generations (Espinoza et al. 2010; Timm 2014).

Their overall sensibility toward social and environmental issues, coupled with their innovation and community-oriented mindsets (Howe & Strauss 2000; Hui et al. 2021), has received increasing attention from researchers and practitioners as critical traits to leverage future economic and social devel-opment. In addition, as millennials enter the workforce in more significant numbers, firms must find a way to capitalize on this generation's positive traits and channel their creativity and values into producing innovative ideas, services, and products for organizational and societal development (Hui et al. 2021).

Researchers have begun to investigate factors that promote creativity and innovation (Tan et al. 2019; Zhang & Zhou 2019) to assess organizational factors that could motivate millennials to reach their potential. Key ele-ments include transformational leadership, ethical leadership, teamwork, and employee empowerment and engagement (Tan et al., 2019; Younas et al. 2018). One of the essential factors is organizational identification, defined as employees' willingness to associate themselves as part of their organization (Aghaz & Hashemi 2014; Hui et al. 2021; Zappalà et al. 2019). Studies on organizational factors highlight the necessity for both firms and managers to adapt their strategies and management style to be more in line with the needs and values of millennial workers to stimulate them effectively.

In this context, the key questions are: (a) what changes are required to organizations and firms, and (b) what kind of organizations are best equipped to capture the potential of millennial people?

The emerging model of Humane Entrepreneurship (HumEnt, Kim et al. 2018; Parente et al. 2018, 2020) could represent the missing link between firms and millennials. The HumEnt model maintains that firms need to inte-grate the traditional orientation toward business and profit (well expressed with the concept of Entrepreneurial Orientation, Covin & Slevin 1989) with two additional elements. These two other elements are attention toward Humane Resources involved in the firm – expressed as Humane Orientation, or HO (Kim et al. 2018) – and attention to the environment and the society in which the firm operates – described as Sustainable Orientation, or SO (Parente et al. 2018, 2020).

By adding Human Resource Management (HRM) to leadership and entrepreneurship, the theory and practice of HumEnt put forth the idea that organizations can initiate an entirely human-centered organizational approach that uplifts millennials, along with all other employees, in new ways. In doing so, firms can activate the potential of their millennial employees, producing positive effects for both the individual and the organization.

From this premise, the chapter aims to analyze how the emerging model of HumEnt could create the necessary conditions to harness the potential of the millennial generation, therefore increasing the innovation and competitiveness of their companies and the wellness of society more broadly.

8.2   MILLENNIAL GENERATION IN THE WORKFORCE CONTEXT

Millennials have attracted attention in the last few years from a practical and research point of view, given their essential role in the current workforce context: they represent the majority of today's workforce. Referred to as generation Y and digital natives due to their familiarity with new technologies and modern communications tools, the term "millennial" was coined in 1991 by Neil Howe and Williams Strauss in their book *Generations: The History of America's Future*. Millennials are generally classified as young people born between 1980 and 2000, reaching adulthood in the early 21st century. With about 1.8 billion people, millennials account for nearly a quarter of the world's population (United Nations 2019).

The literature on the millennial generation (Chatman & Flynn 2001; George 2009; Kowske et al. 2010; Twenge & Campbell 2001) recognizes a set of values, life priorities, goals, aspirations, and lifestyles utterly different from both their preceding and ensuing generations. In particular, millennials have a distinctive vision of work and the workplace. Unlike their generation X and baby boomer counterparts, millennials: exhibit distrust in their employers; search for a balance between work and personal life; do not see the value in upward mobility; and change companies every few years. Their approach to work and career is based mainly on three priorities: compensation, flexibility, and the opportunity to make a difference (Nekuda 2011).

These traits unique to the millennial generation have been negatively understood by their older employers and colleagues, leading to the acceptance of preconceived notions regarding millennials' work ethic (La Core 2015). Millennial employees are commonly labeled as a generation of "spoiled youth who need to wake up to the realities of work, where everything does not revolve around them" (Suleman & Nelson 2011, p. 40). The lack of under-standing between generations has caused challenges in the workplace (Brack 2012), and the diverging values of millennials represent a source of tension and conflict with managers (Espinoza 2012).

The literature on millennial workplace integration has identified various obstacles facing members of this generation (Espinoza 2012; Espinoza et al. 2010; Stewart et al. 2017; Suleman & Nelson 2011). Research shows that the challenges stem from three main factors: (1) management's misperception of who millennials are and what they want; (2) a misalignment between the values and expectations of millennials and those of firms; and (3) the inability of firms and the managers to adapt their organizational culture to engage, retain, and effectively integrate millennials into the workplace (Espinoza 2012).

In addition to the challenges that come from a clash of values, millennials in the workplace face concrete economic growth setbacks caused by worldwide economic events. Specifically, the financial crisis of 2008 and the ongoing COVID-19 pandemic of 2020 have caused more significant major economic setbacks to the average millennial entering the workforce than to older workers. For example, because of the Great Recession, "the average millennial [lost] about 13% of their earnings between 2005 and 2017," which constitutes more significant losses than generation X at 9 percent and baby boomers at 7 percent (Rinz 2019). Moreover, with the recent onset of another economic recession caused by the coronavirus pandemic, the workers most negatively affected are those same millennial workers.

The millennial generation has a difficult path ahead to catch up to previous generations' expected wealth gain; however, their journey is unlike their predecessors with additional troubles involving student loans, auto loans, and credit card debt. Yet, despite the hostile economic and organizational environ-ments facing millennials, they continue to change the workforce wildly.

8.3   MILLENNIALS' POTENTIAL FOR ECONOMIC AND SOCIAL GROWTH

Despite misunderstandings and negative preconceived notions about the millennial generation's work ethic, research reveals that millennials are an extraordinarily talented and well-educated generation of workers (Erickson 2008) and the harbingers of social and economic development (Corgnet et al. 2016; Howe & Strauss 2007; Twenge & Campbell 2001). Furthermore, studies demonstrate that when firms adequately manage the factors affecting millen-nials' workplace integration, millennials positively impact the growth and success of their organizations (Hershatter & Epstein 2010; Stewart et al. 2017; Thompson & Gregory 2012). In other terms, these studies assert that managers can overcome conflicts between millennials and their firms by changing their leadership approach and creating a more comfortable environment that allows millennials to express their potential.

Millennials show several traits that represent critical resources for organizations. First, they are characterized by optimism and confidence in the world. This generation was born in the era of social media and computers, and consequently, they are perceived as an open, interconnected, social generation. Second, they prefer teamwork and value authenticity, ethics, and flexibility over set hierarchies. Third, millennials want to know what is expected of them in their jobs and await feedback on their performance. Fourth, they search for a work-life balance as they consider work a fun hobby; their salary is generally of secondary importance. Finally, millennials are interested in exploring new opportunities for self-development, and therefore they are not afraid of changing their place of employment to achieve personal goals (Smedeby 2011).

Other distinctive characteristics of the millennial generation are their creativity and orientation toward innovation (Gong et al. 2018; Pink 2005). Some researchers define millennial workers as "Millennovators," or Millennial Innovators (Moon 2014). Zhu et al. (2018) argue that the millennial generation has a natural inclination toward developing new ideas and exerts more effort to acquire new knowledge and skills when facing a challenge.

Due to their tendency to innovate, millennials thrive under leaders who support them in their creative pursuits specific to their organizational context and at organizations that value people and originality (Kubiatko 2013). Hamel and Breen (2007) proposed a list of six human capabilities that increase a firm's ability to innovate and reach competitive success: passion, creativity, initiative, intellect, diligence, and obedience. In this regard, millennials are better positioned in passion and creativity but poorly in compliance. The authors also suggest that managers and firms focused on a rule-based hierarchical approach cannot capture millennials' great potential in passion, creativity, initiative, and intellect.

Separate from their characteristics, millennials have grown up in a period of increased attention to the environment, resulting in a unique generational orientation toward social and environmental issues. Many millennials worry about the state of the world and feel personally responsible for making a difference, and therefore are inclined to participate in social causes (Lumesse 2018). With the themes of sustainability and sustainable development at the center of public and political discussions, millennials have cultivated an attitude of global citizenship and an orientation to act for environmental protection. A 2016 Deloitte survey found that about 63 percent of millennials worldwide were involved in social issues and wanted their employers to have a sense of purpose beyond profit. The sensibility of this generation toward social and environmental issues is well summarized by Andrew Swinard of Abundant

Venture Partners, an international venture capital firm: "doing business responsibly is the millennials' new religion" (Swinard 2014).

To channel and retain the potential of the millennial generation, organizations must change their management and leadership style to meet the expectations of millennials and create a work environment more in line with their values and beliefs (*The Economist* 2015). As Espinoza et al. (2010) suggest millennials are not apathetic; they are just indifferent until they find a reason to care about something. In this respect, they are easy to motivate. They want to know why before what. Try to make them see that the organization's goals are an extension of their personal goals.

Many researchers have investigated the motivational factors of millennials (Hui et al. 2021; Tan et al. 2019; Zhang & Zhou 2019), including leadership, teamwork, employee empowerment, and engagement (Tan et al. 2019; Younas et al. 2018). The research highlights that an employee's creative and innovative behavior is strictly related to organizational behavior (Soda et al. 2017). Consequently, Hui et al. (2021) suggest that innovative behavior of individuals can be stimulated and induced when an organization adapts its overall behavior to that of its employees.

These results are the product of organizational identification, which occurs when its values, mission, and vision perfectly fit with its employees. This factor has been defined as employees' willingness to express themselves as part of their organization (Aghaz & Hashemi 2014; Zappalà et al. 2019). Organizational identification occurs when an employee has a sense of belonging and is aware of his role (Abdullah et al. 2017; Cornwell et al. 2018; Lu et al. 2018). Therefore, it is necessary to stimulate creativity among the millennial generation (Hui et al. 2021). To effectively channel the potential of millennial workers, organizations must capitalize on organizational identification (Aghaz & Hashemi 2014; Bednar et al. 2019; Cornwell et al. 2018). When employees perceive a strong organization identification, they are more likely to cooperate and devote effort to improve the organization as a whole (Ghosh 2015; Kim et al. 2018; Zhao et al. 2019). As Hui et al. (2021, p. 1656) summarize, "a strong organization identification can help employees build a close sense of sharing in the organization's outcome and overcome unhappiness in their work."

8.4   THE HUMANE ENTREPRENEURSHIP MODEL: ENABLER OF CREATIVITY OF THE MILLENNIAL GENERATION

Millennials have certainly struggled to find their footing within the workforce, as presented by the analysis in the preceding sections. However, as this new wave of workers continues to establish themselves professionally, researchers and practitioners must look for long-term solutions to the clashes between millennial workers, managers, and organizations.

The key questions facing researchers and firms are: (a) what necessary changes must organizations make to engage and retain millennials, and (b) what kind of organizations are best equipped to capture the potential of millennial people? To address these questions, we might reflect on Peter Drucker's idea of corporations as a human community (Drucker 1993). Millennials demand humaneness to be incorporated into their work experience. To combat the decline in people-oriented culture, millennials have specifically challenged top managers to alter their leadership styles to align with millennial needs. Most leadership theories and strategies assume that "effective leadership refers to the ability of a firm's top managers to select and apply the 'correct' strategic approach or effectively implement an appropriate strategy" (Kim et al. 2018, p. 16). Leadership style is recognized as "a necessary shortcut to business prosperity and perpetuation even in a constantly changing environment of business" (Wobodo 2019, p. 1675), and therefore within the millennial context managerial leaders must work to identify the leadership style that is best for their situation (Hersey & Blanchard 1988).

Although causal research involving real-world organization data is limited, "prominent leadership scholars generally agree that top-level leadership is related to organizational performance outcomes" in their ability to increase worker participation and advance the goals of entrepreneurial orientation (EO) (Kim et al. 2018, p. 17). According to Hersey and Blanchard (1988), a leader's effectiveness is dependent upon their ability to diagnose the readiness level of the follower, show flexibility by using a variety of leadership styles, and a willingness to partner with the follower. In motivating employees, or "followers," to carry out activities determined by leaders, leadership must provide desirable rewards for effective performance or undesirable consequences for poor performance (Hollander 1992). In this perspective, a shift in managerial style could captivate millennials in an entirely new way.

However, millennial workforce integration will not occur solely from adjusting leadership techniques and methods. To spur on integration, we must look beyond leadership. The theory and practice of Humane Entrepreneurship (HumEnt) put forth the more well-rounded approach needed to address the two questions facing organizations today. By adding HRM to the leadership and entrepreneurship mix, the HumEnt model provides a method to initiate an entirely human-centered business approach that uplifts millennials – and employees at large – in ways that have not been previously. The HumEnt model moves beyond the idea of a company doing well for others, be it their customers or surrounding environment as seen in social entrepreneurship, and ensures that the company itself is an example of a human-based and human-focused culture.

Utilizing the tactics of entrepreneurial orientation can bring firm positive results. However, it does not maximize the full potential of employees. More successfully adding a humane component to entrepreneurial orientation leads to rapid and long-term innovation, risk-taking, and proactivity. Many nations and firms, but certainly not all, recognize the importance of HRM and that employee and citizen engagement is a powerful strategy for driving organizational improvement and business results (Carmeli et al. 2011). Going further than leadership and EO to involve human-centered HRM, Humane Entrepreneurial Orientation (H-EO) generates quality employment opportunities for millennials. It creates long-term wealth generation for the millennial generation, which grows national and global economies.

Observing the multidimensional nature of HRM sheds light on the management practices that increase profitability through people, including participation and empowerment, employee ownership, training, and skills development, cross-utilization and cross-training, employment security, selective recruiting, high wages, and information sharing (Pfeffer 1998). Understanding that high-performance HRM can also mean high-commitment HRM, humanistic management is at the centerfold of HumEnt due to its focus on mutual gains for both the employee and employer. Humanistic management describes a style of management that "emphasizes the human condition and is oriented to the development of human virtue, in all its forms, to its fullest extent" (Melé 2003, p. 79). Within this theory, top managers must connect with human needs to motivate employees fully. In doing so, management creates a company culture that considers the ethical impact of actions and motivates people around them to acquire virtues to build a strong community (Melé 2003). In all societies, including the business realm, respect for human dignity demands human freedom. HumEnt seeks to uplift and expand this respect specifically within the workplace.

An organization of any size or stature has the opportunity to enhance its structure and strategy and create an ecosystem that includes and amplifies the millennial generation by exhibiting the four critical components of HumEnt: empathy, equity, enablement, and empowerment. By harnessing these four domains, organizations can create powerful synergies for their internal and external relations and activities (Kim et al. 2018). For example, an empathetic orientation acts as the key driving factor for employee engagement and communicative business culture, which will result in better relations between both organizational members and stakeholders (Choi 2006). Furthermore, as empathy can be utilized to gain insights into other people's understandings and beliefs, it is considered the starting point of design thinking and is essential to understanding customers' needs (Ickes & Simpson 1997).

The level to which an organization expresses the four components of HumEnt qualifies it in one of the four HumEnt status categories: ideal, moderate, negative, and harmful (Kim et al. 2018).

IDEAL HumEnt status includes organizations adhering to a people-centered entrepreneurial orientation, resulting in cyclical growth that benefits all stakeholders. MODERATE HumEnt consists of a social and financial capital clash amongst their EO and H-EO practices, which ultimately leads to mixed results that inhibit continuous cyclical growth. Finally, NEGATIVE HumEnt is absent from a people-centered model from entrepreneurial orientation, causing disadvantageous trends and broken growth cycles.

Finally, HARMFUL HumEnt portrays an organization that directly or indirectly causes active harm to some of their stakeholders, their employees (including millennials), and their surrounding communities, which undoubtedly results in a destructive cycle of growth. It is important to note that in a changing world, such as that of today, the collective conscience seems to be shifting more toward the leveraging of social capital in and for organizational success, which will significantly benefit the commencement of the millennial generation into the workforce (Kim et al. 2018).

8.5   MILLENNIALS AND HUMANE ORIENTED FIRMS: SOME PRACTICAL EVIDENCES

This section describes two organizations that could be considered good examples of firms adhering to a people-centered entrepreneurial orientation. We identified the companies, starting from the rating provided by "Great Place to Work," an international organization that annually gives a ranking of the firms that, from the point of view of approach and relationship with employees, have been recognized by millennials as the ideal workplace.

Loccioni is a medium Italian company located in the Marche Region and operating in the sector of designs and building measurement and control systems for application in different industrial and service businesses (mobility, human care, home, environment, energy). The company is a world leader in the sector with an international presence and four offices worldwide (Germany, USA, China, Japan).

The company's mission is to create in the territory, and spread throughout the world, an entrepreneurial model that goes beyond the logic of profit but aims to generate a sustainable value. The founder defines the company as a technological tailor's shop. Every product is designed and tailored to the customer, integrating the best internal and external skills and technologies and building long-term relationships with customers and suppliers for mutual development.

Loccioni is recognized for its results in product quality and excellence in innovation, as evidenced by several prestigious awards, and for its attention to the territory and environment as shown by many projects promoted and financed by Loccioni aimed to protect and valorize the territory. Loccioni is further recognized for its peculiar humane resource care and approach, as shown by several awards obtained as the best place to work.

People represent the most critical and most significant value for the firm, and the basic idea is that people who work in the firm are not employees but entrepreneurial collaborators. Therefore, the firm's founder, Mr. Enrico Loccioni, sustains the importance of having and developing "intrapreneurs," people with the skills and spirit of initiative necessary to achieve the objectives. In the idea of Mr. Loccioni each collaborator is a shareholder in his work: he must accumulate skills and knowledge that he will use to generate entrepreneurship within the company and outside.

To reach this aim, Loccioni has developed a model of the firm that is not hierarchical, but a horizontal organization, in which people can grow through merit and passion and an open company, open to young people and those with a lot of experience, to customers, suppliers, competitors, the scientific and institutional communities.

The management of people in Loccioni is based on three key elements: cultivating talents, developing talents, and flying skills. To apply this management approach, Loccioni has promoted and realized a program that aims to involve people and talents of all ages: undergraduate, graduate, and postgraduate students, teachers and managers, experts in every field come together to share their knowledge and work on new, challenging projects. The program is divided into three areas.

The so-called "Bluzone," designed to cultivate talents, is a set of projects and education laboratories that involves about 1,000 students at different school levels every year. Bluzone is a "training gym" that stimulates students' creativity and imagination, from elementary to secondary school, also involving students who are about to graduate and doctoral candidates, giving them the possibility to acquire new competencies and guiding them toward the choice of their working future. The aim of Bluzone is first to make young people aware of their potential and prepare them for the future. In the context of the Bluzone program, different initiatives have been realized. For example, the Vivaio project, formalized in 2015, aims to learn a convergence between school and work to improve students' training. The project is realized in collaboration with the schools (elementary, middle, and high schools) of the territory (located within 30–40 minutes from the company). It includes training laboratories for elementary and middle school teachers on specific topics such as coding, robotics, precision agriculture (digital farming). As a result, students can work on an actual project together with a group of selected teachers, giving them the possibility to develop skills and competencies.

Another exciting project is the Bluzone Camp, an educational program realized during the summer involving students from middle and high schools and children and adolescents. The program is based on four laboratories dedicated to students and young people of different ages who can develop a project through work and fun.

Further, Loccioni organizes training projects, orientation activities, welcomes students on internships, and launches projects in collaboration with high schools and universities. For example, high school students are hired through a project that provides schoolwork alternation in the summer and, subsequently, a six-month internship. Even university students (80 percent from STEM courses and 20 percent from economic-managerial and humanities courses) are included in an alternation between school and work, including a six-month internship. At the end of the process, they are hired with a fixed-term contract which can become permanent.

These training projects allow students to learn about the world of work and manage concrete projects before finishing their studies. In this way, they can choose their career path with greater awareness. At the same time, the company trains and selects candidates who have the skills and personality suitable for working successfully within it.

The Redzone is a program dedicated to collaborators aimed to develop talents. The first project was launched in 1998, a training project on skills that consisted of a fact-finding interview, a potential test, and two classroom days. In 2011, the "Talent tutoring" project was launched, a training program voluntarily aimed at fueling the entrepreneurial action of collaborators – 126 out of 302 collaborators answered the call, and 22 were selected to participate in three training days. Further, the company organizes programs aimed at aligning the skills of collaborators to those required by the evolution of the economic environment.

Finally, Silverzone is a program dedicated to people that had finished their professional careers and decided to share their experience, passion, and enthusiasm with the young company's collaborators.

Silver, a retired collaborator, is invited to mentor young people and share his experiences and knowledge. In this way, new opportunities for young students and collaborators can be created. Moreover, the presence of over 65s with long-standing experience, external to the group but with a passion for the Loccioni world, makes a place to renovate, guide and design.

Further, Loccioni offers support and training to collaborators to become entrepreneurs. Thanks to this initiative, about 30 start-ups have been promoted, and many of them collaborate with the company. All these initiatives have been realized in a defined context as the Play Factory. The Play Factory is a new culture of work that encourages creativity, develops active knowledge, experiences, and innovative discoveries. It is not a workplace but a place where collaborators can work, express their potential, and realize themselves personally and professionally.

Cisco is an American multinational technology conglomerate founded in 1984 and located in San Jose, California, in Silicon Valley. Cisco develops, manufactures, and sells networking hardware, software, telecommunications equipment, and other high-technology services and products.

The company is a world leader in the sector and is worldwide recognized for its ability to lead the evolution of network technologies (in 2020, Cisco was classified among the Best Technology Companies (https://fairygodboss.com/best-companies-for-women-technology-2020). But Cisco is also recognized worldwide for the quality of the work environment and the opportunities it offers to its employees, as showed by the fact that in 2019 and 2020, the workplace culture authority Great Place to Work Inc., in conjunction with *Fortune* magazine, has ranked Cisco as first place in the Great Place to Work ranking.

Further, as stated by the market analyst Patrick Moorhead (2019): "emphasis on humanity and respect within the organization is a major differentiator for Cisco. It's why the company has a great employee retention rate, and doubtlessly a major factor in the company's overall market success."

The company's philosophy is based on the idea that combining work and people's happiness is probably a risky approach when it involves profit-oriented companies and multinationals, but it is a possible mission. The basic idea is that to combine profitability and productivity with people's motivation, building an excellent work environment and involving employees indirectly produces better and tangible economic results.

To understand the approach of Cisco toward its employees, the starting point is its "People Deal," a sort of agreement between the firm and its employees based on the centrality of the individual, the respect for aspirations, the respect for diversity, the possibility to give space to the passion of people and on a mutual commitment to growing together, from a professional and human point of view. The People Deal is an agreement expressing what Cisco expects from its employees and what its employees expect from Cisco.

The Deal is based on three components: Connect everything, Innovate everywhere, and Benefit everyone. Connect everything means Cisco promises to connect its employees with people, information, and opportunities. At the same time, it asks its employees to communicate to generate positive outcomes.

With the Innovate everywhere principle, Cisco guarantees employees an "open and agile" environment that encourages employees to explore ideas and challenges, asking in return that employees pursue innovation to create a better future. The Innovate Everywhere Challenge (IEC) is one of the most critical initiatives aimed to apply this principle. The challenge is a program during which employees are encouraged to form teams around an innovative idea based on the company's care about networking, security, collaboration, and more. As a result, every year, about 75,000 employees across 90 countries have the opportunity to show their ideas and bring them to life.

Winning teams receive $25,000 in seed funding, mentoring from Cisco professionals and coaches, and a three-month innovation rotation to focus on developing their solutions. In 2019, about 50 percent of employees participated, and over 2,800 ideas have been submitted. Among the 85 semifinalist teams, five ventures have been adopted by the business and implemented, generating more than $2 billion in business impact (https://newsroom.cisco .com/feature- content?type=webcontent&articleId=2017697).

The third component is to Benefit everyone. The company promises to support its employees' professional development while encouraging and appreciating individual contributions. Another important driver in the HRM approach refers to its company culture strategy as a "Conscious Culture" that is based on the idea that both management and employees develop self-awareness of the environment in which they are and that everyone feels accountable, empowered, and expected to act in a way that is in line with the culture of the company. This framework is divided into three areas. The first environment aims to create a work context in which dignity, respect, fairness, equity, diversity, and inclusion are keywords. The second aspect is Cisco's characteristics that refer to how the company culture is shaped by its behaviors, beliefs, and principles. These principles reflect its corporate social responsibility program and the culture of "giving back" that characterizes it. The third and final component, experiences, refers to the direct experiences its employees have with the company through management, their teams, and their work

8.6   CONCLUSION

By analyzing the millennial generation's workplace opportunities and access, we can establish a culture of HumEnt among organizations that both attract and capture millennials. Recognizing that this population has confronted great adversities throughout their lifetimes, they are ready to innovate in alternative ways. From a place of systemic oppression, this group is proactive in searching for solutions that have yet to be discovered. More significantly, millennials have completely revolutionized the way that we, as a society, interact with communication and technology. In describing how millennials have challenged preconstructed systems and ideas, Tischelle George states:

> Where most knowledge workers today use two forms of communication – written and spoken – the employees of tomorrow [millennials] see endless variations and

protocols. Far from being awed by current technology, kids will find the tools they need to do what they want, or they'll remake software and hardware to get the job done. In short, who needs the IT guy? They will either "hack" it or "huck" it. Another advantage of growing up digital has manifested in that they can do many things at once. Millennials feel powerful. (Espinoza 2012, pp. 24–5)

Organizations and firms must adopt new methods to capture this generation's untapped power to create long-term wealth for the millennial generation, strengthen national and global economies, and build quality employment opportunities. Humane Entrepreneurship and the application of its four fundamental principles represent the missing link between firms and the millennial workforce. By connecting their organizational culture to the value and beliefs of their newest workers, organizations will be able to successfully motivate and profit from the potential of the millennial generation.

8.7   RECOMMENDATION FOR BUSINESS SCHOOLS

In modern society, a new way of doing business and a new approach to managing people involved in the firm is not only possible but necessary. The future of humane entrepreneurship includes empowered employees and well-educated entrepreneurs making intelligent decisions to protect the environment and benefit the world. A new category of entrepreneurs and managers needs to be developed to reach these aims, and education can play a crucial role.

Business schools could act in at least two ways:

1. Adopting a bottom-up approach through the diffusion and the description, in existing management courses of examples of Humane Entrepreneurship and Humane Entrepreneurs to inspire the future generation of managers and entrepreneurs.
2. Adopting a top-down approach by introducing these topics in management courses or through the prevision of new specific courses.

REFERENCES

Abdullah, MI, Ashraf, S and Sarfraz, M 2017, 'The organizational identification perspective of CSR on creative performance: The moderating role of creative self-efficacy,' *Sustainability*, vol. 9, no. 11, p. 1770.
Aghaz, A. and Hashemi, A. 2014, 'Investigating the impact of personality traits on expanded model of organizational identification,' *International Journal of Business and Management*, vol. 9, no. 3, pp. 48–156.
Bednar, JS, Galvin, BM, Ashforth, BE and Hafermalz, E, 2019, 'Organization science putting identification in motion: A dynamic view of organizational identification,' *Organization Science*, vol. 31, no. 1, pp. 200–22.

Brack, J 2012, 'Maximizing millennials in the workplace,' *UNC Executive Development*, pp. 1–14.

Carmeli, AJ, Schaubroeck and Tishler, A. 2011, 'How CEO empowering leadership shapes top management team processes: Implications for firm performance,' *Leadership Quarterly*, vol. 22, pp. 399–411.

Chatman, JA and Flynn, FJ 2001, 'The influence of demographic heterogeneity on the emergence and consequences of cooperative norms in work teams,' *Academy of Management Journal*, vol. 44, pp. 956–74.

Choi, J 2006, 'A motivational theory of charismatic leadership: Envisioning, empathy, and empowerment,' *Journal of Leadership & Organizational Studies*, vol. 13, no. 1, pp. 24–43.

Corgnet, B, Espín, AM and Hernán-González, R 2016, 'Creativity and cognitive skills among millennials: Thinking too much and creating too little,' *Frontiers in Psychology*, 7, Article 1626.

Cornwell, TB, Howard-Grenville, J and Hampel, CE 2018, 'The company you keep: How an organization's horizontal partnerships affect employee organizational identification,' *Academy of Management Review*, vol. 43, no. 4, pp. 772–91.

Covin, JG and Slevin, DP 1989, 'Strategic management of small firms in hostile and benign environments,' *Strategic Management Journal*, vol. 10, no. 1, pp. 75–87.

Drucker, P 1993, *The Concept of the Corporation*, New York: Routledge.

Erickson, TJ 2008, *Plugged in: The Generation Y Guide to Thriving at Work*, Boston, MA: Harvard Business School Press.

Espinoza, C 2012, 'Millennial integration: Challenges millennials face in the workplace and what they can do about them,' PhD. dissertation in Leadership and Change Program of Antioch University.

Espinoza, C, Ukleja, M and Craig R 2010, *Managing the Millennials: Discover the Core Competencies for Managing Today's Workforce*, Hoboken, NJ: John Wiley & Sons.

Fry, R 2015, 'Millennials surpass Gen Xers as the largest generation in U.S. labor force,' FACTANK – News in the Numbers, accessed October 2020 at http://www.pewresearch.Org/fact- tank/2015/05/1 1/millennials-surpass-gen-xers-asthe-la rgest-generation-in-u-s-labor-force/.

George, L 2009, 'Dude, where's my job?,' McLeans.Ca., accessed September 2020 at http://www2.macleans.ca/2009/01/14/dudewhere%E2%80%99s-my-job/.

Ghosh, SK 2015, 'Linking organizational identification to job embeddedness in Indian context: Role of job satisfaction and perceived organizational support,' *International Journal of Business and Management*, vol. 10, no. 12, pp. 258–68.

Gong, B, Ramkissoon, A, Greenwood, RA and Hoyte, DS 2018, 'The generation for change: Millennials, their career orientation, and role innovation,' *Journal of Managerial Issues*, vol. 30, no. 1, pp. 82–6.

Hamel, G and Breen, G 2007, *The Future of Management*, Boston, MA: Harvard Business School Press.

Hanks, K, Odom, W, Roedl, D and Blevis, E 2008, 'Sustainable millennials: Attitudes towards sustainability and the material effects of interactive technologies,' in *Proceedings of the SIGCHI Conference on Human Factors in Computing Systems*, ACM, pp. 333–42.

Hersey, P and Blanchard, K 1988, *Management of Organization Behavior: Utilizing Human Resources* (5th edn), Englewood Cliffs, NJ: Prentice-Hall.

Hershatter, A and Epstein, M 2010, 'Millennials and the world of work: An organization and management perspective,' *Journal of Business Psychology*, vol. 25, pp. 211–23.

Hollander, EP 1992, 'Leadership, followership, self, and others,' *The Leadership Quarterly*, vol. 3, pp. 43–54.

Howe, N and Strauss, W 2000, *Millennials Rising: The Next Great Generation*, New York: Vintage Books.

Howe, N and Strauss, W 2007, *Millennials go to College* (2nd edn), Great Falls, VA: Life Course Associates.

Hui, L, Qun, W, Nazir, S, Mengyu, Z, Asadullah, MA and Khadim, S 2021, 'Organizational identification perceptions and millennials' creativity: Testing the mediating role of work engagement and the moderating role of work values,' *European Journal of Innovation Management*, vol. 24, no. 5, pp. 1653–78. DOI: 10.1108/EJIM-04-2020-0165.

Ickes, W and Simpson, JA 1997, 'Managing empathic accuracy in close relationships,' in W Ickes (ed.), *Empathic Accuracy*, New York: The Guilford Press, pp. 218–50.

Kim, KC, El Tarabishy, A and Bae, ZT 2018, 'Humane entrepreneurship: How focusing on people can drive a new era of wealth and quality job creation in a sustainable world,' *Journal of Small Business Management*, vol. 56, no. S1, pp. 10–29.

Kowske, B, Rasch, R and Wiley, J 2010, 'Millennials' (lack of) attitude problem: An empirical examination of generational effects on work attitudes,' *Journal of Business and Psychology*, vol. 25, pp. 265– 79.

Kubiatko, M 2013, 'The comparison of different age groups on the attitudes toward and the use of ICT,' *Educational Sciences: Theory & Practice*, vol. 13, no. 2, pp. 1263–72.

Kurz C, Li, G, Vine, DJ 2018, 'Are millennials different?,' *Finance and Economics Discussion Series*, 2018-080. Washington, DC: Board of Governors of the Federal Reserve System; 2018.

La Core, E 2015, 'Supporting millennials in the workplace,' *Strategic HR Review*, vol. 14, no. 4, p. 155.

Lu, H, Yue, A, Han, Y and Chen, H 2018, 'Exploring the effect of different performance appraisal purposes on miners' organizational citizenship behavior: The mediating role of organization identification,' *Sustainability*, vol. 10, no. 11, p. 4254.

Lumesse (2018), 'Corporate Social Responsibility is a Key in Attracting Millennials,' Lumesse White Paper, February.

Mackey, J and Sisodia, R 2012, 'Conscious capitalism: Unleashing human energy and creativity for the greater good,' *GDR Creative Intelligence*, vol. 43, pp. 6–11.

Melé, D 2003, 'The challenge of humanistic management,' *Journal of Business Ethics*, vol. 44, no. 1, pp. 77– 88.

Moon, TM 2014, 'Mentoring the next generation for innovation in today's organization,' *Journal of Strategic Leadership*, vol. 5, no. 1, pp. 23–35.

Moorhead, P 2019, *How Cisco Fosters A 'Conscious Culture' Within The Company*, Forbes.

Nekuda, J 2011, 'What millennials want,' Human Capital Lab, accessed September 2020 at http://www.humancapitallabe.org/blog/?p=256.

Parente, R, El Tarabishy, A, Vesci, M and Botti, A 2018, 'The epistemology of humane entrepreneurship: Theory and proposal for future research agenda,' *Journal of Small Business Management*, vol. 56, no. S1, pp. 30–52.

Parente, R, El Tarabishy, A, Botti, A, Vesci, M and Feola, R 2020, 'Humane entrepreneurship: Some steps in the development of a measurement scale,' *Journal of Small Business Management*, pp. 1–25. DOI: 10.1080/00472778.2020.1717292.

Pfeffer, J 1998, *The Human Equation: Building Profits by Putting People First*, Boston, MA: Harvard Business School Press.

Pink, D 2005, *A Whole New Mind*, New York: Riverhead Books.

Rinz, K 2019, 'Did timing matter? Life cycle differences in effects of exposure to the Great Recession', Working paper, Center for Economic Studies, US Census Bureau.

Smedeby, A 2011, 'Trendwatch: Why should you care about Generation Y?' Europa, EAS, Management Matters – February, accessed December 2020 at https://europa .eu/eas/press/Management%20Matters%20-%20February%202011.pdf.

Soda, G, Stea, D and Pedersen, T 2017, 'Network structure, collaborative context and creativity,' *Journal of Management*, vol. 45, no. 4, pp. 1739–65.

Stewart, JS, Oliver, EG, Cravens, KS and Oishi, S 2017, 'Managing millennials: Embracing generational differences,' *Business Horizons*, vol. 60, no. 1, pp. 45–54.

Suleman, R and Nelson, B 2011, 'Motivating the millennials: Tapping into the potential of the youngest generation,' *Leader to Leader*, vol. 62, pp. 39–44.

Swinard, A 2014, 'Corporate social responsibility is millennials' new religion,' accessed March 25, 2014 at http://www.chicagobusiness.com/article/20140325/ OPINION/140329895/corporate-social-responsibility-is-millennials-new-religion.

Tan, CS, Lau, XS, Kung, YT and Kailsan, RA 2019, 'Openness to experience enhances creativity: The mediating role of intrinsic motivation and the creative process engagement,' *Journal of Creative Behavior*, vol. 53, no. 1, pp. 109–19.

The Council of Economic Advisers 2015, 'Economic Factors about Millennials', accessed October 2020 at https://www.whitehouse.gov/sites/default/files/docs/ millennials_rei3ort.pdL.

The Economist 2015, 'Myths about millennials,' *The Economist*, August 1, accessed October 2020 at https://www.economist.com/business/2015/08/01/myths-about -millennials.

Timm, JC 2014, 'Millennials: We care more about the environment', MSNBC, accessed October 2020 at https://www.msnbc.com/morning-joe/millennials-environment -climate-change- msna291876.

Thompson, C and Gregory, JB 2012, 'Managing millennials: A framework for improving attraction, motivation, and retention,' *Psychologist-Manager Journal*, vol. 15, no. 4, pp. 237–46.

Trzesniewski, KH and Donnellan, MB 2010, 'Rethinking "Generation Me": A study of cohort effects from 1976–2006,' *Perspective on Psychological Science*, vol. 5, no. 1, pp. 58–75.

Twenge, JM and Campbell, WK 2001, 'Age and birth cohort differences in self-esteem: A cross- temporal meta-analysis,' *Personality and Social Psychology Review*, vol. 5, no.4, pp. 321–44.

United Nations 2019, 'Revision of World Population Prospects,' accessed October 2020 at https://population.un.org/wpp/.

Van Dam, A 2020, 'The unluckiest generation in U.S. history,' *The Washington Post*, June 5, accessed October 2020 at https://www.washingtonpost.com/business/2020/ 05/27/millennial- recession-covid/.

Wobodo, CC 2019, 'Conflict management strategies and industrial harmony: A theoretical review of Rivers State University, Port Harcourt,' *Strategic Journal of Business & Change Management*, vol. 6, no. 2, pp. 981–94.

Younas, A, Wang, D, Javed, B, Rawwas, MYA, Abdullah, I and Zaffar, MA 2018, 'Positive psychological states and employee creativity: The role of ethical leadership,' *Journal of Creative Behavior*, pp. 1–15.

Zappalà, S, Toscano, F and Licciardello, SA 2019, 'Towards sustainable organizations: Supervisor support, commitment to change and the mediating role of organizational identification,' *Sustainability*, vol. 11, no. 3, p. 805. https://doi.org/10.3390/su11030805.

Zhang, X and Zhou, K 2019, 'Close relationship with the supervisor may impede employee creativity by suppressing vertical task conflict,' *R&D Management*, vol. 49, no. 5, pp. 789–802.

Zhao, H, Liu, W, Li, J and Yu, X 2019, 'Leader–member exchange, organizational identification, and knowledge hiding: The moderating role of relative leader–member exchange,' *Journal of Organizational Behavior*, vol. 40, no. 7, pp. 834–48.

Zhu, YQ, Gardner, DG. and Chen, HG 2018, 'Relationships between work team climate, and individual motivation, and creativity,' *Journal of Management*, vol. 44, no. 5, pp. 2094–115.

Websites

https://gblogs.cisco.com/it/2016/01/25/lavoro-e-felicita-un-connubio-possibile/
https://www.forbes.com/sites/moorinsights/2019/11/01/why-no-one-should-be
-surprised-cisco-named-worlds-best-workplace-for-2019/?sh=69fd16eb3886
https://www.forbes.com/sites/patrickmoorhead/2018/08/08/ciscos-people-deal
-exemplifies-its-cutting-edge-commitment-to-employees/?sh=5e515b707ff7
https://www.forbes.com/sites/forbes-personal-shopper/2020/12/18/best-sales-online
-right-now-this-weekend/?sh=5be96dfb3518
https://www.forbes.com/sites/patrickmoorhead/2019/03/19/how-cisco-fosters-a
-conscious-culture-within-the-company/?sh=7f4a1b8150b7
https://blogs.cisco.com/wearecisco/cisco-worlds-best-workplace
https://www.bestworkplaces.it/aziende/cisco-systems/
https://www.cisco.com/c/en/us/about/careers/we-are-cisco.html
https://www.cisco.com/c/en/us/about/careers/we-are-cisco/conscious-culture.html
https://www.greatplacetowork.com/resources/summit-focus-sessions/it-s-not-about
-avocado-toast-how-cisco-created-a-best-workplace-for-millennials-and-beyond
https://newsroom.cisco.com/feature-content?type=webcontent&articleId=2017697
https://www.industriaitaliana.it/guadagnare-creando-startup/
https://rienergia.staffettaonline.com/articolo/34427/L%E2%80%99impresa+di+
seminare+bellezza/Loccioni
https://espresso.repubblica.it/plus/articoli/2014/07/21/news/enrico-loccioni
-imprenditore-hi-tech-ora-vi-diro-cosa-accadra-nel-2068-1.173957
https://press.loccioni.com/upload/articoli/documenti/1331-articolo.pdf
http://www.marche-manufacturing.it/it/content/aea-srl-gruppo-loccioni

9. System changers – for a new era of value creation

Valeria Budinich, Fernande Raine and Diana Wells

9.1 INTRODUCTION: LEADING IN TIMES OF RAPID CHANGE IS HARD BUT NOT IMPOSSIBLE!

In this current era of complexity, challenges cannot be addressed merely within the confines of one organization alone. The sheer size of the challenges that lie ahead – from climate change and shifting economies to rewiring entire education systems – requires that we imagine solutions at a new scale. Instead of focusing on quick fixes, we must redirect our whole value creation process to solve problems while generating sustainable value within systems. The economy of the future will consist of markets in which transactions serve multiple purposes and create various forms of value for business and society at the same time.

This kind of systems-focused value creation demands a new set of skills and mindsets of leaders, not just in the social sector but also in the corporate world. Adaptability and constant renewal have long been touted as critical for corporate growth, and CEOs are eagerly trying to prepare their teams and institutions to be more agile and innovative. More recently, corporate leaders realized that they are intertwined in complex ecosystems of stakeholders and resources, and they are held accountable for generating or diminishing the value for all those stakeholders. What does this mean for leadership?

Over the past decade, leadership studies have increasingly focused on models that are not hierarchical, such as the model of the servant leader, the empowering leader, the coach, etc. But these models are not quite enough to answer the billion-dollar question of "how do I achieve sustainable, lasting growth while improving systems and increasing the value for all people my business touches?" Providing leadership within a system requires that companies examine their long-term growth and how this will impact different stakeholders. Leaders must fundamentally have a view beyond the walls of their institution and even beyond the business sector to collaborate for collective impact towards a shared goal.

Ashoka's research with 120 world-leading system changers suggests a powerful playbook for business leaders seeking to enable their teams to create and capture value in new ways in today's economy.[1]

Read on to learn about the worldview and leadership capabilities displayed by proven system changers in the world as a guide for leaders in all sectors who want to navigate the rapidly changing world, solve complex problems, and strive to leave a better world for the generations to come.

9.2   THE CASE FOR SYSTEM CHANGE

Given the significant systemic issues facing the planet, it is no wonder that systems change is on people's minds. The economic and social model of the industrial era has created visible stress for society and the planet, creating pressure on leaders from all sectors to actively engage in seeking solutions in the interest of the whole. The World Economic Forum is publishing articles and hosting conversations about systems change (Schwab Foundation n.d.). Business leaders are increasingly under pressure from their shareholders to impact the environment and society positively (Sorkin 2018). Meanwhile, the talent marketplace is orienting itself towards interconnected accountability, a quest for more meaning, and an eagerness to contribute positively (Imperative 2022). Moreover, leaders are beginning to question what systems change means for them and their roles.

System change means that entrepreneurs must continuously remain curious and expand their imagination to allow a fluid view of the entire market system to inform how they develop their product or intervention. Imagine an entrepreneur working in food; this entrepreneur might look at where the product they sell ends up through a system change lens. This investigation may lead to the world of recycling value chains and facilities, where entrepreneurs could analyze the profit model and catch a glimpse of the living and working conditions of the trash-pickers of paper and plastics. Once they see this, they face the choice: choose to ignore it as "not my problem" or engage – as some consumer products companies have – in reimagining the downstream economy of packaging materials.

Willy Foote, who founded Root Capital, started his journey investigating the supply chain of fruit. He ultimately reinvented agricultural business financing, generating $1.6 billion in economic activity while simultaneously improving the conditions of 1.6 million farmers living in environmentally vulnerable areas in Africa and Latin America (Root Capital 2021).

Jos the Blok, a Dutch nurse and social entrepreneur, reimagined the system of home care in the Netherlands with a focus on better care at a lower cost and more flexible working conditions for nurses. He created Buurtzorg (meaning "neighborhood care"), with a network of 850 self-managed autonomous teams involving 10,000 nurses, becoming a reference point for revolutionizing health care worldwide (Buurtzorg International 2022).

Vera Cordeiro reimagined the ecosystem around child patients. She founded the Associação Saúde Criança (or Children's Health Association), which serves as a model for how to radically reduce children's hospitalizations (by 85 percent) through a holistic, family well-being approach (Battilana et al. 2018). She acts systemically, increasing family income and hence the family's ability to take better care of their children while saving public hospitals millions of dollars (Instituto Dara (formerly Saúde Criança Resnacer) 2022).

Canopy is a company that cast a light on an overlooked ingredient in global manufacturing: fibers from endangered forests. Canopy developed a ten-year action plan to save 30 percent or more of the world's forests by 2030 by replacing 50 percent of the forests' global pulp supply with alternative fibers, like agricultural residues, which are currently burned, and cotton textile waste, which ends up in landfills. Nicole Rycroft created this Canadian organization to work with 750 of the forest industry's largest customers globally, from book publishers and printers to leading clothing brands and fashion designers, to help reshape their purchasing practices (Canopy 2020).

The work of leading system changers has also contributed to the creation of multi-billion-dollar industries.[2]

What started in Bangladesh as microlending, an alternative financing mechanism to serve the poor, and then spread around the world by social entrepreneurs, spawned a global US$2.1 trillion microfinance industry.

Similarly, Khan Academy, a free web-based, high-quality educational product, radically expanded the market for online learning and helped develop what is now a US$35.6 billion market (Khan Academy 2022).

Couch Surfing, launched by Casey Fenton as a free network for the exchange of overnight accommodations for university students, paved the way for an entire sharing economy around accommodations with Airbnb as the market leader valued at US$31 billion as of May 2017 (Couchsurfing 2022).

Likewise, Germany's US$35.5 billion energy transition market can be traced back to Elektrizitätswerke Schönau (EWS) local power supply systems, a civil society initiative that took over local power supply systems to enable ecological, decentralized electrical power supply (Anon 2022).

Finding, supporting, and connecting these system changers is at the core of Ashoka's purpose, the organization founded by McKinsey alumnus Bill Drayton (Bornstein 2004). Since 2002, Ashoka has worked together with corporations and system changers to transform industries and solve some of the world's toughest problems (Budinich and Drayton 2010).

This study aims to examine how more business leaders, across industries and geographies, can become system changers who reimagine and reshape industries for the benefit of all.

9.3   OVERVIEW OF RESEARCH METHODOLOGY

Over two years, Ashoka consulted 120 leading system changers through its global network of social entrepreneurs. This research tapped into 40 years of Ashoka's expertise in identifying system changers as "Ashoka Fellows" and integrating them into a global, supportive community (Wells 2018).

Ashoka Fellows are selected through a rigorous process that assesses the impact potential of the new system change idea and the creativity and entrepreneurial skills of the system changer. Most of these Fellows lead citizen sector[3] organizations with national or international impact. As of 2022, Ashoka has elected more than 4,000 Fellows in 90 countries through a selection process that uses consistent criteria.

Building from this strong base of collective knowledge and a global community of peers, the Ashoka research team developed a four-phase research methodology under highly experienced external leadership coaches. A brief description of this two-year process is provided below.

- Phase 1 – Preparation: Desk Review. Conversations with external leadership coaches to develop an initial set of research hypotheses on system changers' worldview and leadership skills. Seek the advice of 30+ Ashoka Venture and Fellowship staff worldwide who nominated what they considered the most advanced Fellows in terms of the scale of impact and leadership. Out of 400 nominations, we selected 120 Fellows as those representing both a diverse pool – geography, themes, gender – as well as the most proven leadership capabilities to shift systems for the good of all.
- Phase 2 – Identification of Competencies: Selection of the Initial Cohort of 20+ Ashoka Fellows for In-depth Interviews. Research further about the work of these Fellows. Develop an in-depth structured interview guide. For this cohort, we used four selection criteria, including (i) the scale of the impact, (ii) how creatively the Fellow had reframed value and how relevant this was from a business world perspective, (iii) the likelihood that the Fellow's work was enabling many to self-identify has changemakers; (iv) the degree to which the Fellow was perceived as having developed innovations to engage others as value creators or changemakers. Conduct 11 in-depth interviews where the Fellows shared critical moments in their leadership journeys, why they do what they do, challenges they face as leaders, and how they engage others in their work.

- Phase 3 – Prioritizing Workshop: Capture and analyze what these 11 Fellows shared during the interview process. Identify key quotes on how they describe their worldview and leadership competencies. Distill key descriptors of their worldview and leadership competencies. Capture the different means through which Fellows enable others – teams and external partners – to impact system change. Produce an initial leadership capability model for system changers.
- Phase 4 – Validation of Findings: Design a survey to validate and prioritize the initial findings. We shared this survey with the original list of 400 Fellows nominated by the Ashoka teams. A total of 109 members of the Ashoka community responded to it. Survey results were analyzed by the Ashoka research team and the external coaches that guided us in defining the original hypothesis. Prioritize the different elements of the leadership capability model. Distill a synthesis of the worldview of system changers and the five leadership competencies shared in this chapter.

We feel confident that this methodology can articulate and validate a shared perspective of system changers' worldview and leadership capabilities. However, we need to recognize that we were overwhelmed by the breadth and the number of innovations shared by the Ashoka Fellows when asked the open-ended question: "Since we consider you either as a system changer and you are exposed to system changers, we would like to hear from you from your experience on the most effective ways to develop system changing mindsets, skills, and behaviors?" Future research efforts will need to dive deeper into the immersive experiences and innovations developed by individual Ashoka Fellows worldwide, as we could only hint here at the richness of these learnings. Section 9.5 below includes selected Ashoka global programs that collaborate with Fellows that impact universities and corporations.

9.4   NEW WORLDVIEW OF SYSTEM CHANGERS

One of the most striking insights emerging from our interviews with these system changers is that they all share a compelling and unique worldview (Figure 9.1).

Every person has a worldview. It is, in essence,

> a commitment, a fundamental orientation of the heart, that can be expressed as a story or in a set of presuppositions (assumptions which may be true, partially true, or entirely false) that we hold (consciously or subconsciously, consistently or inconsistently) about the basic constitution of reality, and that provides the foundation on which we live and move and have our being. (Sire 2020, p. 6)

Our worldview serves as the filter to our everyday lives, affecting how we perceive events and make choices.

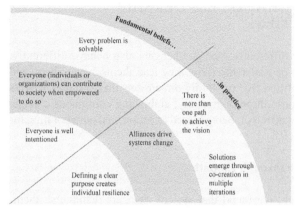

Within the figure:

Fundamental beliefs...

Every problem is solvable

Everyone (individuals or organizations) can contribute to society when empowered to do so

Everyone is well intentioned

...in practice

There is more than one path to achieve the vision

Alliances drive systems change

Solutions emerge through co-creation in multiple iterations

Defining a clear purpose creates individual resilience

Our research shows that system changers see that complex systems can be changed, but it requires people to come together in mutual trust and shared intention.

Source: Ashoka's research on system change capabilities 2016–19.

Figure 9.1   Worldview of system changers

The research shows that system changers see that while complex systems can be changed, they do not operate alone. Systems change requires people to come together in mutual trust and shared intention. In this worldview, system changers see every problem as solvable and that everyone can contribute to society when empowered to do so. Furthermore, they assume that everyone is well intentioned at the core, even when interests and opinions might be conflicting.

This is a critical element of their leadership style, for this belief in good intentions begets trust, and trust is a central ingredient to building partnerships and effective teams. These leaders co-create solutions with others in an iterative process, incorporating many different ideas so that change is felt not only within one value chain but across the entire system. Working across the whole system and value chain necessitates an ability to move fluidly among different and, at times, competing interests and parties. Within the partnerships they form among various stakeholders, system change leaders play a critical role in modeling humility and faith in humankind and crystallizing a shared vision and purpose, keeping the team on course through the inevitable ups and downs they encounter.

While this worldview on its own does not necessarily predict success, it is a foundational mindset that successful system changers share as they work to scale their reach and impact. When asked about it, about 90 percent of system changers found that the worldview resonated with their mindset.

9.5   SYSTEMS CHANGE LEADERSHIP CAPABILITIES

In addition to thinking differently, system changers also behave differently. Across the three levers of leadership (how they lead themselves, others, and systems), we have identified five capability dimensions that system changers manifest: building purpose through empathy, embracing continuous change, having the courage to be different, being biased to action, and collaborating for impact (Figures 9.2 and 9.3).

9.5.1   Build Purpose through Empathy

Throughout our research, we found that system changers distinguish themselves through a sense of purpose through empathy (Baggio et al. 2019). Deeply connecting with the needs of others triggers in them a sense of moral urgency to create a solution and to pursue their vision in collaboration with others. Their deep-rootedness in empathy radiates, attracting and inspiring others. As an example, Stephen Friend, former Senior Vice-President at Merck

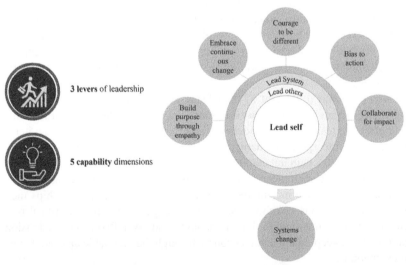

Source: Ashoka's research on system change capabilities 2016–19.

Figure 9.2   *System change leadership*

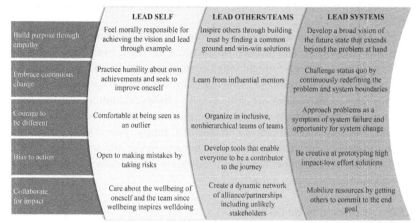

Source: Ashoka's research on system change capabilities 2016–19.

Figure 9.3   System change capabilities

& Co and Co-Founder and President of Sage Bionetworks, designed his work to radically increase data sharing and transparency in the field of biomedical research because he was driven "to quench my desire to more directly provide what people need."

With his unique patient-centric approach, Stephen was able to inspire and build trust across different actors of biomedical research, leading to the creation of a non-competitive space of shared, open-access data where researchers can build on each other's insights (Sage Bionetworks 2022). When recalling his journey, Stephen talks about the sheer amount of "naive optimism" that allowed him to take risks he would not have taken otherwise. "If I knew everything ahead of time, I would not have had the courage to take it on."

Developing a broad vision of the future rooted in his concern for patients and feeling morally responsible for achieving this vision gave him the strength and patience to sustain his efforts to gain others' trust and buy-in and attract funders willing to support high-risk projects like his.

9.5.2   Embracing Continuous Change

Another common theme for system changers is the capacity to embrace continuous change. When reflecting on their achievements, system changers consistently expressed deep humility and a constant quest to improve themselves. Patrick Struebi, Founder and CEO of Fairtrasa, is ambitiously changing the face of fair-trade exportation in Latin America with more than 5,000 farmers. He talks about how his idea continuously matured into what it is now, shaped by changing circumstances and his interactions with these changes (Fairtrasa 2022).

One way system changers adapt is through their propensity for learning from key supporters and influential mentors in their lives. For example, Stephen Friend actively sought advice from scientists and mentors who won Nobel Prizes in medicine. This humility and willingness for continuous learning and improvement are why system changers continuously redefine the problems they address and challenge the status quo. This is how Nicole Rycroft, Founder and Executive Director of Canopy, started with preserving ancient forests by influencing the paper industry in Canada and progressively redefined the mission of her initiative to advocate for sustainable supply chains globally and across many industries.

9.5.3   Courage to Be Different

One thing that system changers never seemed to care about was fitting in. They demonstrated the habit of questioning the status quo, even from an early age. For example, Ai Jen Poo, today Executive Director of the National Domestic Workers Alliance (NDWA) and the Co-Director of Caring Across Generation started questioning the gap between rich and poor as a child and held lengthy conversations with her mother, questioning the racial divide and employment conditions for their household support at home (National Domestic Workers' Alliance 2022).

The courage to be different also applies to how system changers work with others, as they encourage people to imagine the world not as it is but as it could be. Gautam Bharadwaj described his ritual of starting regular meetings with "wouldn't it be lovely if …" – meetings that were in and of themselves different from how things are usually done. In designing a model to transform how low-income workers financially plan for old age, Gautam sought to create a network in which each group triggers a new group to join and work together on the problem. As typical of many system changers, he created a "very horizontal" organization, inclusive and non-hierarchical.

Finally, system changers dare to take a different look at old problems. They perceive problems not as inevitable but as symptoms of a fixable failure in a system. Vera Cordeiro, Founder and Chairwoman of the Board of Associação Saúde Criança, quickly saw that the health outcome disparities in poor communities were not determined by what happened in the hospital, but by what happened "beyond the walls of the hospital." Realizing that there needed to be a holistic focus on the person and even the family behind the disease, she created the Family Action plan that focuses on five areas: health, mother, education, housing, and vocational training.

9.5.4   Bias to Action

System changers are unquestionably biased towards action and take what others perceive as bold risks to test their ideas in practice – even if it means opening them up to early failure. Arnoud Raskin, who launched 40 mobile schools in 20 countries to educate over 60,000 street children annually, first started by designing a backpack/poncho-shelter combination for kids to create a safe pod while on the move. This design was short-lived as Arnoud's colleagues in Colombia thought children would sell this product for drugs. Following his trip to Cartagena, Arnoud realized the flaw in his project and quickly created a new prototype that would become the backbone of the – ultimately highly successful – Mobile School. Today, StreetwiZe, one of his ventures, is developing high-impact learning products for companies, inspired by the complex and competitive reality of street communities (StreetwiZe – Mobile School 2022).

Of the system changers surveyed, 70 percent have developed tools that enable everyone to contribute to the change journey. For Arnoud, empowering youth before educating them was the game-changer and significantly impacted their capabilities. Willy Foote, the system changer reimagining financing mechanisms for small producer farmers, "invested heavily in training to be able to expand geographically and still hire employees locally."

9.5.5   Collaborate for Impact

While entrepreneurship often denotes a highly competitive and aggressive attitude towards others, system changers operate with an open heart and fluid boundaries. By viewing others (even those that might appear as "competitors" or "bad guys") as partners and collaborating with them for impact, system changers create dynamic partnerships with unlikely stakeholders. Celina da Sola, Co-Founder and Vice President of Programs at Glasswing, is a pioneer of catalyzing unlikely partners to break poverty and create economic opportunity in Central America. In her experience, "empowering her staff in the decision-making process" not only enables rapid expansion but allows for very low turnover (Glasswing International 2022).

Rikin Gandhi, CEO of Digital Green, who develops technology to improve agricultural practices in rural India, stressed the importance of a "partnership approach to amplify the work of other organizations and not work around them." By being "very open to adapt the approach" while staying mission-oriented and "uncompromising on the desired goal," Rikin could get organizations to commit to the same goals and partner with them to better use digital technology in supporting farmers (Digital Green 2022).

There are many things to get right. When asked about prioritizing the top three system change capabilities, the winners were – including at the start of a social venture – the ability to develop a broad vision beyond the problem at hand, being able to inspire others through building trust by finding common ground and win-win solutions, and creating a dynamic network of alliance/partnerships including unlikely stakeholders (Figure 9.4).

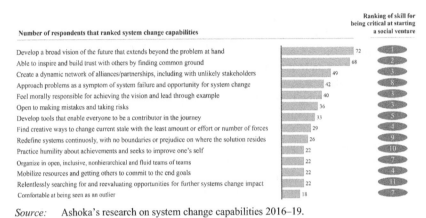

Number of respondents that ranked system change capabilities

Ranking of skill for being critical at starting a social venture

Capability	Number	Ranking
Develop a broad vision of the future that extends beyond the problem at hand	72	1
Able to inspire and build trust with others by finding common ground	68	2
Create a dynamic network of alliances/partnerships, including with unlikely stakeholders	49	3
Approach problems as a symptom of system failure and opportunity for system change	42	8
Feel morally responsible for achieving the vision and lead through example	40	3
Open to making mistakes and taking risks	36	3
Develop tools that enable everyone to be a contributor in the journey	33	5
Find creative ways to change current state with the least amount or effort or number of forces	29	4
Redefine systems continuosly, with no boundaries or prejudice on where the solution resides	26	9
Practice humility about achievements and seeks to improve one's self	22	10
Organize in open, inclusive, nonhierarchical and fluid teams of teams	22	7
Mobilize resources and getting others to commit to the end goals	22	4
Relentlessly searching for and reevaluating opportunities for further systems change impact	22	11
Comfortable at being seen as an outlier	18	7

Source: Ashoka's research on system change capabilities 2016–19.

Figure 9.4   *Ranking of system change capabilities*

9.6   HOW TO GET STARTED

Traditionally, leadership lessons place much pressure on leaders in learning mode to improve themselves to lead others better. This set of insights and lessons amounts to a different prescription.

At its core, system change leadership is not predicated simply on a set of skills and behaviors but emerges from a new worldview. When you *see* differently, that is, when you see everyone as a potential leader when you see people as well intentioned when you see in systemic failure an opportunity to create value, *then* you can *do* differently – you can lead from within, find new areas of growth, motivate others, build partnerships that are based on a proper alignment of goals. You can design highly effective interventions that tip systems for everyone's benefit.

So, how does a changemaker get started? How does one learn or acquire these new mindsets and capabilities? Our research showed that the top five most effective ways identified by systems change leaders all have to do with *learning by doing or immersion* (Figure 9.5), that is,

- Hands-on life experience through projects and working with teams on system change (mainly through trial-and-error).
- Experiential learning, defined as direct experience and focused reflection on learning (e.g., field visits to work sites, facilitated workshops/experiences on system change, learning journeys) (Wurdinger and Carlson 2009).
- Peer-to-peer exchanges and participation in open networks.
- Exposure to role models that exemplify these qualities.
- On-the-job coaching/mentoring around the mindsets and capabilities.

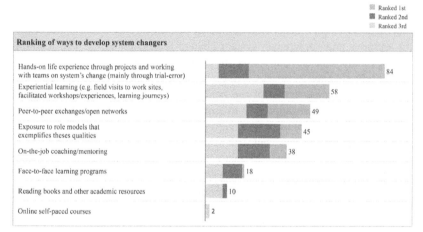

Source: Ashoka's research on system change capabilities 2016–19.

Figure 9.5   *Ways to develop system changer's mindsets and capabilities*

Through these activities, leaders develop a holistic view that helps them see things that used to be externalities as integral parts of a system with potential for value creation. This broadened view of what matters applies not only to elements within the system, such as water supply or recycling. It also applies to who is considered to be part of the team. Stakeholders who would have been marginal in the old leadership framework become partners in unlocking value in the new framework.

9.7   ASHOKA'S EXPERIENTIAL LEARNING JOURNEYS: FROM SYSTEM CHANGE LEADERSHIP TO ENABLING EVERYONE TO BE A VALUE CREATOR

Ashoka has been working with leading system changers since its founding in 1981. As the pioneer in social entrepreneurship, Ashoka has selected over 4,000 systems-changing social entrepreneurs from over 90 countries. What Ashoka may be less known for is its decades-long work to build changemaking mindsets and skills in the business and education sectors and its efforts to help these institutions organize differently to catalyze changemaking value. Ashoka has partnered with hundreds of companies across the globe to this end.

One example is a decade-long partnership with Boehringer Ingelheim (BI), a German-based pharmaceutical company. We prototyped experiential learning journeys and "practiced" system change leadership skills. The learning journeys start with company executives immersing themselves in the work of a system changer for weeks or months. During this time, these executives gain a different perspective of the health system, a new way of looking at problems, and a fresh approach to imagining solutions. As a result, these executives-in-residence often emerge with new ideas for business models and a powerful sense of purpose but with a new worldview, including a new understanding of their role in their company and their role in the world. It is a view in which solutions abound, and value can be created for the good of all. This immersive learning opportunity enables a new conception of self and one's role in the world – one imbued with purpose and value.

Tanja Vermeer, Senior Global People Growth Manager, Boehringer Ingelheim, states: "These immersive experiences have been a game-changer for our employees. Stepping into entirely new environments, they see first-hand the systemic reasons for health inaccessibility in local communities and have new opportunities to further develop the skills required to work in complex systems and act with an entrepreneurial spirit" (Ioan and Bianchi 2021).[4]

In these partnerships, we see the power of system changers to enable others as changemakers (Wells 2018). Social entrepreneurs – as system changers – inspire others to recognize that change is possible and act as role models. In their systems change work, they also create new roles for others to play in their changemaking endeavors.[5] In other words, social entrepreneurs build changemaking mindsets, skills, and abilities in others for the good of all. What began as a philanthropic initiative, shifted to opportunities for site visits and workshops to understand systems change, social innovation, and changemaking. Then, by working with human resources and senior management, the partnership created opportunities for employees to practice changemaking. Today this collaboration, following its name, is about *Making More Health*. In Vermeer's remarks above (Ioan and Bianchi 2021), we also hear the relevance of the immersive experience as a pedagogical model that offers employees a new worldview imbued with purpose. This worldview further offers a self-identity as one who is driven to find and build solutions to lived problems.

Building on what we observed in the work of our Fellows and their systems change capabilities, Ashoka expanded its theory of change to advance an "Everyone a Changemaker" world. As a result, while still finding leading social entrepreneurs and accelerating their solutions, Ashoka is also actively working with higher education and primary and secondary education institutions to mainstream the skills and attitudes needed to participate as changemakers in a world of rapid change.[6]

Since 2008, Ashoka has partnered with colleges and universities around the globe to define and develop changemaking education and to rewire campuses to graduate changemakers. This work began by collaborating with higher education faculty to meet student demand for courses on social entrepreneurship. Over the years, the focus has expanded beyond social entrepreneurship programming. Today, social innovation and changemaking competencies are embedded in academic and co-curricular programming within various programs and colleges across campuses including those for education, engineering, and business. Ashoka U's focus has also expanded from supporting individual programs to integrating changemaking across campuses to graduate changemakers.

This work is about collaborating with university leadership, faculty, and students for engaged scholarship focused on graduating students who are prepared for the rapidly changing world. The program has partnered with 51 institutions designed as Changemaker Campuses, engaged over 600 colleges and universities in Ashoka U programs, and supported over 4,000 educators and senior administrators designing and teaching courses, producing research, and creating and implementing strategy. Creating experiential learning opportunities to advance changemaking and systems change leadership as student learning outcomes and a way of being for educators and administrators has been central to this work

Examples of such learning opportunities include peer-to-peer exchanges at annual conferences and convenings, online cohort-based accelerators for educators and their changemaking projects, and fostering site visits and collaboration grants across Changemaker Campuses (Anon 2021). Committed to systems-level change across higher education itself, Ashoka U codified vital principles, practices, and case examples for changemaking leadership and education so that they can more easily scale (Fuessel 2020).

Today, Ashoka U continues its work with an expanded focus on how higher education can, and is, creating a world where everyone can be a changemaker.

Beyond graduating changemakers, higher education institutions (including business schools) are key players in producing research, catalyzing impact, and creating system-wide shifts in what it means to be successful in a world where the only constant is change.

9.8   HIGHER EDUCATION AND BUSINESS SCHOOLS AS DISSEMINATORS OF A SYSTEMS CHANGE LEADERSHIP

Higher education is a critical means for influencing systems to change leadership across society. As business schools embrace the goal of graduating students with techniques to change worldviews and leadership skills, they will equip the next generation of business leaders to redefine value creation and create greater purpose, accountability, and social and economic impact in their sectors.

When educators graduate from educator preparation programs focused on changemaking, they are equipped to design curricula to foster a new generation of changemakers, including new value creators, regardless of which sector or career they pursue. This skill should not be limited to primary and secondary educators, but should be embraced by educators, faculty, and staff at all levels. To graduate systems change leaders, business schools must incorporate this thinking into their curricula and their educational pathways and institutional strategies, leadership, and culture. It means becoming a Changemaker Institution that lives and breathes systems change leadership itself – whether mobilizing resources and collaborating with its community to address the United Nations' Sustainable Development Goals or empowering collaboration and innovation from anywhere across the campus regardless of department, level, or tenure (Fuessel 2020).

This new world of complexity and accelerated change requires different measures of success. Success should be defined not only by productivity outputs but also the percentage of changemakers in an organization, school, and company. Ashoka is currently prototyping tools to do just this: a changemaker index to measure individual and group mindsets, changemaker density, and a means to measure institutional readiness for enabling changemaking (see Box 9.1).

BOX 9.1   CHANGEMAKING AS VALUE CREATION

Changemakers are people who can visualize a new reality, take action, and collaborate with others to bring that new reality into being for the good of others. In this historic moment where repetition and efficiency are no longer primary drivers, the ability to visualize and create in a rapidly changing world is critical. A new era of value creation demands new measures to assess changemakers' individual and collective abilities in any community. In this regard, system changers offer many examples for both the private and public sectors. As we understand this phenomenon further, we find it equally applicable for businesses and governments to understand and enable changemaker density. Equally important is the need to build ecosystems that will allow changemakers to thrive. Because this is what the system changer worldview enables, it unlocks changemaking and value creation at scale. When we acknowledge this fact, we will have to answer the question: What is the future of business schools?

To identify your most vital changemaking abilities and opportunities to develop new ones, take Ashoka's Changemaker Index, a tool that will continue to evolve and build changemaking resources: https://cmi.ashoka.org.

9.9   THE PRIZE: A WORLD TRANSFORMED

With these learnings, our system changers are collectively helping us see a new future, regardless of the sector or industry. In this future, profit-motivated organizations are managing a financial bottom line and a bottom line that creates value for all stakeholders in a system.

In this future, we see benefits across all levels:

* *Self*: Personal fulfillment through more meaningful work (purpose).
* *Others/Teams*: Increased sense of shared purpose among staff *and core partners* increases productivity, and more empathy and collaboration lead to more innovation and highly effective collective action.
* *System*: New market opportunities and value creation beyond one organization.

If we follow system changers' lessons, it will be possible to dream of this world and create that future today.

As a path forward, we would like to invite you to reflect on questions like:

* How can we ensure that young people grow up with the ability to envision and build solutions to create value for many?
* What could business schools do differently to foster more system changers and *changemakers* with the vision, commitment, and augmented entrepreneurial skills?

Table 9.1   *Quick self-diagnostic for system change readiness*

In the last year, I have gone through at least one experience that shifted my worldview	*Not at all/Slightly/To a large extent/Fully*
I have engaged recently in conversations where I build trust and co-created with <u>unlikely</u> partners	*Not at all/Slightly/To a large extent/Fully*
I have taken steps to map and understand the full system in which my business is operating	*Not at all/Slightly/To a large extent/Fully*
I am engaged regularly in conversations to sense opportunities in the system in which I operate	*Not at all/Slightly/To a large extent/Fully*
I have enabled new kinds of teams to form and encouraged collaborative ways of operating	*Not at all/Slightly/To a large extent/Fully*
In the last months, I have personally had the chance to build trust with stakeholders in the ecosystem of my business	*Not at all/Slightly/To a large extent/Fully*
I have created new types of value through solutions for the broader ecosystem of my business	*Not at all/Slightly/To a large extent/Fully*

- How could business incubators better integrate the work of all types of entrepreneurs, innovators, and *changemakers* who are positioned to shift market systems for broader benefit?
- What pathways would allow large corporations and their teams to be effective co-creators of business, social, and environmental value?
- How can we have more public, philanthropic, and commercial investors *who share the worldview of system changers* and are willing to play a role in enabling new markets for all and system-wide investments?
- What enabling conditions would facilitate trust between citizens and market forces to encourage more ethical/socially conscious business/ exchange?

Finding powerful and long-lasting responses to these and other similar questions requires collective energy and creativity. We hope that if you are reading this, you are either already on this path or open to joining the journey of system changers and innovators worldwide.

But before you leave us, if you are committed to exploring this new era of value creation and to being a changemaker, take a quick self-diagnostic to evaluate your readiness to change systems (Table 9.1). And enjoy the ride!

NOTES

1.   The authors would like to thank Anita Baggio for her invaluable guidance throughout this research. Anita serves as Chief People, Performance, ESG, HSE, Social Responsibility, Communication, Culture Officer at Eneva, an integrated energy company with headquarters in Rio de Janeiro, Brazil.

2. These examples are based in part on a two-month research collaboration between Ashoka and McKinsey Germany that took place in the summer of 2014. The internal report was titled "Today's Social Innovations – Tomorrow's Market Shifts."

3. For definition of the term citizen sector, see Leviner, N., Crutchfield, L.R. and Wells, D. (2006). "Understanding the Impact of Social Entrepreneurs: Ashoka's Answer to Measuring Effectiveness. Association for Research on Nonprofit Organizations and Voluntary Action." The ARNOVA Occasional Paper Series is a publication of the Association for Research on Nonprofit Organizations and Voluntary Action, pp. 89–95. http://www.arnova.org; also available here: https://www.ashoka.org/en/files/understanding-impact-social-entrepreneurspdf.

4. More specifically, "Making More Health" (MMH), the ten-year collaboration between Ashoka and Boehringer Ingelheim (BI) has contributed to accelerating social innovation on health and building business and social value. Together, BI and Ashoka have enabled a peer community of 87 Fellows, social entrepreneurs building system change in health care active in 37 countries and reaching more than 9 million direct beneficiaries. MMH has directly invested €8.55 million in finding and funding these social entrepreneurs. Since 2011, more than 5,000 BI employees around the world have showcased their intrapreneurial skills and helped to bring the social and business sectors together in "win-win" opportunities. MMH also launched three global online challenges to source social health innovation ideas which uncovered 800 new ideas in health care and investments in projects in Kenya, India, Indonesia, and the United States (Ioan and Bianchi 2021).

5. For case examples of Ashoka's system-changing social entrepreneurs, see Bornstein (2004); Schwartz (2012); Rayner and Bonnici (2021).

6. For more information on Ashoka's history, see Bornstein (2004) and Wells (2018). For information about Ashoka's work to reshape education systems to enable changemaking skill acquisition, see Bassi and Wells (2020).

REFERENCES

Anon, 2021. *Innovating Higher Education for the Greater Good (SSIR)* [online]. Stanford Social Innovation Review. Available from: https://ssir.org/innovating _higher_education_for_the_greater_good (accessed October 30, 2021).

Anon, 2022. *atomstromlos. klimafreundlich. bürgereigen* [online]. EWS Schönau. Available from: https://www.ews-schoenau.de/ (accessed January 31, 2022).

Baggio, A., Garner, N., Raine, F. and Budinich, V., 2019. Answering Society's Call: A New Leadership Imperative [online]. McKinsey Quarterly. Available from: https://www.mckinsey.com/business-functions/people-and-organizational-performance/. our-insights/answering-societys-call-a-new-leadership-imperative?cid=other-eml -alt-mcq-mck&hlkid=431088caaede409ca7e908ba269951d6&hctky=2369986& hdpid=0c31eea6-83dc-4aa6-99ac-228df352e294 (accessed January 31, 2022).

Bassi, F. and Wells, D., 2020. A New Framework for the Growing up Years. Available from: https://www.wise-qatar.org/everyone-a-changemaker-ecosystems-a-new -framework-for-the-growing-up-years/ as well as http://www.ashoka.org (accessed October 2020).

Battilana, J., Kimsey, M., Zogbi, P. and Mair, J. Associação Saúde Criança: Trying to Break the Cycle of Poverty and Illness at Scale. Harvard Business School Case 419-048, December 2018. (Revised February 2019.)

Bornstein, D. 2004. *How to Change the World: Social Entrepreneurs and the Power of New Ideas*. Oxford University Press.

Budinich, V. and Drayton, W., 2010. A New Alliance for Social Change. *Harvard Business Review*, September.

Buurtzorg International, 2022. Our Organisation [online]. Buurtzorg International. Available from: https://www.buurtzorg.com/about-us/our-organisation/ (accessed 31 January 2022).

Canopy, 2020. Survival – a Pulp Thriller: A Plan for Saving Forests and Climate [online]. Available from: https://canopyplanet.org/wp-content/uploads/2020/01/SURVIVAL-Next-Gen-Pathway.pdf (accessed January 31, 2022).

Couchsurfing, 2022. About | Couchsurfing [online]. Available from: https://about.couchsurfing.com/about/about-us/ (accessed January 31, 2022).

Digital Green, 2022. About | Digital Green [online]. Available from: https://www.digitalgreen.org/about-us/ (accessed January 31, 2022).

Fairtrasa, 2022. Who We Are | Fairtrasa [online]. Available from: https://fairtrasa.com/we/ (accessed January 31, 2022).

Fuessel, A., 2020. Becoming a Changemaker Institution [online]. Mountain View, CA: Ashoka U. Available from: https://globaleducationforum.org/wp-content/uploads/2021/09/Becoming-a-Changemaker-Institution-s.pdf (accessed October 30, 2021).

Glasswing International, 2022. Our Story [online]. Available from: https://glasswing.org/our-story/ (accessed January 31, 2022)].

Imperative, 2022. Imperative – the Peer Coaching Platform [online]. Available from: https://www.imperative.com/ (accessed January 31, 2022).

Instituto Dara (formerly Saúde Criança Resnacer), 2022. Instituto Dara [online]. Available from: https://www.dara.org.br/ (accessed January 31, 2022).

Ioan, A. and Bianchi, A., 2021. A Transformative Partnership. 10 years & 10 Principles for Effective Collaboration between Business and Civil Society | Ashoka | Everyone a Changemaker [online]. Available from: https://www.ashoka.org/en-us/story/transformative-partnership-10-years-10-principles-effective-collaboration-between-business (accessed January 31, 2022).

Khan Academy, 2022. About [online]. Khan Academy. Available from: https://www.khanacademy.org/about (accessed January 31, 2022).

National Domestic Workers' Alliance (NDWA), 2022. Our Work [online]. Available from: https://www.domesticworkers.org/about-domestic-work/our-work/ (accessed January 31, 2022).

Rayner, C. and Bonnici, F., 2021. *The Systems Work of Social Change*. Oxford University Press.

Root Capital, 2021. Root Capital – Our Impact [online]. Available from: https://rootcapital.org/our-impact/ (accessed January 31, 2022).

Sage Bionetworks, 2022. Our Work [online]. Available from: https://sagebionetworks.org/ (accessed January 31, 2022).

Schwab Foundation, n.d. Five Lessons for Systems Change. Beyond Organizational Scale: How Social Entrepreneurs Create Systems Change [online]. Available from: https://wef.ch/2L4VTmH (accessed January 31, 2022).

Schwartz, B., 2012. *Rippling: How Social Entrepreneurs Spread Innovation throughout the World*. John Wiley & Sons.

Sire, J., 2020. *The Universe Next Door: A Basic Worldview Catalog* (sixth edn). Ivp Academic.

Sorkin, A.R., 2018. BlackRock's Message: Contribute to Society, or Risk Losing Our Support. *The New York Times* [online], January 16. Available from: https://www .nytimes.com/2018/01/15/business/dealbook/blackrock-laurence-fink-letter.html (accessed January 31, 2022).

StreetwiZe Mobile School, 2022. Who We Are [online]. Available from: https://www .streetwize.be/about-us/who-we-are (accessed January 31, 2022).

Wells, D., 2018. From Social Entrepreneurship to Everyone a Changemaker: 40 Years of Social Innovation Point to What's Next. *Social Innovations Journal* [online], 52 (Ashoka Edition). Available from: https://socialinnovationsjournal.org/editions/ issue-52/75-disruptive-innovations/2906-from-social-entrepreneurship-to-everyone -a-changemaker-40-years-of-social-innovation-point-to-what-s-next (accessed January 31, 2022).

Wurdinger, S. and Carlson, J., 2009. Teaching for Experiential Learning: Five Approaches That Work. R&L Education.

10. Partners in learning

Heather Cairns-Lee and Alisée de Tonnac

10.1 INTRODUCTION

We take as our point of departure a question from Karl Weick, "how can we think about reconfiguring management education, when the dynamics of managing keep shifting?" (Weick, 2007, p. 5). Although Weick's question was posed in 2007, it is perhaps even more relevant today in a world that is beset by complex wicked problems that pay no heed to national borders as evidenced by the Covid-19 pandemic. How indeed do business schools educate in a changing and unpredictable world? Drawing on Weick we propose that reconfiguring business schools as learning partners requires each partner to "*acquire* and *drop*" (2007, p. 5) certain assumptions in order to collaborate and learn from each other to address the shifting dynamics of our time.

We proceed as follows. First, we provide a brief retrospective of business schools. We suggest that their focus on "business" has much to do with their etymological origins that foreground commerce and trade over society. We then describe recent calls for business schools to address their purpose, ethics, curricula and research and impact. Recognizing that individuals, organizations and societies alike need to sustain competitive advantage while simultaneously identifying and creating new opportunities, we address how business schools can contribute to a more inclusive and sustainable society through developing entrepreneurial skills (Hitt et al., 2011). Drawing on literature that foregrounds the value of partnerships for business education (Kickul et al., 2012) we share a case study about a learning partnership between the School of Management, Fribourg and Seedstars to develop entrepreneurial learning. We conclude with suggestions and recommendations for future research and practice.

10.2 THE HISTORY AND ETYMOLOGY OF BUSINESS SCHOOLS

A quick tour of history shows that business schools appeared in Europe in the eighteenth century to teach commerce. Perhaps unsurprisingly, the creation of two of the earliest business schools in the world were founded by entrepreneurs who identified a need to develop commercial skills. Jean-Baptiste Say, a French economist and scholar, is credited with inventing the term entrepreneurship in 1800 and founding a school of commerce in Paris in 1819. Joseph Wharton, industrialist and entrepreneur, founded the first US school of business at the University of Pennsylvania 62 years later. By 1917, there were 30 business schools in the US and, according to the Association to Advance Collegiate Schools of Business (AACSB, 2011), there are now 13,000 business schools worldwide. Ironically, despite the involvement of entrepreneurs in the foundation of the schools, many have lost touch with their entrepreneurial origins.

A useful review of business school history from Currie, Davies and Ferlie (2016) identified three time periods that have shaped the development of business schools. In the first phase business schools were expected to develop managerial capabilities to support the economic growth needed by society, resulting in a relatively narrow focus on developing the skills to run businesses. In the second phase from the 1980s, business schools became preoccupied with academic legitimacy by focusing on theoretical research detached from the reality of management practice. They also prioritized programs and research to maximize shareholder value that marginalized wider societal concerns. Although not explicitly stated, business schools at this time were to have a "pro-business and clearly capitalist orientation" (Peters et al., 2018 p. 8). The third phase of business schools that evolved after the financial crisis is shaped by global concerns with complex grand challenges with the purpose of creating social (not only shareholder) value through multi-disciplinary "public interest" approaches (Ferlie et al., 2010).

History is important, it charts the people, decisions and actions that have brought us to the present. However, language is also important because it signals the narratives that comprise "identity and ideology" (Ferlie et al., 2010, p. 60) which convey who and what is valued. As such, it is instructive to look to the history of language to identify the origins, meanings and possible legacy of words. The original purpose of business schools was "commerce," which etymologically meant "social interaction," which shifted to "interchange of goods or property, trade especially trade on a large scale by transportation between countries or different parts of the same country" (Harper, 2001–17). Just as the etymology of commerce shifted from social interaction to trade, business schools have shifted from their entrepreneurial roots with connections to industry, community and society to focus on commercial concerns that prioritize business operations and financial return. This commercial perspective is based on a root metaphor of "trade" that emphasizes buying and selling, profit and loss, shareholder value, market dynamics and prioritizes financial performance. Language based on this root metaphor reflects the transactional nature of trade, that is viewing people as "human resources or human capital" to be deployed for the good of the business. This commercial focus has been criticized for limiting business schools' interaction with society, for inadequately preparing students to deal with challenges in the real world and for reducing their impact (Thomas & Ambrosini, 2021). Returning to the etymological roots of "commerce" as social interaction foregrounds relationships, society and the ways that people interact.

Words matter, they create meaning, they influence our minds and direct attention (Feldman Barrett, 2020). In the world of education words matter enormously. This is not simply a question of semantics. Words are the conduits of meaning and learning and they convey what is valued and what is not. It matters which words and metaphors we choose and there are serious consequences "if we choose unwisely or fail to understand their implications" (Romaine, 1996, p. 192).

To underscore the importance of language, Ferlie et al. (2010) highlight that some schools chose to call themselves "management" schools rather than "business" schools (e.g. Fribourg in Switzerland and Lancaster in the UK). They suggest that these schools of management may consider their purpose more broadly as enhancing the public interest than business schools that might focus more narrowly as reflected in their name. Their argument is that management applies to all kinds of organization beyond business, such as non-governmental organizations (NGOs), charities, communities and entrepreneurs. Similarly, consider the word school, it typically activates memories of schooldays with the associated memories of teachers and students with concomitant expectations for how people behave in these roles including the relative power of the teacher to cover subjects, impart knowledge, grade exams and decide who passes and who fails according to predetermined criteria. We suggest that the shift in language from business schools to partners in learning is a significant signal about purpose and the nature of the relationship. Partners in learning broadens the focus from purely commercial concerns and teaching with its associated power dynamics to signal a relationship of equals focused on co-created learning which is essential to address the complex concerns of society.

10.3   THE PURPOSE AND IMPACT OF MANAGEMENT EDUCATION

There have been multiple calls to examine the purpose, morality and impact of business schools evidenced by thousands of books, articles and special journal issues dedicated to examining these questions (Pettigrew & Starkey, 2016; Svensson & Wood, 2006). Business schools sit at the uneasy intersection of business and education, in turn criticized for being too distant from business to be relevant or too close to business to be objective, controlled through funding and client demands (Ferlie et al., 2010). Although there has been increasing criticism of business schools, perhaps most radically by Parker (2018) who argues they should be shut down, the criticism is hardly new. Concerns about the overly scientific approach to management education led to the emergence of readable management books from the 1980s onwards, for example Porter's (1980) *Competitive Strategy* and Collins's (2001) *Good to Great*. While these books made management thinking more accessible to practicing managers, their launch highlighted a major challenge for business schools, namely, how to gain and manage academic legitimacy AND have real-world impact (Pettigrew & Starkey, 2016; Thomas et al., 2013). This challenge is evident in criticism concerning the perceived disconnect between business school curricula and the real-world dilemmas of practicing managers (Ghoshal, 2005) and for schools' preoccupation with rankings and reputation based on A-listed journal publications over more integrative progressive research relevant to the world of managers (Adler & Harzing, 2009).

Twenty years ago, Gioia warned that unless business schools challenged their own assumptions they were in danger of training managers "bereft of socially responsible values" (2002, p. 143). Following the financial crisis, these warnings were heightened by Podolny (2009) who claimed "that people have come to believe that business schools are harmful to society, fostering self-interested, unethical, and even illegal behavior" (p. 63).

From these critiques, it is apparent that the purpose of business schools is questioned and we welcome the contribution of this book to consider their future. According to Petriglieri and Petriglieri, "the questions we need to ask of business schools are not only how they develop leaders but for what purpose and on whose behalf" (2015, p. 642). Traditionally, the purpose of business schools has been to socialize managers and legitimize management (Grey, 2002). This tends to preserve the status quo and can lead to silence on issues that are not deemed mainstream to management. Instead of socializing, Grey suggests that schools should aim to "responsibilize" (2002, p. 499) managers which requires them "to make sense of their experience" (p. 506). When schools conceive their purpose broadly as "responsibilizing" themselves and their participants to respond to the needs of society, they enroll participants as active "partners" in the learning process rather than as passive recipients of accumulated wisdom. Yet, beyond the individual level at which participants learn, when schools conceive purpose in terms of responsibility it supports them to make a deliberate commitment to enhancing their contribution to societal value and away from an instrumental pursuit of more narrowly defined economic outcomes (Kitchener & Delbridge, 2020).

If the purpose of business schools is to responsibilize for the benefit of individuals and society, how can they develop leaders? Two aspects are important. One is to form connections within and across society through partnerships and the other is to develop the skillset and mindset that equip people to deal with an uncertain future through an entrepreneurial education. We address these two considerations in turn before illustrating these points with a case study.

10.4 PARTNERSHIPS FOR ENTREPRENEURIAL EDUCATION TO ADDRESS EMERGING CHALLENGES

It has long been acknowledged that addressing complex issues lies outside the competency of business schools alone. Indeed, "It is rare to find complex, adaptive, social problems that do not require collaboration among key stake-holders from nonprofit, public, and private sectors" (Kickul et al., 2012, p. 481). We draw on the United Nations to suggest that the willingness to form innovative partnerships to address complex multi-dimensional problems is essential.

> The achievement of the 2030 Agenda for Sustainable Development and the Sustainable Development Goals require all hands on deck. It requires different sectors and actors working together in an integrated manner by pooling financial resources, knowledge and expertise. For achieving the sustainable Future We Want, cross sectorial and innovative multi-stakeholder partnerships will play a crucial role for getting us to where we need by the year 2030. (United Nations, 2021)

Partnerships enable creative and meaningful engagement with complex issues in three ways: (1) they multiply the resources and impact of the partners; (2) they provide the opportunity to challenge each partner's assumptions and through this (3) they enable the development of new forms of knowledge and solutions that correspond with emerging challenges. While partnerships have many advantages, it is important that participants "lower walls" of interaction (Currie et al., 2016) in order for collaboration to flourish. This is a useful reminder that learning partners need to be prepared to both "acquire and drop" (Weick, 2007, p. 5) familiar ways of thinking and acting in order to learn and grow.

While partnerships enable the sharing of assumptions, resources and action to address issues, it is also important to address the actual skills and mindsets that equip people to deal with future adaptive challenges and for this we turn to entrepreneurial education, which is fundamental to the ability of individuals, organizations and society to shift with changing times. This is much more than learning the skills of managing a business, which is core to MBA programs, it is a profound form of education that contributes to a more holistic curriculum (Rynes & Bartunek, 2013). Yet there are debates whether entrepreneurship – a skill/mindset that is often seen to exist outside of traditional management – can be taught and if so, how?

With well-publicized stories of entrepreneurs starting multi-billion dollar businesses without finishing college or attending business school, it is questioned whether entrepreneurship can be taught. For example, Bhatia and Levina (2020, p. 323) ask whether "imagination, disruption, and counterintuitive actions" are inherent to entrepreneurs and if so whether these characteristics are compatible with business education? They recognize that entrepreneurship has matured as a discipline and is indeed taught at business schools although the approaches to teaching vary depending on the epistemic stance adopted by the school. These epistemic stances frame what counts as knowledge including how entrepreneurship and entrepreneurs are defined, the practices of relating to people and the environment and styles of thinking and inquiry (Rowbottom & Bueno, 2011).

Different stances will influence what counts as knowledge, what is taught about entrepreneurship, the attitudes and beliefs of those teaching and how knowledge is conveyed. If entrepreneurship is narrowly defined as a predisposition of a subset of people, it can present hurdles if people do not identify as an entrepreneur which can affect their confidence to learn entrepreneurship. If, on the other hand, entrepreneurship is defined more broadly as a potential path for all, this opens up possibilities for students to learn the craft of entrepreneurship and for them to develop greater self-efficacy about entrepreneurial work. Different stances may underscore tensions in teaching entrepreneurship. For example, if it is taught and justified through accepted business school methods and logics this can limit ground-breaking modes of engagement, teaching and learning. Furthermore, different attitudes towards relating to people can influence styles of engagement. For example, Bhatia and Levina (2020) explored the stances to engagement in three US business schools, Darden, Rotman and Wharton, that offered entrepreneurial education. They found that all schools valued the importance of developing strategic partnerships, albeit for different reasons. For example, access to resources, support with commercialization or searching for new market opportunities, underscoring that partnerships are crucial to effective learning about entrepreneurship.

In order to illustrate a learning partnership in action, we now share a case study between Seedstars and the School of Management at Fribourg.

10.5   LEARNING PARTNERS SCHOOL OF MANAGEMENT (HEG) FRIBOURG AND SEEDSTARS

Entrepreneurship is integral to the school of management (HEG) in Fribourg (https://www.heg-fr.ch/en/about-us/), as articulated in its mission to:

> support, prepare and empower leaders and international entrepreneurs to apply actionable executive skills to address global challenges faced in business and society. We are committed to creating a positive impact through the students, participants and partners, all of whom will benefit from our programs and activities in three core areas: Entrepreneurship, Innovation and Internationalization.

The school's mission statement is noteworthy not only due to its identification of entrepreneurs as a core audience and entrepreneurship as a core area but also due to its focus on partners. This focus on partnership is rooted in the position that Fribourg is at a linguistic crossroad between French and German-speaking Switzerland. Bridging linguistic borders supports the school to adopt a multi-cultural and open-minded attitude to relationships. In addition to the focus of teaching entrepreneurship to entrepreneurs, one of the school's noteworthy research outputs is the annual Global Entrepreneurship Monitor.

Seedstars (https://www.seedstars.com/) was founded in 2013 to make a positive difference in emerging markets through technology, entrepreneurship and the development of startup ecosystems. It also focuses on important themes for education including childhood development, upskilling for the twenty-first century and Edtech. The organization focuses on emerging markets because even though these markets account for 85 percent of the world's population, many still lack basic services including education, energy and healthcare. Despite the massive opportunity for growth, these emerging markets only account for 3.6 percent of global venture capital investment (EMPEA, 2020). Seedstars supports entrepreneurs from across the globe through incubation programs, acceleration events and direct investments in tech-enabled impact startups and investment fundraising. Its platform is an opportunity for startups to hone and pitch their ideas to potential investors and meet mentors in the service of achieving their next milestone. It has a global community of over 250,000 members, 5,000 investors, 75 mentors and 500 training programs. The startups they have worked with have created over 5,000 jobs and raised over $250 million in over 113 countries.

Both Seedstars and the School of Management Fribourg are based in Switzerland, and both have strong international outlooks. For example, Fribourg offers trilingual education and Seedstars has tech-hubs in 15 locations around the world. The two organizations collaborate to develop entrepreneurial skills for the future. Beyond sharing a purpose based on strong international presence and entrepreneurial focus, the two organizations also share similar epistemic stances. They both aim to develop entrepreneurial skills for society, rather than focusing more narrowly on the education of entrepreneurs. Their approach to educating skills in responsible entrepreneurship is pragmatic and mutually beneficial. While HEG Fribourg provides education in entrepreneurial skills for the private sector and Seedstars develops entrepreneurial talent for startups, they share a goal to bridge the gap between traditional academic education that tends to operate in transmission mode (Löbler, 2006) and the need for entrepreneurial skills in society. They both view entrepreneurial education as an imperative for the leaders society needs now and in the future, and they have partnered to create a win-win situation for their institutions and as a contribution to fostering an entrepreneurial mindset in society. They share a belief that everyone needs entrepreneurial acumen for the future to deal with the new skills of artificial intelligence (AI), coding and robotization but also to have the entrepreneurial drive and creativity to make sense of a fast-changing world. These skills are important, along with the "soft skills" of communication and managing relationships even if people may not found their own companies. These skills contribute to socially responsible citizens who are able to make a difference globally.

Underlying the partnership is a match in values between HEG Fribourg and Seedstars working at individual, economic and societal levels to contribute to individual potential and society's triple bottom line: social, environmental and financial. This triple level impact is depicted in HEG's societal engagement and impact framework (Figure 10.1).

Target	HEG-FR field of action (aligned with our mission and strategy)	Our goal
Individuals	Teaching in a family culture Equality and diversity	Empowering individuals to reach their full potential within our society
Economy	Educate with high practical relevance Valorization of new technology for business and society Support entrepreneurship and innovation for the entrepreneurial ecosystem	Contribute to an efficient and sustainably successful economy, which we see as part of the society
Society	Conveying multilingual, intercultural competences Global challenge in business and society: sustainability, impact, purpose	Making our small contribution to the positive development of society

Figure 10.1   HEG Fribourg's societal engagement and impact framework

The cooperation between HEG Fribourg and Seedstars started in 2014 and is marked by practical and international learning for students including internships and career acceleration, by the insights generated into emerging markets, and the networking activities. HEG Fribourg gives the education prize at the annual final Seedstars Summit which symbolizes the philosophy of both organizations to advance entrepreneurial education.

Each year students from HEG Fribourg, especially those in the Master program in Entrepreneurship, have the opportunity to attend the Summit to meet people from all over the world and experience the mélange across cultures. Before the Summit, workshops are held with the students. These one-day workshops involve one of the Co-Founders or team members of Seedstars sharing stories about entrepreneurs and presenting case studies of startups to open the students' eyes to opportunities in emerging markets. Seedstars and HEG Fribourg want their partnership to be about more than the transmission of ideas and case studies and so they have worked to involve the entrepreneurship students actively in the organization of the Summit. The aim is to train students in an entrepreneurial environment focused on Emerging Markets while working on specific projects. This approach, based on the collaboration of the Learning Partners – Seedstars and HEG Fribourg – provides students with vital professional skills and leadership and entrepreneurial mindset, making their education more concrete than case studies. The highest performing students are selected for interviews to join the Seedstars team, creating a mutual benefit for students and Seedstars.

On the one hand, the Summit is a form of international importance. This means that the students experience first-hand what it means to organize an event of this magnitude. They are involved in various tasks such as sales; in-kind partners; content and speakers; and workshops. They have the opportunity to take on essential administrative tasks and thus implement and build upon the experience from their educational courses. They also have the chance to get in touch with venture capitalists, entrepreneurs and key people to expand their network and enhance their possibilities in job search. The program helps students to develop core skills, learn more about the different startup ecosystems, and impact for their business. In addition, it is an excellent opportunity to play an essential role in organizing one of the most significant global events dedicated to startups and emerging markets. Finally, this hands-on activity includes entrepreneurial thinking, acting, leadership and agility, providing a unique experience for the students.

Beyond the collaboration around Seedstars Summit, there are other noteworthy aspects to the partnership. One of these is Seedstars' participation in HEG Fribourg's international summer school "How to lead with purpose and global impact." Another aspect is in partnering to facilitate the development of entrepreneurial talent more broadly in Switzerland and globally. For example,

Seedstars is an official partner of the Innovation Lab Fribourg, an incubator hub founded at HEG Fribourg in 2016 to promote collaboration and connections to accelerate innovation. Furthermore, Seedstars fosters and supports the network of HEG Fribourg concerning research grants, for example, with B lab Geneva, part of the Swiss branch of a global NGO that aims to accelerate the role of business to address societal challenges, or the Swiss SME Ricola. Finally, Seedstars and HEG Fribourg collaborate with the *Financial Times* for the FTxSDG Challenge. The Sustainable Development Goals Challenge is dedicated to empowering impact-driven entrepreneurs in emerging markets through a startup competition, split into thematic challenges based on six of the United Nation's Sustainable Development Goals – gender equality, climate action, quality education (sponsored by HEG Fribourg), good jobs and economic growth, reduced inequalities and good health and wellbeing.

This example of the collaboration between HEG Fribourg and Seedstars shows how management learning can be enhanced through learning partnerships that create more innovative and impactful approaches to education than would be possible by a solo player. It is a collaboration that combines education and entrepreneurship to develop the entrepreneurial mindset and skills needed to face the future.

10.6 DROPPING AND ACQUIRING TOOLS IN A LEARNING PARTNERSHIP

Partnership can exist at different levels, as identified by Epstein et al. (2002), from limited one-time collaborations to full partnerships in which organizations with shared values, goals and power contribute complementary skills to create new value based on a relationship of mutual trust and respect. Effective learning partnerships embody these shared values, trust, respect and goals. They are born when stakeholders recognize that value is co-created with others, which requires forming relationships and the creation of safe spaces to discuss knowledge gaps and divergent views (Thomas & Ambrosini, 2021).

Learning partnerships provide multiple perspectives, different types of learning opportunities and the ability to connect and learn with communities, creating ecosystems that collaborate for the common good. This provides the advantages of situated learning (Lave & Wenger, 1991), through the practices of groups that are created over time and that develop through shared experiences. Three components are essential to a successful partnership: a shared enterprise, mutual engagement and a shared repertoire. A shared enterprise relates to the purpose of the community that is crafted and negotiated over time. Mutual engagement brings people together for the purpose of a shared goal in an ongoing partnership and a shared repertoire involves the way that people work together over time including style, behavior and artifacts. These three components create overlapping spheres of influence.

Partnerships are successful when divergent thinking from the different partners supports systems to become aware of possible blindspots and problems because this is "associated with (their) ability to act on them" (Westrum, 1993, p. 340). The importance of being able to notice what we might otherwise not notice and hence the need for collaboration with others is beautifully encapsulated in an apposite quote by Goleman (1985, p. 24):

> The range of what we think and do is limited by what we fail to notice. And because we fail to notice that we fail to notice there is little we can do to change until we notice how failing to notice shapes our thoughts and deeds.

Openness to the thinking of others through partnerships is one way that business schools can "drop" their habituated ways of seeing by finding people who understand a situation differently or better and deferring to them (Weick, 2007). Hence learning partners can help each other see what might otherwise be invisible so that that their familiar assumptions, practices and actions do not preclude new ways of seeing situations. Returning to Weick, learning what to keep and what to drop is essential to thrive in a complex world and, we would contend in learning partnerships, as "Knowledge involves acquiring. Wisdom involves dropping" (2007, p. 15).

10.7   CONCLUSION

This chapter outlines the recasting of business schools as partners in learning. Doing so addresses some of the criticism of business schools as overly focused on commercial concerns. We suggest that recasting "business schools" as "partners in learning" can help to reconfigure management education by broadening the remit from "business" to "society" and from "school" to "learning." Words matter – they reflect and perpetuate root metaphors that have implications for action. In addition to changing the root metaphor for management education, when schools create partnerships based on aligned attitudes to how knowledge is created and shared, they can enhance their contribution to society. Partnerships that provide an entrepreneurial education develop adaptive, innovative solutions for today and tomorrow. Our sincere hope is that schools will be proactive and receptive in seeking out partners in learning to enhance their purpose and practices to create a better tomorrow for the good of humanity.

REFERENCES

AACSB. (2011). *Globalization of management education: Changing international structure, adaptive strategies and the impact on institutions*. Bingley, UK: Emerald.

Adler, N.J., and Harzing, A.-W. (2009). When knowledge wins: Transcending the sense and nonsense of academic rankings. *Academy of Management Learning & Education, 8*(1), 72–95.

Bhatia, A.K., and Levina, N. (2020). Diverse rationalities of entrepreneurship education: An epistemic stance perspective. *Academy of Management Learning & Education, 19*(3), 323–44.

Collins, J.C. (2001). *Good to great*. New York: Harper Collins.

Currie, G., Davies, J., and Ferlie, E. (2016). A call for university-based business schools to "lower their walls": Collaborating with other academic departments in pursuit of social value. *Academy of Management Learning & Education, 15*(4), 742–55.

EMPEA. (2020). *Trends in global VC+Tech*. New York: Global Private Capital Association.

Epstein, J.L., Sanders, M.G., Simon, B.S., Salinas, K.C., Jansorn, N.R., and Voorhis, F.L.V. (2002). *School, family and community partnerships: Your handbook for action* (second edn). Thousand Oaks, CA: Corwin Press.

Feldman Barrett, L. (2020). People's words and actions can actually shape your brain – a neuroscientist explains how. Retrieved December 31, 2021 from https://ideas.ted.com/peoples-words-and-actions-can-actually-shape-your-brain-a-neuroscientist-explains-how/?fbclid=IwAR1rmwlAGo_cWU4j-Eeaq8sIqYG4imOEoKqTf6exzxFqPX0VIKgUJnkPMWc

Ferlie, E., McGivern, G., and De Moraes, A. (2010). Developing a public interest school of management. *British Journal of Management, 21*, s60–s70.

Ghoshal, S. (2005). Bad management theories are destroying good management practices. *Academy of Management Learning & Education, 4*(1), 75–91.

Gioia, D.A. (2002). Business education's role in the crisis of corporate confidence. *Academy of Management Perspectives, 16*(3), 142–4.

Goleman, D. (1985). *Vital lies, simple truths: The psychology of self-deception*. New York: Simon & Schuster.

Grey, C. (2002). What are business schools for? On silence and voice in management education. *Journal of Management Education, 26*(5), 496–511.

Harper, D. (2001–17). Online etymology dictionary. Retrieved December 6, 2017 from http://www.etymonline.com/

Hitt, M.A., Ireland, R.D., Sirmon, D.G., and Trahms, C.A. (2011). Strategic entrepreneurship: Creating value for individuals, organizations, and society. *Academy of Management Perspectives, 25*(2), 57–75.

Kickul, J., Janssen-Selvadurai, C., and Griffiths, M.D. (2012). A blended value framework for educating the next cadre of social entrepreneurs. *Academy of Management Learning & Education, 11*(3), 479–93.

Kitchener, M., and Delbridge, R. (2020). Lessons from creating a business school for public good: Obliquity, waysetting, and wayfinding in substantively rational change. *Academy of Management Learning & Education, 19*(3), 307–22.

Lave, J., and Wenger, E. (1991). *Situated learning: Legitimate peripheral participation*. Cambridge: Cambridge University Press.

Löbler, H. (2006). Learning entrepreneurship from a constructivist perspective. *Technology Analysis & Strategic Management, 18*(1), 19–38.

Parker, M. (2018). *Shut down the business school: What's wrong with management education?* London: Pluto Press.

Peters, K., Thomas, H., and Smith, R.R. (2018). The business of business schools. *Global Focus – European Foundation for Management Development, 12*(1), 6–11.

Petriglieri, G., and Petriglieri, J.L. (2015). Can business schools humanize leadership? *Academy of Management Learning & Education, 14*(4), 625–47.

Pettigrew, A., and Starkey, K. (2016). From the guest editors: The legitimacy and impact of kbusiness schools – Key issues and a research agenda. *Academy of Management Learning & Education, 15*(4), 649–64.

Podolny, J.M. (2009). The buck stops (and starts) at business school. *Harvard Business Review*, June, 62–7.

Porter, M.E. (1980). *Competitive strategy*. New York: Free Press.

Romaine, S. (1996). War and peace in the global greenhouse: Metaphors we die by. *Metaphor & Symbolic Activity, 11*(3), 175.

Rowbottom, D.P., and Bueno, O. (2011). How to change it: Modes of engagement, rationality, and stance voluntarism. *Synthese, 178*(1), 7–17.

Rynes, S.L., and Bartunek, J.M. (2013). Curriculum matters: Toward more holistic graduate education. In E.C. Dierdorff and B. Holtom (eds), *Disrupt or be disrupted: Evidence-based strategies for graduate business school* (pp. 179–218). Hoboken, NJ: Wiley & Sons.

Svensson, G., and Wood, G. (2006). Special issue on business schools or schools for scholars? *European Business Review, 18*(4).

Thomas, H., Thomas, L., and Wilson, A. (2013). The unfulfilled promise of management education (ME): The role, value and purposes of ME. *Journal of Management Development, 32*(5), 460–76.

Thomas, L., and Ambrosini, V. (2021). The future role of the business school: A value cocreation perspective. *Academy of Management Learning & Education, 20*(2), 249–69.

United Nations. (2021). Multi-stakeholder partnerships and voluntary commitments. Retrieved 16 January, 2022 from https://sdgs.un.org/topics/multi-stakeholder -partnerships-and-voluntary-commitments

Weick, K.E. (2007). Drop your tools: On reconfiguring management education. *Journal of Management Education, 31*(1), 5–16.

Westrum, R. (1993). *Thinking by groups, organizations, and networks: A sociologist's view of the social psychology of science and technology*. New York: Guilford.

PART III

Performance of business schools: recent trends, views on pertinence and use of management education

11. The manager of the future will either be resilient and empathetic, or not at all!

Inés Gabarret and Marcela Schweitzer

11.1 INTRODUCTION

It is common knowledge that we live in a world of organizations, and organizations mean management. As Canadian professor Henry Mintzberg of McGill University explained in his seminal book from 1989, our society has become a society of organizations. Organizations are formal and coordinated groups of people who function to achieve particular goals. These goals cannot be achieved by individuals working independently. The Austrian American professor Peter Drucker, one of the most influential thinkers and writers on the subject of management theory and practice, explains that organizations depend on managers, are built by managers, and are directed and held together by managers (Drucker, 1973). From the small or medium-sized owner-managed company to the multinational enterprise (MNE) whose shares are traded on the stock exchange, managers play a critical role in planning, organizing, and directing the activities of the firm and, all the while, leading, encouraging, and coaching their teams to higher levels of productivity.

Whatever the organizational context, the effectiveness of the manager will depend on the ability to understand the organization and the environment, and the capacity to get things done through it. Therefore, management is about facilitating human collaboration (Mintzberg, 1989), as well as getting results with the cooperation of other people (Drucker, 1973).

Looking retrospectively, managerial roles have evolved as organizations have changed. In the past, managerial functions were based on a command-and-control model, as explained by Henri Fayol already at the end of the 19th century. His definition of the process of management was centered on a cycle of planning – organizing – commanding – coordinating – controlling. Over time – and as society became more complex – managerial roles have evolved to rise to the challenge inherent in greater complexity. According to Mintzberg (1989), the manager develops interpersonal roles, informational roles, and decisional roles, leading to a variety of activities (strategic planning, coordinating, empowering, facilitating, coaching, etc.).

The current global health crisis provides an opportune moment to reassess managerial roles and ask new questions about leadership. Considering that business schools prepare the leaders of the future, what are the competencies the managers of the future must develop? And how can business schools help students develop such competencies?

Brené Brown, in her book *Dare to Lead* (2018), explains that leadership has always been associated with courage and being brave in times of crisis. However, according to the author, leadership is also about empathy, vulnerability, and self-care. Brené Brown (2018) considers vulnerability as uncertainty, risk, and emotional exposure. It is not weakness; it is the most accurate measurement of courage. In complex and uncertain environments, a leader who can meet vulnerability with empathy will be able to feel compassion, to build connections, and turn crises into learning experiences. Learning from mistakes is possible when responding to vulnerability and shame with empathy and compassion (Brown, 2018).

Moreover, a leader's emotions have an impact on the emotions of everyone on the team. Leaders who can manage their own emotions are better prepared to deal with uncertainty and to improve productivity and working conditions for the team.

Based on those ideas, our proposition is that along with awareness about ethics, corporate social responsibility, and sustainability, it is also necessary to develop competencies to deal with extreme uncertainty. Such competencies can be resumed as flexibility, resilience, and empathy. Business schools must therefore consider preparing their students to develop both hard and soft skills.

11.2 MANAGERS SHAPED BY THE BUSINESS SCHOOLS

The advent of the business schools is a critical event in the evolution of the discipline of management theory and practice. Business schools are educational institutions that specialize in teaching courses and programs related to business and/or management (Kaplan, 2018), and they have been shaping the management of these organizations since the beginning of its existence, starting by the creation of ESCP Europe in 1819, considered as the world's oldest business school. In Europe, the history of the European business schools is analyzed through two periods. The first one is from 1819 to 1944. The second one started on 1944 and it lasts until today (Kaplan, 2014). The second period shows the influence of globalization and lately, the emphasis on research.

During this second period, and because of the globalization, European business schools were influenced by the American management model. With a certain amount of justification, they were identified as the key culprits for the undue focus on financial management which, it may be argued, was a driving force in the subprime crisis. As Currie et al. (2010) consider, concentrating the obligations of managers on improving shareholder value was not a good recipe and business schools need to become more introspective and look critically at what they teach. In the special issue of the *British Journal of Management* that they coordinated in 2010, several authors provide important approaches to management education, through integration, leadership, and through a critical re-evaluation of the model for the future business school. In this focus, Ford et al. (2010) develop a profound analysis about the critical management education. According to the authors, business school programs and teaching will influence students in ways that are impossible to predict.

Along with the evolution of business schools, Christensen et al. (2007) explain how the development of curricula focus on Corporate Social Responsibility (CSR) as well as Sustainable Management criteria, meaning the preservation of resources for future generations.

It is principally the 2008 financial crisis that has encouraged researchers and managers to focus on ethics, questioning how businesses must be conducted, and how business schools can provide solid ethics educations to their students (Sigurjonsson et al., 2014). Moreover, the increasing number of corporate scandals show the importance of reinforcing ethics education in business schools (Sigurjonsson et al., 2015). Christensen et al. (2007) assume that ethics education in business schools has shifted the focus from just teaching ethics to a more integrated approach including the concepts of CSR and sustainability.

Other topics of discussion concerning business schools include their role (specifically in the current competitive scope), the impact of business schools' rankings in the hierarchization of activities, and the different consequences of the global competition. Durand and Dameron (2011) explain that there is a need "to engage in strategic conversations" to redesign management education and research in Europe and beyond. Kaplan (2018) talks about major shifts in business education, major challenges driving him to the realization that we are facing the emergence of a "new era in the history of business education" (Kaplan, 2018, p. 599).

Looking critically to give an answer to the problem of the adequacy of the business schools given the complexities of the global challenges, different approaches are proposed. Among them, Gröschl and Gabaldon (2018) focus on the need for responsible leadership and use Edgar Morin's notion of trans-disciplinarity to develop a humanistic vision and awareness that challenges simplistic thinking. Painter-Morland and Slegers (2018) focus on the "Giving Voice to Values" (GVV) pedagogy to allow students to behave according to their tacit values and understand economic theory with a morally appropriate focus.

Beyond the problems of the economic crisis and corporate scandals of the past decades, the global health crisis has placed business schools face to face with new challenges. The manager of the future must be able to deal with increased uncertainty. To better prepare those managers, a possibility for business schools is to complete their academic curricula with complementary approaches based on soft skills. Important aspects to consider are the capacity to develop resilient attitudes and empathetic abilities, thought to be fundamental to be able to manage in times of crisis.

11.3 RESILIENCE AND EMPATHY AS KEY ASPECTS FOR THE FUTURE MANAGERIAL ROLES

Beyond classic hard skills, curricula must also include soft skills. Introducing the development of emotional intelligence into business school programs is a fundamental point in the construction of the manager of the future. Among the many soft skills and competencies from the conceptual approach of the psychology of emotions, resilience and empathy seems to be principal to deal with extreme uncertainty.

11.3.1 Emotional Intelligence, What Is It About?

Emotional intelligence is the ability of an individual to understand his/her own feelings and express his/her emotions constructively while being able to understand the feelings of others (Goleman, 1998). According to the author, emotional intelligence is composed of five aspects: self-awareness, empathy, relationship management, management of feelings, and motivations. This model was redesigned in 2002 with four domains: self-awareness, self-management, social awareness, and relationship management.

Self-awareness is the ability to read and understand your emotions as well as recognize their impact on others (Goleman, 2014). Two important elements are self-confidence and the ability to self-assess. We can experience feelings that are the result of an emotion and we can understand the meaning of that emotion. We cannot avoid emotions, but we can change our thoughts about them (self-evaluation).

The second aspect is self-management, or self-regulation. It is the ability to orient ourselves towards our goals, overcome problems and manage stress. It is linked to resilience, reliability, adaptability, initiative, and the ability to make the right decisions. Self-regulation provides a sense of well-being, self-efficacy, and confidence.

Social awareness is the ability to understand the emotions of others taking their perspective and developing empathy. According to Goleman (2014), social awareness is linked to our social conscience and empathy by exploring different perspectives, namely:

- Interest and empathy for the problems of others;
- Deep listening;
- The ability to decode the emotional state of a group;
- The ability to optimize the emotional potential of his work team;
- The ability to encourage dialogue and debate;
- The ability to understand organizations.

Relationship management, the fourth aspect, is the ability to combine one's own emotions, the emotions of others, and the context to manage social interactions successfully. It is our ability to communicate (Goleman, 2014):

- Help others to progress;
- Positively influence others;
- Be competent in conflict management;
- Be a catalyst for change;
- Have leadership skills;
- Have the ability to work in a team;
- Have the ability to build relationships, make deals, and connect with others in a positive and respectful manner.

Salovey and Mayer (1990) consider emotional intelligence as a form of intelligence that involves the ability to control one's feelings and emotions and those of others, to distinguish between them, and to use that information to guide one's thoughts and feelings. This definition connects emotion and cognition. According to the authors, our emotions will guide our thoughts and actions.

For two decades now, researchers in psychology, neurosciences, and artificial intelligence have developed theories and models that integrate the interactions between emotion and cognition (Sander and Scherer, 2019).

Emotional intelligence is also known to have positive effects on resilience. Sarrionandia et al. (2018) show how the ability of individuals to identify and manage their own emotions, as well as other's emotions, seems to have a predictive impact on their ability to cope with developmental tasks despite the risks.

11.3.1.1 Empathy for connected leaders
Empathy is the capacity to connect to the emotion another person is experiencing and not the actual experience (Brown, 2018). In English, the word comes from the Greek root *pathos*, which means emotion, feeling, suffering,

or pity. The term also comes from the German word *Einfühlung* (Titchener, 1909) which means "feeling into" or "to feel oneself in." According to Decety (2010), empathy must be considered when a person experiences an emotional response to another's emotion. It is thus necessary to distinguish between oneself and the other and be able to regulate one's own emotion. Decety (2010) puts forward that its components influence each other.

Although empathy is a complex skill, it can be developed with practice (Brown, 2018). For instance, Denmark is teaching empathy at school as a compulsory course in the same vein as mathematics (see Danish law of 1993 on education[1]). This country thus prepares the new generations for the experience of projecting themselves into the situation of the other, to decode their mental state, and to develop reconstructive empathy through experiential simulation.

In March 2018, teams from the University of Cambridge, the Institut Pasteur, and the University of Paris Diderot published a study in *Translational Psychiatry* showing that some certain empathy abilities are genetically determined. They estimate that about 10 percent of the variations in empathy between individuals are linked to genetics (Warrier et al., 2018). We can therefore infer from the results of this study that the environment plays a role in the development of empathy through training.

Brené Brown (2018) considers courage as a set of four skills that can be observed, measured, and taught. The four skill sets are: rumbling with vulnerability, living into our values, braving trust, and learning to rise. According to Brown (2018), empathy is not possible without vulnerability. Vulnerability allows tough conversations, builds trust, and reinforces empathy. It therefore seems that vulnerability is a common foundation on which the concepts of empathy and leadership are based.

According to Eklund and Meranius (2020), the terms and aspects generally linked to empathy are automatisms (mechanisms and neurons), observation, management, care, behavior, listening abilities, avoidance of judgment, understanding others, and awareness of oneself and others. There is a consensus that empathy is related to awareness of self and others and understanding and sharing each other's feelings.

11.3.1.2 Resilience in the face of uncertainty

Resilience is the ability to overcome and adapt after adverse circumstances (Bullough et al., 2014). On an individual level, resilience allows the individual to stabilize her/his emotions and broaden her/his scope of attention (Fredrickson et al., 2003; Waugh et al., 2008). On a social level, resilience is the capacity to build with others (Danaher, 2014).

Resilience is complex, multidimensional, and dynamic (Southwick et al., 2011). A resilient individual is able to find meaning in adverse events and considers adversity as a challenge (Southwick et al., 2011).

Resilience was first considered a personality trait reflecting flexibility to adapt to emotional events (Genet and Siemer, 2011). It was also considered a dynamic process to deal with uncertainty (Sutcliffe and Vogus, 2003). This dynamic process can be taught and developed over time with practice (de Vries and Shields, 2006; Luthans et al., 2007).

Individual resilience concerns two psychological mechanisms: the regulation of emotion (emotional resilience) and the flexibility of thought (cognitive resilience). Emotions, even if they are transitory, lead to different ways of action. A negative event or stressful situation provokes negative emotional states. Resilient individuals are capable of adjusting their emotions (Waugh et al., 2008) and to transform the negative emotional state into a neutral or positive one. Once the regulation of emotion is done, cognitive resilience will allow the search for information and the exploration of other possibilities (Isen, 2001; Fredrickson and Branigan, 2005). Thanks to the cognitive flexibility, individuals can recognize essential from non-essential information and adapt to a changing environment (Genet and Siemer, 2011). According to Inés (2001) cognitive flexibility enables individuals "to switch perspectives and see things in multiple ways and come up with viable solutions." Cognitive resilience involves two cognitive process: inhibition and shifting (Genet and Siemer, 2011). Inhibition means to eliminate irrelevant information (Miyake et al., 2000). Shifting means to switch back and forth between multiple mental sets (Miyake et al., 2000).

The development of resilience is necessary for the decision-making process in uncertainty and will allow for an opening towards different solutions, within the framework of a flexible approach, since flexibility is considered an adaptive change to the events of the environment (Clément, 2006). Flexibility refers to new ways of apprehending the situation by developing procedures that are not part of the repertoire (Clément, 2006). In the context of a problem, repertoire means patterns of action activated in individuals that cannot be applied directly to the situation. The discovery of a solution thus depends on the restructuring of the patterns by way of considering the constraints of the situation and the transformations accomplished or to be accomplished.

Several theoretical approaches consider flexibility as a component of the creative thinking (Clément, 2006). In addition to this, resilience as a process allows flexibility of thought and, as such, the creation of innovative approaches where the old ways of solving problems have been proved ineffective.

11.4   BUSINESS SCHOOLS' CURRICULA FOR NEW MANAGERIAL ROLES

Business schools must follow and adapt to changes in society, providing qualitative education for the new generations of leaders. In this scope, business schools must orient their curricula to the needs of society at each moment in time.

Nowadays, the necessity of empathetic, flexible, and resilient leaders is a certainty. Business schools are the best place to form leaders with those characteristics, through the development of programs on emotional intelligence to complement those on rational intelligence. While rational intelligence consists of objective analysis of facts and figures, emotional intelligence helps to understand others' emotions as well as your own.

11.4.1 Developing Empathy and Resilience in Business Schools

The implementation of a program on emotional intelligence, allowing the school to develop empathy and resilience among their students, must be a strategic decision incorporating all the stakeholders. It will consider three levels: school management, faculty, and students.

The proposed program is transversal and longitudinal. It means that emotional intelligence concepts must be developed through seminars and specific courses, but also incorporated into all curricula and all over the learning process, from the first year of studies to the last.

To successfully accomplish this task, faculty must be trained in pedagogical theories, methods, and approaches of the emotional intelligence before starting to implement these concepts in curricula.

Concerning students, the starting point is a personalized diagnosis at their incorporation at the business school. Competencies in emotional intelligence can be tested through questions, role plays, case studies, or experiential simulations.

The following action is to introduce a new learning model based on the development of emotional skills with the objective of a behavioral evolution of students. A process of conceptual and behavioral change implies four different steps: ignorance, contemplation, preparation, and action (Goleman, 2014). The four steps will help develop a behavioral change and thus a change of the mental representations concerning the emotional approach.

Ignorance is the first stage. The individual fails to see the problem and does not feel a need to change. The second is contemplation. The individual begins to understand the interest and need for behavioral change and comes to express it. The third step is preparation. At this level, the individual is aware of the problem and can formulate a detailed plan for action. The last is action level. It is the time for change – the individual sets up the plan, develops it, changes his/her way of acting, changes his/her emotional patterns, and his/her vision of her-/himself and others.

Each level builds on the previous one allowing a process of behavioral change. So how can we support this development? Which pedagogical methods to adopt? We propose an emotional intelligence and management program built on the development of awareness, conceptualization, self-assessment, and finally, the co-construction of a new model of management with the students.

Business schools can think about the program as a mini laboratory. Inspired by the conceptual recommendations of Goleman (2014), they can orient courses based on the analysis of behavior, as well as the understanding of the emotional and social skills developed by the managers on every situation to infer the influence and the impact they can have at the level of groups and the organization. To do this, a logic of contents for a five-year program is recommended. The aim is to work at two levels: the construction of emotional competencies, and the construction of social competencies.

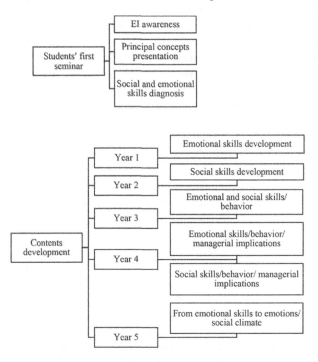

Figure 11.1   Emotional intelligence program in five years

11.4.1.1 The construction of emotional competencies

Emotional competencies such as self-knowledge, self-regulation, and motivation are the first to be developed in this program. The aim of this first stage is to improve the recognition of the different emotional states, being aware of feelings, emotions, preferences, as well as emotional resources, to develop emotional awareness. Emotional Awareness (EA) involves not only recognizing one's emotions but also the effects of EA. In this approach, self-assessment will be at the center of the process. Each student will be able to know her/his strengths and their limits on an emotional level. Not to mention that all this work directly improves self-confidence by realizing one's own self-worth and capacities.

The second conceptual element is self-regulation. This phase of training is essential for the management of internal states, negative impulses, and thought-less emotional behavior. Self-control is a key element to be developed. It can be done in the context of experiential simulations or role playing, followed by analytical work within each working group. Self-regulation is considered the first mechanism of individual resilience (Fredrickson and Branigan, 2005).

The third element of this first part of our program proposal is motivation. Motivation is a concept that is sometimes difficult to teach. How to be moti-vated and remain so? How to recognize this force, to engage and seize oppor-tunities, to move forward? The proposition is to approach motivation through the analysis of lived experiences.

11.4.1.2 Behavioral translation of the construction of emotional skills in future managers

The second step of the program must be based on the analysis of behavior of individuals endowed with emotional skills, and the construction of hypotheses on the consequences of managerial actions within organizations.

This phase of the program focuses on the co-construction of patterns: emotional skills/managerial behavior/involvement for employees and organ-izations. The aim is to understand the advantage for a future manager of making firm decisions despite uncertainties and pressures, with benevolence and empathy.

What can the vision and reaction of employees be when faced with a manager who admits her/his own mistakes and confronts others with their unethical acts? What can be the vision of employees and the consequences for an organization, to have proactive, thoughtful, committed, and flexible managers? How can employees react to a manager who is open to honest and well-meaning criticism, new perspectives, lifelong learning, and personal development?

We will appeal here to an active and reflective participation of students, in a pedagogical approach based on Vygotskian theory in which meanings are first constructed in the social group (interpsychic level) to then be apprehended in an intrapsychic way. The central place should be given to group work in the conceptualization of the relationships between emotions/managerial behavior/ implications for employees and organizations. In this stage the teacher's role will be that of mediator between learners and knowledge by maximizing positive feedback. Feedback helps support learning, improves subsequent performance, and develops students' autonomy. It can contribute to the development of a positive perception of competence and the feeling of self-efficacy (Bandura, 1982).

11.4.1.3 The construction of social competencies

The concept of empathy is at the center of the development of social competencies. At this stage, we recommend working on the need to understand others by involving students in themes related to the development of this skill that we consider key for the leaders of tomorrow.

What does empathy mean in a managerial role? Under what circumstances can a manager be empathetic?

Being empathetic does not only imply understanding the other – it is also being attentive to the other's needs and interests, supporting employee development within organizations, developing employees' skills, being sensitive to difference and providing opportunities that show equal treatment, being able to interpret the emotional currents of groups, and being able to manage power relations within an organization.

The empathetic posture of a manager is directly related to the quality of his/her social skills, namely:

- be charismatic, having the ability to stimulate the desired reactions in others;
- be a good communicator, have a clear and true language, also know how to listen;
- be a good manager in conflict situations, have the ability to defuse problematic situations;
- be a leader, have the ability to inspire and guide others;
- be a catalyst for change;
- be a person who brings others together, creates links, promotes group synergy within organizations.

In this phase of the program, students must be trained in change management, in verbal and non-verbal communication, in interpersonal communication with an emphasis on clarity, empathy, and openness. Other components of communication should be treated such as the phatic and conative functions. Leadership skills can be approached through experiential methods, social interactive learning, and reflective learning.

11.4.1.4 Behavioral translation of the construction of social skills in future managers

As explained above in the case of emotional skills, the behavioral translation of the construction of social skills starts with the analysis of the behavior of individuals endowed with social skills, then continues with the construction of hypotheses on the consequences of managerial behavior within organizations. This phase of the program focuses on the co-construction of patterns: social skills/managerial behavior/involvement for employees and organizations.

To complete the emotional intelligence training program, we suggest that students move from emotional competence (self-knowledge, empathy, resilience, etc.) to the study of emotions (pride, satisfaction, relief, guilt, shame, envy, contempt, etc.), and the positive and negative implications of each type of emotion in individuals and groups. We refer to the classes of emotions studied by Garcia-Prieto, Tran and Vranik in 2005 (Sander and Scherer, 2019, pp. 348, 349).

This approach allows to develop the concept of "social climate" within organizations. The social climate is based on emotions, and on social representations that members of an organization share, all translated into a collective phenomenon (Sander and Scherer, 2019). Individuals from the same organization coexist in the same social environment. This environment is made up of its own organizational structure, working conditions, and type of leadership. According to Sander and Scherer (2019), these elements contribute to the emergence of common cognitive assessments and therefore to the production of similar emotions in groups of individuals in response to specific events. This set of components makes up the culture or climate of the company, of which our future managers will be the guarantors.

11.5   CONCLUSION

In this chapter we raise questions about the competencies needed for the managerial roles of the future. Facing the emergence of a "new era in the history of business education" as evoked by Kaplan (2018), it is necessary to prepare future generations of managers for the post-crisis period and potential future upheavals. According to Sander and Scherer (2019), emotions are essential determinants of behavior and achievement at work. They influence the social climate and productivity of companies. Emotions are an essential part of organizational life (Ashforth and Humphrey, 1995).

Knowing how to deal with emotions is an important skill for managers. Empathy and resilience are fundamental capacities to allow managers to deal with uncertain and complex environments, and, in this way, they are undoubtedly the keys to be favored. This new posture implies the emergence of a new leadership model.

Michele Borba (2016), a psychologist specialized in education, explains that the lack of empathy is a consequence of the increasing narcissism that can be seen among the younger generations. A leadership model based on empathy and focused more on cooperation than on individual work can provide the impetus for a paradigm shift, and privilege values in line with the challenges of sustainable development, essential components for any company and any manager in the post-crisis period.

Introducing emotional intelligence training and courses in business schools seems to be an essential condition in today's world. Past experience has shown that we have known whole rational experience (cold cognition approaches). The interaction between cognition and emotion in the construction of training programs is the good path to take.

The content we propose goes beyond simple interventions on the development of soft skills, as it is very common to observe. Our proposal invites students to study, understand, and conceptualize in action. To analyze emotional skills/emotions/behaviors and implications for individuals and organizations, with a systemic and reflective approach putting the learner at the center of the knowledge-building process.

Empathy and resilience, and more broadly emotional intelligence, can be learnt and therefore, can be taught. The aim of this chapter is to propose an insightful approach to the understanding of emotions and insights on how to help the managers of the future develop abilities such as empathy and resilience to better succeed in a complex and uncertain world.

The world will need resilient managers solving problems with flexibility and adaptation, developing empathetic approaches, and working with others in constructive and cooperative ways. This means that the manager of the future will be resilient and empathetic, or will not be.

NOTE

1.   https://www.retsinformation.dk/eli/lta/1993/509, last accessed 1 May 2021.

REFERENCES

Ashforth, B.E., and Humphrey, R.H. (1995). Emotion in the workplace: A reappraisal. *Human Relations*, 48(2), 97–125. https://doi.org/10.1177/001872679504800201

Bandura, A. (1982). Self-efficacy mechanism in human agency. *American Psychologist*, 37(2), 122–47.

Borba, M. (2016). *UnSelfie: Why Empathetic Kids Succeed in Our All-About-Me World*. Touchstone, Simon & Schuster, New York.

Brown, B. (2018). *Dare to Lead, Brave Work, Tough Conversations, Whole Hearts*. Random House, New York.

Bullough, A., Renko, M., and Myatt, T. (2014). Danger zone entrepreneurs: The importance of resilience and self-efficacy for entrepreneurial intentions. *Entrepreneurship Theory and Practice*, 38(3), 473–99.

Christensen, L.J., Peirce, E., Hartman, L.P., Hoffman, W.M., and Carrier J. (2007). Ethics, CSR, and Sustainability Education in the Financial Times Top 50 Global

Business Schools: Baseline data and future research directions. *Journal of Business Ethics*, 73, 347–68.

Clemént, E. (2006). Approche de la flexibilité cognitive dans la problématique de la résolution de problème. *L'Année psychologique*, 106(3), 415–34.

Currie, G., Knights, D., and Starkey, K. (2010). Introduction: A post-crisis critical reflection on business schools. *British Journal of Management*, 21, S1–S5.

Danaher, P.A. (2014). *Contemporary Capacity-Building in Educational Contexts*. Palgrave Macmillan, Basingstoke, UK.

de Vries, H., and Shields, M. (2006). Towards a theory of entrepreneurial resilience: A case study analysis of New Zealand SME owner operators. *Applied Research Journal*, 5(1), 33–43.

Decety, J. (2010). The neurodevelopment of empathy in humans. *Developmental Neuroscience*, 3, 16–24.

Drucker, P. (1973). *Management: Tasks, Responsibilities, Practices*. Harper & Row, New York

Durand, T., and Dameron, S. (2011). Where have all the business schools gone? *British Journal of Management*, 22, 559–63.

Eklund, J.H., and Meranius, M.S. (2020). Toward a consensus on the nature of empathy: A review of reviews. *Patient Education and Counseling*. doi: https://doi.org/10.1016/j.pec.2020.08.022.

Ford, J., Harding, N., and Learmonth, M. (2010). Who is it that would make business schools more critical? Critical reflections on critical management studies. *British Journal of Management*, 21, S71–S81.

Fredrickson, B., and Branigan, C. (2005). Positive emotions broaden the scope of attention and thought-action repertoires. *Cognition and Emotion*, 19(3), 313–32.

Fredrickson, B.L., Tugade, M.M., Waugh, C.E., and Larkin, G. (2003). What good are positive emotions in crises? A prospective study of resilience and emotions following the terrorist attacks on the United States on September 11th, 2001. *Journal of Personality and Social Psychology*, 84(2), 365–76.

Genet, J., and Siemer, M. (2011). Flexible control in processing affective and non-affective material predicts individual differences in trait resilience. *Cognition and Emotion*, 25(2), 380–8.

Goleman, D. (1998). *Working with Emotional Intelligence*. Bantam Books, New York.

Goleman, D. (2014). *What Makes a Leader: Why Emotional Intelligence Matters*. More than Sound LLC, Florence, MA.

Gröschl, S., and Gabaldon, P. (2018). Business Schools and the development of responsible leaders: A proposition of Edgar Morin's Transdisciplinarity. *Journal of Business Ethics*, 153, 185–95.

Inés, A. (2001). An influence of positive affect on decision making in complex situations: Theoretical issues with practical implications. *Journal of Consumer Psychology*, 11(2), 75–85.

Kaplan, A. (2014). European management and European business schools: Insights from the history of business schools. *European Management Journal*, 32, 529–34.

Kaplan, A. (2018). A school is "a building that has four walls … with tomorrow inside": Toward the reinvention of the business school. *Business Horizons*, 61, 599–608.

Luthans, F., Avolio, B., Avey, J., and Norman, S. (2007). Positive psychological capital: Measurement and relationship with performance and satisfaction. *Personnel Psychology*, 60, 541–72.

Mintzberg, H. (1989). *Mintzberg on Management. Inside Our Strange Word of Organizations*. The Free Press, New York

Miyake, A., Friedman, N.P., Emerson, M.J., Witzki, A.H., and Howerter, A. (2000). The unity and diversity of executive functions and their contributions to complex "frontal lobe" tasks: A latent variable analysis. *Cognitive Psychology*, 41(1), 49–100.

Painter-Morland, M., and Slegers, R. (2018). Strengthening "Giving Voice to Values" in business schools by reconsidering the "invisible hand" metaphor. *Journal of Business Ethics*, 147, 807–19.

Salovey, P., and Mayer, J.D. (1990). Emotional intelligence. *Imagination, Cognition and Personality*, 9(3), 185–211. doi:10.2190/DUGG-P24E-52WK-6CDG.

Sander, D., and Scherer, K. (2019). *Traité de psychologie des émotions*. Dunod, Paris.

Sarrionandia, A., Ramos-Diaz, E., and Fernandez-Lasarte, O. (2018). Resilience as a mediator of emotional intelligence and perceived stress: A cross-country study. *Frontiers in Psychology*, 9:2653. doi: 10.3389/fpsyg.2018.02653.

Sigurjonsson, T.O., Vaiman, V., and Arnardottir, A.A. (2014). The role of business schools in ethics education in Iceland: The managers' perspective. *Journal of Business Ethics*, 122, 25–38.

Sigurjonsson, T.O., Arnardottir, A.A., Vaiman, V., and Rikhardsson P. (2015). Managers' views on ethics education in business schools: An empirical study. *Journal of Business Ethics*, 130, 1–13.

Southwick, S.M., Litz, B., Charney, D.S., and Friedman, M.J. (eds) (2011). *Resilience and Mental Health: Challenges across the Lifespan*. Cambridge: Cambridge University Press.

Sutcliffe, K.M., and Vogus, T.J. (2003). Organizing for resilience. In Cameron, K., Dutton, J.E., and Quinn, R.E. (eds), *Positive Organizational Scholarship*. Berrett-Koehler, San Francisco, CA, pp: 94–110.

Titchener, E.B. (1909). *Lectures on the Experimental Psychology of the Thought-Processes*. Macmillan, New York.

Warrier, V., Toro, R., Chakrabarti, B. et al. (2018). Genome-wide analyses of self-reported empathy: Correlations with autism, schizophrenia, and anorexia nervosa. *Translational Psychiatry*, 8 (1), 35. doi: 10.1038/s41398-017-0082-6.

Waugh, C.E., Fredrickson, B.L., and Taylor, S.F. (2008). Adapting to life's slings and arrows: Individual differences in resilience when recovering from an anticipated threat. *Journal of Research in Personality*, 42(1), 1031–46.

12. How do Business Schools interpret business values?

Paul G. Davies and Louisa Huxtable-Thomas

12.1 INTRODUCTION

This chapter provides a case study of a Business School seeking to embed a new critical purpose, that of preparing learners for uncertainty in an organizational environment increasingly dominated by evolving perspectives on society's values. The aim is to provide the antidote to the transactional, 4-box-model-Maslow-quoting-'zombie' managers as we call them. If this sounds critical of the established norms, it is intended to. The new manager would be values led, seek to create responsible business not just because it is attractive to customers but because it is a sustainable model for growth. In addition, the new manager would have interpersonal skills and be critical of the business-as-usual. In doing so they would be critical thinkers, enabling proactive resilience in their organizations instead of knee-jerk reactions. Introducing management tools does not automatically enable an ability to discern when and how to utilize them responsibly. Reaching for the metaphorical drill regardless of the task at hand is not an encouraging sign of ability and reduces confidence in the skills of the individual. Responsible management has increasingly appeared as an attractive notion globally, with shared value emerging as an interesting foundational concept to examine the purpose of business (Rao et al., 2013; Muff, 2017). Questions need to be asked, such as who benefits from the value created and to what extent it can be shared? To offer a lens through which to explore and interpret business practice (Hogan et al., 2021).

In this chapter we challenge the traditional purpose and function of Business Schools, recognizing a timely opportunity of converging forces that are shaping the way that business will evolve and a chance for Universities to remain relevant in the face of that change. The chapter initially sets out the nature of the challenge, providing a context for the MBA example being used. Following this scene setting, the chapter introduces the example of the MBA developed by Swansea University's School of Management, UK. The case explores the rethinking of the MBA course and the process that was adopted in order to successfully design and implement the new MBA. Finally, reflections on the experience are provided, drawing on the importance of creating space for course design and development to be effectively managed alongside an awareness of the existing systems that a course needs to integrate into. The conclusion articulates these points as lessons that we hope can be instructive for others in shaping practice.

12.2   THE CHALLENGE

Over the past 70 years, Business Schools in the UK and their early prede-cessors have inhabited a complex position within Universities. Providing learners with knowledge directly applicable to the workplace, whilst bridging the academic and industry worlds has created a cash cow for institutions (Zimmerman, 2001). This should not be surprising – the first UK Business Schools were set up to both address a post-war lack of management and pro-ductivity expertise in the late 1940s, but also to fund expensive technology and science projects elsewhere in the University (Ivory et al., 2006). The funding gap between research income and delivery of blue-sky research is still filled by the contribution made by Business Schools.

Being a unit of the higher education ecosystem focused on preparing stu-dents for organizational reality presents Business Schools with an interesting mix of stakeholders to cater to and long recognized contradictions (Carton et al., 2018). The need to structure along subject or discipline lines internally, arbitrarily dividing programmes of study into bite-sized modules or units, chafes against the desire to incorporate research and student understanding in the way that individuals need to integrate all of these disciplines in their every-day activity in the workplace. A more fundamental concern is found in the actual nomenclature, that is, are they schools of Business or Management and what does this distinction signify? To paraphrase Shakespeare, is it a School by any other name?

Since the first Business Schools opened their doors, subtle changes have occurred that affect what and how they teach with different traditions evident within Europe and the US (Kaplan, 2014). It made sense that multi- and inter-disciplinary approaches would be utilized in the early Business Schools – they had to be staffed by a mix of academics and practitioners that had no theoretical business education themselves because it simply had not been available. This has led to each Business School becoming a chimera of the available knowl-edge; psychologists rub shoulders with economists to understand why people make poor decisions, ecologists and accountants work together to consider new models for predicting sediment movement in our estuaries. However, this valuable mixing pot is increasingly disappearing. We are now seeing second and third generation business academics; lecturers who were taught by lecturers who studied at Business Schools. At a time when interdisciplinarity is needed to address complex challenges, there is a danger it is being replaced by 'vanilla' business education that is still predominantly founded in a business environment that existed in the 1960s but is almost certainly extinct today.

In the past, seeking efficiencies, outcompeting the rest of the sector and bottom-line profits were enough to achieve success (Ivory et al., 2006). Today's organizations are being affected by persistent waves of fast-paced changes and cultural shocks that have changed the emphasis of what success looks like. At the time of writing, the changes wrought to businesses and Universities by COVID-19 are still being understood, but they are just the most recent example of change. A series of wicked problems encapsulating factors such as climate change, Industry 4.0, ageing populations, social justice and globalization have been troubling contemporary organizations. Each of these challenges affects an organization differently, and this has an inevitable impact on the Business School. However, these examples are by their nature complex; the answers to some challenges are contradictory to others. As a result, the challenges to the concept of business-as-usual are vast. In this particularly challenging business environment, Business Schools are attempting to prepare the next generation of managers and leaders. But it can be argued that the vanilla approach that has worked so far has stopped being effective (Lambert, 2019).

Profits are no longer the only indicator of success. Moral and cultural values may be considered to be the core basis of business success in a world where technology is less and less a limiting factor. Consumers are increasingly well educated about the tools that businesses use to gain their wallet share. Global and multinational organizations have eschewed the triple-bottom-line focus in favour of co-creation, trust and creating shared experiences (Randall et al., 2011). Add to this that Google can now tell you everything – what is the value of just imparting tools and knowledge that can be gained from YouTube in seven minutes?

While big business is questioning the value of simplified profit-orientated business thinking, an increasingly transactional and customer-like student outlook (Jabbar et al., 2018) is perversely forcing more of it to proliferate. In the UK, there has been an observable shift since the introduction of University fees, from a student population focused on enriching themselves with a variety of transformative educational experiences (Ashwin et al., 2016), to that of buying a service, and buying a degree certificate to enable them to compete in a highly competitive jobs market (Naidoo and Jamieson, 2005). This in turn has had consequences on the policies made with regard to student recruitment and retention in Universities, with higher education staff encouraged to think about degrees as productized knowledge (Jabbar et al., 2018) and increasingly incentivized through time and resource constraints to simplify and standardize knowledge in order to teach more students more efficiently.

The danger for Business Schools is that the space to think continues to shrink and as a result, business education becomes a series of tick-box exercises designed to recreate the management clones of the 1980s but fails to address the needs of society (Gosling and Mintzberg, 2003). This is exacerbated by the pressures on Deans of Business Schools globally that have not been addressed since they were first identified in the mid-1990s (Bolton, 1996). The MBA, in particular, is a staple of Business Schools and has received a degree of criticism in relation to the way that it can produce corporate clones to take their place in the management positions of organizations – having plenty of business theory but with no management skills (Gosling and Mintzberg, 2003; Mintzberg, 2004; Bennis and O'Toole, 2005).

Into this tension between increasingly values-driven industries and market-driven but arguably out of touch Universities comes a third consideration. At the time of writing, lecturers, researchers and administrators who paid student fees for their own education are playing the role of educational decision makers for the first time. Their own experience of education differs from their predecessors; those who experienced higher education when it was provided for free and with graduates left in a job market hungry for their qualifications.

In summary, the ways in which Business Schools have thrived in the past have been eroded during the 21st century leaving Universities and Business Schools with the need to balance the needs of today and tomorrow's organizations with the immediate challenges of being financially sustainable and relevant. Like any organization facing an existential challenge as it matures, it is time to reconsider what society needs and innovate to provide the answer, so remaining relevant. In this period of competing priorities between student, employer and educator set against a macroenvironment that is by turns volatile and ambiguous, Business Schools in the UK have an opportunity to reimagine what value looks like to the full range of stakeholders

12.3   THE CASE: SWANSEA UNIVERSITY SCHOOL OF MANAGEMENT, MBA

Into this context we now introduce the case study of the redesign of the MBA at Swansea University, UK. The University recently celebrated its centenary having been established in 1920 and is proud of its strong reputation for teaching quality; it was awarded a Gold in the Teaching Excellence Framework. Echoing this culture, the School of Management draws on a strong research reputation to inform its teaching, achieving a top 30 position in the last Research Excellence submission (Research Excellence Framework, 2014). As with many Business Schools, the course portfolio contains a strong range of general and specialist awards at undergraduate and postgraduate level reflecting the need to effectively prepare graduates for the myriad career opportunities across a range of sectors in the UK as well as globally. Indeed, the international nature of the student body is a strength of the School in creating a diverse experience in the classroom and the campus generally. Underpinning the relevance of teaching and research activity within the School is a vibrant network of industry partners. Links to industry play a fundamental role in contextualizing the subjects for students through well-established routes such as placement opportunities, guest lectures, client projects, etc. and bring a valuable experiential element to the learning environment.

The next sections of the chapter will outline the process and theory behind the redesign of the course and provide an example to illustrate the way a number of tensions within Business Schools were held up for examination. We argue that responsible management affords not only a powerful frame of reference for students to develop critical questioning skills but also challenges Business Schools to fully reflect on their role and value to Universities and wider society.

12.3.1   Rethinking of the MBA

The MBA was designed from a blank sheet of paper, informed by the philosophy of shared value, and taking into account the many and varied competing societal pressures that face graduates in their working lives. A period of change within the School produced an opportunity to refresh the course portfolio and particularly, rethink the role of the MBA as a flagship course within management education. Furthermore, the arrival of new staff enabled fresh perspectives to add to the School, bringing experience and innovation from other institutions to complement the existing knowledge base.

External pressure on MBAs informed the need to consider the role and purpose of the MBA within the School. Criticisms of the corporate domination in MBA content and career development builds on the views of critics such as Mintzberg to emphasize the experiential nature of an MBA. Such perspectives echo the way the postgraduate portfolio within the School seeks to clearly meet the aims and ambitions of recent graduates as well as those with post experience. The belief that the MBA should be a post experience qualification that can utilize students' prior background to contextualize content and stimulate debate is a factor in distinguishing from other courses within the School but more importantly recognizes the strategic nature of the course and the way that it examines the tools that an effective manager needs in their toolbox and how they can be applied.

The need for a more critical/questioning ethos to management education has already been alluded to in earlier sections. Recognizing disparate business models and the increasingly complex understanding of the way value is understood and experienced shapes business activity. Thus, it is imperative for courses to engage with such complexities in order to provide a framework for students to work within. The MBA can provide a powerful space where the ability to introduce and explore ambiguity and contradictory stakeholder motivations is the catalyst for student learning. The temptation to provide students with the answer to business problems should be avoided for one simple reason. Being armed with an answer to be applied regardless of the situation is a dangerous simplification of the business world. The ability to understand the nature of a situation is a profoundly greater skill, particularly for the strategic focus underpinning an MBA.

Furthermore, the idea of a 'situation' rather than a 'problem' offers a more positive framing of the way analysis and decision making can inform and shape the future direction of an organization (Checkland, 1999). Surely, it is the role of management education to prepare learners for the way to think in their roles, as varied and disparate as they are likely to be for an increasingly global student body. If this is the case, then the ability to question and reflect on experiences within a guided setting offers relevant and valuable scholarship.

12.3.2   Process

As we have established in the earlier sections of this chapter, the resuscitation of the same old, fossilized MBA was not the ambition for the School. Rather, the opportunity to review the potentially tired three letters was one that afforded a chance to take a broader perspective. A comparator between the old and the new MBA programmes is provided in Table 12.1, providing a context for the examples to follow.

Input from across the School's disciplines incorporating business and management, finance, accounting and economics was a significant factor in the programme's development. Firstly, the nature of the MBA cuts across the range of disciplines to enhance the strategic understanding of organizations. Secondly, the programme benefitted from a range of voices to shape the programme outcomes and content. The starting point was the underpinning philosophy of the course as this provided the locus for subsequent discussion and decisions. 'A concern for human values as well as shareholder value' emerged as the heart of the course and articulated the desire to explore the ambiguity and complexity of organizational life. Pleasingly, this philosophy has resonated with a wide range of stakeholders, particularly students, demonstrating a desire to engage with a more nuanced exploration of values. The first year of the course has received glowing feedback from the cohort of 12, predominantly international, students from countries including India, Nigeria, Jamaica, China and the Middle East.

Table 12.1   *Comparison of old and new MBA programmes*

Design Factor	Previous	New
Driver for MBA creation	Increase in student numbers Reputation	To provide a foundation for purposeful business United Nation's Principles of Responsible Management Education (UNPRME) commitment
Philosophy	Business process improvement and internationalization	Purposeful business in periods of uncertainty and unpredictable change
Typical student	1–3 years post full-time education Post experience (2+ years) 50% international	3–6 years post full-time education Managerial experience (3+ years) 70% international
Full time/Part time	Full time, September entry point	Full time, Part time, September entry points
Modules/Curriculum	Cultures and organizations (10c) Strategic case analysis (15c)	Exploring organizational purpose (30c)
	Corporate social responsibility and business ethics (10c)	Navigating innovation and change (30c)
	Leadership (10c) Managing people (15c) Management skills (15c)	Leading with integrity (15c) Data analysis and decision making (15c)
	Managing processes (15c) Managing markets (15c)	Creating sustainable value (15c)
	Managing finance (15c)	Understanding finance (15c)
	Management report (dissertation; 60c) Semester 3	Research in action (work-based project; 60c) Semesters 1, 2 and 3
Structures	Traditional taught modules	Collaborative discussion-based learning and discovery
Role of research in teaching	None	Novel research is introduced in all modules, research methods are taught throughout the programme
Learning environment	Classroom	Online In person – classroom In person – informal settings
Delivery mode(s)	Traditional lectures and seminars	Discussion groups, workshops, lectures, online tutorials, reflection, interactive seminars, experiential learning and work-based learning

The construction of a course is always an interesting experience as the interests of a range of subjects are discussed and debated. The practicalities of the space available and the subjects to fit into it embody the potential for compromise that can undermine the ambition of initial course design. How is this restriction of aspiration to be avoided? A compelling approach is to seek integration rather than confrontation (Follett, 1918). The onus here is to identify the shared element that links motivations, enabled by a clear philosophical base to the course. Thus, a more creative method is encouraged to explore the way that outcomes can accommodate the distinct starting points. Several examples illustrate the way this informed course development and led to the innovative practice that we believe can be informative to others.

12.3.2.1 Example 1

The first example centres on the credits framing the level of study. Within any course design the credit structure shapes many elements, that is, the number of separate modules that are to be studied, the contact hours for each and the amount of independent study expected within a module. The typical module design in the School is informed by a 15-credit (equivalent to 7.5 ECTS) structure. If accepted without question, the discussion around course structure can easily assume the number of modules available and enter into a negotiation around how they are filled without truly questioning whether this is still the right approach.

Adopting an iterative process, the MBA team explored the way that module structure itself needed to be examined. Informing this method was a desire to make more explicit the connection between subject areas being studied. One of the unavoidable consequences of a modular structure is the unintended siloing of subjects. This is further exacerbated by timetabling that is shaped by a lecture/seminar split. The use of three-hour 'lectorials' has been utilized to provide the space for a flexible approach to the classroom. Thus, elements of more formal lecture content can be easily integrated with activities, discussions, etc. that promote the desired critical thinking amongst students. Reducing the number of modules was explored to examine how the content could be delivered in a more integrated manner. One iteration proposed 4 × 30 credit modules, making up the compulsory 120 credit requirement for the taught component of the course.

Eventually, 2 × 30 credit modules were designed to allow for this integrated approach. The revision was agreed upon in order to enable progression of students through the programme of study; in particular it was felt that having just four modules provided too great an opportunity for failure, making it overly complicated for students to redeem any failed individual assignments. These two 30 credit 'super modules' entitled 'Exploring Organizational Purpose' and 'Navigating Innovation and Change' establish foundational elements around the grand challenges facing business today, using the disciplinary perspectives of strategy, organizational behaviour, innovation and change to examine them. The ability to introduce connections within the module also sets the expectation for the way students should be exploring other modules. The remaining 60 credits were formed around more specific areas of MBA requirements, for example, Leadership, Data analysis, Finance and 'sustainable value' which brings together marketing, sales, customer relationships and operations. Having to teach these separately is one of the practicalities that inevitably impinge on emergent ideas in course design. Thus, the balance and format of these modules remains an area to reflect on during initial deliveries of the course.

12.3.2.2 Example 2
The second example exemplifies the way that innovation informed the programme design and more fully considered the skills that MBA students require in their studies and future careers. Research within a taught management course is often clearly delineated as part of a capstone dissertation or project. The provision of a Research Methods module is included as a separate module or part of the dissertation/project in order to establish the skills required to successfully complete the final project. As a means of conducting a piece of management research the positioning of the research methods makes sense and provides a neat bridge into the individual project.

Yet, it also appears to make a major assumption about the role of research in a management course. That is, research is a distinct activity for producing a thesis/project evident in the range of textbooks focusing on this specific activity. The danger of this assumption is that the role of research in a broader context is simply implied, or even ignored, rather than being seen as a fundamental skill that informs study across the whole. In order to overcome some of the challenges that we have identified in this chapter it is imperative that learners appreciate that research underpins all decision making and should be articulated explicitly at the outset. For a skill to be improved one must be aware of its existence (Buoncristiani and Buoncristiani, 2012). Thus, the 'Research In Action' module runs alongside all other modules throughout the course; introducing the importance of research in effective learning, culminating in a major project as the capstone of the course.

12.3.2.3 Example 3
The third example is based on the capstone element of an MBA, traditionally the thesis exploring a research question. In our MBA the thesis is now a client project that places the student as a researcher addressing a real issue for an industry partner, producing an analysis offering effective value to the organization. The client project is a good example of the way that assessment needs to be an integral part of an innovative course design. The traditional dissertation has ceased to become the default form of student project across a number of leading Business School MBAs, replaced by the client-based management

project. The rationale behind this change is not too difficult to understand if we consider that the purpose of the course is to discern the nature of management problems and explore ways to analyze and identify effective solutions. Indeed, in many ways, it is perhaps surprising that more MBA courses still cling to a theoretical model more suited to providing the foundation for doctoral study.

The range of assessment testing learning outcomes provides an articulation in the way a course is designed and reflects the degree of innovation and creativity among the team. Exams and essays, or a combination of the two, form the traditional assessment methods not just in MBAs but across management studies. Fortunately, innovative ideas of how to effectively assess learning have become more embedded in higher education (Bryan and Clegg, 2019). Key to this change in culture is a desire to incorporate a variety of ways for students to demonstrate a range of skills to illustrate their degree of learning. Coupled with this is a more stimulating experience for the students that can enable more engaged studies. Alongside the client report as the end product of the research and analysis students are also introduced to reflective practice. The value of this is integral to understanding research as a core skill underpinning critical thinking. We have already talked about the space that we as a course team benefitted from in discussing and developing the MBA. Similarly, students need the space to reflect on the way that they are undertaking the client project and how aspects of the course are informing the work. Furthermore, reflection is critical in providing a means for future practice to be shaped by experiences. Initial responses from students and industry partners have been excellent with organizations keen to be involved. Not only do they see the value in having an analysis provided but there is also a desire to support the learning environment that supports the philosophical basis that we identified at the heart of our MBA. Again, an ability to integrate strengthens the overall learning environment.

12.3.3   General Thoughts

We have argued in this chapter that a fundamental purpose of a course such as an MBA is to promote critical thinking skills relevant to the management challenges that will face graduates. Therefore, it is imperative to include the voices of external industry partners to ensure our perspective chimes with the needs of a disparate landscape. Here, the focus on understanding situations in order to determine suitable actions resonates with the myriad organizational forms and contexts graduates will encounter. The School's vibrant industry networks informed the course design in informal and formal ways. Informally, the philosophy and structure of the course was shaped by our regular interactions with industry colleagues. Inevitably, the conversations shape the tacit knowledge that is brought into the course design and play a powerful role in contextualizing the business challenges that we want to reflect in the course content.

However, a more formal recognition is also essential in clearly articulating the value of the course to the management practice in its broadest sense, recognizing the disparate organizational forms as we have already indicated. Practically, the engagement of an industry panel provides a valuable sense check on the ideas that have informed the course design. It is easy to get carried away when a group of academics are on a roll and the potential of an approach becomes seductive, making perfect sense for those involved in the conversation. The need for a cold-water approach to practical application is to be encouraged and grounds the course design in a real-world value. Pragmatically, the thought of approaching a validation panel without having included the opinions of the community that the course importantly contributes to would appear naive, if not foolhardy. However, this conversation is not meant to be one-sided. The ideas shaping the course are designed to question and critically think about management practice so it is pleasing that comments from industry partners have indicated the course is providing a different lens to bring to management study and practice and not merely mirroring existing norms.

Alongside engagement with industry it goes without saying that the quality standards of benchmarks such as the QAA played a guiding role in the way programme learning outcomes were designed. Within this overarching framework the modular learning outcomes can be shaped to ensure graduates display the desired MBA attributes. These are elemental aspects of course design but it is instructive to consider them as there exists a danger that the standards are reflected in a passive manner. Surely, for Business Schools to challenge and shape practice the way in which standards are established should be from a critical perspective, that is, how can they be used in a creative and questioning sense?

12.4   REFLECTIONS

To this point we have set out a series of challenges we feel are facing Business Schools and explored the development of an MBA course in addressing some of these challenges. In this section we want to reflect on key aspects of the MBA course design and implementation before moving on to a broader consideration of how this can inform Business Schools more widely in the following section.

The first point that emerges on thinking about the experience is the importance of the space for bringing colleagues together to discuss the course design. Significantly, this created the environment where ideas could be presented and constructively discussed in order to fully examine the value and potential unintended consequences. The example of four large modules as the structure for the course introduced in the earlier section is a good one to exemplify the way that the initial idea could be held up for examination and evolved into a more robust outcome. Indeed, having two large modules at the start of the course has been well received by the first cohort in establishing foundational themes and concepts across the studies.

The philosophy of the MBA also emerged from this space and acted as an important focal point for the way modules were created and how the course has been managed. The response from a range of stakeholders and regular comments from people already holding a Masters who wished they had been able to study our course reinforces the strength of this central ethos. Therefore, a clear identity informing the course structure and subsequent decisions presents itself as a powerful way to frame conversations and decisions, binding disparate perspectives together. Importantly, the philosophy aids the integration of ideas into a coherent whole.

We have talked in earlier sections about the role and value of cementing the students' ability for critical thinking as a key part of a learning environment. The Swansea MBA as a whole is designed to enable and support this ambition, but one element in particular articulates it most clearly. The understanding of research as an essential skill in supporting critical thinking is an expression of the way that the purpose and practical aspects of learning can be considered in more innovative ways.

As the reflections illustrate, the creation of the MBA has been a positive experience. Yet, it is important to consider elements that proved frustrating as they inevitably impact on the way the course has evolved and exists. We are talking about Business Schools within this chapter and have touched on the role they play as a revenue stream for Universities. However, there is also a more practical aspect that informs any course development; namely, the existing systems that operate within a complex organization. The nature of the way systems work within the University inevitably shapes some of the decision making. The example of the initial thinking around four large modules evolved as realities of the practical systems that support student learning became more apparent. Understandably, systems in relation to enrolment, progression, etc. need to accommodate a range of disparate Schools and courses. At times this can feel as if the 'tail is wagging the dog' but is a reality of how a complex organization needs to function. Similarly, practicalities around timetabling can inform the way that delivery of modules is realized.

Here, the potential for programme-level assessment becomes an interesting area to balance the ambitions for more innovative delivery with the practical experience of students to ensure a coherent understanding of the subject areas being studied. Several strands of the course creation that we have introduced are relevant to illustrate the way that the programme level of thinking can be enabled. Firstly, the underpinning philosophy of the course is critical as it provides a 'hook' that modules link into, helping to undermine the silo mentality that can afflict courses. Secondly, the use of the two large foundational modules creates the space for integrated themes to be explored and understood by students. Links are fostered and set the expectation for connections to be made between the content covered within the course. Finally, the Research In Action module specifically sets a group assignment early in the course that draws on the theory covered in the other modules being studied. This is designed to practically enable the students to work together, so fostering the supportive learning environment that is integral to all study, not just an MBA. Furthermore, the specific requirement to think about all of the modules being studied at that stage articulates clearly that subjects are not to be considered as stand-alone entities.

Our reflections identify important elements that have shaped the way the MBA course has been designed. However, the course is in its infancy and continuing reflection is a necessity as the MBA is a living entity and the experience of students, academics and industry partners are vital to understand how these perspectives can shape the way the course evolves to fully realize the philosophy and the critical thinking skills we believe are central to student learning for a modern organizational reality.

12.5   CONCLUSION

In this chapter we have set out a series of challenges that we believe are important for Business Schools to consider. The example of the MBA course development provides an illustration of the way that we sought to address these challenges to create a relevant and stimulating learning environment that can equip graduates for varied careers in an increasingly complex and changeable environment. In this last section we reflect on some of the key points and hope that they provide valuable lessons that can inform practice across Business Schools more widely. The concept of lessons is an important one as there are inevitably shared experiences that will have resonated as you were reading the previous sections. Yet, each institution is its own distinct entity, hence our offering of lessons to stimulate thinking and inform practice.

Creating a critical thinker is a fundamental purpose of education and is at the heart of Swansea School of Management. So how is this realized? An important first step is a clear idea of the purpose of the course that is being designed. Understandably, some perspectives will see the purpose to increase student numbers and thus the revenue streams of the School and institution. This is an inevitable pressure but misses the point that we are making. If the course does not have a clear identity, it is harder to demonstrate the value to prospective students. A transactional aspect to course choices has always been part of the decision-making process, though may be more pronounced in recent times. Students are not a homogeneous entity and multiple reasons will inform course choices. However, we argue that a clear philosophy to the course provides a stronger base on which to build the critical thinking skills that are essential to create more informed decision makers. Early reaction to our new MBA from a range of stakeholders, particularly students, supports this and illustrates the course as a space for critical thinking to flourish.

The second lesson relates to a more practical consideration. A contradiction often exists within Business Schools and Universities more generally. Innovation is encouraged, even demanded in order to maintain a competitive position. Yet, long-established systems are in place that are not always comfortable with change. The feeling of banging your head against a brick wall can be a result, particularly where systems have been founded on a full-time undergraduate model that is still predicated on a September–May learning calendar. We recognize that there are many examples of innovative practice in course design within Business Schools but raise this point to articulate that a course does not exist in isolation. It is imperative to understand the systems that the course will be part of in order to avoid unrealistic expectations and more fatally impractical learning experiences for students.

In conclusion, the two lessons that we offer from our experience marry the philosophical basis of a course with the pragmatic reality of the structures that inform any learning environment. We argue that understanding the balance of these two elements can enable innovative practice that furthers the potential of Business Schools to foster critical thinkers who will shape the wider organizational practice into the future.

REFERENCES

Ashwin, P.W.H., Abbas, A., and McLean, M. (2016). Conceptualising transformative undergraduate experiences: A phenomenographic exploration of students' personal projects. *British Educational Research Journal, 42*(6), 962–77.

Bennis, W.G., and O'Toole, J. (2005). How business schools have lost their way. *Harvard Business Review, 83*(5), 96–104.

Bolton, A. (1996). The leadership challenge in universities: The case of business schools. *Higher Education, 31*(4), 491–506.

Bryan, C., and Clegg, K. (2019). *Innovative Assessment in Higher Education: A Handbook for Academic Practitioners*, 2nd edn. Routledge, London.

Buoncristiani, M., and Buoncristiani, P.E. (2012). *Developing Mindful Students, Skillful Thinkers, Thoughtful School*. Corwin, Thousand Oaks, CA.

Carton, G., McMillan, C., and Overall, J. (2018). Strategic capacities in US universities – the role of business schools as institutional builders. *Problems and Perspectives in Management, 16*(1), 186–98.

Checkland, P. (1999). *Systems Thinking, Systems Practice*. Wiley, Chichester.

Follett, M.P. (1918). *The New State: Group Organization the Solution of Popular Government*. Longmans, London.

Gosling, J., and Mintzberg, H. (2003). The five minds of a manager. *Harvard Business Eeview, 81*(11), 54–63.

Hogan, O., Kortt, M.A., and Charles, M.B. (2021). Mission impossible? Are Australian business schools creating public value? *International Journal of Public Administration, 44*(4), 280–9.

Ivory, C., Miskell, P., Shipton, H., White, H., White, A., Moeslein, K., and Neely, A. (2006). UK business schools: Historical contexts and future scenarios. Summary Report from an EBK. AIM Management Research Forum, Advanced Institute of Management Research, ISBN No: 0-9551850-7-6.

Jabbar, A., Analoui, B., Kong, K., and Mirza, M. (2018). Consumerisation in UK higher education business schools: Higher fees, greater stress and debatable outcomes. *Higher Education, 76*(1), 85–100.

Kaplan, A. (2014). European Management and European Business Schools: Insights from the history of business schools. *European Management Journal, 32*, 529–34.

Lambert, D.M. (2019). Rediscovering relevance. *International Journal of Logistics Management, 3*(2), 382–94.

Mintzberg, H. (2004). Managers not MBAs: A hard look at the soft practice of managing and management development. *Language, 12*(464), 24.

Muff, K. (2017). How the Circle Model can purpose-orient entrepreneurial universities and business schools to truly serve society. *Journal of Management Development, 36*(2), 146–62.

Naidoo, R., and Jamieson, I. (2005). Empowering participants or corroding learning? Towards a research agenda on the impact of student consumerism in higher education. *Journal of Education Policy, 20*(3), 267–81.

Randall, W.S., Gravier, M.J., and Prybutok, V.R. (2011). Connection, trust, and commitment: Dimensions of co-creation. *Journal of Strategic Marketing, 19*(1), 3–24.

Rao, P., Patil, Y., and Gupte, R. (2013). Education for sustainable development: Trends in Indian business schools and universities in a post liberalization era. In *Sustainability Assessment Tools in Higher Education Institutions* (pp. 417–32). Springer, Cham.

Research Excellence Framework (2014). Research Excellence Framework 2014: The results. Bristol.

Zimmerman, J.L. (2001). Can American business schools survive? Simon School of Business Working Paper No. FR, 01-16.

13. Bridging the gap: from instruction to co-construction in higher education

Gaby Probst and Laura Zizka

13.1 INTRODUCTION

In a traditional business school, Bachelor studies consist of courses within a frame defined by the institution to ascertain that the learning objectives have been met. All teaching methods, activities, and assessment methods are defined by faculty members and presented in a classroom. However, with the arrival of the Covid-19 pandemic, these procedures shifted. For business schools worldwide, the move towards distant or remote learning and the subsequent hybrid teaching models introduced from that point on were not a deliberate choice but a sudden obligation. Pre-existing online models were not necessarily useful (Krishnamurthy, 2020), as the time pressure to keep business studies on track obliged faculty members and students to adapt to a new and all-encompassing challenge of teaching and learning remotely.

In the first semester affected by the pandemic, the discrepancies or inequalities in teaching and learning were accentuated in the emergency remote environment, which is not to be mistaken with online learning. To clarify, emergency remote teaching is defined as "a temporary shift of instructional delivery to an alternate delivery mode due to crisis circumstances to provide temporary access to instruction and instructional supports in a manner that is quick to set up and is reliably available during an emergency or crisis" (Hodges et al., 2020, p. 1). Online learning is defined as "an arranged educational experience that provides study materials via an e-learning innovation and an internet browser, which can be absorbed by students in their own way" (Alzahrani & Seth, 2021, p. 6789). Over the past semesters of changing sanitary restrictions and lockdowns, business schools have been obliged to adapt their teaching and learning to accommodate the Covid-19 crisis. Nevertheless, the pandemic has also offered opportunities to reshape, reframe, and reconsider business school practices especially when it comes to the development of a responsible and sustainable pedagogy. Now, two years later, business schools can become better than they were before.

In this chapter, we attempt to bridge the gap between instruction and co-construction, between traditional and sustainable education, basing our analysis on an ongoing collection of data gathered from faculty members and students at various stages during the pandemic. We provide an innovative sustainable model of HyFlex learning for business schools that promotes a holistic experience to ensure engagement from all business school stakeholders. Hybrid flexible, or *HyFlex*, is defined as "an instructional approach that combines face-to-face (F2F) and online learning. Students (and faculty members) can decide how to participate. The HyFlex approach provides students autonomy, flexibility, and seamless engagement, no matter where, how, or when they engage in the course" (EDUCAUSE, 2020, p. 1). The term HyFlex is seemingly the most inclusive and can be adapted partially or entirely to any business school. At the end of this chapter, we have a tube map to share, a map with no set beginning nor ending place; a map that incorporates the essence of what worked over the past two years based on student and faculty survey results from a business school in Switzerland. In short, we hope to provide a new image of business education, that is inclusive and flexible to meet all stakeholders' needs.

13.2   RESEARCH METHODOLOGY

Due to the pandemic, courses moved completely online at the School of Management of Fribourg in the spring semester 2020. The following timeline summarizes the different teaching approaches during our study:

- March 2020 – courses were stopped due to Covid-19 pandemic during a week for special faculty training; emergency remote teaching until the end of the Spring semester, including online exams.
- September 17, 2020 – courses onsite in traditional classrooms.
- October 23, 2020 – courses moved online for the rest of the semester (exams included).
- February 20, 2021 – spring semester began and remained online.

In December 2020 and June 2021, surveys were conducted with faculty members and students via Lime. Their experiences and attitudes toward online teaching were evaluated. The surveys included open questions to allow participants to express opinions and describe the emotional experience. These open questions were answered extensively, as seen in Table 13.1.

The resulting comments were collected and analyzed according to principles of open coding, defined by Glaser and Strauss (1967), resulting in categories of first and second order (Gioia, 2020). The most prevalent categories deriving from the student comments included time, self-efficacy, autonomy,

Table 13.1   *Distribution of comments in the surveys treating the online teaching at Fribourg Business School*

Date of Survey	Survey – December 2020		Survey – June 2021	
Public of Survey	Faculty	Students	Faculty	Students
Participation	58/87 = 66.7%	291/559 = 52.1%	67/90 = 74.4%	249/524 = 47.5%
Number of open questions	7	6	8	7
Number of comments	199	565	201	733
Average comment per person	3.4	1.9	3.0	2.9
Average length of words per comment	25.5	38.4	21.5	23.1

engagement, and real-world skills. The categories from the faculty members' comments were time, technology, teaching online, engagement, interaction, and the future of education.

From these categories, the most relevant comments were chosen, translated from French and German, and quoted throughout this chapter to give voice to our students and faculty members and show the connections between theory and real experience (Gioia, 2020). Through their voices, we examine their trepidations, but also their successes when faced with various models of online teaching and learning to demonstrate what business schools can take from this exceptional experience.

13.2   RESULTS AND DISCUSSION

With the rapid shift from onsite to online courses, both faculty members and students felt lost. It quickly became clear that traditional onsite courses do not automatically and magically morph into an online setting. Many faculty members created new materials, recorded content, or contemplated alternative assessment options. For students, after the initial confusion where to log-in, online learning developed into hours spent in front of the computer screen. Many students and faculty members faced Internet connection issues, technology gaps, or disruption in their teaching and learning journey. At first, nobody had a suitable map at hand with proper indications where to turn or which direction to choose. While online learning was not new in teaching, it was new to many business schools worldwide. To better examine the changes in business school education, we have broken the chapter into three main sections: Learning and Teaching Models, Sustainable Teaching, and Sustainable Learning.

13.3   LEARNING AND TEACHING MODELS

At any business school, the learning of content and the acquisition of competencies is focused on what is needed in the economy of the 21st century. This professional context is characterized by a fast pace and a changing professional context, provoking changes in knowledge, competencies, and behavior, thus requiring "task-solving activities that contain a high degree of complexity" (Schneckenberg et al., 2010, p. 752). This begs the question: what does "learning" mean under these conditions?

Students need to be offered authentic learning environments that engage them in developing their skills in critical thinking, problem solving, collaboration, and self-directed learning (Becker et al., 2017). Generally, according to traditional pedagogical concepts, faculty members are solely responsible for the learning. But learning is an individual process (Knowles, 1975). According to the model of constructivism (Weegar et al., 2012), knowledge is constructed within the learner, linking any new piece of information to prior knowledge. This know-how is then activated and leads to the integration of the new information. If learners are invited to go beyond listening to asking questions and taking notes, they reflect on the given information, and, subsequently, develop their insights. Within passive learning mode, students only receive information through silent reading or passively watching videos. The information is then stored in an isolated or encapsulated form, whereas the active learning methods create profound knowledge which can more easily be applied in new contexts.

Our students experienced this lack of activation online which impeded their concentration as illustrated in this comment: "Some courses were rather boring. Due to the online lessons, you sometimes sit in front of the laptop for 10 hours, especially if you study half-time as I do. In the evening you are exhausted and have to focus hard to listen to the lecturers with full concentration. Some teachers seem to lack the sensitivity when to omit or shorten course activities." This suggests a real need for teachers to engage with the students. Of course, it is not time alone that makes online courses interesting or tedious: "Any education scheme worth its salt must not only deliver knowledge but do so in a way that is highly engaging – and then activate that knowledge, so its owner can do real work in the world" (Sarma & Yoquinto, 2020, p. 20).

Active learning settings integrate the needs of the students and explain the value of the course content in a specific context. This shift from the distributive learning mode to a collaborative way is urgently needed in a fast-changing and unpredictable professional context where the increasing complexity of decision taking requires task-solving competencies (van der Heijde and van der Heijden, 2006). The School of Management of Fribourg is perfectly aware of this demand. Their vision is "to be an agile and inspiring business school," underlined by guiding principles such as "Teaching staff and people in leadership positions act as role models; ... innovative behaviour is duly noted; ... creativity, courage and freedom are supported and collaborative innovation initiatives are implemented" (HEG Website).

One step forward is to engage students in a competence-oriented learning and teaching setting and to move away from inert knowledge being taught without any relation to the day-to-day concerns of students or, in other words, to teach with "more hands-on, real-world experiences for students" (Becker et al., 2017, p. 10). "These processes require social interaction, conflicts and irritation, problem solving and a high degree of authenticity in learning situations" (Schneckenberg et al., 2010, p. 754), creating interaction and cooperation between faculty members and students (Bates, 2019). This reinforces the meaning of *competence*, that is, the knowledge, skills, and attitudes allowing its user to act and react appropriately by combining and mobilizing resources in different contexts (Le Boterf, 2006).

In April 2020, the new online setting obliged many faculty members to rethink their course methodology. One faculty member stated: "This experience allowed me to learn other ways of teaching and to create other forms of interaction." Students noticed these efforts: "Some lecturers have made progress in the design of online teaching. This has been a pleasure and shows that they are committed to their course and to the students." Andreas Schleicher, an educational expert, was quoted in a weekly newspaper: "What teachers learned in one year of Corona, they otherwise would not have learned in 20 years" (Burchard, 2021). Apparently, significant efforts have been made by the faculty members.

The main challenge during the pandemic was to translate the personal teaching concept of every faculty member immediately into functioning online courses. E-learning means "any *planned* education that utilizes electronic media, which includes distance learning through the internet" (Glancy & Isenberg, 2013, p. 22, emphasis added) and is not new; computers made their way into the classroom in the 1980s (Sarma & Yoquinto, 2020, p. xii). However, never before have faculty members been obliged to adopt new teaching styles with so little time for preparation. E-learning can be declined in different forms, linking onsite elements with online activities leading to different combinations such as blended learning models. *Blended learning* is defined as a combination of personal instruction and technologically based lessons where students benefit from temporal and geographic flexibility (Porter et al., 2014). Although blended learning was not an option during this quick shift to online courses, this model should be considered as a longer-term strategy to better meet the needs of students and faculty.

What is the future of business education? For one student: "Online teaching revealed that physical presence is no longer necessary for some courses. The material can be worked on independently and the sporadic meetings with the lecturer can be used for questions. You still have a certain amount of guidance from the lecturer, but you can set your own pace and work yourself." A faculty member agreed: "The future is a mix between face-to-face and distance learning depending on the topics and activities, since certain activities are much more effective online, whereas others are better suited for face-to-face-courses." Although the literature mentions the positive effects of online learning (Alzahrani & Seth, 2021), there is still resistance from faculty members as "faculty continue to be sceptical about the efficacy of online learning" (Krishnamurthy, 2020, p. 1). Some of our faculty members clearly noted the potential of online courses but were not convinced of the necessity or utility of all classes being taught online.

Both students and faculty members mention the suitability of activities and their distribution mode. This is indeed the crucial point of learning and teaching methods, especially in the HyFlex learning format. It is essential to distinguish between those elements that work best in onsite courses versus those in online courses. Faculty members and students must revise their teaching or learning practices to increase active methods. Active learning is known to improve not only lecture attendance, but also engagement and the "acquisition of expert attitudes toward the discipline" on the side of the students (Deslauriers et al., 2019). In that way, faculty members can avoid the cognitive load (Kirschner, 2002) of too long, abstract, or dense explanations and put the students in the center of the course. Although active learning methods are clearly better for the students, they do not always like them, as it demands a significant shift in their habits: Their "negative response to this intense style of active learning is a result of the disfluency they experience in this cognitively demanding environment" (Deslauriers et al., 2019, p. 19255). Passing knowledge and competencies onto the next generation needs the implementation of new and more sustainable learning and teaching methods (Thomas & Ambrosini, 2021), and ample support from all stakeholders: Teaching and learning in business schools must change, potentially through co-construction!

13.4 SUSTAINABLE TEACHING

According to the literature, sustainable teaching focuses on flexibility, inclusion, accessibility and technology, longevity, and Communities of Practice (CoPs). Teaching in business education has never been as challenging or rewarding, as the pandemic has accentuated the differences between faculty members and the possibilities to include new activities, methods, and assessments within their courses. The traditional lecturing format has often been criticized in the past: "Today's teachers have to learn to communicate in the language and style of their students. This does not mean changing the meaning of what is important, of good thinking skills. But it does mean going faster, less step-by-step, more in parallel, with more random access, among other things" (Prensky, 2001, p. 4). The move to online courses and remote learning exacerbated this aspect. Faculty members shifted dramatically from the "all-knowing" fountain of knowledge "teacher" to facilitator, moderator, coach, or organizer of learning (Boettcher & Conrad, 2016). Indeed, competencies cannot be memorized; instead, they must be developed through students' own experiences and interactive learning scenarios (Schneckenberg et al., 2010). During the Covid-19 pandemic, faculty members faced many changes they may not have been prepared for nor envisioned. To help them succeed, business schools need to offer safe places for faculty members to brainstorm new ideas, experiment with innovative assessments, or have access to training in the pedagogical use of technological tools. Faculty members need to know that it is acceptable to feel uncertainty in an uncertain time.

CoPs can provide the response faculty members seek (Monaghan, 2010). CoPs offer a sense of belonging to a meaningful learning community (Nortvig et al., 2018) where faculty members exchange best practices or discuss issues with their colleagues. Sustainable teaching requires a considerate and friendly environment for the teachers to grow in and thrive, and numerous faculty members seemed much more willing to share and experiment with innovative methods. "The challenges of this historical moment create a window of opportunity for initiatives that allow for deep reflection leadership development, and meaningful networking with other academic leaders who are encountering seemingly insurmountable obstacles" (Gigliotti, 2021, p. 444). According to one faculty member: "This time, I worked in a project group to create courses that included theory and application with the goal of improving the quality of my teaching and the learning of my students."

Another positive aspect was the commute. There was more time to prepare for courses without the daily travel to and from the physical campus. For one faculty member: "Very demanding semester, but the flexibility of the teaching location is very good." And faculty members recognized the benefits for the students as well: "I would very much like to see online teaching remain an option for students, especially in evening classes for part-time students, which allows them to avoid long journeys and stress after work to get to class and then back late at night." With fewer commutes, both students and faculty members saved precious time. Nonetheless, many faculty members felt an additional pressure regarding the time it takes to prepare classes for an online environment. One faculty member wrote: "Setting up and organizing this virtual 'infrastructure' is time-consuming" and "online teaching requires a lot of preparation time. We are at the stage where everything has been done in a hurry and we need to put things in order before reusing the material created."

One of the greatest shifts since the first shutdown in March 2020 was the need to use or learn to use new technology for teaching. In traditional teacher education, the teacher training predominantly revolves around classroom teaching. In a study by Marshall et al. (2020), 92.4 percent of teachers had never taught online before the pandemic. As one participant noted: "All of my pedagogical training assumed that teaching would take place in a face-to-face environment" (Marshall et al., 2020, p. 48). This was echoed in our survey results: "The stress and urgency did not allow for the proper use of the tools at hand. It was a bit like driving without a license and without knowing the rules of the road while hoping not to have an accident." The need of training and support is imminent when adapting to online education (Chauhan et al., 2021).

Nonetheless, by the end of the second semester of HyFlex teaching, some faculty members felt more comfortable with this new technology as they found they could reuse material produced in the semester, which will save time in the long run. However, as can be seen in the literature, it is important that adding technology just to add technology is not the answer. Faculty members must choose suitable technology that begins with learning objectives and ends with the acquisition of the necessary competencies. According to Chauhan et al. (2021), "there should be a sturdy fit between digital classroom technology and the tasks to be performed. If business schools start to institutionalise online learning, then it will be possible to find out the gaps and void factors hindering such a fit at the right time" (p. 1611). Faculty members will be obliged to reconsider what they have done in the previous semesters and choose what to keep, what to refine, and what to discard.

The topic of motivation (and demotivation) was frequently reported by faculty members and students. For faculty members, the remote learning environment obliged them to question their teaching practices and define the most important content that students needed immediately to be productive in this new setting. Yet, it also led to disappointment with the online teaching environments. One faculty member stated: "I didn't enjoy teaching under these conditions. I got involved only with the future of the students in mind." Faculty members were concerned that students were getting bored; thus, an additional pressure to redouble the efforts to keep the students motivated emerged.

Student perspectives were also mixed regarding the quality of teaching during this time. One student commented: "The teaching in this online semester was adequate except for some subjects. The quality of the internet connection is however very important, during one class, the professor had a very low quality of bandwidth which did not allow to follow the course properly." As seen before, some students were blatantly aware that the faculty members were struggling with the additional burden of distance teaching. Thus, moving forward, faculty members will need to address the effectiveness of the online elements they may continue using in the future.

In short, sustainable teaching requires a safe and inclusive environment for all faculty members. As seen in the comments from the faculty members and students, many efforts were recognized but more work needs to be done. A mixed bag of satisfaction and dissatisfaction seems to summarize how the faculty members felt about their efforts during these exceptional semesters, but there is a glimmer of hope. What if their efforts paid off and led to authentic learning after all? Let's see what the perception of learning was.

13.5   SUSTAINABLE LEARNING

In this section, we focus on the student's perception through the topics of self-efficacy, support/technology, communication and feedback, engagement/motivation, networks/community, sometimes affecting both communities. All these factors contribute to creating sustainable learning. Today's students are considered as "experts" in technology as they have never known a time when information and communication technologies (ICTs) were not a part of daily life. However, this stereotype has led to misunderstandings of the competencies and ease students have regarding technology. While using technology is second nature for many students, the rapid online shift to learning via technology was challenging for even the most technologically savvy students.

Another concern with the online semesters was the loss of social contact. Frankly, technology is cold. Students have spent hours alone, online, looking at a screen and communicating virtually. While new technology such as apps through mobile devices offer faculty members and students "two-way communication in real time … and gateways to personalized working and learning environments" (Becker et al., 2017), this technology only promotes communication possibilities. However, communication through technology does not automatically create connectivity (Pflugler, 2020) or ensure authentic and sustainable relationships between students and faculty members. Our students consequently lost the "presence" they felt in the traditional classroom, leading to a decline in engagement and a loss of motivation (Marshall et al., 2020). "Learning is seen as essentially a social process, requiring communication between learner, teacher and others" (Bates, 2019, p. 70). For this reason, when moving forward in sustainable HyFlex learning, students need to build relationships in networks and communities, which requires creating a focus on social presence even in an online setting (Lim et al., 2021). One student stated: "I don't think it makes any difference to listen to the teacher at home or at school but it's true that I miss the contact with the other students, we helped each other a lot." Faculty members felt this loss of social contact as well when students refused to turn on the camera if they attended the class at all. According to one faculty member: "Even if the distance learning courses are going well, I am looking forward to meeting the students again. Contacts are essential to enrich and vary the pedagogical approaches and keep the students motivated."

On the other hand, there was an excessive demand for group work, which was complicated by group members who tuned out and did not contribute. "This semester, there was a lot of group work during the lessons, which was not at all conducive to the learning effect due to the lack of participation by group members." In a traditional classroom, these students would be called out for their lack of participation; this proved much more difficult in the remote setting. Nonetheless, group work is an example of collaborative learning which involves students working together in groups or pairs with an emphasis on interaction (Becker et al., 2017); students need this interaction for authentic learning experiences.

Students also need feedback through body language and facial gestures which lacked online compared to face-to-face learning (Zembylas, 2008). One student noted: "The lack of qualitative feedback on intermediate products or final reports does not allow us to draw personal lessons on the work provided." However, feedback is a two-way street. For one faculty member: "The interaction is so much more difficult with large groups and demands a positive psychological attitude especially when the students don't give feedback or interact." Thus, both the students and faculty members felt a feedback deficiency. These observations show that the need for timely and effective feedback in online settings is as important if not more so than in traditional classrooms, otherwise demotivation takes over.

Indeed, motivation was a significant struggle, too. One student commented: "This teaching is mostly of good quality, but we find it difficult to find motivation. It's really not the same as face-to-face." Some students explicitly stated that they were not motivated or incapable of motivating themselves. This was proliferated by faculty members who overloaded the lessons with extra activities and additional homework. Students felt that faculty members needed a more comprehensive view of the student (Krishnamurthy, 2020) to empathize with their struggles to learn. Students posited that it was the faculty members' obligation to make the courses entertaining and active. For one student: "Distance learning works well when teachers take the trouble (and remain) engaged to make their courses attractive."

Sustainable learning requires support for students to keep them engaged, otherwise, attrition and drop-out are the results. Some students seemed determined to continue their studies despite the constant and unsettling changes and could see the advantages for their personal development. As one student stated: "From one day to the next, we had to be more autonomous and more responsible. Setting goals for ourselves, finding information on our own. I feel that this period has shown the determination, intrinsic motivation and desire to succeed of each and every student. I have never had so much difficulty in motivating myself and staying motivated, in maintaining my concentration over time and in being organised and rigorous in my work. I think that not only did we develop enormous adaptability, but also other values specific to all of us that allowed us to succeed despite the difficult situation."

According to Broadbent (2017), learners are responsible for their learning process by planning, setting goals, and engaging in strategies to achieve those goals which can be difficult. Nonetheless, some students and faculty members thrived in the online and HyFlex learning environment. Those who were particularly successful in these environments displayed the well-documented capacities of time management, information organization, effective use of learning tools, and resilience to stay motivated (Veletsianos, 2020). Faculty members who remained positive toward the online switch were able to do what was necessary, including seeking help when necessary. In their willingness and openness to trying new things, faculty members and students increased their feelings of self-confidence, self-efficacy, and self-worth. *Self-efficacy* was defined by Bandura (1994) as "people's beliefs about their capabilities to produce designated levels of performance that exercise influence over events that affect their lives." These beliefs determine how people motivate themselves, whereas *online learning self-efficacy* is defined as a combination of "technical competencies with a more general competency for learning" (Lim et al., 2021, p. 546). Chauhan et al. (2021), too, insist on the fact that learning success depends on the ability of using digital technology. One example of self-efficacy emerged from the shift to online exams through technology. Some students welcomed the opportunity to do online exams as it offered a new possibility to take responsibility for their learning journey. Nonetheless, most of the self-efficacy examples emanating from the students focused on setting goals, being autonomous, and finding information on their own. Students recognized the new skills acquired: "Indeed, what our generation will have experienced is something exceptional at all levels: knowing how to manage a crisis situation and adapt to it/using new tools/discovering new teaching methods/helping each other more than usual." These competencies can be transferred into the future workplace environment: "The new trend now is part-time teleworking. I feel less scared about it now that I've learned how to organise myself to make my tasks on time." If the objective of business schools is to prepare the new generation of competent graduates for the workplace (Krishnamurthy, 2020), some of these skills, albeit hors-curriculum, can be advantageous for the future.

13.6   OUR TUBE MAP PLAN

In this section, we present our tube map linking learning and teaching models, sustainable teaching, and sustainable learning to the real context of business education post-pandemic. The stations stand for key concepts that are marked in bold. Although neither faculty members nor students chose to teach and learn online in such extreme circumstances, the learning curve has adapted, and the comments here reflect this shift. It is for this reason that we have chosen to listen to THEIR voices and to share THEIR thoughts with you. Business school stakeholders have been more resilient and flexible than they could have ever imagined. Our tube map model simultaneously opens the debate and sparks a discussion on how business schools can continue to innovate in the future. It is only by co-creating with all business school stakeholders that we can indeed "mind the gap" in business education.

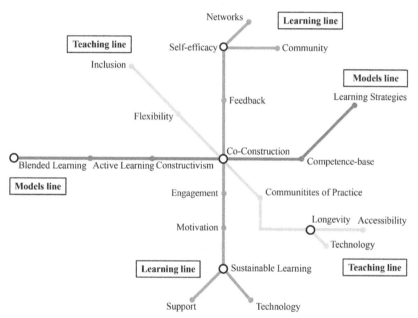

Source: © Gaby Probst, 2022; created with https://beno.uk/metromapcreator

Figure 13.1   Metro map

As seen on the tube map (Figure 13.1), teaching and learning in a remote context is not linear and does not need to be so. Reflection on how to teach and learn can start anywhere. Choosing the Models line, faculty members can reflect on the models of teaching and learning and begin where they feel it is most relevant to them. From *blended learning* through to *learning strategies,* faculty members may spend more time at a specific "stop" honing existing skills or learning new ones. They may pause at *active learning* to examine innovative possibilities to create more effective and engaging learning environments. But perhaps they have a strong pedagogical background already and only need input for teaching practice. In that case, faculty members may choose to enter the tube in the teaching line for sustainable teaching. This line may serve as a catalyst in establishing new practices for the new teaching culture we have experienced in the past two years. The need for *inclusion* and more *flexibility* with or without *technology* has become a topic for faculty members to consider. Through *Communities of Practice*, faculty members may share ideas in a "safe" environment and feel less pressure to find solutions alone. Nonetheless, teaching is only one "route" to take; a great teacher needs to consider what and how the students are learning. To do so, the faculty member may choose the line for sustainable learning. Students need *networks* and *communities* to thrive in when they change their teaching and learning, especially when it comes to remote or HyFlex learning or teaching modes. Both need prompt *feedback* to *motivate* them and help them *engage* with the course. We witnessed mixed levels of *self-efficacy* amongst our students and faculty as well as mixed feelings about learning and teaching remotely over these past semesters. For this reason, additional pedagogical and *technological support* are necessary.

In the tube map model, all three tube lines cross at one junction, the junction of *co-construction*, one of the key points of our chapter. The days of yore where the teacher was the all-compassing master of knowledge and the students were the diligent and passive learners are gone. In our model, the need for co-construction is crucial for the future of higher education business studies. However, co-construction is not a new topic. This concept has been discussed in the literature for decades as an interesting proposal that was just not feasible at this time. Each time it has been introduced, it was shelved away until a "better time." Our proposition in this chapter is the following: NOW is that time! After two years of upheaval in education, this is the perfect moment to engage with all business school stakeholders to co-create innovative courses and programs. It is the moment to step out of the business school mold and disrupt the traditional system. Courses need to be built based on active learning, real-life experiences that meet the needs of the 21st century. If our role is to prepare the graduates to face the world challenges of tomorrow, we need to step out of our traditional roles and open ourselves to innovative ideas deriving from all stakeholders along the way.

13.7 FINAL WORDS

As we complete this chapter, the situation for education is still uncertain. While most business schools worldwide are planning a return to on-campus education, the traditional experience is being questioned. The pandemic has forced business schools to reflect on what they are teaching and how they are doing it. If we have learned nothing else, we have learned that business schools can change and change for the better! Can we go back to where we were before? Should we? Our answer is "no." We should keep what worked well (even better) and discard what didn't work. That is part of the evolution of business schools, an evolution that was long coming. Thus, while the journey from instruction to co-construction might appear complex/tedious/complicated/exciting/liberating/other (choose your word!), it looks promising for the learning and teaching experience of the future. There are many possibilities to integrate rewarding elements as shown in our tube map plan. Do not hesitate to stop at any station, and you can bridge the gap! Remember: Using the tube map of teaching – you've got a road map – you cannot get lost …

REFERENCES

Alzahrani, L., and Seth, K.P. (2021). Factors influencing students' satisfaction with continuous use of learning management systems during the COVID-19 pandemic: An empirical study. *Education and Information Technologies 26*(6), 6787–805. https://doi.org/10.1007/s10639-021-10492-5

Bandura, A. (1994). Self-efficacy. In V.S. Ramachaudran (ed.), *Encyclopedia of Human Behavior* (Vol. 4, pp. 71–81). New York: Academic Press. https://www.uky.edu/~eushe2/Bandura/BanEncy.html (accessed September 2, 2021).

Bates, A.W. (2019). Teaching in a digital age: Guidelines for designing teaching and learning. https://opentextbc.ca/teachinginadigitalage

Becker, A.S., Cummins, M., Davis, A., Freeman, A., Hall Giesinger, C., and Ananthanarayanan, V. (2017). *NMC Horizon Report: 2017 Higher Education Edition*. Austin, Ts: The New Media Consortium. https://library.educause.edu/-/media/files/library/2017/2/2017horizonreporthe.pdf

Boettcher, J.V., and Conrad, R.-M. (2016). *The Online Teaching Survival Guide* (2nd edn). San Francisco, CA: Josey-Bass.

Broadbent, J. (2017). Comparing online and blended learner's self-regulated learning strategies and academic performance. *Internet and Higher Education 33*, 24–32. https://doi.org/10.1016/j.iheduc.2017.01.004

Burchard, A. (2021). Bildungsexperten warnen vor Rückkehr zum klassischen Frontalunterricht. *Der Tagesspiegel*, September 20. https://www.tagesspiegel.de/wissen/digitale-schule-nach-corona-bildungsexperten-warnen-vor-rueckkehr-zum-klassischen-frontalunterricht/27630456.html

Chauhan, S., Goyal, S., Bhardwaj, A.K. and Sergi, B.S. (2021). Examining continuance intention in business schools with digital classroom methods during COVID-19: A comparative study of India and Italy. *Behaviour & Information Technology* 1596–1619. https://doi.org/10.1080/0144929x.2021.1892191

Deslauriers, L., McCarty, L.S., Miller, K., Callaghan, K., and Kestin, G. (2019). Measuring actual learning versus feeling of learning in response to being actively engaged in the classroom. *Proceedings of the National Academy of Sciences of the United States of America 116*(39), 19251–7. https://doi:org/10.1073/pnas.1821936116

EDUCAUSE (2020). The HyFlex course model. https://library.educause.edu/-/media/files/library/2020/7/eli7173.pdf

Gigliotti, R.A. (2021). The impact of COVID-19 on academic department chairs: Heightened complexity, accentuated liminality, and competing perceptions of reinvention. *Innovative Higher Education 46*(4), 429–44. https://doi.org/10.1007/s10755-021-09545-x

Gioia, D. (2020). A systematic methodology for doing qualitative research. *Journal of Applied Behavioral Science 57*(1), 20–9. https://doi.org/10.1177/0021886320982715

Glancy, F.H., and Isenberg, S.K. (2013). A conceptual learner-centered e-Learning framework. *Journal of Higher Education Theory and Practice* 13/2013), 22–35. http://t.www.na-businesspress.com/JHETP/GlancyFH_Web13_3__4_.pdf

Glaser, B.G., and Strauss, A.L. (1967). *The Discovery of Grounded Theory. Strategies for Qualitative Research*. Chicago, IL: Aldine Publishing.

HEG Website. https://www.heg-fr.ch/en/about-us/vision-and-mission (accessed August 16, 2021).

Hodges, C., Moore, S., Lockee, B., Trust, T., and Bond, A. (2020). The difference between emergency remote teaching and online learning. *Educause Review*. https://er.educause.edu/articles/2020/3/the-difference-between-emergency-remote-teaching-and-online-learning (accessed August 20, 2021).

Kirschner, P.A. (2002). Cognitive load theory: Implications of cognitive load theory on the design of learning. *Learning and Instruction 12*(1), 1–10. https://doi.org/10.1016/s0959-4752(01)00014-7

Knowles, M.S. (1975). *Self-directed Learning: A Guide for Learners and Teachers*. Cambridge: Adult Education.

Krishnamurthy, S. (2020). The future of business education: A commentary in the shadow of the Covid-19 pandemic. *Journal of Business Research 117*, 1–5. https://doi.org/10.1016/j.jbusres.2020.05.034

Le Boterf, G. (2006). *Engineering and Competency Assessment* (5th edn). Paris: Eyrolles. (Originally published as Ingénierie et évaluation des compétences.)

Lim, J.R.N., Rosenthal, S., Sim, Y.J.M., Lim, Z.Y., and Oh, K.R. (2021). Making online learning more satisfying: The effects of online-learning self-efficacy, social presence and content structure. *Technology, Pedagogy and Education 30*(4), 543–56. https://doi.org/10.1080/1475939x.2021.1934102

Marshall, D.T., Shannon, D.M., and Love, S.M. (2020). How teachers experienced the COVID-19 transition to remote instruction. *Phi Delta Kappan 102*(3), 46–50. https://doi.org/10.1177/0031721720970702

Monaghan, C.H. (2010). Communities of Practice: A learning strategy for management education. *Journal of Management Education 35*(3), 428–53. https://doi.org/10.1177/1052562910387536

Nortvig, A.M., Petersen, A.K., and Balle, S.H. (2018). A literature review of the factors influencing e-learning and blended learning in relation to learning outcome, student satisfaction, and engagement. *Electronic Journal of e-Learning 16*(1), 46–55. http://www.ejel.org

Pflugler, S. (2020). *Kommunikation für die digitale Ära*. München: Redline.

Porter, W., Graham, C.R., Spring, R.A., and Kyle, R.W. (2014). Blended learning in higher education: Institutional adoption and implementation. *Computers & Education 75*, 185–95. doi: 10.1016/j.compedu.2014.02.011

Prensky, M. (2001). Digital natives, digital immigrants. *On the Horizon 4*(9), 1–6. https://doi.org/10.1108/10748120110424816

Sarma, S., and Yoquinto, L. (2020). *Grasp: The Science Transforming How We Learn.* New York: Doubleday.

Schneckenberg, D., Ehlers, U., and Adelsberger, H. (2010). Web 2.0 and competence-oriented design of learning – potentials and implications for higher education. *British Journal of Educational Technology 42*(5), 747–62. doi.org/10.1111/j.1467-8535.2020.01092.x

Thomas, L. and Ambrosini, V. (2021). The future role of the business school: A value cocreation perspective. *Academy of Management Learning & Education 20*(2), 249–69. https://doi.org/10.5465/amle.2019.0239

Van der Heijde, C.M., and Van der Heijden, B.I.J.M. (2006). A competence-based and multidimensional operationalization and measurement of employability. *Human Resource Management 45*(3), 449–76. doi: 10.1002/hrm.20119

Veletsianos, G. (2020). *Learning Online: The Student Experience.* Baltimore, MD: Johns Hopkins University Press.

Weegar, M.A., and Pacis, D. (2012). A comparison of two theories of learning – Behaviorism and Constructivism as applied to face-to-face and online learning. http://www.g-casa.com/conferences/manila/papers/Weegar.pdf (accessed September 13, 2021).

Zembylas, M. (2008). Adult learners' emotions in online learning. *Distance Education 29*(1), 71–87. doi: 10.1080/01587910802004852

14. The imminent computational MBA degree

Mark Darius Juszczak

14.1 INTRODUCTION

There are many articles, and books, devoted to the subject of the future of the MBA (Master of Business Administration) degree. It might appear, from the title, that this chapter is yet another iteration of that future; that it is analysis of where the MBA degree is going. Nothing could be further from the truth. This is not a chapter about the future of the MBA degree. It is a chapter about the emergence of a new kind of MBA degree, based on a different set of methodological tools that draw from the field of computational finance and from other computational social science graduate degree programs. This computational MBA degree is not a replacement or evolution of a computational finance degree either. It is a specific and distinct type of degree that appears to be imminent because, for the first time, a number of tools in computational social science and computational finance are becoming increasingly available to non-technical users. This democratization of computational tools, a result of dropping costs of cloud computing and supercomputer cluster access, and increasingly sophisticated intermediate user-interface tools that lower technical barriers to use, will lead directly to a broader integration of computational tools into traditional academic disciplines. The MBA is no exception to this trend. This chapter is an attempt to contextualize the structure, function and significance of this trend from the lens of a new type of MBA degree.

14.2 THE STATE OF THE CURRENT MBA DEGREE MODEL

The success of the business degree as a construct, since World War II, is largely unquestioned. The American market, and subsequent global markets, have rapidly adopted and expanded this specific model of education. 'With respect to undergraduate post-secondary education, business is by far the most popular subject of study in the US with approximately 318,000 having received undergraduate business degrees during the 2005–2006 academic year (National Center for Education Statistics, 2007)' (Herrington, 2010, p. 75). The success of the MBA degree follows closely on the heels of undergraduate education in business. 'By 2006, approximately 146,000 Master's degrees in business were awarded in the U.S. (National Center for Education Statistics, 2007). That number represents 25 percent of all Master's degrees conferred in the U.S. during 2006; in popularity, the MBA had become second only to Master's degrees in education' (Herrington, 2010, p. 63).

However, this model is not without its critics or limitations. One of the biggest challenges that business education research identifies is that of where the degree should focus. 'A debate over whether the MBA degree should focus strictly on general skills or allow students to specialize has raged for many years' (Daniel, 1998). One side of the debate argues that MBA curricula should focus 'exclusively on general skills which help students develop intellectual and reasoning abilities' (Rehder & Porter, 1983). The other camp posits that 'even at higher levels of management MBA graduates must be able to manage specific functional areas, thus requiring specialized knowledge' (Hunt & Speck, 1986; Herrington, 2010). This debate between generalists and specialists has its origins in the more fundamental question of whether or not management as a competency can be separated from the particular industry that it happens to be situated in.

If management is a science then it should pass the test of its own discipline and provide scientifically testable outcomes independent of the specific industry in which one happens to practice that art. We know this to be true in physics and chemistry. Whether we drop a ball on Earth or on the Moon, the laws of physics are the same laws. This same issue has never been completely resolved within the domain of management, however. Critics argue that 'the MBA is too often informed by a literature that on the one hand lacks scientific rigor but on the other provides no opportunity for clinical training' (Brocklehurst et al., 2007, p. 380). But the absence of scientific rigor is not the only issue. At the same time, 'Business schools will increasingly need to expose their students to complex decision problems that permit them to exercise managerial judgment' (Schlegemilch & Thomas, 2011, p. 479). This reference to the need for complex problem solving and complex decision making is not just a passing critique. Rather, it is a fundamental question that is closely linked to the need for a computational MBA degree.

Increasingly, researchers and critics are recognizing that the spectrum between generalists and specialists is not the only axis of variance that challenges the standard model of the MBA degree as the only model. A methodological axis also exists. One the one hand, there is an acknowledgment of the need for different types of analytical skills. According to one study, there are numerous 'Opportunities to address unmet needs: shifting angles to frame problems holistically; learning to make decisions based on multiple, often conflicting, functional perspectives; and building judgment and intuition into messy, unstructured situations' (Datar et al., 2010, pp. 8–9). On the other hand, there is also a need for different types of practical skill set. 'The right answer for each school depends on that school's strategy, challenges, constraints, and skill sets. Yet, re-balancing from the current focus on knowing or analytical knowledge to more of what we call doing (skills) and being (a sense of purpose and identity) must occur' (Lagace, 2010). This methodological axis, between analytical and practical skills,] is not the only problem, however. While researchers can employ terms such as analytical skills or practical skills, the simple fact is that, over the past four decades, nearly every industry has become intertwined with increasingly complex information and industrial technology systems that result in higher-order dependencies and inter-dependencies.

If we step back for a moment and analyze the gap in both of these axes from a historical analogical perspective, it will become immediately clear. We don't question or teach reading or literacy in MBA programs, because we assume that every manager can read. That was not always the case historically, but it has been the case for the last several decades. We have this base assumption about literacy because it is so diffuse and so wired into everything we do that we couldn't possibly imagine functioning without it. The same is increasingly becoming true with complex computational systems. I am not referring to the more specific cultural concept of computer literacy. I am referring to the much broader and more significant set of tools that constitute computational literacy – the ability to read, understand and make decisions that are influenced by computational systems. It is this specific literacy that is increasingly causing gaps in decision making and strategy. Not because managers are lacking in decision making or strategic skills, but because managers do not even have, in many cases, the most basic literacy in what computational systems are and in the breadth of their participation in the minutiae of everyday global commerce. In virtually every corner of management, there is now a computational agent, actor or system working behind the scenes.

14.3   THE NEED FOR A COMPUTATIONAL MBA DEGREE

One of the best examples of this phenomenon comes in the quest for alpha. Alpha, a variable critical to hedge fund performance, measures 'the excess return on an investment after adjusting for market-related volatility and random fluctuations.' Two words in this standard definition from Investopedia, excess return, actually refer to skill, more specifically the aggregate set of competencies of investors, managers and decision makers to provide a return-on-investment (ROI) that is uniquely and specifically theirs – as opposed to the result of general market forces or luck.

The shifting nature of those competencies is at the heart of this chapter – and is also the reason why the current MBA market needs not just more courses in computational finance, but an actual computational MBA degree as a stand-alone degree. While the need for better alpha represents a small sample of labor market demand for the competencies acquired in MBA degrees, it does represent a broader trend across the financial, management, supply chain and global business development sectors: the need for new tools to better understand complexity, chaos and interrelatedness of hidden variables. 'In the past, stock market indexes were forecasted by simple technical analysis such as a moving average and linear regression models … Traditional forecasting methods are limited in their effectiveness as they make assumptions about the distribution of the underlying data, and often fail to recognize the interrelatedness of variables' (Fok et al., 2008, p. 1).

On the other hand, computational neural networks performs better than other linear models, specifically, for more 'irregular series and for multiple-period-ahead forecasting' (Fok et al., 2008, p. 1). Numerous studies about the performance of computational neural networks in forecasting complex market dynamics (Cao & Tay, 2001; Chen et al., 2003; Kamruzzman & Sarker, 2003, 2004) consistently demonstrate that computational modeling, and the ability to manage and design computational business research, are critical factors in competitive advantage.

This competitive advantage is not merely about competencies linked to computational finance (as numerous courses in this area already exist). It is about the need for non-technical management to open the computational black box and begin understanding its integral parts. This applies to global hedge funds and to small business alike. 'Asset managers around the world are … striving to deliver alpha in a way that sets them apart from other firms. The quest for alpha traditionally has been associated with investment strategy and performance, but it is now increasingly understood and accepted that a similar concept also applies to operations' (Merrell, 2016, p. 113). That concept is nothing new – alpha, in the form of experience operating as wisdom, has always been the most significant asset a company can have. But, what is new is the need for non-technical managers, decision makers and investors to consistently (as opposed to haphazardly) plan and draw on the computational world to conduct research and make decisions (McCourt, 2006; Landau, 2008; Sugurmaran et al., 2017).

That need, for business generalists who speak, understand and can use the tools of the computational world, is very different than the need for technical computational finance specialists. While there are computational finance degrees, there does not yet appear to be a true computational MBA degree available to students in the US. The computational MBA degree, from the lens of the competencies just articulated, should be seen not as a derivative of computational finance, but as interdisciplinary integration of computational sociology, computational economics, computational behavioral science and computational finance.

At the current time, the degree that comes the closest to a computational MBA degree is a MS degree in computational finance, or a certificate in the same. Purdue is one of the first universities in the US to offer an MBA degree with a specialization in computational finance. And it is not alone. Georgia Tech's Scheller College of Business offers an immersive track in the MBA degree in computational finance. The Saunders College of Business at RIT (Rochester Institute of Technology) offers an MS in computational finance as does Carnegie Mellon University.

While this degree is really a derivative of a more common MS degree offered in numerous universities, the financial engineering degree, the opportunity for traditional MBA students to specialize in computational finance is relatively uncommon. Although both degrees deal with finance, they have been largely treated as (to use the famous phrase of Stephen Jay Gould) 'non-overlapping magisteria.' Nor should we treat a computational MBA degree as an upgrade or broadening of a computational finance degree. While the computational MBA degree will draw on some of the same methodological tools, it is, and always will be, a fundamentally different degree. That is because the two degrees answer different questions with different tools – and the two fields do not really speak to each other. Part of the problem appears to be a market misconception – the conflation of all things computer with all things 'compu-tational.' Little recognition is given to the true distinction of computational science as being a fundamentally different field of theoretical science – with analogues in the traditional sciences. Instead, big data, data analytics, artificial intelligence (AI) and computational science are often perceived as belonging to a single core of computer-based tools.

Computational science is not simply 'working with computers.' That liter-acy, commonly referred to as digital literacy, has to do with the way in which consumers interact with digital technologies. Whereas computational literacy is really about fundamental science and the way in which scientific tools advance business strategies, decisions and technologies. As such, literacy in computational sciences is a literacy of a specific and non-empirical scientific method.

14.4   WHAT IS COMPUTATIONAL SCIENCE?

Ever since the Monte Carlo method was developed by Stanislaw Ulam and John Von Neumann, under the broader umbrella of the Manhattan Project in the 1940s (Eckhardt, 1987), there has been a broad recognition by the scientific community that computational science is a field of science that is distinct from its empirical analogues, no matter the amount or type of data contained within that broader empirical field.

A cursory examination of the field of chemistry versus that of computational chemistry can most easily highlight this distinction: within the field of chemistry, chemists study, as but one example, water molecular dynamics. They do this through the empirical method: testing, re-testing, observing and analyzing the behavior of water. Computational chemists who work in the field of computational water molecular dynamics never work with water itself. They do not conduct empirical experiments with water molecules. They conduct computational simulations with computational water molecules developed and stored in computational molecular libraries. This method has existed for over 30 years (Pranata & Jorgensen, 1991). Instead of walking to a tap to fill up a beaker with water, a computational water molecular chemist goes to an online repository to access a computational water molecule and then conducts experiments in supercomputer simulations to develop theories and solve problems in the real world.

As but one example of this type of program, Michigan State University is one of the growing number of major universities in the US to offer a computational variant of a traditional Master's degree. Their MS program in Computational Chemistry is a typical example of one of these programs. Their program description states:

> The Master of Science with a major in Computational Chemistry is designed to prepare individuals to implement, manage, and support all aspects of the application of computers and computing in chemistry within academic, governmental, and industrial scientific settings. Graduates will also be equipped to serve as professional resources for visualization, modeling, and database activities.

Several specific components of the program objective are of particular interest in the context of a computational MBA degree. In fact, if we substitute the word chemistry for the word business, we can see right away the fundamental logic in a computational MBA curriculum:

> The Master of Business Administration with a major in Computational Business Administration is designed to prepare individuals to implement, manage, and support all aspects of the application of computers and computing in business and business decision-making within corporate, B2B, B2G and B2C markets. Graduates will also be equipped to serve as professional resources for visualization, modeling, and database activities.

The juxtaposition may, at first glance, seem jarring. However, if we look closely at the language of substitution we can see that a computational MBA degree appears perfectly rationale – as long as we approach it from a methods-based perspective.

Computational science does not use the empirical method. No matter how sophisticated the algorithms or analytics may be, traditional MBA programs, in all of their course work, are fundamentally reliant on the empirical method to sift and filter truth from opinion. To quote one of the major proponents of computational scientific methods, Stephen Wolfram,

> In the existing sciences much of the emphasis has been on breaking systems down to find their underlying parts ... But, just how these components act together to produce even some of the most obvious features ... has in the past remained an almost complete mystery. Within the framework of the new kind of [computational] science ... it is finally possible to address such a question. (Wolfram, 2002, p. 3)

In this regard, computational science is not merely about statistical sampling and inference. Rather, it is about the reconstruction of a simulated reality through the mechanism of simple components to observe the emergence of complex behaviors. 'The principle of computational equivalence [states] that whenever one sees behavior that is not obviously simple – in essentially any system – it can be thought of as corresponding to a computation of equivalent sophistication' (Wolfram, 2002, p. 719).

For many years, the overriding practiced assumption of universities has been that computational sciences can only derive from natural sciences. And while much attention and funding has been given to the development of computational natural science fields, little attention has been paid to the development of computational social science fields, until recently. However, the opportunities for theoretical advancement within the social sciences are no lesser than for their natural counterparts.

> From economics to psychology there has been a widespread if controversial assumption ... that solid theories must always be formulated in terms of numbers, equations and traditional mathematics. But I suspect that one will often have a much better chance of capturing fundamental mechanisms for phenomena in the social sciences by using instead the new kind of [computational] science ... based on simple programs. (Wolfram, 2002, p. 9)

By programs, Wolfram is not referring to programs of study. Rather, he is referring to tools such as cellular automata. The general principle behind such work in computational social science is simple: complex and emergent behaviors of intelligent agents (humans and other sentient embodied and disembodied agents) can be best understood, theorized and predicted, by constructing such agents from the 'ground up' as aggregated sets of simple rules and parts.

14.5   THE HISTORICAL CONTEXT OF A COMPUTATIONAL MBA DEGREE

We can look at the imminent development of a computational MBA degree in a broader historical context – and can, therefore, better understand the relationship between tools, theories and degree programs. The Amos Tuck School of Administration and Finance developed the first graduate degree in business in 1900 (Meacham, 2007). Five years earlier, Frederick Winslow Taylor had published his first major paper on the field of scientific management that eventually bore his name, Taylorism. That paper, 'A piece rate system' was presented to the American Society of Mechanical Engineers in June 1896 (Copley, 1923). Taylor was not alone in his attempts to rationalize and bring empirical order to the world of business.

Rather, he wrote and eventually became professor at the Tuck School (D'Aveni, 2007), during the progressive era; a period defined by two different forces – Roosevelt's progressivism that sought to bring rights and dignity to the common worker and the relentless march of scientific progress. The Tuck graduate degree in business, followed a few years later by Harvard, was not so much an evolution in theory, as it was an evolution in tool sets. Ever since Darwin's publication of the *Origin of the Species* (1859), there had been an interest in applying the empirical method in natural science to the social sciences. Taylor's scientific management, and the acceptance by universities of an empirical approach to business, was the natural outcome of that evolution.

The same transformation appears to be taking place today: for several decades computational methods have matured and evolved within the natural sciences. Universities take it for granted that there are degree programs in both biology and computational biology, or in astrophysics and computational astrophysics. And they are not seen as subsets. IE, the computational astrophysics Master's degree is not a specialization. It is a different degree – it uses different tools and different theoretical models and it investigates different things; things that astrophysicists cannot. As but one example, an emerging subfield within computational astrophysics is numerical relativity, where theoreticians can experiment with boundary constructs in time and space that do not exist in the known universe – and can then apply the outcomes of their research to solving real-world problems.

Universities are beginning to accept that same significant distinction in the social sciences: that a degree in computational sociology is fundamentally different from a degree in sociology. This is principally because, just as in the late 19th century, the tools of this new science have been increasingly democ-ratized. As industrial wealth has led to an increase in the ability of scientists to run experiments in more places, with more precision and with more data, an increase in supercomputer capacity is leading to an increase in the ability of graduate students and scientists to conduct computational science experi-ments. Major companies such as IBM and Amazon are working hard to bring down the cost of supercomputer access (Morgan, 2019) and there is a broad expectation that, just as HTML (Hyper Text Markup Language) has evolved from a complex language requiring technical knowledge in programming to multi-layered WYSIWYGs (What You See Is What You Get) for amateur users, the same will happen (and is happening) with supercomputers. In short, as the tools of data scientists are democratized, there will be a general increase in access and tool use for computational social sciences.

The computational MBA is one of the natural next steps for the MBA degree. A democratization of access to supercomputers, and a strong founda-tion of tools, methods, ABMs (Agent-Based Models) and theories in computa-tional sociology, finance and economics means that a functional computational MBA program is within reach within the next 2–5 years.

14.6   THE CURRENT SPACE OF COMPUTATIONAL GRADUATE STUDIES

Universities have been developing, over the past three decades, distinct tracks and programs in the computational natural sciences that do exactly this. At the current time, the following represents but a small sampling of the Master's degree in computational studies that graduate students can pursue: computational astrophysics, computational chemistry, computational molec-ular biology, computational evolutionary biology, computational genomics, computational physics, computational thermodynamics, etc.

The jump to computational social science graduate degrees is the next obvious step. A select few top universities in the US have recently begun offering computational social science degrees for several years. These include: the University of Chicago, UC Davis, UMASS Amherst and the UCLA Computational Sociology working group. In addition, Chapman University offers an interdisciplinary MS degree in computational economics.

If we look more closely at the actual subfields of research within compu-tational social science we can see the link to a computational MBA degree. Principal existing fields of study that are unified under the umbrella of 'com-putational social science' include: artificial life, catastrophe theory, chaos theory, complexity theory, AI theory, cybernetics, dynamical systems theory and evolution theory, to name but a few. Of these, the three C's (catastrophe, chaos and complexity) have always been central to the study of business strategy and theory – except that their investigation has principally been based on empirical models of dissected existing data. When it comes to the behavior of markets, the study of risk, the study of supply chain management and the study of long-term trends, new theoretical approaches to the three C's are critical to the evolution of the MBA degree, and, logically, lead to the development of a computational MBA degree.

14.7 FOUNDATIONAL PIECES OF A COMPUTATIONAL MBA DEGREE

The computational degree will pass the test of market utility in those cases where computational methods can be used to advance theory and provide answers (to use the overused phrase) better, faster and cheaper. In addition, it is important to situate the computational MBA degree within the broader nexus of supercomputer technologies, quantum computer technologies (ideal in many ways for solving optimization problems that are dominant in MBA studies) and computational social science theories and tool sets.

The emergence of a computational MBA degree, as a distinct degree from a traditional MBA, must be considered not merely in the context of its imminence (it's about to occur because the tools that enable it have become broadly enough available for it to be feasible), but also in the context of its utility. In other words, if the computational MBA degree does exist, then that existence cannot merely be because students want to earn that degree. It must also be because the competencies acquired in that computational MBA degree are different enough from, and meet a market need that, the traditional MBA degree cannot meet.

Let us consider this question of utility from a user perspective – the potential employer of a graduate of a computational MBA program. That employer must determine that the specific skills acquired in the computational MBA degree are better suited to the business problems at hand. What kinds of problems might those be? The short answer, and the answer on which both the emergence and the persistence of the computational MBA degree rests, is complexity.

Complexity can, in many cases, be solved through systems analysis, logistics and data analytics courses. All courses available in a traditional MBA degree. What kind of complexity, however, cannot be resolved through such tools? In other words, under what conditions are the types of analysis that are currently possible through an 'empirical framework' not capable of providing answers?

The type of complexity that I am referring to here is a complexity of non-deterministic agents operating in an environment with many hidden variables. In other words, there are certain types of businesses that are highly stable and have highly predictable problems. These businesses can be optimized and rely heavily on analysis from the fields of finance, systems analysis, data analytics, predictive analytics and so on. The key factor here is one of 'bounded complexity.' While there may be many variables, they are known variables.

However, a different type of problem occurs in certain industries and businesses that are highly contingent. In other words, their persistence, emergence or evolution is contingent on a number of externalities that are hidden, incredibly complex and/or unknown and, more specifically, unknowable. We see these types of businesses most clearly at the technological envelope of R&D.

As but one example, consider a company such as Colossal, a Siberian company attempting to bring back the Woolly Mammoth. This company, which has raised over 15 million USD in seed capital, operates in a space of absolute contingency and uncertainty. While 'the sequencing of woolly mammoth genome, have opened the opportunity for the revival of extinct species' (Pina-Aguilar et al., 2009), the business dimension of this potential technology is not so clear-cut as the science. Not only is the business model uncertain, the technology is uncertain, as are numerous parameters of its manifestation. And yet, it exists. And it has problems. Problems that a traditional MBA degree graduate cannot solve because those problems are unsolvable through an empirical framework.

Instead, those problems can only be *approached*. They can't be solved. They can be approximated. They can be simulated. We don't know how to perform a 'data analytics' operation on the relationship between woolly mammoth populations and carbon dioxide emissions in the arctic tundra because NO DATA exists for this specific eventuality. At best, we can simulate it. To do so, we need someone trained in competencies that are at the intersection of business and the various multidisciplinary factors that affect this type of operation; factors that are themselves speculative.

In other words, Colossal has no need for a traditional MBA graduate. Because they have no data. They only have contingencies. As such, an empirical approach to analysis will fail. Instead, a simulative approach, rooted in computational research is the only possible alternative. At the current time, however, these competencies are stuck in the hard sciences. In other words, we may find a computational evolutionary biologist, since that type of graduate program exists. And we may find a computational chemist who can run simulations on soil and carbon dioxide capture in the context of arctic megafauna. But we cannot find in the marketplace, at the current time, a graduate who is able to synthesize those simulations in hard sciences with a business focus and in a business environment.

That competency set does not yet exist as a self-contained competency set from a graduate program. Because the computational MBA does not yet exist. There are thousands of other companies like Colossal that are working at the cutting edge of a technology envelope that need non-empirical answers. Because the data does not yet exist for them to draw conclusions. As such, the computational MBA graduate will provide the marketplace with a unique skill set – capable of bringing non-empirical science into the domain of business.

14.8 WHY ISN'T A COMPUTATIONAL FINANCE GRADUATE DEGREE ENOUGH?

A better understanding of that skill set can be best understood if we look at the limitations of current computational finance degree programs. These limitations are not a critique of computational finance programs. Rather, they represent conceptual limitations in program design that result in the competency gap alluded to in the case of Colossal attempting to resurrect the woolly mammoth.

It is tempting to assume that the computational MBA degree ought to be a computational finance degree with some social science simulation courses added. This would, however, be a categorical mistake, because it would assume that the MBA degree is, itself, an extension of finance theory alone. More than a century of MBA education has demonstrated that this is clearly not the case. The origins of the MBA degree are not in finance alone. Rather, they are in the holistic strategic management of business – a theoretical task which encompasses numerous disciplines, ranging from systems analysis to behavioral psychology to economics.

As such, the computational MBA degree should not be seen as an extension of a computational finance degree. It should be seen as an MBA degree program that has shifted its primary tool base from empirical modeling to simulative modeling and has done so with the explicit intention of broadening the scope and range of analysis available to competent program graduates.

To understand this distinction, and its effect on the core syllabus of a computational MBA degree, we have to first look at the limitations of core courses offered in computational finance degrees. Carnegie Mellon University, which offers one of the oldest MS degrees in computational finance, is an instructive place to begin. According to the program website, 'Carnegie Mellon's MSC program in Computational Finance has been running for the past 27 years. Unlike traditional MS finance programs, this one, like other Computational Finance programs, is focused on simulation.' An example of this can be seen in one of several courses in the MSC program that focus explicitly on simulation tool competencies. The following, from the Carnegie Mellon University website, is an overview of one these courses: Simulation Methods for Option Pricing (Course Number 46932):

> This course initially presents standard topics in simulation including random variable generation, statistical analysis of simulation output and variance reduction

methods including antithetic variables, control variables, importance sampling, conditional Monte Carlo, stratification and martingale control variables. The course then addresses the use of Monte Carlo simulation in solving applied problems on derivative pricing and risk management discussed in the finance literature. Application areas include the estimation of the 'Greeks,' pricing of American options, pricing interest rate dependent claims, and credit risk.

A close analysis of the course overview is instructive. The course is principally based on derivatives of the Monte Carlo method, an approach to scientific inquiry that is rooted in random sampling; using randomness to solve problems that are, in principle, deterministic. In the world of finance, this is an acceptable framework for simulation because the underlying logic of any financial transaction is bound by a singular known variable – price. Computational finance may be situated in a world of unknowns, where the complexity of markets and actors is such that outcomes appear random, but the single variable that drives the logic of any type of experimentation is price.

This is not true in the world of business. While the 'score card' of a business's success or failure may be measurable in money, the task of running a business consists of many variables far beyond price alone. There are variables linked to human motivation and desire, variables linked to human trust and temptation, variables linked to esoteric tacit knowledge resident in the minds of employees and shareholders. There are so many non-financial variables that the microcosm of finance cannot serve as the foundation alone for the jump from a computational finance degree program to a computational MBA program.

In addition, there is a secondary consideration that further propels the argument for the computational MBA degree necessarily being separate in its foundations from a computational finance degree. HFT (High Frequency Trading) and the automation of many types of transactions based on AI systems has resulted in a parallel non-human financial market actively operating in the world of humans. 'Financial markets ... [are] a collective capitalist brain through which capital cognitively organizes the extraction of value, only hampered by occasional and random catastrophe associated with high-frequency trading (HFT) (Terranova 2013: 66)' (Beverungen, 2019, p. 78).

This collective capitalist brain is a direct result of computational financial experiments, analysis and direct integration into market systems. 'The important aspect to note is the way in which human consciousness and cognition become increasingly irrelevant to markets and are ultimately discounted, with a market conceived as a person-machine system, a hybrid computational device, with the thinking off loaded onto things' (Beverungen, 2019, p. 79). In essence, a disproportionate amount of trading volume occurring as a result of automated trading means that the market is actually running on an internal logic of its own, divorced from reality. Rather, it is operating according to auto-mated heuristics that are themselves the products of simulations. As Mirowski and Nik-Khah put it: 'Agents would be folded into the person-machine system, no longer deemed capable of understanding why they made the decisions that they do. Think of their predicament as Artificial Ignorance (2017: 238–239)' (Beverungen, 2019, p. 79).

In order to properly study this symbiotic field of computational finance (as both actor and observer), a new set of analytic tools is needed. In other words, computational finance has spawned a world of real-world financial actors that themselves need to be researched with computational tools. A new type of understanding of the relationship between human actors (as business agents) and their epistemological products is required as a baseline for understanding financial markets. IE, the day-to-day effect of computational financial instruments, is so powerful and so pervasive that it needs its own new kind of 'computational police' – the computational MBA graduates who can properly understand and analyze what is actually happening in this new daily interaction between computational agents and human agents.

14.9 MARKET GOALS OF A COMPUTATIONAL MBA DEGREE

In empirical science, the distinction between universal meaning heuristics and cultural products is not relevant, since the data that is analyzed is 'pre-existing.' In other words, data sets already exist and already contain the biases built into them by the respective cultural agents that manufactured that data. However, in a computational space, that difference matters and results in three different goals, regardless of the type of social science computational degree program that we are speaking about. Those goals are: the determination of hidden correlation and causation, the prediction of the future and the replication of human reasoning in non-human agents. While these may not seem to be business-specific goals, we must bear in mind the purpose of the computational MBA degree. It is not to replicate the goals of an MBA degree with advanced computational tools. The three goals outlined above are not goals of business. They are goals of methodological maturity.

Concerning the first, the determination of hidden correlations and causation, we can examine the problem of pattern recognition in financial markets. Despite the constant search for alpha or the contribution of the analyst and despite the fact that millions of individuals spend countless hours analyzing market data, patterns and trends, 'The seemingly improbable happens all the time in financial markets. A year earlier, the Dow had fallen 7.7 percent in one day. (Probability: one in 50 billion.) In July 2002, the index recorded three steep falls within seven trading days. (Probability: one in four trillion.)'

(Hudson & Mandelbrot, 2008, p. 4). No matter what, events occur in complex systems that are seemingly always disproportionate to the odds of their occurrence. Neither a small number of people communicating orally nor capacity for storage and collection of data about billions of people can avoid the fundamental problem of non-universality in meaningmaking. As a result, even with all of the data available, a paradox will always exist: perfect information will not necessarily lead to equal outcomes. The first goal of the computational MBA degree is to teach competencies in simulation tools that provide us with a way of shedding some light on this problem. While we can never have perfect information, we can better understand HOW agents that are sentient might behave given a specific change in variables.

Concerning the second goal, the prediction of the future, we must examine the construct of induction. The science fiction author and cybernetics philosopher Stanislaw Lem best summarized this specific problem:

> For hundreds of years, philosophers have been trying to prove logically the validity of induction: a form of reasoning that anticipates the future on the basis of past experience. None of them have succeeded in doing so. They could not have succeeded because induction is an attempt to transform incomplete into complete information. (Lem, 2013, p. 124)

Here a second paradox confronts us: the attempt to create complete information from incomplete information among sentient beings that possess variances in meaningmaking will, in almost all cases, function as a recursive loop: the attempt itself will influence the future and the future will reflect the attempt to know the future and not the actual past as it was before such an attempt was made. The second goal of the computational MBA degree, then, is not to predict the future. Rather, it is to synthesize futures in simulation that inform on the present moment.

Concerning the third goal, the replication of human intelligence, we must investigate the fundamental architecture of neural networks from a rather unique perspective: that of epistemological procreation. The primary tools that have developed within data science over the past 50 years for the replication of human intelligence are: 'Principal Component Analysis, Least Square and Polynomial Fitting, Constrained Linear Regression, K-Means Clustering, Logistic Regression, Feed-Forward Neural Networks (FFNs), Convolutional Neural Networks (CNNs), Recurrent Neural Networks (RNNs), Conditional Random Fields (CRFs) and decision trees' (TDS, 2019). What is interesting about these tools is that the majority of them are based on a weighting function that is meant to mimic brain function in humans. To be more specific: the origins of neural network mathematics and clustering are based on a singular premise: that ascribing preferential status to cognitive or logical pathways based on prior events and exposure is critical to learning and improved performance. While this is true, from a perspective of both neuroscience and the function of artificial neural networks, it does not alter a simple fact: in humans weighting functions are genetically and biologically deterministic and therefore hidden from direct human control, but weighting functions in any tool or scientific object in data science are both deliberate and prescriptive. How much a certain pathway is weighted and how much that pathway is influenced by exposure to prior stimuli is a decision that is made by a data scientist.

That decision is a direct function of what matters to that analyst. As a result, the meaning we can extrapolate from any data set, no matter its size or complexity, is both constrained by our individual meaningmaking and by the perception of significance and importance of the data analyst that constructed the weighting mechanisms in the first place. From this perspective, we can conceptualize computational tools as a technology for the artificial reproduction of individual bias. We are, in constructing neural networks, doing nothing more than creating cognitive children of ourselves. We are epistemological parents creating epistemological children that reside in the various neural networks and clustering functions. This is not math. It is procreation. The third and most important goal of a computational MBA program is then the awareness of that deep bias that infiltrates all of the non-human actors that we create and then deploy into the global world of business.

14.10   CONCLUSION

This chapter examines the computational MBA degree from a process and methods perspective. As in other computational fields of study, the issue is not one of content. There is no rationale, in this context, for either describing or advocating for significant changes in the information presented to students in a traditional MBA degree.

Rather, the emphasis in the computational MBA degree is on process – on achieving through non-empirical methods the types of insights that can transform cutting-edge businesses and industries. We can look at the analogue field in computational astrophysics to understand what I mean. Computational astrophysicists can conduct experiments in a supercomputer that they could never conduct in the real world, such as the collision of two black holes under specific conditions. The same is true for a computational MBA graduate. They can conduct experiments that could not be conducted in the real world – such as the impact that a functional fusion reactor would have on oil prices, or the effect of a singular patent on climate change, etc.

The tool set is different and, as a result, the application of that tool set is different. Graduates of a computational MBA degree will be pulled towards those businesses that operate with high degrees of uncertainty. They will have competencies that traditional MBA graduates do not have and do not have a need for. Rather, they will be sought out by companies and employers that operate under unique environments of technological risk, social uncertainty and other forms of complexity that do not bear equally on all markets.

It is my hope in this chapter to outline a new type of degree program that the world needs – a computational MBA program that will meet the challenges faced by companies operating in theaters of unusual complexity and uncertainty.

REFERENCES

Beverungen, A. (2019). Algorithmic trading, artificial intelligence and the politics of cognition. Retrieved August 10, 2022 from: https://mediarep.org/bitstream/handle/doc/14476/Democratization-of-Artificial-Intelligence_77-93_Beverungen_Algorithmic-Trading.pdf?sequence=1

Brocklehurst, M., Sturdy, A., Winstanley, D. and Driver, M. (2007). Introduction: Whither the MBA? Factions, fault lines and the future. *Management Learning*, 38(4), 379–88.

Cao, L. and Tay, F. (2001). Financial forecasting using support vector machines. *Neural Computing & Applications*, 10, 184–92.

Chen, A., Leung, M. and Daouk, H. (2003). Application of neural networks to an emerging financial market: forecasting and trading the Taiwan Stock Index. *Computer & Operations Research*, 30, 901–3.

Copley, F.B. (1923). *Frederick W. Taylor: Father of Scientific Management*. Harper and Brothers. p. 467.

Daniel, C.A. (1998). MBA: The First Century. Cranbury, New Jersey: Associated University Presses (no page number available).

D'Aveni, Richard A. (2007). On changing the conversation: Tuck and the field of strategy. Tuck School of Business. Archived from the original on August 4, 2007.

Datar, S.M., Garvin, D.A. and Cullen, P.G., 2010. Rethinking the MBA. *Business Education at a Crossroads*, 30(5), 451.

Eckhardt, R. (1987). Stan Ulam, John von Neumann, and the Monte Carlo method (PDF). *Los Alamos Science*, 15, 131–7.

Fok, W.W., Tam, V.W. and Ng, H. (2008). Computational neural network for global stock indexes prediction. In *Proceedings of the World Congress on Engineering* (Vol. 2, pp. 2–4).

Herrington, J. (2010). MBA: Past, present and future. *Academy of Educational Leadership Journal*, 14(1), 63.

Hudson, R.L. and Mandelbrot, B.B. (2008). *The Misbehavior of Markets: A Fractal View of Risk, Ruin, and Reward*. Profile.

Hunt, S.D. and Speck, P.S. (1986). Specialization and the MBA: Is the broad MBA passe? *California Management Review*, 28(3), 159–75

Kamruzzaman, J. and Sarker, R. (2003), Forecasting of currency exchange rates using ANN: A case study. In *Proceedings of IEEE International Conference on Neural Networks & Signal Processing* (ICNNSP03), pp. 793–7.

Kamruzzaman, J. and Sarker, R. (2004). ANN-based forecasting of foreign currency exchange rates. *Neural Information Processing – Letters and Reviews*, 3(2), May, 49.

Lagace, M. (2010). What is the future of MBA education? *Harvard Business School Working Knowledge*, 3.

Landau, R.H. (2008). What to teach? Computational Science as an improved model for science education. Oregon State University, March.

Lem, S. (2013). *Summa technologiae*. Suhrkamp Verlag.

Mandelbrot, B.B. and Hudson, R.L. (2010). *The (Mis)Behaviour of Markets: A Fractal View of Risk, Ruin and Reward*. Profile Books.

McCourt, F.R. (2006). Computational science: An intermingling of science, mathematics, and computer science. In *International Conference on Computational Science* (May, pp. 193–8). Springer.

Meacham, S. (2007). Business Education History. Dartmo.com: The Buildings of Dartmouth College. Retrieved November 9, 2007 from: https://www.dartmo.com/

Merrell, T.W. (2016). Operational alpha and reconciliation solutions for growing asset managers. *Journal of Securities Operations & Custody*, 8(2), 113–18.

Morgan, T.P. (2019) Bending the supercomputing cost curve down. Retrieved August 10, 2022 from: https://www.nextplatform.com/2019/12/02/bending-the-supercomputing-cost-curve-down/

Pina-Aguilar, R.E., Lopez-Saucedo, J., Sheffield, R., Ruiz-Galaz, L.I., de J. Barroso-Padilla, J. and Gutiérrez-Gutiérrez, A. (2009). Revival of extinct species using nuclear transfer: Hope for the mammoth, true for the Pyrenean ibex, but is it time for 'conservation cloning'? *Cloning and Stem Cells*, 11(3), 341–6.

Pranata, J. and Jorgensen, W.L. (1991). Computational studies on FK506: Conformational search and molecular dynamics simulation in water. *Journal of the American Chemical Society*, 113(25), 9483–93.

Rehder, R.R. and Porter, J.L. (1983). The creative MBA: A new proposal for balancing the science and the art of management. *Business Horizons*, 26(6), 52–4.

Schlegelmilch, B.B. and Thomas, H. (2011). The MBA in 2020: Will there still be one? *Journal of Management Development*, 30(5), 479.

Sugumaran, V., Sangaiah, A.K. and Thangavelu, A. (eds) (2017). *Computational Intelligence Applications in Business Intelligence and Big Data Analytics*. CRC Press.

TDS (2019). Retrieved August 10, 2022 from: https://towardsdatascience.com/top-10-machine-learning-algorithms-for-data-science-cdb0400a25f9

Wolfram, S. (2002). *A New Kind of Science*. Wolfram Media.

15. Is higher education hybrid-ready or not? An open call for business schools' ongoing dual transformation

Francesca Pucciarelli, Francesco Rattalino and Francesco Venuti

15.1 INTRODUCTION: THE EVER-CHANGING LANDSCAPE OF BUSINESS AND MANAGEMENT EDUCATION

Change is part of everybody lives, thus individuals and organization, business schools included, must learn how to cope with an uncertain future, become more agile and resilient, as well as more focused on innovation. 2020 will be remembered as the year of COVID-19, a global pandemic, but also a sudden, profound and unavoidable external shock that forcedly accelerated many of the trends already in place in our society (e.g., digital transformation, quest for more ethicalness in business management, agility, etc.), and imposed completely new endeavours (e.g., personal protection devices, social distancing, etc.). Even if the magnitude of the implications of the pandemic varies a lot, from industry to industry, from country to country, a common denominator is the capacity of COVID-19 in rebooting the public and scholarly debate on digital transformation, and more specifically on the potential of hybrid models of working and learning, and its impacts for businesses, universities and society at large.

COVID-19 forced companies to quickly shut down many activities as well as their offices and to completely reorganize the ways of work, adopting technologies of remote working. In the same manner, the COVID-19 pandemic and the closing down of the universities and business schools' campuses strongly affected the way education is and will be delivered. With the evolution of the pandemic situation and the gradual reopening of campuses and classes, reflection on the online and hybrid educational model became a major issue for all the institutions involved. As the effects of this pandemic continue to unfold, an understanding of online disruption and emerging hybrid models is needed (Meiller, 2020).

Some companies, such as Adecco, LinkedIn, Twitter among many others, are taking a serious stake on remote and hybrid working, publicly committed to supporting a hybrid future and promising significant forms of flexibility. Employees are split between those who wants to continue with remote working only, those that consider the office to be the best place to work, and the remaining part, actually the majority of employees, that are in favour of some sort of hybrid model.[1] Yet, many issues and challenges about this situation are still not clear, as well as a number of open questions about the real cost and sustainability of the work-at-home and hybrid working flexibility that are receiving increasing attention in the public debate.

As a matter of fact, technology has always had a great impact on higher education and the way it is delivered (Hamilton et al., 2016). E-learning, remote learning, blended learning has been around for a long time, evolving gradually and remaining on the fringe. While several signals indicate that higher education is at the crossroads of disruption, higher education resistance to change and aversion to risk often act as a constraint (Kaplan, 2021), slowing, limiting or even impeding significant change from taking place.

The COVID-19 pandemic forced universities to shut down their offices and campuses indefinitely, imposing a sudden and massive transition to online. As a consequence, online learning has become mainstream (Chakraborty et al., 2021) and the rapidness and smoothness of the transition to hybrid education models can change the present, and the future, of any business schools (Greenberg and Hibbert, 2020). It is important to notice that this enduring health crisis (like other major global crises previously), in addition to new international issues that have recently emerged (such as the war in Ukraine and in other area of the world, which might impose additional restrictions to travelling or to being physically present in a certain place at a precise moment), represents an important moment of self-reflection for academia at large on the role and on the future of business schools. And we shouldn't miss the precious opportunity of this crisis to reinvent the higher education system at large (Lozano, 2012; Yang and Huang, 2021), refocusing the business schools in the forward direction of more responsible management education practices (RME), to equip students to thrive in an uncertain and challenging future (Moratis and Melissen, 2020; Goedegebuure and Meek, 2021; Pucciarelli and Kaplan, 2022).

The chapter aims at illustrating the consequences of the passage to a hybrid educational model amidst COVID-19 using the case of a top league European business school, namely, ESCP Business School, describing its transition to hybrid education to explore the opportunities, challenges and open questions that all business schools are called to address in this unprecedented moment.

The chapter is organized as follows: in the next section an illustration of the key elements of a hybrid education model is presented, within a well-known theoretical framework. The SAMR framework is used to help readers in understanding the shift to a hybrid education model. SAMR stands for the four degrees of technology integration in supporting learning, namely, Substitution, Augmentation, Modification and Redefinition. The chapter concludes by highlighting that the future of business schools cannot be divorced by the digital transformation and the hybrid education model could (and should) expedite more sustainable practices in management education.

15.2 BUSINESS SCHOOLS IN A GLOBAL PANDEMIC: ONLINE EMERGENCY TEACHING AND HYBRID EDUCATION MODEL

Higher education institutions aim at serving society, by focusing on learning (rather than just teaching; Kaplan, 2021), developing research with impact (rather than focusing merely on journal impact factor; Gorska et al., 2020); and eventually enabling active agents in shaping tomorrow (Király and Géring, 2019) and addressing the grand challenges of our times (Goedegebuure and Meek, 2021).

Furthermore, the Principles for Responsible Management Education (PRME) noted that 'business and management schools as well as other management-related higher education institutions play a key role in shaping the mindsets and skills of future leaders and can be powerful drivers of corporate sustainability'.[2]

Business schools in fact have enormous educational power and duty (Lozano, 2012), as these institutions are where future leaders are educated, embedding both hard and soft skills, as well as cultural intelligence, and adequate perspectives, to inspire them to act responsibly to deal with an increasingly complex an uncertain future (Venuti et al., 2022).

In 2020 we participated in the massive and global higher education experiment of digital transformation (Kaplan, 2021). The normal use and capacity of classes, amphitheatres and campuses was halted to conform to COVID-19 restrictions and to limiting the spread of the virus. The only available alternative for universities and business schools, in order to offer the due pedagogical contents and ECTs to already enrolled students, consisted in quickly moving to fully online learning (Greenberg and Hibbert, 2020; Moldoveanu, 2020; Kaplan, 2021), and then, in a second moment, when confinement passed, to campuses reopening with reduced classroom capacity use and social distancing – to a hybrid education model. The way universities and business schools deliver educational programmes is undergoing and will definitively undergo a change, forcing individuals, institutions and the academic community at large to work more closely together to cope with this new educational environment (Greenberg and Hibbert, 2020).

The case of ESCP Business School is used as an example to explore the hybrid education model, a mixture of asynchronous and synchronous, online and offline teaching proposed by many business schools in the last year to balance the need for agility (in case another overnight switch to fully online will be required), and the need for inclusion, social interaction and peer interactions, premises for team spirit, students' performances and satisfaction.

15.3 THEORETICAL BACKGROUND AND LITERATURE ON HYBRID MODELS IN HIGHER EDUCATION

Neither online instruction nor hybrid education are new concepts in education, and specifically in higher education. According to Doering and Veletsianos (2008), hybrid and distance learning have been in existence since the late 1800s, with rapid increases especially in lower levels of education, and specifically in more recent times. In the same study, the authors introduced the difference between inservice and preservice teachers to explain the success of new models in education and switched the focus from quantifying technology integration in classroom ('how much?') to the ways technology has actually been integrated in the classroom ('how?').

Also in higher education, hybrid models are not new. Aspen University proposed its first fully online MBA back in 1987, while in 1994 it was the turn of the Executive MBA programme to go fully online at Athabasca University in Canada. Since then, a plethora of fully online universities and programmes have appeared in the market, in parallel with the development of globalization and the increase in international mobility of people, students and workers.

Throughout the decades, there have been more technological advancements and recognition of the centrality of technology in higher education. For example, 2012 was proclaimed by the *New York Times* as the year of the MOOC (Massive Open Online Course), explaining that EdTech incumbents (e.g., online courses delivering platforms such as Coursera, edX and Udacity) would disrupt the higher education sector. But, in reality, not much happened, and business schools were actually opting to focus on strengthening their value proposition and brand reputation, building on innovation at the pedagogical level, but also on the togetherness allowed by the in-campus social exchanges (Pucciarelli and Kaplan, 2019; Venuti et al., 2022). Business schools started to add on some degree of face-to-face experiences to their online programmes, blending in fact the two educational delivery modes. Herein the name 'blended programmes' – also called hybrid education – which in the pre-pandemic version consisted of a mix of online contents delivered asynchronously and some in-campus seminars. ESCP Business School, for example, opened its online doors to the Executive Master in International Business (EMIB) in 2016 and in 2018 it also started offering EMIB in the blended programs, proposing seminars and electives in ESCP Business Schools campuses.

Yet, the disruption caused by COVID-19 forced a wind of change in higher education globally. The only option for universities and business schools to cope with lockdowns and months of confinements was to embrace a fully online educational model and, little by little, once countries gradually reopened with social distancing and limited classrooms capacities, to adjust their models to hybrid education to balance the need to bring back as many students as possible in class and not leave behind those who could not participate face-to-face (Kaplan, 2021).

Hybrid models differ from the existing blended model as a combination of remote and face-to-face education is available simultaneously and at scale, enabling each student to alternatively choose the mode preferred for each educational activity (Pucciarelli and Kaplan, 2022), with a consequent significant increase in the 'customization' and 'personalization' of learning. Hybrid education could represent the next 'new normal' higher education model, because of its advantages (Dorn et al., 2020), for example, in term of flexibility and sustainability. But are we sure that business schools are really hybrid-ready? In order to also be effective in their educational mission, higher education institutions probably still need to complete a redesign of their pedagogy and their approach to this new model. And, then, are business schools really able and willing to continue the (re)definition of their educational model or will they just go back to normal (when it is possible)?

To provide a preliminary answer to the above stated questions, the chapter continues by elaborating on advantages and barriers of hybrid models of education presented by the latest academic and managerial literature on the topic, and then illustrates the case of the transition of ESCP Business School to hybrid education.

15.3.1   Hybrid Education Advantages and Barriers

Just like when telework became the norm for company employees, transforming rapidly the initial confusion and distress of being forced to be at home into appreciation of the advantages of the new flexibility in where and when to work, getting quickly used to the benefits that come with it (Gratton, 2021), it didn't take long for students, professors, staff and business schools' administrators to realize the advantages of remote learning at the dawn of the hybrid model (Dorn et al., 2020; Pucciarelli and Kaplan, 2022).

The mechanics of the new hybrid teaching model has been subject to vivid discussion because the increased digitalization of higher education and the implementation of hybrid education call for new open questions to be addressed by business school Deans and top management boards. For example, what is the role of online asynchronous self-learning and what is the role of in-person classes? Or how to guarantee the social experience, socialization and team spirit in an online and/or hybrid teaching model, etc.

The SAMR theoretical framework, originally proposed by Dr. Puentedura (2014), suggests that there are four stages for technology implementation in the classroom, namely, *substitution, augmentation, modification and redefinition*. The first two steps are technological enhancement of the learning experience, meaning that technology acts as a direct, more convenient *substitute* of traditional practices (e.g., using online quizzes rather than paper and pencil) and as *augmentation* of the learning process, making it more independent, student-centric and engaging (e.g., students using EdTech app to gamifiy contents). In the two stages, namely, modification and redefinition stages, the use of technology becomes increasingly sophisticated, and it transforms the educational experience, making new things possible, for example, *modifying* the way tasks are designed towards interactive and dynamic tasks (e.g., student producing a video presentation or a podcast instead of a standard oral presentation) or even *redefining* the entire experience (e.g., producing short films and publishing their work online where it can be watched by peers), to open new doors (e.g., strong technological soft skills as digital collaboration, how to critically access web 2.0 for a web-based research, etc.), regardless of how sophisticated the technology used.

This SAMR theoretical model was originally developed by its authors as a tool for promoting and generally encouraging the use of technology. However, in some studies and in some applied research, it has also been effectively considered as a powerful tool for instructional designers to evaluate learning activities and their effectiveness (Romrell et al., 2014).

The case of the shift to online and hybrid during the COVID-19 pandemic has undoubtfully advanced all these four dimensions at once, but with differences in the speed and depth for each dimension. Professors and students, obliged to experience emergency online teaching, experimented in how difficult and frustrating it could be to retain a high level of attention during online classes, especially when attempting to deliver the same content and learning processes online that had been used successfully in physical classes (Venuti et al., 2022). In sum, fervid individual and institutional experimentations produced a lot of benefits (e.g., in the capability of business schools to work closely together, in the flexibility in choosing where and when to learn, etc.), but also a lot of frustrations, a sense of isolation, and emotional disconnection from the business school.

15.3.1.1 Advantages of hybrid education

The first and foremost benefit of hybrid models is flexibility (Gratton, 2021). Flexibility in the organization of classes, flexibility to choose the mode that best fits individual student needs in participating in each and every curricular and extra-curricular activity (Hall and Villareal, 2015). Access to the synchronous activities is available face-to-face in class, as well as via portable PC, tablet or mobile device, both to be utilized simultaneously or deferred (by watching the session's recording), enabling students to transcend space and time when it comes to learning (Loh et al., 2021). Space that can alternatively be the campus, or potentially everywhere else, as learning in hybrid models is accessible also synchronously from any connected device. Other interesting benefits include environmental sustainability (as it reduces or limits travelling) and time saving, as there is no longer the need to commute to attend classes, and this time can be used for other educational activities, for nurturing interest or even to dedicate time available to volunteering (Pucciarelli and Kaplan, 2022).

The overnight shift to online-only instruction deepened the comprehension of the difference existing between online teaching and online education (Yang and Huang, 2021), as simply moving courses online has proven to be insufficient to have class attention and avoid students turning off their cameras, or even worse their brains (Venuti et al., 2022). Teachers need to be safe and equipped to teach, so that students can (and must) take accountability for the educational experience and must feel safe and equipped to learn (Dorn et al., 2020).

On the other hand, almost everybody sooner or later has discovered that digital tools and online pedagogy can also add value to learning effectiveness. For example, a number of studies investigating the online learning experience during the COVID-19 pandemic as perceived by business schools' students reported on students' mixed feelings. The majority of the students involved in the Chakraborty and colleagues (2021) study agreed or strongly agreed that learning in a physical classroom is preferable to the online one (65.9 per cent), including because they can interact better with the professor face-to face (75.1 per cent). Surveyed students also acknowledged the positive side of online education, mentioning it as a viable alternative in some circumstances, such as the one we are living in (i.e., the COVID pandemic, 77.9 per cent of respondents), adding that the use of chat box during lectures makes professors-students communication more interactive (76.3 per cent), that online tools can enrich courses (72.1 per cent), and they also felt professors have improved their online teaching skills since the beginning of the pandemic (68.1 per cent) (Chakraborty et al., 2021, p. 360).

The pandemic forced universities and colleagues to shift all programs to the internet, while striving to maintain the quality and function of higher education, moving in fact all of the business school virtually (e.g., classes, but also career fairs, networking events and other forms of gathering) to fully incorporate the richness of social curricular and extra-curricular interactions (Pucciarelli and Kaplan, 2022). Furthermore, the increased use of technology in education could also mean a more inclusive education capable of having a larger impact outside classrooms, fostering new forms of participation and engagement in society (Pedersen et al., 2018).

Hence, the benefits of such a large-scale migration to online and hybrid education have produced valuable educational experiments and experience that deserve to be preserved and leveraged in the future (Yang and Huang, 2020; Kaplan, 2021).

15.3.1.2 Disadvantages of hybrid education

With the rise in popularity of hybrid education, model scholars are also concentrating on the unknowns and the negative influences of this educational model on business schools' key stakeholders.

One of the more frequent words repeated in scholarly papers commenting on the forced innovation that happened during the pandemic is disruption, not only in terms of accelerated digital disruption, but also in disrupting 'management academics' work, careers, and academic identities' (Greenberg and Hibbert, 2020, p. 123).

Frustration, isolation and reflections are the predominant sensations that permeate the analysis of Goedegebuure and Meek (2021, pp. 3–4). Frustration proven by the instructors 'of not being able to engage as deeply with our students as we would have liked and have done in the past … and probably more, there is a true sense of not delivering to our students what they came to our institutions for in the first place' (p. 3).

A number of studies look at the early students' educational experience during the COVID-19 pandemic, reporting the increased level of technostress and exhaustion (Loh et al., 2021), affecting students' daily life both in term of metal health and social life (Chakraborty et al., 2021). The list of stress factors reported by these studies include among others: the overuse of digital technologies, the excessive screen time, together with phobia of losing connectivity and the anxiety of online assessment (bigger than onsite ones). Furthermore, students also felt that online education is exposing the digital divide among them (Chakraborty et al., 2021, p. 360).

Furthermore, there is an overall agreement on the fact that the digitalization of the educational experience calls for the need for restabilizing the social dimension of learning (Mucharraz y Cano and Venuti, 2020; Kaplan, 2021). The sense of isolation, due to prolonged confinement and lockdown, contributed in re-establishing the power and importance of being physically together. The urgency to get back to the classroom varies by circumstances, such as type of programme (Kaplan, 2021), students' arrangements in term of parental support in returning back to school, student personal risk, etc. (Dorn, 2020). And one of the aspects of the hybrid education model that still needs to be validated consists in finding the right balance between online and face-to-face experience (Venuti et al., 2022). Also, in consideration of the fact that the *Know* and *Do* components of the learning experience can be easily enhanced, substituted and augmented by technology (Puentedura, 2014), yet they must come alongside the *Be* component[3] of the learning experience (Datar et al., 2010).

In the following section, the case study of ESCP Business School's transition to the hybrid education model is presented and discussed in the light of the SAMR theoretical framework and the existing literature.

15.4   THE SHIFT TOWARDS A HYBRID EDUCATION MODEL: THE CASE OF ESCP BUSINESS SCHOOL

ESCP Business School is the world's oldest business school, with over 200 years of history and a unique truly international and innovative pedagogy, consisting of enhancing student learning, intercultural and social experience, by studying in at least two different campuses across Europe (up to four of the six countries in which the Business School has its facilities).

In the short term providing education as usual to enrolled student was the priority during the first outbreak of COVID-19, and it has been managed mostly at local level, with Italy at the forefront of the pandemic and the Turin campus experimenting, adopting and pivoting emergency solutions. A task force involving the Turin campus Dean, faculty and members of the programme office was established to ensure a smooth and prompt transition to fully online education. ESCP Business School Turin campus was closed for one week and it reopened fully virtually on 2 March 2020 (ten days prior to the official announcement by the Italian Government of national lockdown). The task force daily meetings were meant to cover all necessary themes to ensure the continuity of educational activities. Topics included: evaluation of possible online tools in addition and/or substitute to Blackboard e-learning platform in use to make course material available to students, Blackboard Collaborate Ultra (feature already available in the e-platform, and hardly used pre-pandemic) self-training through best practices sharing sessions' online resources, as well as training of sessional professors and follow-up; redesign and reorganization of the courses and calendars, etc.

At this very first stage, right at the very beginning of the pandemic spread, the 'Substitution' moment of the SAMR model was still predominant, although 'Augmentation' was also taking place (as new tools were immediately implemented and activated, improving immediately some of the benefits of remote learning).

Once the complete transition to online activities was finalized, the task force scope changed, and the new mission become the fine-tuning of the online educational model. This step marked the transition to the subsequent phases of the SAMR model towards the modification of the educational practices. Encompassing activities, such as collecting feedback across programmes, monitoring personnel and student sentiment, as well as supporting the other campuses that were entering the COVID-19 pandemic too.

In the meantime, ESCP Business Schools promptly invested in new technologies (e.g., to more integrated and interacting e-learning platforms), classroom equipment, in personnel recruitment (e.g., internalizing e-learning specialists), as well as in equipping and elevating staff and faculty's capabilities to make effective, innovative, and efficient use of this technology.

The mechanics of the new hybrid teaching model have been subject to vivid internal discussion, in trying to address key questions needing a common unique ESCP Business School answer. Such as: What is the role of online asynchronous self-learning and what is the role of in-person classes? How to guarantee the social experience, socialization and team spirit in an online and/ or hybrid teaching model, still characterized by social distancing and impossibility of group in-class activities as usual? Etc.

The medium-term answer to the pandemic adopted by many business schools – such as London Business School, ESCP, ESSEC, Insead, SDA Bocconi, among others – is the hybrid teaching model, where hybrid teaching model refers to those teaching pedagogies that combine (socially distanced) face-to-face and online learning. In the case of ESCP Business School, hybrid education means a continuous alternation and mix of asynchronous online material and synchronous sessions, available in campus and live broadcasted. The online asynchronous self-learn component is meant to harmonize familiarity and proficiency with a given theme, allowing the student to study at his/her own speed, even re-watching at his/her convenience the educational material; the synchronous component is meant to enrich the learning experience through active learning, team-working, case-based and more practice-oriented discussion, as well as socialization.

The results of hybrid teaching are far from being perfect, but the balance of the first month of this new hybrid model is quite satisfactory and beneficial from many perspectives. The flexibility of the hybrid teaching model is a key undeniable benefit. Students have the flexibility to move between on-campus and remote learning. Business schools and programme decision makers have the flexibility to adjust, according to the developing situation, a congruous mix of in-person versus online learning, proposed social and professional development activities, almost in real time from one day to the next. Flexibility, also in the sense that there is no limit to class seat numbers for asynchronous online learning, so students have the chance to attend more courses or even to re-watch all their courses when revising. Another benefit consisted in community engagement, both in terms of stronger cohesion and collaboration – within the faculty and between faculty and administrative staff to face the emergency – and also in terms of better and broader use of the alumni network, thanks to the possibility to host speakers online, who would not be able to fly to Turin.

From a pedagogical perspective and to turn criticalities into opportunities, new active learning projects were tested. For example, matching the availability of students unable to run their internship due to the lockdown and the need of local businesses to navigate the pandemic, the so-called 'Local Business COVID-19 projects', launched to provide local small and medium-sized enterprises (SMEs) with team of students working for them, reinforcing the linkages and active contribution of ESCP Business School to local business community recovery, and providing hand-on experience to its students.,

There has been immediate student appreciation of the prompt transition to online and the hybrid teaching model. This may be less indulgent in the near future, and the more hybrid teaching is used operatively, the more students' expectations on the quality of overall augmented education experience may rise. Moreover, what has clearly emerged is the need to balance the flexibility and scalability of remote learning to provide knowledge and skills to students, with the need to provide the 'being' component of the learning experience, the personal development of the student, the values, attitudes and beliefs that form managers' world view and professional identities (Datar et al., 2010). In other words, those in campus social experiences and interactions with peers, essential in achieving a satisfactory student experience, reinforcing a sense of belonging and long-term bonds of alumni with their Alma Mater (Kaplan, 2018, 2021).

At the end of the academic year 2020/2021 (i.e., in June 2021), a consistent and significant reflection in consolidating the new pedagogical approach and to formalize a permanent mix of online and onsite was on its way at ESCP. The School Dean, Professor Frank Bournois, publicly announced that the school will permanently adopt a very simple rule of designing all its courses, programmes and educational activities with no less than 20 per cent online activities and no less than 40 per cent onsite. All courses' pedagogy and delivery mode will be redesigned and implemented according to this new format. This redesign of the pedagogical model definitely corresponds to the fourth stage of the SAMR model, that is, 'Redefine', to redesign the experience for the students.

Nevertheless, the deep rethinking of how to provide education as usual in a very unusual situation, also represents an unmissable opportunity to use the fierce lesson from the pandemic as a platform to critically reflect on the future of business schools (Pucciarelli and Kaplan, 2022).

15.5 CONCLUSIONS

With the ongoing challenges facing higher education, the future success of any business school is closely linked to the capacity to innovate its value proposition along two strategic dimensions: the digital transformation and the sustainability transition.

In fact, COVID-19 accelerated a dual transformation of higher education, urging universities and business schools in every corner of the world to rethink their educational offering to fully leverage the potential of remote and hybrid education, while presenting a second and equally needed opportunity of using this wind of a change to bring forward the sustainability agenda.

Over the latest 18 months, business schools demonstrated that they are able to change, and they are able to quickly reconfigure their education delivery mode, combining top-down and bottom-up approaches, engaging students, professors, staff, alumnus, local businesses and other crucial stakeholders in the (reimagining and) implementation of the new educational model. During the pandemic the smoothness of digital transformation, the implementation of the shift to online pedagogies, were the key focus of many business school Deans, as a means to limit the spread of the virus, to keep everyone safe and to continue delivering educational contents to enrolled students. Yet, as a result of the redesign of campus practices, a number of new and more sustainable endeavours were experimented with and deployed, serving thus as an accelerator of the sustainable transition.

The case of ESCP Business School is used as an example of how a leading European business school has responded to the forced shift to online emergency teaching, first, and then to the hybrid teaching model. The hybrid education model combined augmented online instruction with additional social activities that add on meaning to the learning experience. There are many benefits and barriers in the deployment of the hybrid model. On the one hand, the hybrid model ensures accessibility and scalability of remote learning; becoming even a way to cut costs, once the initial investment in technology, professors and staff, new skills equipment, new material in new formats production, is repaid. On the other hand, it complements the offering with a number of curricular and extra-curricular activities, open to a variety of key stakeholders (e.g., present, past and future potential students, as well as local business, among others), to enrich their personal experience, create fulfilling moments and memories, and ultimately increase the sense of belonging to Alma Mater.

NOTES

1. In the case of the 80,000 employees of a Japanese company analyzed by Gratton (2021), in February 2020, 75 per cent of employees considered the office the best place to work. In May 2020, after having experienced home working since March 2020, 30 per cent of employees considered their home to be the best place to work compared to the 15 per cent responding the office is the best place to work, and 55 per cent preferring a hybrid working model. In the US, according to Global Workplace Analytics (GWA), both employees and employers are willing to further adopt hybrid working, and in April 2020 three in five US workers who have been doing their jobs from home during the first outbreak of COVID-19 would prefer to work remotely as much as possible also after the pandemic. GWA forecasts that 25–50 per cent of the US workforce will be working from home one or more days a week after the pandemic (see https://glob alworkplaceanalytics.com/work-at-home-after-covid-19-our-forecast (accessed 12 September 2021)). Moving to Europe, early estimates from Eurofound (2020) suggest that nearly 40 per cent of EU workers began to telework full time due to the first outbreak of the pandemic (March 2020), while in 2019, only 5.4 per cent of workers in the EU-27 worked from home more often than not.
2. http://www.unprme.org/index.php
3. Datar et al. (2010) in their analysis on the necessary rethinking of the MBA programme propose the '*Be, Know, Do*' components of the learning experience in a business school. Without the 'doing' part, the skills, 'knowing' per se is of little value, but 'doing' skills will be ineffective and direction-less without the self-awareness and reflection on values and beliefs that come from developing 'being', the person and his/her value set for to be a more responsible and critical thinker future manager and/or leader.

REFERENCES

Chakraborty, P., Mittal, P., Gupta, M.S., Yadav, S. and Arora, A., 2021. Opinion of students on online education during the COVID-19 pandemic. *Human Behavior and Emerging Technologies*, 3(3), 357–65.

Datar, S.M., Garvin, D.A. and Cullen, P.G., 2010. Rethinking the MBA. *Business Education at a Crossroads*, 30(5), 451.

Doering, A. and Veletsianos, G., 2008. Hybrid online education: Identifying integration models using adventure learning. *Journal of Research on Technology in Education*, 41(1), 23–41.

Dorn, E., Panier, F., Probst, N. and Sarakatsannis, J., 2020. Back to school: A framework for remote and hybrid learning amid COVID-19. McKinsey & Company.

Eurofound, 2020. *Living, Working and COVID-19*. COVID-19 series. Publications Office of the European Union, Luxembourg. Available at: https://www.eurofound .europa.eu/sites/default/files/ef_publication/field_ef_document/ef20059en.pdf (accessed 12 September 2021).

Goedegebuure, L. and Meek, L., 2021. Crisis – What crisis? *Studies in Higher Education*, 46(1), 1–4.

Gorska, A., Korzynski, P., Mazurek, G. and Pucciarelli, F., 2020. The role of social media in scholarly collaboration: An enabler of international research team's activation? *Journal of Global Information Technology Management*, 23(4), 273–91.

Gratton, L., 2021. How to do hybrid right. *Harvard Business Review*, 99(3), 65–74.

Greenberg, D. and Hibbert, P., 2020. From the editors – Covid-19: Learning to hope and hoping to learn. *Academy of Management Learning & Education*, 19(2), 123–30.

Hall, S. and Villareal, D., 2015. The hybrid advantage: Graduate student perspectives of hybrid education courses. *International Journal of Teaching and Learning in Higher Education*, 27(1), 69–80.

Hamilton, E.R., Rosenberg, J.M. and Akcaoglu, M., 2016. The substitution augmentation modification redefinition (SAMR) model: A critical review and suggestions for its use. *TechTrends*, 60(5), 433–41.

Loh, X.K., Lee, V.H., Loh, X.M., Tan, G.W.H., Ooi, K.B. and Dwivedi, Y.K., 2021. The dark side of mobile learning via social media: How bad can it get? *Information Systems Frontiers*, 1–18.

Lozano, J.F., 2012. Educating responsible managers. The role of university ethos. *Journal of Academic Ethics*, 10(3), 213–26.

Kaplan, A., 2018. A school is 'a building that has four walls … with tomorrow inside': Toward the reinvention of the business school. *Business Horizons*, 61(4), 599–608.

Kaplan, A., 2021. *Higher Education at the Crossroads of Disruption: The University of the 21st Century*. Bingley, UK: Emerald Group Publishing.

Király, G. and Géring, Z., 2019. Introduction to 'Futures of Higher Education' special issue. *Futures*, 111, 123–9.

Meiller, Y., 2020. Digital transformation, covid-19 crisis, digital transformation. Managing a postcovid19 rra. *ESCP Impact Papers*. eBook. Paris: ESCP Research Institute of Management (ERIM), pp. 171–8.

Moldoveanu, M., 2020. A post-COVID Higher Ed: Which programs will thrive, which won't, and why. *Harvard Business Review* online, 24 July. Available at: https://hbsp.harvard.edu/inspiring-minds/a-post-covid-higher-ed-which-programs-will-thrive-which-wont-and-why (accessed 30 September 2021).

Moratis, L. and Melissen, F., 2020. Responding responsibly. BizEd, AACSB International. Available at: https://bized.aacsb.edu/articles/2020/july/responding-responsibly (accessed 26 September 2020).

Mucharraz y Cano, Y and Venuti, F., 2020. Online learning can still be social: 10 keys to building a supportive digital community of learners. Available at: https://hbsp.harvard.edu/inspiring-minds/online-learning-can-still-be-social (accessed 7 October 2021).

Pedersen, A.Y., Nørgaard, R.T. and Köppe, C., 2018. Patterns of inclusion: Fostering digital citizenship through hybrid education. *Journal of Educational Technology & Society*, 21(1), 225–36.

Pucciarelli, F. and Kaplan, A., 2019. Competition in higher education. In *Strategic Brand Management in Higher Education* (pp. 74–88). New York: Routledge.

Pucciarelli, F. and Kaplan, A., 2022. Transition to a hybrid teaching model as a step forward toward responsible management education? *Journal of Global Responsibility*, 13(1), 7–20. https://doi.org/10.1108/JGR-12-2020-0111.

Puentedura, R., 2014. Learning, technology, and the SAMR model: Goals, processes, and practice. *Ruben R. Puentedura's Weblog*.

Romrell, D., Kidder, L. and Wood, E., 2014. The SAMR model as a framework for evaluating mLearning. *Online Learning Journal*, 18(2). Available at: https://www.learntechlib.org/p/183753/ (accessed 27 March 2022).

Venuti, F., Rattalino, F. and Pucciarelli, F., 2022. The importance of the international and social dimensions of learning in the post-COVID higher education. In

Borderlands: The Internationalisation of Higher Education Teaching Practices. In press.

Yang, B. and Huang, C., 2021. Turn crisis into opportunity in response to COVID-19: Experience from a Chinese University and future prospects. *Studies in Higher Education*, 46(1), 121–32.

16. Looking to the future: will male students underperform in the business school (too)?

Kristian J. Sund

16.1 INTRODUCTION

Business schools play an important role in providing access to the job market, and ultimately to management positions, for people of all genders and minorities. After centuries of inequality favouring men in higher education, the trends appear to have reversed over the past decades. In the case of the UK, all the way into the 1980s three out of four students obtaining higher degrees were still men (Hillman and Robinson, 2016). Today, men continue to make up the majority of academic staff, are over-represented among professors and senior managers, are over-represented in governing boards, and have higher pay (ECU, 2015; Sherer and Zakaria, 2018). However, compared to women, they now seem less likely to complete their degrees or achieve high grades (Higher Education Academy, 2014). This has led to the emergence of both a popular and academic argument that males underperform in both lower and higher education. But can we trust this conclusion in the context of the business school? Is there a sex effect in the performance of business school students? That is the question examined empirically in this chapter.

In 2014/15, Higher Education Statistics Agency (HESA) data showed that 73 per cent of women gained a good degree, that is, a 2:1 or above in the UK system, compared to 69 per cent of men. Women thus now appear to achieve higher grade point averages (Cantwell et al., 2001; Dobson and Skuja, 2005), leading to higher degree classifications overall. Men are considered by some to be the new underachievers of higher education.[1] From a societal perspective, there has been increasing alarm relating to the underachievement of males within education in general. An entire body of academic work, and what by some is referred to as the "boy discourse", has emerged looking at male underachievement from primary, through secondary, and into higher education (Lahelma, 2014). Like any discourse, it has the potential to shape policy

(Trowler, 2001; Vingaard Johansen et al., 2017). At the heart of this discourse is a form of moral panic about the educational performance of males at all ages (Epstein et al., 1998; Francis and Skelton, 2005; Kimmel, 2010). The assumption within this strand of literature is not that young men are performing badly in absolute terms, but that they are underachieving relative to young women, and that the problem is found at all levels of education.

Intuitively, there is a connection between academic performance in early schooling and later stages within the educational trajectory (Scheeren et al., 2018). This has, to some extent, been confirmed empirically. A study by Smith and Naylor (2001) of 48,000 students across universities in the UK found that high pre-university achievement markedly increased the likelihood of receiving higher grades at university. Therefore, if boys underperform in school, they are likely to underperform in higher education as well. The boy discourse has not gone unnoticed in the practitioner and popular press. For instance, the feature story on the front page of the *Times Higher Education* magazine in the week of 10 May 2018, elaborated on the statistics of female over-representation in higher education under the title, "Why are boys underachieving across all stages of education?", while a *Newsweek* article in the week of 10 December 2018, elaborated on the disappearance of white British men from some universities under the title, "Are white males a minority group? Two universities say yes, launch recruitment drive". But, can we generalize the boy discourse to all subject areas?

In a somewhat overlooked policy document commissioned by the Higher Education Academy of the United Kingdom (HEA), using data from HESA and the National Student Survey (NSS), Fielding et al. (2008) investigated differences in degree attainment between males and females, as well as different ethnic groups. Their initial analysis of over 60,000 UK students found that females generally perform better than males in higher education, echoing the findings of other studies. Females are also reported to have an advantage over males in getting "first class" (summa cum laude) degree classifications. However, they also report that sex differentials in higher education attainment vary significantly according to subject area. In some subjects there seems to be a female advantage, and in other subjects not so. They thus mention that it is "unduly simplistic to take as a stylized fact the net female advantage overall" (Fielding et al., 2008, p. 67). This warning has so far largely been ignored in the discussion. In this chapter, the warning is taken seriously, and the relationship between sex and degree outcome is investigated for business and management studies, using data gathered on close to 400 undergraduate students at a large London business school.

16.2   EXPLAINING ACHIEVEMENT

Student achievement can be linked to both student characteristics and the learning environment (Astin, 1993; Bignoux and Sund, 2018). Although the focus here is on differences linked to the sex of a student, age and ability at entry are other student characteristic variables commonly examined in literature, and that will be briefly discussed in this section.

16.2.1   Sex and Degree Achievement

The literature states several reasons underlying male underachievement. First and foremost, various behavioural differences between the sexes have been hypothesized to have an effect on learning and educational achievement. One argument is that men don't like to read, according to which boys and young men read too little, read poorly, or do it in all the wrong ways (Hillman and Robinson, 2016; Asplund and Pérez Prieto, 2018). Instead, young men spend much of their leisure time playing collaborative video games as opposed to reading (OECD, 2015). A growing body of research indicates a positive link between reading skills, especially leisure reading, and the development of cognitive skills, education attainment, and social mobility (Sullivan and Brown, 2015).

It has also been suggested that young men have less self-discipline than young women. One study reports that young women spend an average of one hour longer on their homework, start their homework approximately 20 minutes earlier, and watch less television (Duckworth and Seligman, 2006, p. 201). It may also be that young men have a negative attitude to education. Young women have a stronger tendency towards values encouraged at school, such as achievement, hard work, and ambition (Deutsche Shell, 2006, p. 175). School-aged boys are more likely than girls to arrive late for school. Boys are less likely than girls to engage in school-related work out of intrinsic motivation (Quenzel and Hurrelmann, 2013; Hillman and Robinson, 2016). At the higher education level, women are more likely to conform to institutional requirements, and to attend lectures (Woodfield et al., 2006). Finally, one might speculate that attendance behaviours could differ, but this is not empirically clear in the context of higher education (Sund and Bignoux, 2018). Cultural gender norms may play a role in some of these behavioural differences. In one study, the children of African immigrants were found to equate an anti-school attitude with masculinity (Jackson, 1998, p. 89), with the implication that active participation in class is "feminizing" (Epstein et al., 1998, p. 100).

Another argument has to do with cognitive biases. There are now more female teachers than male within primary and secondary schools in many countries (Hillman and Robinson, 2016). This inequality could cause a problem for the educational outcomes of boys and young men. For example, a recent teacher bias experiment found that female teachers systematically allocated lower marks to male pupils, as compared to the marks awarded by external examiners (Ouazad and Page, 2013). However, this conclusion can be questioned by evidence showing that male educational outcome may not significantly benefit from having a male teacher in the classroom (Ludowkye, 2001). In any case, there appears to be a growing perception that there are "too few" male teachers (McGrath and Sinclair, 2013).

The above paints a rather dismal picture of the present and future for males within education. However, the "boy discourse" is not without its detractors and it is being challenged. In their large-scale study, Fielding et al. (2008, p. 67) caution that it is "unduly simplistic to take as a stylized fact the net female advantage overall", given evidence of significant variation across disciplines (Higher Education Authority, 2014). Even if higher education is becoming more feminized, this may not be a problem if it "represents different employment preferences or tastes for schooling", and thus "may not be a matter for great societal concern" (Jacob, 2002, p. 589). Men and women have traditionally chosen different pathways to success (Lahelma, 2014). Formal schooling is organized so that education leading to traditionally male occupations (e.g., electrician, mechanic, or plumber) takes place at the upper secondary level and then further education, not at higher education and university education level (Lahelma, 2014).

There is also contradictory evidence relating to women's success in education. For example, men still comprise the majority of entrants at the highest-tariff institutions in the UK, such as Oxford University and Cambridge University, while women make up the majority of entrants at the lower-tariff institutions (UCAS, 2015, p. 112; Hillman and Robinson, 2016). In 2015, 18-year-old UK women were 45 per cent more likely to enter a lower-tariff institution, 33 per cent more likely to enter a medium-tariff institution, and only 28 per cent more likely to enter a higher-tariff institution than 18-year-old men. In 2014/15, at Oxford and Cambridge, 46 per cent of undergraduates and 44 per cent of postgraduates were women (UCAS, 2015). Men also outnumber women in the science and technology (STEM) subjects (DeAro et al., 2019; Van Miegroet et al., 2019). When we look at the entire higher education sector in the UK, and discount for students taking subjects linked to medicine and education, the difference between the total number of male and female education students reduces itself from around 281,000 to 34,000 (Hillman and Robinson, 2016). Finally, there is some evidence from other countries that gender influences choice of subject major (Noël et al., 2016), but not overall academic performance in the business school context (Khaola, 2012).

16.2.2   Age and Degree Achievement

The evidence for a relationship between age and academic achievement is contradictory. Some studies show that mature students perform better than direct-entry high school students in higher education, while others show the opposite. Some studies report that mature undergraduate students would seem to perform better on intermediate and final grade point averages (Naderi et al., 2009; Sheard, 2009), and achieve higher degree classifications (Hoskins et al., 1997). The greater success of mature students has been attributed to factors such as higher motivation (McInnis et al., 1995; Eppler and Harju, 1997), superior study skills, and superior time management skills (Murray-Harvey, 1993; Richardson, 1994; Trueman and Hartley, 1996). Mature students are also reported to be more likely to think that their university has met their expectations, and are less interested in socializing, presumably making them more focused on their studies (Krause et al., 2005).

However, other studies report that younger students outperform mature ones (Koh and Koh, 1999). Also, mature students have higher dropout rates than direct-entry high school students (National Audit Office, 2002). A more refined view finds that it depends on the discipline (Richardson and Woodley, 2003). According to this, direct-entry high school students may have an advantage in science-, technology-, and engineering-based disciplines, whereas mature students have an advantage in other disciplines (Bourner and Hamed, 1987). It appears that the advantages that mature students bring to higher education, such as increased motivation and superior study skills, diminishes in importance in certain disciplines, as core knowledge and continuity provide younger students with an advantage (Burke da Silva et al., 2008). In some disciplines, mature students do not benefit from the integration of life experience and study (Knapper and Cropley, 2000), while other disciplines require high contact hours, which appear to work against mature students (Burke da Silva et al., 2008).

Another consideration is how rapidly technical knowledge gained in high school erodes, and how rapidly life skills such as time management are developed. Thus, other studies provide a more nuanced view by showing that the age effect depends on the duration of the gap between high school and higher education, and on the reasons for deferred entry. Students who take a one-year gap between high school and university perform better than direct-entry high school students (Martin et al., 2013). A gap year to pursue "developmental" activities, such as travel, volunteering, short courses of interest, and so on, may resolve a lack of academic motivation and high school uncertainty, and assist higher education students in developing adaptive behaviours important for academic success (Martin, 2010). Related work shows that engaging in various activities prior to higher education enhances an individual's economic, social, and cultural capital, which then has advantages in subsequent education (Brown and Hesketh, 2004; Heath, 2007).

In one recent study, Martin et al. (2013) find that gap-year entries and more mature age entries both have higher achievement. However, mature students (students over the age of 21 in their study) do not have a performance advantage over gap-year students. A gap year yields additional performance benefits. However, once again, performance depends on why a student has deferred their entry into university. If the reason is to gain experience, then late entry may be beneficial. However, if the reason is the result of accumulated responsibilities, such as parental responsibilities, then late entry may be detrimental. In another study, Roksa and Velez (2012) find that many students deferring entry to university in the United States are from disadvantaged backgrounds, may be in parental roles, or have to work because of their life circumstances. They argue that a student who defers entry for these reasons will have a performance disadvantage. This performance disadvantage is further accentuated by welfare systems that are calibrated to encourage work rather than education. Many of these life course factors explained the negative relationship between deferred entry and university achievement in their study. However, when factors such as parenting duties, employment, and social disadvantage are controlled for, the effects of deferment are no longer significantly negative. These results all suggest that the beneficial or deleterious effects of late entry into higher education on degree attainment are discipline- and context-specific.

16.2.3 Ability at Entry and Degree Achievement

Ability at entry refers to a student's general academic ability at the point of university entry. This academic ability at entry is often captured by standardized tests, such as high school grades ('A'-level scores in the UK context) and/ or university entry scoring (Universities and Colleges Admissions Service, or UCAS, scores, in the UK context). The evidence is clear, and the pattern develops early, whereby there is a positive and significant link between prior academic achievement and overall degree performance. When studying the sex–performance relationship, it is therefore necessary to control for students' abilities at entry. For instance, in a recent study, Alfarhan and Dauletova (2019) examine psychometric factors that could explain why female students outperform male students at a university in Oman. They find that high school grades are a significant predictor of subsequent university performance. In the UK context, it has been found that the higher the UCAS score, the more likely students are able to complete university-entry foundation courses and achieve a higher grade average (Smith and Naylor, 2001; Schofield and Dismore, 2010). In an early meta-analysis of 20 studies investigating prior academic achievement and overall degree achievement in higher education, Peers and Johnston (1994) reported an overall correlation of 28 per cent between grades attained at A level (the normal school-leaving examination in the UK) and final degree performance. In a long-term study of medical graduates in the UK, McManus et al. (2005) concluded that previous academic achievement (as measured by A-level results) not only predicted outcomes in a medical course but also outcomes of subsequent careers. The same pattern is found in comparable countries. For example, Mercer and Puddey (2011) investigate the influence of cognitive factors on final-degree grade point average in a single undergraduate cohort. They find that previous academic performance captured by the Australian Tertiary Entrance Rank was a major positive predictor of performance in a medical course. Such an effect of previous academic achievement is consistent with previous research findings both in medical courses (Ferguson et al., 2002; Hughes, 2002) and for tertiary study in general (Dobson and Skuja, 2005; Win and Miller, 2005; Birch and Miller, 2007).

Only a few studies have questioned this longitudinal effect. For example, Bartlett et al. (1993) did not report a significant relationship between school examination performance and academic achievement in higher education. Peers and Johnston (1994) similarly questioned the predictive utility of A-level grades for degree performance. The relevance of prior academic achievement to future academic performance is supported by a vast majority of earlier studies and the findings of educational bodies, making this an important control variable in any study of sex and academic achievement.

16.3 METHOD

To test for the sex effect on overall academic performance in a business school context, data was collated on undergraduate students on the general management programme at a large London-based business school. The dataset was derived from a larger set previously described in a study by Sund and Bignoux (2018). Students included were those who embarked on their final year of study between 2011 and 2014 (four cohorts), and who at the time of sampling had completed their studies and been awarded an exit award (bachelor's degree or other). This yielded an initial sample of 911 students. Sex was measured based on official university records, with all students categorized as male or female.

Overall academic performance was measured using final degree classification. The classification provides a measure of average student achievement over the final two years of study. The scheme used by the university in question is provided in Table 16.1, which shows the equivalent in percentage

Table 16.1   Degree classifications

Degree Classification	Percentage Range (%)
First class honours	70 +
Upper second class	60–69
Lower second class	50–59
Third class	44–49
Third class	40–43
Fail	0–39

terms for the reader's convenience. Degree classification was "first class", "upper second class", "lower second class", "third class", and in the case of missing credits, "ordinary degree". In a few exceptional cases, students failed to achieve sufficient credit, and received only a diploma or certificate. For the sake of the analysis, ordinary degree and other exit awards were grouped together in a single "Other" category. The reasoning was that these students all had in common a lack of credits, typically the result of failing courses repeatedly, or dropping out.

As discussed in the literature overview, control variables included the student's general academic abilities or ability at entry. In the case of UK universities, this is typically coded as the UCAS entry, or tariff, score. This score ranges from 5 to a theoretically maximally achievable 768 points, with higher entry qualifications and grades achieving higher tariff points. The score is not collected for students entering the university with non-UK qualifications, and certain types of other entrants. From the total initial sample of 911 students, it was possible to identify a UCAS entry tariff score for 378 students. This is perhaps the greatest limitation in the dataset, as it means results are representative only of students entering the university from the UK. The study thus examines the sex effect for UK students only. This is not a problem per se, but as this particular university recruits many foreign students, the final sample size is significantly reduced.

As discussed in the literature overview, mature entrants may present different motivations, or be subject to other pressures, than direct-entry students, so age was measured at study start. Finally, cohort dummy variables were introduced to control for any cohort effects. Owing to a few missing data points, the final sample size for this study was 364 students. The descriptive statistics for the sample are shown in Table 16.2.

The link between sex, age at entry, UCAS entry score, and classification was studied by conducting a series of multinomial regressions. The dependent variable was final classification, whilst sex, age at university entry, UCAS entry score, and the cohort dummy variables were all independent variables.

Table 16.2   Descriptive statistics for continuous variables in model sample

	N	Sample Proportion	Mean	Std. Deviation
Sex Female	161	44.2%		
Cohort 2010/11	50	13.7%		
Cohort 2011/12	82	22.5%		
Cohort 2012/13	108	29.7%		
Cohort 2013/14	124	34.1%		
Classification First	84	23%		
Classification Upper Second	154	42.2%		
Classification Lower Second	80	21.9%		
Classification Third	7	1.9%		
Classification Other	30	8.2%		
Age at Start	364		19.02	2.055
Entry Tariff	365		190.36	89.274

A similar procedure to that described by Fielding et al. (2008) was followed, removing independent variables one by one to capture any interaction effects.

16.4   RESULTS

The ensuing models are outlined in Table 6.3, labelled models 1, 2, 3, and 4. The results indicate no significant cohort effects, no effect of age at entry, and no sex effect. However, there is a UCAS effect whereby a student with a one-point higher entry score has his/her log-odds raised by 0.005 units of subsequently obtaining a first-class classification, rather than an upper second-class classification. This effect is consistent in size and is statistically significant in all models. The model's (model 4) predictive accuracy is 47.2 per cent.

In this sample of students, sex and age at entry do not predict degree classification. Only ability at entry, as measured by UCAS entry score, appears to have a small predictive effect on the likelihood of ending up with the highest degree classification. These results appear consistent with those of Fielding et al. (2008),[2] who found no sex effect for business schools.

Table 16.3   Summary of multinomial regression models with variables predicting final classification

Classification (reference is Upper Second)	Model 1 Sig. = .196[a] B	SE	Model 2 Sig. = .077[a] B	SE	Model 3 Sig. = .017[a] B	SE	Model 4 Sig. = .002[a] B	SE
Ordinary Intercept	-2.835		-2.491		-2.337		-2.517	
EntryTariff	.002	.003	.001	.003	.001	.003	.001	.003
AGE_START	.017	.136						
[Sex = F]	-.617	.568	-.615	.568	-.653	.565		
[Academic year = 2010–11]	-.841	1.170	-.858	1.166				
[Academic year = 2011–12]	.733	.713	.714	.705				
[Academic year = 2012–13]	.104	.713	.092	.712				
Third Intercept	-.687		-2.382		-3.422		-3.240	
Entry Tariff	-.001	.005	-.001	.004	.000	.004	.001	.004
AGE_START	-.087	.336						
[Sex = F]	.440	.788	.425	.787	.444	.784		
[Academic year = 2010–11]	-1.068	1.184	-1.026	1.182				
[Academic year = 2011–12]	-1.197	1.173	-1.136	1.160				
[Academic year = 2012–13]	-1.614	1.150	-1.576	1.145				

	Model 1		Model 2		Model 3		Model 4	
	Sig. = .196[a]		Sig. = .077[a]		Sig. = .017[a]		Sig. = .002[a]	
Second Lower Intercept	-.502		-.205		-.436		-.458	
Entry Tariff	-.001	.002**	-.002	.002***	-.001	.002	-.001	.002
AGE_START	.012	.069			-.065	.274		
[Sex = F]	-.075	.278	-.047	.277				
[Academic year = 2010–11]	-.559	.460	-.616	.455				
[Academic year = 2011–12]	.262	.373	.208	.367				
[Academic year = 2012–13]	-.428	.368	-.476	.364				
First Intercept	-2.065		-1.353		-1.657		-1.715	
Entry Tariff	.005	.002**	.005	.002***	.005	.002****	.005	.002****
AGE_START	.036	.063			-.187	.276		
[Sex = F]	-.188	.277	-.186	.277				
[Academic year = 2010–11]	-.488	.469	-.521	.465				
[Academic year = 2011–12]	-.179	.399	-.214	.394				
[Academic year = 2012–13]	-.199	.340	-.218	.338				

Notes: * p < .1; ** p < .05; *** p < .01; **** p < .001.
[a] Likelihood chi-square ratio test significance.

16.5   CONCLUDING DISCUSSION

A main conclusion from this data is that in the business school context, the boy discourse does not seem to hold true. In an era in which higher education policy discourse in general appears highly focused on employability (Vingaard Johansen et al., 2017), what are the implications for a business school? One implication could be that the lack of a sex effect suggests there is no need to consider sex as an issue in the design of programmes, or in pedagogical considerations. Having stated this, even within a general management programme, there are courses with a more mathematical or statistical focus, and others with a more linguistic or sociological one. The lack of a sex effect for overall degree achievement could well mask more fine-grained differences at the level of individual courses and management disciplines. A more refined study would collate data on performance at course level as well. What can be concluded for now is that the stylized fact of generalized higher female achievement may not hold true for the business school context, and the associated "boy discourse" is best avoided in this context.

Although not the main focus of this study, in terms of mature university entrants, an implication of this study could be that there is no need for particular school-level support for such entrants. There is no evidence that such students are any more or less disadvantaged than direct entrants, once ability at entry is controlled for. Only if mature entrants are systematically academically weaker at entry would it be warranted for a business school to provide particular academic support to those students. In this case, late entrance would be a proxy for weak abilities at entry. On the other hand, as discussed in the review of the literature, mature students are more likely to struggle with balancing multiple demands on their time, such as balancing family life, work life, and study life. They have therefore been found to be more likely to drop out of their studies than direct-entry students. The sample here includes only those students that made it to the third year of study. It is possible that among the students dropping out in the first or second year, there was a different distribution of ability at entry (or sex for that matter) than in the sample. There is no way of verifying this.

Two limitations emerged related to sampling. Future work in this area may be needed to overcome these. The first relates to dropouts, and the second to the availability of ability-at-entry data. Dropouts represent a potential drawback to this type of study, as they do to all studies examining relationships to degree achievement. Students dropping out early in their studies, or who fail to show up at all at the start of their studies, may not be a problem, but for students dropping out later in their studies, the issue of potential sample bias needs to be considered. In this study, students dropping out in the middle of the year would automatically qualify for an exit award (a certificate in business administration as a minimum) and be included in the sample. The overall non-completion rate in the degree programme is known to be around 25 per cent, but no data was available to assess the impact of this potential sample bias. The effect would be limited to dropouts in years 1 and 2, making for a real non-completion figure well below 25 per cent, since these are the only ones to receive no exit award in this particular university system.

The second limitation in the study is that standardized ability at entry (UCAS) scores exist for home students only, not for overseas students. This study thus examines the sex effect for UK students only. This is not a problem per se, but as this particular university recruits many foreign students, the final sample size is consequently reduced. Finding better ways to estimate ability at entry, for all students, would be a major advance for this kind of study. This could be achieved if all students at the start of their studies were subjected to a standardized entry test. Few universities currently use such tests at the bachelor's degree level, but certain programmes, such as MBA programmes, do use standardized tests, such as the GMAT (Graduate Management Admission Test), which has been found to be highly valid as a measure of ability (Oh et al., 2008).

Although purely speculative, an interesting thought experiment would be to consider what would happen if the sex effect found in other disciplines was to spill over to the business school context. Based on the evidence presented here, it appears that business school achievement is currently sex neutral. Given that participation in business schools is also almost exactly equal among men and women (Hillman and Robinson, 2016), as long as employers do not engage in any gender discrimination in graduate work recruitment, male and female graduates would have equal employment opportunities. What if the performance balance tipped in favour of females in the business school too? Already now, in the UK, women earn more than men in the 22- to 29-year age group, and possibly also in the 30- to 39-year age group (according to data from the Annual Survey of Hours and Earnings). This gap could be accentuated if there are more women graduating from, and achieving higher grades in, business schools. As the few areas in the economy where males are still over-represented are gradually being automated, such as manual and technical positions, one might in time expect a higher rate of unemployment, and lower salaries, among men than women. Could pay structures and promotions in business eventually favour women? Might men be the ones facing a glass ceiling in the not-too-distant future? Time will tell. But for now, the boy discourse seems irrelevant for the business school.

ACKNOWLEDGEMENT

I would like to sincerely thank Stephane Bignoux for his invaluable contributions to this study, including, but not limited to, the data collection on the original dataset as described by Sund and Bignoux (2018).

NOTES

1.   Underachievers are defined here as a group whose mean achievement falls below that of a selected reference group. The assumption is made that there should be no difference between the two groups under comparison and thus if there is a difference, then the difference is described as underachievement by one group (Plewis, 1991).
2.   It should be noted that Fielding et al. (2008) get a different result for age, but they coded this as a dummy variable of over or under the age of 22, whereas this study uses the actual age. The age variables are therefore not directly comparable.

REFERENCES

Alfarhan, U.F. and Dauletova, V. 2019. "Revisiting the gender academic achievement gap: evidence from a unique environment". *Gender and Education*, vol. 31, no. 7, pp. 827–48.
Asplund, S.B. and Pérez Prieto, H. 2018. "Young working-class men do not read: or do they? Challenging the dominant discourse of reading". *Gender and Education,* vol. 30, no. 8, pp. 1048–64.
Astin, A. 1993. *Assessment for excellence: the philosophy and practice of assessment and evaluation in higher education*, Phoenix, AZ: The Oryx Press.
Bartlett, S., Peel, M.J. and Pendlebury, M. 1993. "From fresher to finalist 1", *Accounting Education*, vol. 2, pp. 111–22.
Bignoux, S. and Sund, K.J. 2018. "Tutoring executives online: what drives perceived quality?" *Behaviour & Information Technology*, vol. 37, no. 7, pp. 703–13.
Birch, E.R. and Miller, P. 2007. "Tertiary entrance scores: can we do better?" *Education Research and Perspectives*, vol. 34, pp. 1–23.
Bourner, T. and Hamed, M. 1987. *Entry qualifications and degree performance*, London: Council for National Academic Awardsn.
Brown, P. and Hesketh, A. 2004. *The mismanagement of talent: employability and jobs in the knowledge economy*. Oxford: Oxford University Press.
Burke da Silva, K.L., Hunter, N.C. and Auburn, Z. 2008. "First year biology: a dilemma for mature age students", Paper presented at *An apple for the learner: celebrating the first year experience*, 11th Pacific Rim first year in higher education conference.
Cantwell, R., Archer J. and Bourke, S. 2001. "A comparison of the academic experiences and achievement of university students entering by traditional and non-traditional means", *Assessment and Evaluation in Higher Education*, vol. 26, pp. 221–34.
DeAro, J., Bird S. and Mitchell Ryan, S. 2019. "NSF ADVANCE and gender equity: past, present and future of systemic institutional transformation strategies", *Equality, Diversity and Inclusion*, vol. 38, pp. 131–9.

Deutsche Shell. 2006. "Jugend 2006: 15. Shell Jugendstudie. Conceptualization and co-conceptualization and coordination", in Hurrelmann, K., Albert, M. and TNS (eds), *Infratest sozialforschung*, Frankfurt: Fischer Taschenbuch verlag.

Dobson, I. and Skuja, E. 2005. "Secondary schooling, tertiary entry ranks and university performance", *People and Place*, vol. 13, p. 53.

Duckworth, A.L. and Seligman, M. 2006. "Self-discipline gives girls the edge: gender in self-discipline, grades, and achievement test scores", *Journal of Educational Psychology*, vol. 98, pp. 198–208.

ECU (Equality Challenge Unit). 2015. *Equality in higher education: statistical report 2015, Part 1: staff*, London: ECU.

Eppler, M. and Harju, B. 1997. "Achievement motivation goals in relation to academic performance in traditional and non-traditional college students", *Research in Higher Education*, vol. 38, pp. 557–73.

Epstein, D., Elwood, J., Hey, V. and Maw, J. 1998. *Failing boys? Issues in gender and achievement*, Buckingham, UK: Open University Press.

Ferguson, E., James D. and Madeley, L. 2002. "Factors associated with success in medical school: systematic review of the literature", *BMJ*, vol. 324, pp. 952–7.

Fielding, A., Charlton, C., Kounali, D. and Leckie, G. 2008. *Degree attainment, ethnicity and gender: interactions and the modification of effects*, report available from The Higher Education Academy: https://www.bristol.ac.uk/media-library/sites/cmm/migrated/documents/degree-eth-gender.pdf, accessed 9 April 2019.

Francis, B. and Skelton, C. 2005. *Reassessing gender and achievement*, London: Routledge.

Heath, S. 2007. "Widening the gap: pre-university gap years and the economy of experience", *British Journal of Sociology of Education*, vol. 28, pp. 89–103.

Higher Education Academy. 2014. *Undergraduate retention and attainment across the disciplines*, York, UK: HEA.

Hillman, N. and Robinson, N. 2016. *Boys to men: the underachievement of young men in higher education – and how to start tackling it*, Oxford: Higher Education Policy Institute.

Hoskins, S., Newstead S. and Dennis, I. 1997. "Degree performance as a function of age, gender, prior qualifications and discipline studied", *Assessment and Evaluation in Higher Education*, vol. 22, pp. 317–28.

Hughes, P. 2002. "Can we improve on how we select medical students?" *Journal of the Royal Society of Medicine*, vol. 95, pp. 18–22.

Jackson, D. 1998. "Breaking out of the binary trap: boys' underachievement, schooling and gender relations", in Epstein, D., Elwood, J., Hey, V. and Maw, J. (eds), *Failing boys? Issues in gender and achievement*, Buckingham, UK: Open University Press, pp. 77–95.

Jacob, B. 2002. "Where the boys aren't: non-cognitive skills, returns to school and the gender gap in higher education", *Economics of Education Review*, vol. 21, pp. 589–98.

Khaola, P.P. 2012. "Explaining performance in the Postgraduate Diploma in HRM at the National University of Lesotho". *International Journal of Management Education*, vol. 10, pp. 215–22.

Kimmel, M. 2010. "Boys and school: a background paper on the 'boy crisis'", SOU 2010, Swedish Government Official Reports, Ministry of Education Research, Sweden.

Knapper, C. and Cropley, A. 2000. *Lifelong learning in higher education*, 3rd edn, London: Kogan Page.

Koh, M.Y. and Koh, H.C. 1999. "The determinants of performance in an accountancy degree programme", *Accounting Education*, vol. 8, pp. 13–29.

Krause, K.L. et al. 2005. *The first year experience in Australian universities: findings from a decade of national studies*, Canberra, CA: Australian Department of Education, Science and Training.

Lahelma, E. 2014. "Troubling discourses on gender and education", *Educational Research*, vol. 56, pp. 171–83.

Ludowyke, J. 2001. "Directing change: national enquiry into boys' education", *Professional Voice*, vol. 1, pp. 6–8.

Martin, A. 2010. "Should students have a gap year? Motivation and performance factors relevant to time out after completing school", *Journal of Educational Psychology*, vol. 102, p. 561.

Martin, A., Wilson, R., Liem, G.A. and Ginns, P. 2013. "Academic momentum at university college: exploring the roles of prior learning, life experience, and ongoing performance in academic achievement across time", *Journal of Higher Education*, vol. 84, pp. 640–74.

McGrath, K. and Sinclair, M. 2013. "More male primary-school teachers? Social benefits for boys and girls", *Gender and Education*, vol. 25, no. 5, pp. 531–47.

McInnis, C., James, R. and McNaught, C. 1995. *First year on campus: diversity in the initial experiences of Australian undergraduates*, Canberra: Australian Government Publishing Service.

McManus, I.C., Powis, D.A., Wakeford, R., et al. 2005. "Intellectual aptitude tests and A levels for selecting UK school leaver entrants for medical school", *BMJ*, vol. 331, pp. 555–9.

Mercer, A. and Puddey, I. 2011. "Admission selection criteria as predictors of outcomes in an undergraduate medical course: a prospective study", *Medical Teacher*, vol. 33, pp. 997–1004.

Murray-Harvey, R. 1993. "Identifying characteristics of successful tertiary students using path analysis", *Australian Educational Researcher*, vol. 20, pp. 63–81.

Naderi, H., Abdullah, H.T., Sharir, J. and Kumar, V. 2009. "Creativity, age and gender as predictors of academic achievement among undergraduate students", *Journal of American Science*, vol. 5, pp. 101–12.

National Audit Office. 2002. *Improving student achievement in English higher education*, London: National Audit Office.

Noël, N.M., Trocchia, P. and Luckett, M. (2016). "A predictive psychometric model to identify personality and gender differences of college majors", *International Journal of Management Education*, vol. 14, pp. 240–47.

OECD. 2015. *The ABC of gender equality in education: aptitude, behaviour, confidence*, Paris: OECD.

Oh, I.S., Schmidt, F.L., Shaffer, J.A. and Le, H. 2008. "The Graduate Management Admission Test (GMAT) is even more valid than we thought: a new development in meta-analysis and its implications for the validity of the GMAT", *Academy of Management Learning & Education*, vol. 7, no. 4, pp. 563–70.

Ouazad, A. and Page, L. 2013. "Students' perceptions of teacher biases: experimental economics in schools", *Journal of Public Economics*, vol. 105, pp. 116–30.

Peers, I. and Johnston, M. 1994. "Influence of learning context on the relationship between A-level attainment and final degree performance: a meta-analytic review", *British Journal of Educational Psychology*, vol. 64, pp. 1–18.

Plewis, I. 1991. "Underachievement: a case of conceptual confusion", *British Educational Research Journal*, vol. 17, pp. 377–85.

Quenzel, G. and Hurrelmann, K. 2013. "The growing gender gap in education", *International Journal of Adolescence and Youth*, vol. 18, pp. 69–84.

Richardson, J. 1994. "Mature students in higher education: I. A literature survey on approaches to studying", *Studies in Higher Education*, vol. 19, pp. 309–25.

Richardson, J. and Woodley, A. 2003. "Another look at the role of age, gender and subject as predictors of academic attainment in higher education", *Studies in Higher Education*, vol. 28, pp. 475–93.

Roksa, J. and Velez, M. 2012. "A late start: delayed entry, life course transitions and bachelor's degree completion", *Social Forces*, vol. 90, pp. 769–94.

Scheeren, L., Van de Werfhorst, H. and Bol, T. 2018. "The gender revolution in context: how later tracking in education benefits girls", *Social Forces*, vol. 97, pp. 193–220.

Sheard, M. 2009. "Hardiness commitment, gender, and age differentiate university academic performance", *British Journal of Educational Psychology*, vol. 79, pp. 189–204.

Sherer, M. and Zakaria, I. 2018. "Mind that gap! An investigation of gender imbalance on the governing bodies of UK universities", *Studies in Higher Education*, vol. 43, pp. 719–36.

Schofield, C. and Dismore, H. 2010. "Predictors of retention and achievement of higher education students within a further education context", *Journal of Further and Higher Education*, vol. 34, pp. 207–21.

Smith, J. and Naylor, R. 2001. "Determinants of degree performance in UK universities: a statistical analysis of the 1993 student cohort", *Oxford Bulletin of Economics and Statistics*, vol. 63, pp. 29–60.

Sullivan, A. and Brown, M. 2015. "Reading for pleasure and progress in vocabulary and mathematics", *British Educational Research Journal*, vol. 41, pp. 971–91.

Sund, K.J. and Bignoux, S. 2018. "Can the performance effect be ignored in the attendance policy discussion?" *Higher Education Quarterly*, vol. 72, no. 4, pp. 360–74.

Trowler, P. 2001. "Captured by the discourse? The socially constitutive power of new higher education discourse in the UK", *Organization*, vol. 8, pp. 183–201.

Trueman, M. and Hartley, J. 1996. "A comparison between the time-management skills and academic performance of mature and traditional-entry university students", *Higher Education*, vol. 32, pp. 199–215.

UCAS. 2015. *End of cycle report 2015*, available from: https://www.ucas.com/sites/default/files/eoc-report-2015-v2.pdf, accessed 10 March 2019.

Van Miegroet, H., Glass, C., Callister, R.R. and Sullivan, K. 2019. "Unclogging the pipeline: advancement to full professor in academic STEM", *Equality, Diversity and Inclusion*, vol. 38, pp. 246–64.

Vingaard Johansen, U., Knudsen, F.B., Engelbrecht Kristoffersen, C., Stellfeld Rasmussen, J., Saaby Steffen, E. and Sund, K.J. 2017. "Political discourse on higher education in Denmark: from enlightened citizen to homo economicus", *Studies in Higher Education*, vol. 42, no. 2, pp. 264–77.

Win, R. and Miller, P. 2005. "The effects of individual and school factors on university students' academic performance", *Australian Economic Review*, vol. 38, pp. 1–18.

Woodfield, R., Jessop, D. and McMillan, L. 2006. "Gender differences in undergraduate attendance rates", *Studies in Higher Education*, vol. 31, pp. 1–22.

Index

Printed and bound by CPI Group (UK) Ltd, Croydon, CR0 4YY

16/04/2025

14658484-0003